Demography

Second Edition

Demography

The Study of Human Population

Second Edition

David Yaukey

Professor Emeritus
University of Massachusetts, Amherst

Douglas L. Anderton

Director, Social and Demographic Research Institute
University of Massachusetts, Amherst

WAVELAND
PRESS, INC.
Prospect Heights, Illinois

For information about this book, write or call:
Waveland Press, Inc.
P.O. Box 400
Prospect Heights, Illinois 60070
(847) 634-0081
www.waveland.com

Cover photo: Roger Allyn Lee/SuperStock

Contents

4 Age and Sex Structure   75

Preface

"Demography is changing." This sentence opened the preface to David Yaukey's 1985 edition of this textbook. There is hardly a more appropriate entry to the preface of this much-anticipated second edition, revised by Douglas Anderton. In recent years the field of demography and demographic conditions throughout the world have changed both rapidly and radically. The dominant focus of demography during the 1960s and 1970s, especially in undergraduate classes, had been on fertility and an impending population explosion. The monolithic focus on fertility has since given way to a more varied and rich discipline. Fertility declines have spread to many of the less-developed countries and have led to below-replacement-level fertility in many more-developed regions of the world. Meanwhile, HIV/AIDS and tobacco pandemics have taken devastating tolls on world health, especially in sub-Saharan Africa and parts of Asia. Concerns with mortality and morbidity have risen in prominence as those with fertility have tempered. Alternative forms of stable sexual unions have increasingly come to the attention of American demographers as they have become more common in the United States. And issues of immigration, aging, and segregation all have risen in prominence in the more-developed regions of the world and have assumed a more prominent role in the discipline. These are just a few of the substantial demographic changes that have influenced the much-revised content of this book.

In revising this text we naturally have been influenced by the success of the first edition. However, the second edition is not simply an updating of the data in that text. The entire content of each chapter has been reevaluated and rewritten. To accommodate changing interests and the growing breadth of demographic research, two entirely new chapters have been added: chapter 6 on "Morbidity and Health" and chapter 11 on "Population Diversity." Population diversity is left to the last chapter in the text, where a focus on the United States to illustrate diversity issues does not detract from the global scope of the remainder of the text. Fertility and migration, each of which had two chapters in the first edition, have been replaced with single, longer chapters emphasizing the full range of contemporary theories that have replaced simpler paradigms of the past.

On the other hand, we have retained the familiar chapter structure of the original text and the text's overarching emphasis on the discussion of demographic "problems." Typical chapters include not only substantive summaries but also short treatments of data sources and measurement issues. As in the original text, chapters end with simple exercises and propositions for class debate. The eleven chapters are designed for use in a typical semester, or quarter, course.

One difficulty in preparing a textbook is the continual challenge of keeping material examples up-to-date. During the preparation of this text the United Nations' revised 1998 population projections were released. Wherever possible, tables and text were updated to reflect that revision. The reader also will note that tables often reference the latest Internet-released data from the Census Bureau, the Immigration and Naturalization Service, and so forth.

We have made several efforts to accommodate this rapidly accelerating data availability and to insure the text remains up-to-date for a considerable time. First, we have included in chapter 2 a listing of Internet sites from which students can get the latest data on the subjects discussed in each chapter. Second, we have made liberal use of short-term projections of relatively stable demographic trends to carry the text well into, or even through, the first decades of the century. Third, we have designed each chapter with the intention of facilitating the exploration of the most recent data available over the Internet. The text is, in short, a guide for students both to the subject of demography and to the interpretation and use of the most recent data available.

Each of us has many debts to acknowledge in the production of this text. Foremost we thank our staff and colleagues at the Social and Demographic Research Institute. Karen Mason spent countless hours editing our innumerable revisions. Susan Hautaniemi assisted with primary library research and data graphics. Dee Weber helped us acquire the latest database resources required. David's loyal wife, Barbara, has now survived two editions of this book and deserves to share his retirement. And Douglas' courageous spouse, Terri, has proven our endurance in adversity is but a shadow of her own. Without their aid and support, completing the text would have been a much more difficult, and less satisfying, task. Finally, we thank Neil Rowe of Waveland Press for his persistence in encouraging this overdue revision. And, of course, we are grateful to the continued users of the first edition, whose loyalty justified the revision. We hope the product rewards their patience.

1 Introduction

Most of you will be reading this book as a text for a course, rather than on your own. You may already have attended one or more class sessions. If so, what were the first things you noticed about that class? Probably you looked around to see how large the class was and whether the room was crowded. Perhaps you noted what proportion of the students were men and women, or whether the other students seemed to be older or younger than yourself. You may even have chatted with neighbors to find out what their intended majors were. If so, what you did was demography. You studied the size and composition of a specific population—your class.

Most of us seem to sketch a quick demographic description as a first step in coping with a new social situation. We know intuitively that the size and composition of groups with which we are dealing are important. The same logic applies on a larger scale to communities, regions, nations, even planets.

If demographic analysis is a widespread human tendency, what then is demography as a discipline?

DEMOGRAPHY DEFINED

Our students tell us that an *informal* definition is a gentle way to start. Let us define demography, then, in terms of the *questions* it tries to answer. In the vernacular, these are:

- How many people, of what kind, are where?
- How come?
- And so what?

More *formal* definitions of demography (e.g. Pressat, 1985; IUSSP, 1982) say much the same thing in a bit more precise terms. Demography is the study of:

1) the *size* and *composition* of populations according to diverse criteria (age, sex, marital status, educational attainment, spatial distribution, etc.);

1

2) dynamic life-course processes that *change* this composition (birth, death, marriage, migration, etc.); and

3) relationships between population composition and change, and the broader social and physical environment in which they exist.

Formal and informal definitions make the same points. Demography describes population size and composition. It studies the causes (or determinants) of changes in size and composition. And it studies the effects (or consequences) of these population trends.

Demography overlaps with many neighboring disciplines. Most demographers—at least in the United States—also identify themselves as sociologists, economists, anthropologists, geographers, biologists, and so on. Demographic inquiry may be narrowly focused on demographic variables alone or broadly concerned with society, economy, and culture. The terms *pure demography* and *formal demography* are sometimes used to distinguish more narrowly focused interests in population composition and demographic dynamics, dealing entirely with demographic variables. An example of formal demographic analysis would be developing a theoretical model specifying the relationship between changes in fertility (treated as a cause) and changes in age composition (treated as an effect). A more extensive and less narrowly focused approach to demography is implied by the phrase *population studies*, which includes all of the above but also encompasses the study of relationships between demographic and nondemographic variables. The far-reaching implications of demographic variables in other disciplines have generated broad interest in such fields of study as *social demography, economic demography, anthropological demography,* and *historical demography,* to name a few.

Two more preliminary remarks need to be made. One is that demography deals with *aggregates* (or collections) of people, not individual people. The very term "population" refers to the numbers of people resident in some specified geographic area, be it a classroom or a nation. Likewise, demography describes characteristics of populations, not of individual members in those populations. Thus, the cartoon shown in Figure 1-1 is something of a demographers' inside joke.

The second point is that demography is generally *quantitative* and statistical, although some demographers also use qualitative methods (see Kertzer and Fricke, 1997; Bogue et al., 1993, ch. 27). Demography deals with populations, and the features of populations are most often measured by counting the people in the total population, or in segments of it, and comparing those counts. That means that demography can easily present basic population descriptions in tables and graphs. Paging ahead through the tables and figures of this text will illustrate the quantitative nature of demographic descriptions to the reader.

Furthermore, because the subject is so numerical, readers will get used to following simple demographic arithmetic in the course of reading this text. Almost all chapters end with straightforward exercises that provide guidance and practice. By doing these exercises, you will have accumulated a basic set of demographic tools by the end of this book.

Figure 1-1 "They Tell Me You're a Demographer . . ."

"They tell me you're a demographer. Whatever happened
to Fred Biddlingmeyer?"

Source: Cartoon by Peter Steiner, *Science '83.*

CURRENT POPULATION SIZE AND COMPOSITION

Absolute Size, Distribution, and Density

Population size has three facets. First is *absolute size.* The absolute size of the earth's population reached 6 billion in the latter part of 1999 and will most likely grow by about another billion before the end of the year 2020. The ten countries with the largest populations in the world are shown in Table 1-1, with the absolute size of their population in column 1. Figure 1-2 goes beyond the ten largest nations and maps all the countries of the world, shaded according to the absolute sizes of their populations.

Absolute size has its own consequences. To use our classroom illustration, large classes have to be taught differently than small classes, more by lecture than by discussion. The immense cities of today have different problems than did the villages and towns of yesterday, and they have developed different kinds of governments to handle them. China is home to well over a billion, and India to just over a billion, people. In both cases very large population size has had significant effects on the politics, culture, and economic development of these nations.

A second facet of population size is *distribution*, or relative size. If we compare the populations in Table 1-1, we see that China and India together have over a third of the world's entire population of 6 billion. These ten countries together have more than half (3.6 billion) of the world's population living in them. The United States is third in size—a little more than one-fourth the size of India's population.

Distribution, as well, has its own consequences. For instance, citizens of Western countries tend to be alarmed that the people of non-Western countries outnumber

them now and will outnumber them by even more (see chapter 3). Distribution of population within nations also is a subject of concern. For example, many less-developed
countries are worried about premature and extreme urbanization (see chapter 10).

The third facet of population size is *density*. One of the main consequences of
large size and uneven population distribution is that they can lead to very crowded, or
densely settled, populations. In our classroom illustration, if you noticed how

Table 1-1

**Ten Countries with the Largest Absolute Population Size, and Their
Population Density per Square Kilometer, 2000**

Country	Population in 1,000s (1)	Density per sq. km. (2)
China	1,261,833	132
India	1,014,004	309
United States	275,563	29
Indonesia	224,784	118
Brazil	172,860	20
Russia	146,001	9
Pakistan	141,554	178
Bangladesh	129,194	897
Japan	126,550	335
Nigeria	123,338	133

Source: U.S. Bureau of the Census, International Database Projections, 3/21/00.

Figure 1-2   World Countries Classified by Absolute Population Size, 1999

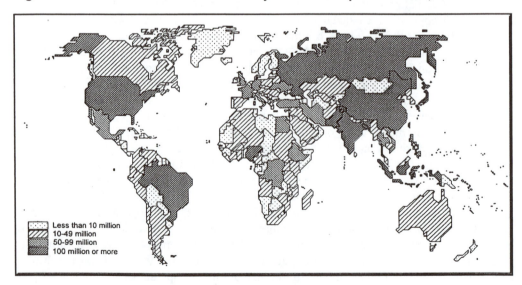

Source: United Nations, *Charting the Progress of Populations*, 2000, fig. 1.1. The United Nations is the author of the original
material. Used with permission.

crowded (or if you are lucky, uncrowded) the room was, you were noticing density. It refers, in its most restricted use, to the relationship between population size and the space in which the population is located. For large geographic units, one might measure density in persons per square mile or kilometer.

The largest populations of the world are not those with the highest density. In fact, some of the very smallest countries in terms of geographic area and population are the densest—for instance, Monaco or Macau have about 32,000 people per square kilometer. The second column of Table 1-1 shows the density for the ten largest populations. Of these countries, Bangladesh is by far the most densely settled because it has an unusual combination of large population and small land area.

Density, too, has its own negative and positive consequences. Epidemic diseases can spread more easily in densely settled populations, but so can knowledge and ideas. For most people who face daily crowds, noise, and air pollution, the negative aspects of density are most obvious. Indeed, the concept of "overpopulation" (chapter 3) implies a concern over too dense a population in a given environment.

Composition

The topic of composition recalls our first demographic question, with added emphasis: How many people, *of what kind*, are where? In our classroom illustration, you were observing composition when you counted the males and females, those younger and older than yourself, and the numbers from various majors. Demographers go beyond simply counting the absolute numbers in categories and *compare* the numbers, focusing on the *relative* size of categories. Thus, you will see heavy use of percentage distributions and various ratios in demographic descriptions of population composition.

Which traits do demographers use to classify population composition? The list is potentially limitless; however, some kinds of characteristics turn out to be more useful than others. For example, characteristics that either do not change easily or change in a predictable fashion tend to be useful. Therefore, sex, age, and ethnic identity are more useful than body weight, satisfaction with the president, or number of cars owned.

Demographers also focus on traits that are inherently related to altering population size and composition, such as giving birth, dying, or moving from one population to another. Variables like age and sex are again important in this context since these traits are clearly related to basic biological behavior. As the students in your class grow older they will face an increasingly higher chance of dying each year. Most college students also are approaching the ages at which they are more likely to have children. Women in the class will have different lives, in part, due to childbearing. This affects the different subcultures of men and women even for those who choose not to have children. In fact, because age and sex are related to many behaviors, we can make reasonable guesses about some of the major characteristics of people's lives knowing only their age and sex.

Demographers also have concern for characteristics of the composition that are used as a basis for ascribing societal roles. Because so much of behavior is related to age and sex, these characteristics are also used by people to ascribe social roles. Few of the people in the class are "children" or "elders," but most are young adults. Role ascription, to sociologists, means assigning people to roles on the basis of traits over which the individual has no control. All societies use sex and age to some degree in ascribing roles, whether we like it or not.

Although age and sex are basic dimensions of population composition, many other social and economic characteristics also are used to ascribe social roles; for example, how we categorize people and what their social roles may be are influenced by their ethnicity, literacy and education, occupation, and income. Governments are concerned with the economic welfare of their populations and with their populations as workforces for their economies. So most demographic censuses collect information on the economic composition of the population. Governments also are concerned with identifying vulnerable groups that have special policy needs and the characteristics of these groups, thus many demographic surveys are focused on such specific groups and policy-relevant population characteristics. And, finally, the public is concerned with the size and distribution of identifiable subgroups within the nation, so most national censuses deal in some way with the subject of ethnic identity, be it by race, ethnicity, religious affiliation, or native language.

Age and sex are the most universally studied dimensions of population composition because they change predictably, are related to demographic behavior, and are basic to social ascription of roles. However, the study of population composition is not a closed book. The characteristics related to behavior and used to ascribe social roles can, and do, change over time and vary across cultures.

POPULATION CHANGE

So far, we have been dealing with population description as of a given moment. Clearly, that can be only the beginning. The future population is the one we anticipate and plan for, not the present one. Indeed, describing a present population helps mainly to the degree that it tells us something about that population in the future. Thus, most demography focuses on the study of population change, including change in size.

Population Growth and Its Components

To demographers, "growth" means change in population size. It is called growth even if it is negative growth. The amount of growth is obtained by subtracting some earlier population count (P_1) from some later count (P_2). Clearly, the difference can be either positive or negative. Most populations in developing countries are experiencing positive growth, but some of the more-developed countries are, in fact, experiencing negative growth.

What are the immediate causes of population growth? That is, what could happen to alter a population size from P_1 to P_2? Common sense furnishes the answer. If we are considering the world's population, it can change in only two ways: people can be born into the world, increasing the population, and people can die, decreasing the population. Any population such as the world's in which people cannot come or go is a *closed population* and can increase or decrease only through births or deaths. In terms of an equation:

$$P_2 - P_1 = B_{(1,2)} - D_{(1,2)}$$

which says simply that the population change in a closed population from an earlier (subscript 1) time to a later (subscript 2) time is increased by the number of births that occurred between the two times and decreased by the number of deaths between the two times. The difference between births and deaths *(B–D)* is called the *natural increase* of the population. Thus, in a closed population, population growth is the *natural increase*; that is, the difference between births and deaths.

Figure 1-3 dramatizes this imbalance on the world level for the year 2000. The figure shows the births *(B)*, deaths *(D)*, and natural increase *(B–D)* for the world's population in the year 2000, as well as for an average month, day, hour, minute, and second of that year. In the average minute, for example, there were about 249 births and 103 deaths, resulting in a natural increase, or growth in the world's population, of about 146 people per minute.

Most populations, however, are not closed. That is, people also come and go. In an *open population* there are four—and only four—ways in which a geographic area can add or subtract from its population. Again, people can be born into it or can die out of it. But in addition, people can cross a border into it or people can cross a border out of it. In this case the growth equation is a bit more complicated:

$$P_2 - P_1 = B_{(1,2)} - D_{(1,2)} + M_{(1,2)}$$

Figure 1-3   World Growth and Natural Increase per Year, Month, Day, Hour, Minute, and Second, for the Year 2000

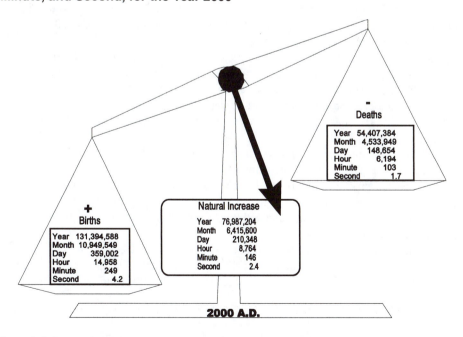

Source: U.S. Bureau of the Census, International Data Base Projections, 4/4/00.

In words, this growth equation for an open population says that the change in size of the population of a specified area during a specified time interval equals the number of births (B) over that time, minus the number of deaths (D), plus the net migration into the population (M) over the same period of time. *Net migration* is the imbalance between the movers-in and the movers-out and can, of course, be either positive or negative. Thus, even a population with a negative natural increase can grow or maintain its size with a substantial net migration of others into the population. This is in fact the case for countries in some of the more-developed regions of the world. An exercise at the end of this chapter offers practice in using these equations.

Growth Components as Population Processes

So far we have been talking about the causes of population growth as events. Each birth, each death, each move across a border is a population event. However, demographers—and indeed the general public—are accustomed to thinking of these individual events as expressions of underlying collective processes. That is, we think of the number of births that occur in a population as an expression of the collective *fertility* of that population; the number of deaths is the manifestation of its force of *mortality*; and the number of moves across the border (in and out) is the process of *migration*.

The simplest measure of a population process is a *crude rate*. But before we discuss it, we should ask: Why construct rates at all? Why not simply count the number of events and let that total be the measure of the process? Perhaps the best answers to these questions may be obtained by asking you to think about the following reasoning: Suppose that exactly the same number of deaths had occurred in the United States during 1900 as occurred during 2000. Can one conclude that the mortality of the United States was the same in 1900 as in 2000? Most readers will recognize that such a statement is misleading. There were many more people available to die in the year 2000 than there were in 1900. If the same number of people had actually died in both years then a much smaller percentage of the population would have died in 2000 than did in 1900. Or, as demographers would express it, the population at *risk* of dying was greater in 2000, and that should be taken into account when measuring how likely it was that these events occurred.

The basic demographic strategy for doing this is to divide the number of events that occur over a given time by the population that was at risk of experiencing those events. This step produces one of the fundamental measurements demographers use, that is, *rates*. The numerator is the number of events; the denominator is the population at risk. Generally speaking, rates tell us the probability that a member of the population at risk participated in one of the events.

A *crude* approximation of the population at risk for demographic processes is the size of the total population during the specified year. Dividing the number of events by the estimated total population produces *crude rates*. A general formula for crude rates is

$$\frac{E}{P_m} \times n$$

where E is the number of events (either births, deaths, etc.) occurring in the specified place and year. P_m refers to the estimated total population. Since the size of the population varies throughout the year, the mid-year population (indicated by the subscript m) is often used as a representative figure for the total population at risk during the year.

Finally, most crude rates are multiplied by a number or *base* of the rate, n, to express the rate as the number of events occurring for every n people. A common convention, for example, is to multiply by 1,000, which makes the rate the number of events per 1,000 population, which is quite reasonable for births, deaths, and migration. The base can be changed to give the rate per $n=1$ person, as a percentage of every $n=100$ persons, or, for very rare events, per 100,000 people. The base is chosen to minimize the decimal places in crude rates or, equivalently, to adjust for the fact that some events occur to only small fractions of the population in any given time.

The adjective "crude" in these rates is not accidental. Not everybody in the total population is equally at risk of dying, or of producing a baby, or of migrating. We will introduce more refined demographic rates and measures in later chapters. Crude rates, however, provide a quick, and for many purposes adequate, measure of demographic processes. An exercise at the end of this chapter offers practice in constructing crude rates.

The growth equation, which we expressed earlier in terms of absolute numbers, can also be written in terms of crude rates. If we take each term in the growth equation and divide by the midyear population, P_m, like this

$$\frac{P_2 - P_1}{P_m} = \frac{B_{(1,2)}}{P_m} - \frac{D_{(1,2)}}{P_m} + \frac{M_{(1,2)}}{P_m}$$

each of these terms becomes a crude rate. We can, of course, also multiply each term by a base such as 1,000 to express them as rates per 1,000 population. In either case, in words this equation says:

growth rate = birth rate – death rate + rate of net migration

To illustrate this form of the growth equation, Figure 1-4 traces components in the population growth history of the United States from 1910 forward, projected to 2010. Each of the components is expressed as a crude rate per 1,000 population. The top panel of the graph shows the crude birth rate (the highest line) and the crude death rate (the lowest line) over this period. The higher birth rate at the turn of the twentieth century and the baby boom of the late 1940s and early 1950s can be seen in the crude birth rate. The effects of the worldwide influenza epidemic and World War I can be seen in the peak of the crude death rate just before the 1920s. The difference between these birth and death rates is the rate of natural increase in the population. Note the reduction in natural increase, for example, that occurred at the time of World War II (where the arrows labeling natural increase appear). During this time deaths rose at the same time births declined, minimizing the imbalance. Then, in the postwar years, births rose dramatically as deaths declined slowly and steadily, resulting in a large imbalance and natural increase.

The second panel of Figure 1-4 shows the net migration rate (the lower line), which is added to the natural increase from the previous panel to give the population growth rate (the higher line). Notice that growth rates prior to the Great Depression, before the 1930s, were erratic and highly affected by changes in the year-to-year net

Figure 1-4   Birth, Death, Natural Increase, Net Migration, and Growth Rates, United States, 1910–2010

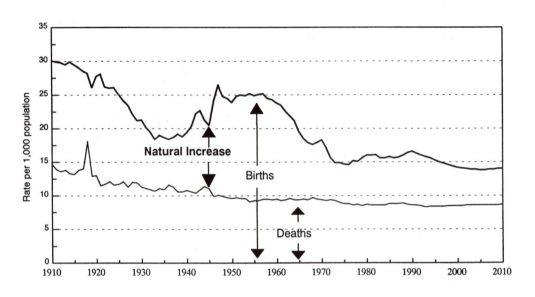

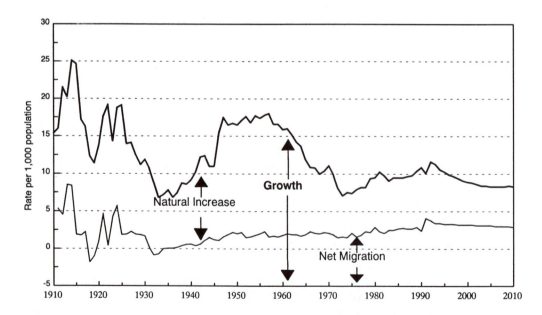

Source: Anderton et al., *Population of the United States*, 1997, fig. 1-1. Reprinted with permission of The Free Press, a division of Simon & Schuster, Inc.

migration rate. Twice during this time net migration dropped below zero, indicating a net loss of migrants. After the early 1930s the growth rate is much more heavily dependent upon the rate of natural increase, and net migration is more stable than the rate of births.

Population Change: Growth and Reclassification

So far we have been dealing only with population growth, that is, change in population *size*. Demographers also study change in population *composition*, though less exhaustively. What are the processes involved in a change in population composition?

All four components of growth can affect the size of a population category or subpopulation, just as they do the size of a total population. For instance, the number of Catholic Americans grows (positively or negatively) in response to births and deaths among Catholic residents and the international migration patterns of Catholics into or out of the United States. However, unlike the case for total population growth, category growth can be influenced by an additional process, which we will call *reclassification*. Thus, Catholics can change their religious affiliation to another religion and others can become Catholics, thereby influencing the size of the Catholic population without involving mortality, fertility, or migration. Reclassification is, in a sense, a migration among subpopulations.

The process of classification is hard to simplify. For some traits, such as gender, the changes produced by reclassification are still very limited. For other traits, such as age, reclassification proceeds predictably. And for still others, such as occupation, it involves individual choices that follow no simple pattern. In fact, the study of changing subpopulation composition, and the complex forces that may affect the demography of subpopulations such as occupational groups, income groups, educational attainment groups, etc., is a research trend throughout the social and behavioral sciences.

One reclassification process has enjoyed special attention from demographers. It is *nuptiality*, the process of changing marital status. Marriage is of special interest for several reasons. One is that marital status does seem to have direct and indirect impacts upon the growth processes, as it influences birth, death, and migration. Another reason is that marriage (and in some cultures related behavior such as cohabitation or same-sex couples) implies a jointly functioning social unit that shares resources and demographic decisions. It is also the case that couples are viewed differently by governments and that conventional demographic data systems often gather evidence of marital events and of marital relations within households.

POPULATION PROBLEMS

In each chapter of this book we discuss not only demographic methods, statistics, and trends, but what may be called population "problems." Population problems are socially defined, just as are other social problems. They may seem to be self-evident and beyond dispute at a given moment of public consensus, but the history of population problems shows that a public can be alarmed about a given population trend and then, some years later, view the same trend with indifference. Moreover, one public's problem trend may be another public's blessing. To understand this, let us look sociologically at the mechanics of defining population problems.

Public Definition

"Problem" is a label awarded by the public. That labeling requires two mental steps by the public: 1) accepting some belief of cause and effect and 2) passing a negative value judgment on the alleged effect. Let us elaborate the role of the cause-effect belief, using as an illustration the aging U.S. population. As we shall see in chapter 4, the average age of the U.S. population is increasing and will increase in the future if our fertility stays low. That, in itself, is not a problem unless the U.S. public believes one or more of the various theories about how that change in age composition will influence other variables. For instance, there is an economic theory that the increase in the proportion of the population that is of retirement age will shrink the proportional size of the workforce and thus the collective productivity of the economy. There is the general belief that, as the average age of the workforce increases, as more workers enter their late middle age, the workforce will tend to become less innovative, less willing to accept new ideas, and less energetic. There is the belief that older workers are less willing to move away from areas of low employment to areas of employment opportunity, adding rigidity to the economy. The point is, each of these theories or beliefs represents a statement of a relationship between some demographic variable (population aging in our example) that is seen as a cause, and some nondemographic social or economic variable that is seen as an effect. Looking back to our definition of demography, this means that some purely demographic variable is viewed as a cause of some social, economic, or environmental variable that is publicly defined as a social problem.

Those things we choose to label as population problems depend on our population theories, our beliefs about cause and effect, and even the adequacy of the demographic information we have available. That has important implications. It means the accuracy of pinpointing population problems depends on our success in what we have defined earlier as *population studies*, which treat the relationships between demographic and nondemographic variables. It also means our definition of population problems at a given moment may be based upon a fallacy, an erroneous belief about a cause-effect relationship, or a lack of foresight into other effects that change the equation of our anticipations. Indeed, population studies can solve population problems simply by disproving fallacious beliefs about cause and effect, and can also improve upon our anticipations by helping us understand the variety of influences that might alter demographic trends in the near future. On the other hand, it means that as-yet unknown consequences of population trends would be labeled "problems" if our theories were better.

Let us get back to the value-judgment component of the problem-definition process. It is easy to overlook the fact that every definition of a problem involves an implicit value judgment regarding the alleged effect of the population trend. The main reason for this is that people tend to talk to other people who share their own values and consequently are unaware that somebody else might evaluate the trends quite differently. A simpler illustration is the concern over the changing ethnic composition of the United

States and Western Europe. In the past these countries welcomed ethnic immigrants as migrants, farm workers, and "guest" workers. Ethnic immigrants were perceived as filling a necessary labor need in the developed economies. However, in more recent times host countries are alarmed that those guests have stayed, creating cultural enclaves and in fact growing to larger and larger proportions of the population. This is a problem to some natives. Concern over immigration in the United States, for example, is seen in California's 1994 passage of Proposition 187, seeking to end education and nonemergency medical care to illegal immigrants; in the 1995 bipartisan panel of Congress recommendation to gradually reduce immigration; and in the 1996 immigration reform bill designed to end illegal immigration. But is this a problem to the immigrants? Maybe they would be happier if there were more of their former countrymen in their new home country to increase their political power, protect them from discrimination, and surround them with their familiar culture. At the least, it is likely that immigrants do not consider themselves to be the problem seen by segments of the native population. Those population trends one calls "problems" depends very much on where one sits.

Population Problems in This Textbook

In decades past, concern over population problems was the impetus for introductory courses in demography or population studies. In our own university—and, we will wager, most others—such courses used to be titled "Population Problems," or something very similar. A focus on what was then considered the single most important demographic problem—the world population explosion alarm of the late 1960s—led to demography courses that were universally oversubscribed by socially and ecologically minded young people.

Things have changed. World population growth has slowed (but by no means stopped). In addition, some environmental conditions have improved despite growing populations, demonstrating growth alone is not to blame for environmental degradation. Panic over a looming population catastrophe has, as a result, become less widespread. Nowadays, demographic concern with population growth tends to be about insuring universal opportunities for human development and with more reasoned concern over cumulative environmental effects of population growth. Demographers have come to appreciate the complexity of human demographic systems and the likelihood of an unanticipated future turn when making long-range demographic forecasts.

Similarly, most students turn to this course for more pragmatic reasons than in the past. Some are looking for demographic literacy, while others seek an understanding of demographic effects on our lives and environment, or fundamental skills which are useful in virtually any career. Accordingly, they are less likely to focus on population problems. Or, to state it more positively, they may be more inclined to recognize the subjective and relative nature of population problems and to consider a whole range of potential problems rather than follow any one current public obsession.

This book's treatment of population problems is based on this framework. The subject of population problems is reserved until the end of the chapter, after important trends have been described in detail. Then, emphasizing the subjective nature of demographic problems, we speculate about three questions regarding each potential problem raised for discussion: Who is alarmed by the trend? What specific effects do these people consider problematic? And, why do they judge these effects to be negative? Each chapter also contains a section of topics for discussion that often focus on possible population problems. We have chosen these topics to stimulate discussion of alternative perspectives and to illustrate the fact that identifying population problems generally involves making judgments of value.

SUMMARY

Demography is the study of the *size* and *composition* of populations, the processes that *change* this size and composition, and the relationships of population characteristics with the broader social and cultural *environment*. A narrow definition, *formal demography*, emphasizes the study of the demographic variables and their interrelationships. A broader definition, *population studies*, includes the study of the nondemographic determinants and consequences of the demographic variables. There are many population characteristics of demographic interest when describing population composition, but age and sex are the most fundamental.

Demography not only describes population traits as of a given moment but also analyzes the dynamic processes by which populations change in size and composition. The growth equation is a fundamental feature of demography and describes the relation between growth and births, deaths, and migratory moves. Collectively, such population events are seen as manifestations of population processes: fertility, mortality, and migration. Demographers employ *rates* to measure the force of these processes, the simplest examples being *crude* rates. Change in population composition is determined not only by fertility, mortality, and migration, but also by the complex processes of *reclassification*.

One source of public interest in demography is concern over population problems. Population problems are social problems and as such are defined subjectively by the public and by governments. Labeling a population trend as a problem involves believing some theory about its consequences and making a negative value judgment about those consequences. Current population "problems" are raised for discussion in context at the end of each chapter in this textbook. However, demographers have learned to appreciate the changeable nature of demographic behavior, and even the changeability of even more transitory definitions of population problems.

EXERCISES

1. Table E1-1 gives estimated demographic data for the United States and Mexico for the calendar year 2000. Use these data to calculate the estimated net migration for Mexico. Use the blank cells in the table for recording your computations and use the United States column as an example. Remember, the formula needed for these calculations is the growth equation for an open population:

$$P_2 - P_1 = B_{(1,2)} - D_{(1,2)} + M_{(1,2)}$$

Table E1-1
Population Data for the United States and Mexico, 2000[a]

	United States (1)	Mexico (2)
Population at the beginning of 2000	274,329	99,603
Population at the beginning of 2001	276,797	101,097
Growth during 2000	2,468	
Births during 2000	3,858	2,308
Deaths during 2000	2,480	502
Natural increase during 2000	1,378	
Net migration during 2000	1,090	

[a]In thousands.
Source: U.S. Bureau of the Census, International Database Projections, 4/27/00.

2. Compute the estimated crude rates for Mexico in Table E1-2. Use the data from Table E1-1 to compute these rates, and the United States column of Table E1-2 as a model. The formula for a crude rate, again, is

$$\frac{E}{P_m} \times 1,000$$

Compute your estimated mid-year population (P_m) by finding the arithmetic mean of P_1 and P_2; that is, add the beginning-of-2000 and beginning-of-2001 populations together and divide by two. Finally, since these are only rough estimates by the Census Bureau's International Data Base, round your rates to whole numbers. Also, remember that the crude growth rate is a percent (per hundred), while the others are expressed as crude rates per thousand.

Table E1-2
Crude Rates for the United States and Mexico, 2000

	United States (1)	Mexico (2)
Estimated mid-year population[a]	275,563	
Crude birth rate, 2000	14	
Crude death rate, 2000	9	
Crude rate of natural increase, 2000	6	
Crude growth rate (%), 2000	0.9	

[a]In thousands.
Source: U.S. Bureau of the Census, International Database Projections, 4/27/00.

▶ **PROPOSITIONS FOR DEBATE**

1. Population "problems" should not be a matter of opinion; they only appear so in the short run because of our imperfect knowledge of the future.

2. The population problems in the headlines today will still be there in ___ years.

3. A world population explosion catastrophe is still happening; demographers just aren't paying any attention to it.

4. The demography of the population (i.e. size and composition, processes of change, and relationships of these with the environment) will, or will not, affect personal decisions I make while in college.

▶ REFERENCES AND SUGGESTED READINGS

Anderton, Douglas L., Richard E. Barrett, and Donald J. Bogue. 1997. *The Population of the United States.* 3rd ed. New York: Free Press.

Bogue, Donald, Eduardo Arriaga, and Douglas L. Anderton, eds. 1993. *Readings in Population Research Methodology.* United Nations Fund for Population Activities. Chicago: Social Development Center.

Gelbard, Alene, Carl Haub, and Mary M. Kent. 1999. "World Population Beyond Six Billion." *Population Bulletin* 54(1).

International Union for the Scientific Study of Population (IUSSP). 1982. *Multilingual Demographic Dictionary.* English Section. Liege, Belgium: Ordina Editions.

Kertzer, David I., and Tom Fricke, eds. 1997. *Anthropological Demography: Toward a New Synthesis.* Chicago: University of Chicago Press.

McFalls, Joseph A., Jr. 2000. *Population: A Lively Introduction.* Washington, DC: Population Reference Bureau.

Population Reference Bureau. 2000. *1999 World Population Data Sheet.* Washington, DC: Population Reference Bureau.

Pressat, Roland. 1985. *The Dictionary of Demography.* Edited by Christopher Wilson. New York: Basil Blackwell Ltd.

United Nations. 1998. *World Resources 1998–99.* A Report by the World Resources Institute. Oxford: Oxford University Press.

———. 1999. *Revision of the World Population Estimates and Projections, 1998 briefing packet.* New York: United Nations.

———. 2000. *Charting the Progress of Populations.* ST/ESA/SER.R/151. New York: United Nations.

United States Bureau of the Census. 1999. *World Population Profile: 1998.* Report WP/98. Washington, DC: Government Printing Office.

2

Demographic Data

As civilizations arise and as nations develop, governments build systems for gathering information about their people. Minimally, they wish to know how many of what kind are where. The current standard data-gathering system, evolved in the West, has as its foundation the decennial census. But a census tells only about one moment. Therefore, censuses are supplemented in this system by registration of population events (births, deaths) and/or by sample surveys. Even with the most sophisticated combination of these elements, however, gaps remain that must be filled by estimation. This chapter treats these interrelated elements in order: censuses, registration, sample surveys, and estimation.

POPULATION CENSUSES

In modern times, the practice of taking population censuses spread through Western countries in the 1800s, and from there to the rest of the world. That is not to say that earlier civilizations had not at their peaks done something very similar. According to the New Testament (Luke 2: 1–7), Joseph and Mary were reporting to Bethlehem for a Roman census when she gave birth on what has since been called Christmas Eve. But the worldwide spread of census taking, promoted by the United Nations, is basically a post-World War II phenomenon.

The United Nations Statistics Division (1999) reports that over 99.5% of the world's population live in countries that have taken, or will take, a census in the 1995 to 2004 round. During that decade, only nineteen countries have not taken, and do not plan to take, a census. Countries without censuses are often small (e.g. Andorra, Pitcairn, Faeroe Islands) or those with recent political strife (e.g. Afghanistan, Angola, Liberia, Somalia). Despite these lapses, census data are increasingly available for the world's population.

Basic Features

What is a census? The United Nations, where international standards evolve, says that a census should have four basic features. First, it should be *individual;* each person is to be recorded separately along with his or her traits. This allows later cross-classification of individuals in the tabulation process. Second, it should be *universal;* everybody in the specified territory should be counted and described. Third, it should be *simultaneous;* enumerators should specify each person's location and traits as of some particular "census moment." Fourth, censuses should be *periodic;* they should be carried out at regular intervals. Regularity makes it easier to describe trends and to check on consistency between censuses. The United Nations recommends decennial censuses and, further, has attempted to nudge countries into taking them in years ending in zero to allow international comparability (United Nations, 1998).

Consistent with these goals, modern census taking has evolved into a set of conventional steps taken by the government:

1) It specifies the geographic boundaries of the area to be covered. Further, it specifies the geographic boundaries of the subareas about which it ultimately wants separate information. Subareas should be small enough so that each can be the responsibility of an individual enumerator.

2) The government decides which traits it needs to know about for each of its people and settles upon a questionnaire.

3) Simultaneously, within all of the subareas, the government sends out the assigned enumerator to visit households and to list all of the individuals in each household. At the same time, the enumerator is to gather questionnaire information about each of the individuals. Conventionally, the enumerator visits each household, finds a qualified informant there, and gathers information about each individual residing in the household, filling it into a separate row or column on the questionnaire.

4) The government compiles the information from the subareas, tabulating numbers of people by subarea (distribution) and by category of individual trait (composition).

5) The government reports the findings to the sponsoring citizenry.

Particular governments may choose, for good reasons, to deviate from this set of traditions. For instance, recent U.S. censuses have deviated in two ways from the steps just summarized: 1) they have used a mail-out/mail-back procedure instead of face-to-face interviews for most of the population and 2) they have asked some questions of only a sample of the total population. (A later section of this chapter describes the evolution of the U.S. census.) Increasingly, as populations grow and technology evolves the question of how much information should be collected using modern sampling methods versus complete population censuses has become a central issue in designing censuses.

Census Topics

Bases for choice. How should a government decide what topics to cover in its censuses? The criteria recommended by the United Nations (1998) fall into two categories, political and technical.

On the *political* side, the United Nations recognizes the priority of national over international needs in determining census content. Each nation should decide its questions through its normal political processes. In a democracy, this usually involves lengthy hearings and debates dealing with demographic priorities, rights to privacy, and, inevitably, financial constraints. Being political, the decisions reflect swings in public concern. For instance, U.S. censuses from the 1920s contain more coverage of ethnicity, reflecting that era's support for legislation restricting immigration (Weeks, 1996). More recently, a great deal of discussion has revolved around ethnicity and race questions because of the rising numbers of children from parents with different ethnic backgrounds, calling for a more comprehensive multiethnic classification (Edmonston and Schultze, 1995).

On the *technical* side, demographers need data that are complete and comparable. Nations can enhance international comparability by taking censuses in standard years (those ending in zero), by covering the same topics, and by using the same definitions. They can enhance time comparability by covering the same topics repeatedly in their census series, allowing them to identify trends. Another consideration is one the United Nations calls "suitability": a census should not ask questions that respondents are unable to answer or find offensive, as such a procedure is unrealistic and may jeopardize the census.

International priorities. Figure 2-1 describes the considerable international accord as to which questions should be asked on current national population censuses. The consensus was reached in a series of regional conferences held in preparation for the 2000 round of national censuses (United Nations, 1998). Some explanation about categories of questions for population censuses may help.

Topic 1, geographical information, concerns place of residence and allows counting total population for particular areas as well as for categories of areas, such as urban versus rural. Incidentally, one issue governments have to decide is whether it serves them better to record as a person's residence where he or she was found at the "census moment" (*defacto* residence) or his usual place of residence (*dejure* residence). Most nations compromise, with the United States leaning toward the *dejure* principle. Information on duration of residence and comparison of previous with present residence provide partial information on migration.

Topic 2 focuses on households rather than individuals. Knowing the relationship of each individual to the family or household head (or other reference member) allows description of the household and family composition. A major change in the 1980 U.S. census was the elimination of the *head*-of-household concept and its replacement with a reference-member approach. This dodges the irrelevant issue of power within the household, a thorny one in days of sensitivity to sexism.

Topics 3, 5, 6, 7, and 8 all contain questions on population composition. As one might expect, age and sex universally are top-priority topics. Some questions on economic activities and human resources (literacy and educational attainment) also are general. Questions dealing with ethnic identity (i.e. religion, language, national or ethnic group) are judged useful but not necessarily of highest priority for all world regions. Questions on nativity and international migration status were added to the United Nations recommendations for 1990 censuses; those on disability have been added for the 2000 censuses. In both cases these questions were added because censuses are likely to be the only reliable source of data for these topics.

Figure 2-1 United Nations List of Topics for 2000 Censuses

1. Geographical and Migration Characteristics

Place of usual residence	Place of residence at a specified date in the past
Where present at time of census	Total population
Place of birth	Locality
Duration of residence	Urban or rural
Place of previous residence	

2. Household and Family Characteristics

Household and family composition	Household and family status
Relationship to head (or other reference member of household)	

3. Demographic and Social Characteristics

Sex	Religion
Age	Language
Marital status	National and/or ethnic group
Citizenship	

4. Fertility and Mortality

Children ever born	Maternal or paternal orphanhood
Children living	Age, date, or duration of first marriage
Date of birth of last child	Age of mother at birth of first child
Deaths in the past 12 months	

5. Educational Characteristics

Educational attainment	School attendance
Literacy	Field of education and qualifications

6. Economic Characteristics

Activity status	Time worked
Occupation	Income
Industry	Sector of employment
Status in employment	Place of work

7. International Migration Characteristics

Country of birth	Citizenship
Year or period of arrival	

8. Disability Characteristics

Disability	Impairment and handicap
Causes of disability	

Source: United Nations, *Principles and Recommendations for Population and Housing Censuses,* 1998, pp. x–xii.

Topic 4, concerning fertility and mortality, has a special purpose. The general type of question in censuses deals with traits of persons at the moment of the census. However, demographers want to deal not only with population characteristics at a given moment but also the processes by which size and composition change: mortality, fertility, and migration. Civil registration and sample surveys, dealt with later in this chapter, provide direct information about the population processes. To supplement and cross-check with these two sources, demographers habitually include *retrospective* questions about some past vital events in censuses.

Census Errors

Errors of coverage. No census is perfect. All suffer from two kinds of errors. The most obvious is coverage error, counting some people more than once or, more likely, not at all. In the 1990 U.S. census, the undercounting of people increased for the first time in fifty years. In fact, the undercount of the population nearly doubled (Edmonston, 1999). Even when enumeration is almost complete on the average, particular types of people are more likely to be overlooked. Marginal segments of the population are particularly vulnerable: minorities, the homeless, and the isolated. Revisiting a sample of the population to determine coverage errors of the 1990 U.S. census, the Census Bureau found that 5.7% of the black population, but only 1.3% of the white population, were omitted from the census (Robinson et al., 1993, p. 13). While undercounting of population has generally declined prior to 1990, it declined less for the black population. So, as a proportion of the population the underreporting of blacks has become relatively more severe over time (Edmonston, 1999). Of course,

Figure 2-2   1880 Political Cartoon

"Wonderful effect of the appearance of the census enumerator."

Source: Francese, "The 1980 Census," 1979, p. 34.

the major problem with such coverage errors is that they are difficult to identify without some additional information beyond the initial enumeration of the population.

Errors of content. These arise when respondents misreport information about the people being enumerated or when the interviewer misrecords the information given. Misreporting can be due to ignorance of the facts, a desire to look better in the eyes of the interviewer, or a belief that the answer is none of the government's business. Such misreporting is difficult to identify even using standard Census Bureau procedures (Iversen et al., 1999). Remember, just because a government wants to gather facts from its populace does not mean that the populace has those facts to give or cares to report them accurately. For example, although most people in the world can report their sex (gender) accurately, it is surprising how few know (or care about) their precise age. The tendency of people to round their reported ages to even years, the nearest five years, or even the nearest ten years, results in higher percentages of people reporting these ages, a phenomenon so common that demographers have a term for it, *age heaping*. Many individuals with parents of different race or ethnic groups also have difficulty determining which categories of race and ethnicity apply to them. (To address this problem in the year 2000 census respondents were offered the chance to check more than one racial category.) Such errors of content arise in large part because census data are self-reported and because even central demographic concepts such as race or ethnicity can be ambiguous to respondents.

Estimating errors. An integral part of the census enterprise, according to the United Nations, should be estimating result errors. There are several ways to validate or correct census errors: post-enumeration surveys, data validation, and comparison with secondary data sources. In the first and most reliable of these methods, census bureaus can reenumerate with special care a sample of the census respondents and compare the results with the original enumeration. In both the 1990 and 2000 U.S. censuses, the Census Bureau conducted just such a Post-Enumeration Survey (PES) to obtain complete coverage and correct information for a sample of the geographic areas covered by the censuses.

A second way of estimating and correcting for census errors is simply to insure that the data recorded are accurate, internally consistent, and plausible. Census bureaus can, and do, develop a variety of means to make sure the data is entered correctly in the first place. Recent censuses have, for example, used computer-assisted data collection for both personal and telephone interviews (U.S. Bureau of the Census, 1999). Information is entered as it is collected, and errors or inconsistencies are identified for correction during the data collection itself. For instance, a woman reporting her age as twenty-five years is unlikely to have twenty living children. If this information were entered by the enumerator the computer might ask the interviewer to repeat the question or make further inquiries to resolve the inconsistency.

Finally, in countries that are statistically developed, bureaus can compare census statistics against other statistical records. For instance, the total number of children enumerated under age ten should bear some correspondence to total number of births and childhood deaths that have been registered over the past ten years. Moreover, as more and more information is available about individuals in other administrative, or *secondary,* record-keeping systems, the United Nations is considering these data as a possible replacement to a traditional census (Suliman, 1996). In the United States, the Census Bureau is "evaluating the feasibility of using administrative records to supplement or improve traditional data collection methods" in the 2010 census (U.S. Bureau of the Census, 1999).

Census bureaus seldom can correct erroneous individual records, but they can and do correct aggregate tabulations for sets of individuals. They also pass on warnings to consumers about the degree and direction of such errors. These corrections are often in the form of estimated underreporting of various categories of people. Such revised or corrected estimates of population characteristics that adjust for estimated errors are being used for most purposes in the year 2000 U.S. census.

EVOLUTION OF THE U.S. CENSUS

The United States has the longest modern series of censuses on record (Edmonston and Schultze, 1995; Shryock, 1982). The first U.S. census was taken in 1790; the twenty-second in 2000. This primacy probably is explained by the political basis for the birth of the nation. As the first postrevolutionary Western nation to be established, it had a strong philosophical commitment to the idea of popular suffrage. Accordingly, its very constitution provided for a census, initially for the purpose of apportioning seats in the House of Representatives and for directing taxes among the states.

However, the first census probably bore little resemblance to the last. It was not until 1902, more than halfway through the U.S. history of census taking, that a permanent census bureau was established; prior to that censuses must have been *ad hoc* affairs handled by temporary organizations. In contrast, the present U.S. Bureau of the Census continuously plans for the next decennial census and processes the last (and also administers a variety of smaller, related data-gathering efforts). The cost of the census has risen dramatically in recent years, with the cost of the 2000 census pegged at $4.8 billion (Edmonston, 1999).

Over its two centuries, the decennial census has been transformed. It has expanded its coverage in several ways. Obviously the territory covered has spread along with national boundaries, but in addition there has been a move to cover all parts of the nation and its affiliated territories. In parallel, there has been a tendency to include all, not part, of the population therein. Content, as well, has grown from a rudimentary noting of existence and location of individuals to a detailed description of them. Since 1940 it has been a census of population and housing (Anderton et al., 1997). With professionalization came a steady reduction of errors—until a rise in undercounts in the 1990 census. Extensive efforts were made in the year 2000 census to continue the trend of improving census quality. As public confidence in the results have grown and as the needs of modern society for information have exploded, the ways of processing the reports have also become more sophisticated and varied. The latest census information is now regularly distributed with considerable speed over the Internet, through a system of State Data Centers, and on CD-ROMs to many government repositories in major libraries. As the dissemination of census data has improved, and as computing facilities have become more accessible, there has been a continual growth in the use of census data in both the public and private sectors. The following sections detail these changes.

Coverage

Not only did the geographic coverage of the U.S. census follow the frontier across the coterminous United States, it also followed the expansion of the American empire beyond those borders. "Alaska was first included in 1880; the Philippine Islands, Puerto Rico, Hawaii, Guam, and American Samoa in 1900; the Canal Zone and Midway in 1910; the Virgin Islands in 1920; certain small Pacific and Caribbean Islands in 1940; and the Trust Territory of the Pacific Islands in 1950" (Shryock, 1982, p. 142). Moreover, coverage reached even beyond the "empire" to include Americans living outside: armed forces and federal civilian employees (and their dependents), crews of merchant vessels, and so forth.

As in ancient censuses, the earlier U.S. counts did not treat all residents equally. In the first six censuses, only the head of household was listed by name; other members were simply tallied into categories for an aggregate description. Listing all persons by name, along with their characteristics, was the great innovation of the census of 1850 (Shryock, 1982, p. 138). Moreover, categories of peoples simply ignored or only partially described in the past (slaves, Native Americans) have been included more and more in recent censuses.

In 1990 attempts to expand coverage to the homeless population included a special one-night "Shelter and Street Night" count of persons found at various locations where homeless people might congregate. In the 2000 census this effort was expanded through a "Special Place Facility Questionnaire" to enumerate people who do not live in traditional housing units and a "Transient Night (T-Night)" survey to enumerate people at campgrounds, fairs and carnivals, marinas, and so on. The 2000 census also included the population living on maritime vessels and a remote Alaskan enumeration. As such efforts to expand coverage continue, the census is rapidly approaching universal coverage of the population. These efforts are, of course, limited by the fact that some people in the United States, such as illegal immigrants or recluses, may wish to evade enumeration.

Census Geography

Not only has geographic coverage increased but also the geographic detail of reporting. The basic census strategy is to map small geographic units of responsibility, each to be assigned to a specific enumerator. This means small units are capable of being assembled into meaningful larger units for reporting purposes. The bureau increasingly has taken advantage of this opportunity, reporting not only by administrative units (town, county, state) but also using its data partially for defining other meaningful social units (parts of cities, standard metropolitan statistical areas, census regions, divisions of the country, and so forth.).

Figure 2-3 lists some of the geographical units that the Census Bureau uses to report population data. The top panel of the figure shows the hierarchy of contiguous geographic units, from largest to smallest. There are four census *regions* (Northeast, Midwest, South, and West) and each region has two to three *subdivisions* made up of anywhere from three to nine states. Almost all census data are regionally organized. However, we are most often interested in population data for smaller areas. *States (*and *territories*) form natural divisions within the regions as do *counties* within states.

Moving to smaller areas becomes more complicated and areas delineated are often unique to the design of the census (see Anderton et al., 1997, ch. 2 for a more complete discussion). *County subdivisions* are designed by the Census Bureau in cooperation with state and local officials. Within these smaller areas the Census Bureau identifies *incorporated places,* or cities and towns, as well as *census designated places* in equivalent areas. Since the 1990 census, all areas of the country also are divided into small areas called *census tracts.* Portions of the country were divided into tracts in earlier censuses. Tracts are defined by local officials working within Census Bureau guidelines and so reflect, as well as any defined area, local communities or neighborhoods. Most tracts have a population of several thousand and average around 4,500 people. Much of the research conducted using census data has been done using census tracts, and computerized census data is generally available for these areas. For even smaller areas of analysis the Census Bureau defines *blocks* and *block groups.* Blocks are small areas bounded on all sides by visible features such as streets, roads, streams, etc., or other political property boundaries. Blocks are often used to study small areas. However, because blocks are so small, the Census Bureau regularly suppresses block-level information that might identify specific individuals.

Figure 2-3 Geographic Specification in the U.S. Census: Selected Areas Used in Reporting Census Data

General Hierarchy
United States
  Region
    State
      County (Metropolitan & Nonmetropolitan)
        County Subdivision
          Place or part (Incorporated & Census Designated)
            Census Tract/Block Numbering Area or part
              Block Group or part
                Block

Other Selected Reporting Units
Metropolitan Statistical Area
  Central City
Urban and Rural
Urbanized Areas
Zip Codes
Congressional Districts
School Districts

Source: U.S. Bureau of the Census, *1990 Census of Population,* 1992.

Looking at the lower panel of Figure 2-3, we see that a number of other categories are used in reporting census data. Data generally are available for *metropolitan statistical areas* (MSAs) consisting of a large population nucleus and adjacent communities that are socially or economically integrated with the population center. *Central cities* in the MSA are also designated. Census tabulations are frequently divided into *urban* and *rural* areas, but the Census Bureau designates *urbanized areas* consisting of a central place and its adjacent, densely settled, urban fringe to better capture this distinction. Less frequently used categories include *Zip Code* areas, *congressional districts, school districts,* etc. As demands for data have risen the variety of geographic areas delineated by the Census Bureau has increased, and areas identified in Figure 2-3 are just some of the more commonly used designations.

Content

Until recently, the trend has been to expand the topics covered in the census, along with the people covered. "Several of the Founding Fathers, including Thomas Jefferson and James Madison, labored mightily to persuade the Congress to add items that would provide information on manpower, industrial composition, and national origins" (Shryock, 1982, p. 138). This expansion was gradual, peaking in 1890.

But expansion took place within a political context and therefore reflected (and still reflects) the public preoccupations of the particular era (Weeks, 1996). For the first century, more or less, Congress was directly responsible for establishing the content. After the establishment of the Census Bureau in 1902, the director made these decisions, though undoubtedly remaining sensitive to political as well as technical considerations. Some items on the census are directly legislated by Congress. Since 1950, the process of deciding not only questionnaire content but also priorities regarding tabulations has been the work of an elaborate network of advisory committees, public hearings, and correspondence culminating in congressional approval (see U.S. Bureau of the Census, 1999, fig. V-1). This process now takes years before the actual census date.

As one might expect, the topics normally covered in recent U.S. censuses go beyond the priority items recommended by the United Nations in Figure 2-1. Table 2-1 shows major items included in the U.S. census between 1960 and 2000. However, not all of these topics are covered for each individual in the population. Progressively since 1940, in the interests of economy, the census questionnaires have been divided into a "short form" (questions asked of everybody) and one or more "long forms" (including supplementary questions for specified samples of people).

Table 2-1 indicates which questions were asked of everyone on the short form and which were asked of a sample of people on one or more long forms in each U.S. decennial census from 1960 to 2000. Generally, in each decade fewer questions are asked on the short form and more information is collected on only a sample of the population. In the year 2000 census the short form no longer collected information on the number of rooms, units at an address, or the value of property. These items were still collected on the long form administered to a sample. Questions dropped altogether from the 2000 census included those on age or date of first marriage, children

Table 2-1
Availability of Selected Questions on the U.S. Decennial Census: 1960–2000

(S indicates item is available on short form, L indicates long form of any sample)

Census Information[a]	1960 (1)	1970 (2)	1980 (3)	1990 (4)	2000 (5)
Population Items					
Age	S	S	S	S	S
Sex	S	S	S	S	S
Race	S	S	S	S	S
Hispanic Origin		L	S	S	S
Relationship to Household Head	S	S	S	S	S
Age or Date of First Marriage	L	L	L		
Children Born to Mother	L	L	L	L	
School Attendance and Attainment	L	L	L	L	L
Place of Birth	L	L	L	L	L
Place of Birth Mother and Father	L	L			
Ancestry			L	L	L
Language Spoken at Home	L	L	L	L	L
Residence 5 Years Ago	L	L	L	L	L
Work Disability		L	L	L	L
Employment Status	L	L	L	L	L
Hours Worked Last Week	L	L	L	L	L
Year Last Worked	L	L	L	L	
Industry, Occupation, and Class	L	L	L	L	L
Means of Transportation	L	L	L	L	L
Income from Earnings	L	L	L	L	L
Farm Income, Soc. Sec., and Assistance		L	L	L	L
All Other Income	L	L	L	L	L
Housing Items					
Owned or Rented	S	S	S	S	S
Number of Rooms	S	S	S	S	L
Units at Address	S	S	S	S	L
Value	S	S	S	S	L
Mortgage and Insurance			L	L	L
Detailed Utility Costs	L	L	L	L	L
Year Built	L	L	L	L	L
Number of Bedrooms	L	L	L	L	L
Source of Water	L	L	L	L	
Sewage Disposal	L	L	L	L	
Heating Fuel	L	L	L	L	L
Telephone Available	L	S	L	L	L
Automobiles	L	L	L	L	L

[a]Some items listed represent consistent blocks of multiple questions on the census.
Source: Edmonston and Schultze, eds., *Modernizing the U.S. Census,* 1995, appndx. A, table A-2; U.S. Bureau of the Census, *Census 2000 Operational Plan,* 1999, table V-1.

born to the mother, year last worked, and housing questions on sewage disposal and water supply (U.S. Bureau of the Census, 1999). These questions were dropped because there was no legislation requiring their collection by the Census Bureau, and one question, about caregiving by grandparents, was added because new legislation mandated it. These decisions reflect both the increasing concern for the cost of conducting a census and an increasing political influence on census content.

Data Collection

Prior to World War II, census-taking procedures in the United States were conventional; that is, they involved the gathering of full information about all individuals by means of personal interviews with household informants. Since then, a series of fundamental changes have been made.

The first innovation, actually started in 1940, is asking some questions about only a *sample* of the population and making generalizations, from the sample, about the total population. By 2000, only six items in Table 2-1 were on the census short form, asked in all households; the remaining long-form questions were asked only in a sample containing about 17% of the nation's households (U.S. Bureau of the Census, 1999). The justification, obviously, is economy: by sampling, the bureau saved money that then could be spent for improving the quality of enumeration.

The second innovation is obtaining answers through the *mail* rather than by face-to-face interviews. As mentioned, throughout its history, the U.S. census has cleaved more to the idea of *dejure* than *defacto* residence. The idea of locating people through their mailing addresses seems consistent with this tradition. The mail-out, mail-back procedure started in 1960. And, since 1980, individual interviews have been used only for the population living in remote areas and for transients and persons without fixed addresses, found in special sweeps (U.S. Bureau of the Census, 1999; Shryock, 1982). Obviously the mailing procedure puts a premium on the careful preparation of address lists and probably is workable only in a society where mail service is virtually universal.

The third, most recent, innovation is the incorporation of both *telephone* and *computer* (via the Internet) interaction in the 2000 census. Actually, this is more a body of innovations than a single change: as mentioned earlier, in the 2000 census a special edit was incorporated to review submitted questionnaires for missing, incomplete, or inconsistent data that might affect census coverage. When questionnaires failed coverage edits, a telephone follow-up survey was conducted to resolve any issues. The Census Bureau also used toll-free multilingual telephone assistance numbers and an Internet site offering assistance in completing the census questionnaire, and individuals were allowed to submit their responses over the Internet using a computerized (English-only) version of the short form. Use of the Internet in conducting censuses will likely expand in coming decades.

Finally, there was the controversial proposal by the Census Bureau to use statistical sampling methods as an alternative to enumeration for the 2000 census (see, for example, Wright, 1998; and Edmonston and Schultze, 1995, ch. 5). The Bureau, and most demographers, believed that it had done its best to perfect the administration of traditional census methods in 1990, yet had still experienced difficulties that resulted in an undercounting of hard-to-reach segments of the population. Congressional discussion over the use of sampling was quickly politicized. Republicans saw the proposal as a method that would increase the political clout of normally Democratic constituencies, such as ethnic minorities and the poor. Democrats viewed Republican reluctance as maintaining an unfair political status quo, justified by an irrational sentiment for traditional census methods. The Supreme Court took a position that traditional enumeration was constitutionally required for allocating federal legislative representation to areas, but that sampling may be used for other census purposes. The Census Bureau has resolved to use sampling to provide the best estimates possible for all uses other than allocation. The issue of sampling, however, will continue to be controversial and hotly contested.

Processing and Publication

Until 1890, U.S. census returns were tabulated by hand. This was a time-consuming and error-plagued process, and its inadequacies grew in proportion to the population being counted. Highly motivated as it was, the Census Bureau became the source of data-processing innovations that since have spread to other organizations. Herman Hollerith developed a tabulating machine that was used from 1890 to 1910;

All census forms are now processed first through optical scanning, but the Census Bureau still employs hundreds of clerks to tie up loose ends.

an improved "unit counter" using punched cards was developed at the Bureau and used through 1950; electronic computers were in partial use in 1950, and now virtually all census tabulations are made with them; optical scanning devices, along with pre-coded questionnaires, have been in heavy use for decades. By 1980, questions on the short form were pre-coded for optical scanning. By the 2000 census all questions and written answers were processed first through optical scanning with manual data entry done only to resolve difficult to process write-in items.

Modernization has also permitted a transformation in census reporting. Since 1980, when the census data were published in great detail, the Census Bureau has moved away from the production of increasingly detailed published tabulations. Instead, access to census data is increasingly provided in electronic form over the Internet, on CD-Rom, on computer tapes, and so on. An integrated system called the *American FactFinder* is being used to distribute data products and tabulations from the year 2000 census. This system provides access to census data for small geographic areas such as blocks and tracts (similar to that provided in the 1990 census *Summary Tape Files*) and a sample of individual-level data with identifying information deleted (i.e. the widely used *Public Use Microdata Samples,* or *PUMS*). The interactive provision of census data has given census data users the ability to extract customized tables, charts, graphs, maps, etc., for either standard Census Bureau geographic areas or user-defined geographic areas. The system also supports on-line documentation and help in accessing the data. Of course, summary data will continue to be published in hard copy for general use.

Registration and Vital Statistics

Suppose that a country does have a decennial census. That supplies it with information only about its population size and composition as of the "census moment." It does not tell the size and composition during the years between censuses. Nor does it tell about the events (births, deaths, migrations) that continuously are changing that population, except for the meager information from a few retrospective questions on the census.

In the Western demographic tradition, the system that has evolved to complement censuses is the registration of population events as they occur. The relationship between the two systems is analogous to that between stock and flow data in commerce, or to that between prevalence and incidence statistics in the study of public health (Seltzer, 1982). This registration strategy has been applied better to deaths and births than to migrations. Since these two events refer to the starting and stopping of life, counting the registered events results in "vital statistics." Most demographers use that term more broadly to include events that change marital status, such as marriages and divorces. This inclusion is understandable since deaths, births, and marital events originally were registered as part of the same process.

Evolution of Vital Statistics Systems

For many centuries, long before Europe took censuses, Christian priests kept track of their flocks in writing. They evolved local parish registers, recording not only the existence and status of all members of the flock but also the status-changing events as they occurred. As we shall see in chapter 7, these early parish registers have provided a wealth of information for the field of historical demography. For the present, their importance to us is in their role as precursors of conventional Western vital statistics systems.

Western nationalism secularized this tradition of local registration. It evolved into a system of civil registration of major changes in individual status and documentation of those changes in certificates of birth, death, marriage, and divorce. The main additional step necessary for creating a *vital event registration system,* once registration is in place, is the continuous and exhaustive compilation of the local records in some central location. In the United States, birth and death certificates are collected from local registers by each state, which then transmits them to the National Center for Health Statistics, or NCHS (Hetzel, 1997).

A final step in the development of vital statistics systems was to expand the information gathered about the nature of the event and the people involved; for example, the cause of death as well as its occurrence, the sex of the new child as well as its birth, and the age and marital status of the mother. It is this additional information, and particularly the age and sex of those involved, that allows registration data to be combined with census data in population analysis. In the United States, NCHS provides standard forms and model procedures to the states, which administer birth and death registration. A revision of the standard death data collected in the United States (e.g. inclusion of a Hispanic identifier, decedents' education and socioeconomic status) is planned for the year 2002.

Just as with censuses, a key element in a national registration system is a system of dissemination and access to the collected data. NCHS distributes a variety of reports on a regular basis from the vital registration system. Increasingly these reports are being provided in electronic form over the Internet. NCHS also provides public-use files from registration data over the Internet with on-line documentation. In addition to vital statistics, NCHS oversees a number of large national surveys (e.g., some of those in Figure 2-4) and, similarly, provides public-use access to these data.

Difficulties

The maintenance of an effective registration system probably is more of an administrative accomplishment than carrying out decennial population censuses. Whereas a census can involve periodic crash efforts, civil registration requires maintaining a permanent bureaucracy in every locality in the country. Because of this, most countries have more confidence in data from their censuses than vital statistics data from their registration systems. This, combined with their costliness, has caused many countries to curtail their registration systems. As a result, "In many developing countries registration is either weak or almost entirely lacking" (United Nations, 1999, p. 20).

Even in the United States, the NCHS made a change of historic proportions in vital registration when it stopped collecting national marriage and divorce registration data in 1996. Marriage and divorce data had been collected by the government since 1867. NCHS discontinued this registration system "to prioritize programs in a period of tightened resource constraints" (Federal Register, 1995) and because of "concerns about the completeness and quality of detailed marriage and divorce data" (Broome,

1995). Changes in marital status in the United States will, as vital events in many developing countries are, have to be learned from sample surveys and information reported in census years.

Population Registers

While most countries with standardized reporting of vital statistics now maintain event registration systems similar to the United States, population registers provide an alternative means of monitoring vital events. Registers, much like those of early Western European parishes, are kept on a centralized, secular, national basis. They provide continuous recording of data on particular events that occur to each individual, as well as selected characteristics describing those individuals. The key difference from event registrations is, then, that registers organize a continuous record of events into a life history for each individual in the register. Such systems are found in some Scandinavian countries, Eastern Europe, and the Far East. Where present, they provide a data system potentially independent of that provided by the combination of the census and vital statistics.

The alert reader may notice that no mention has been made of registering the third population process: *migration*. Most nations do attempt to register crossing of their national borders, but they do this so incompletely that registration does not play a central role in measuring migration, as it does in measuring fertility and mortality. The complexities of migration estimation are treated separately in chapter 9.

SAMPLE SURVEYS

Demographic sample surveys have become so widespread, in less-developed countries as well as those more-developed, that they now are an integral part of national data systems, along with censuses and registration (United Nations, 1999). Surveys are used to improve the quality of the other data sources, even to substitute for them, and to supplement them with detail.

As we just noted, systems for registering births and deaths are especially difficult for less-developed countries to maintain. Sample surveys in these countries often substitute for registration in estimating national fertility and mortality. True, such surveys cannot provide the kind of accounting—continuous and for all localities—that a sophisticated registration system can. On the other hand, they can provide national-level data of richer detail through such features as detailed retrospective questions.

Census bureaus also use such surveys as one way to form intercensal or postcensal *estimates* of the population (see next section). Census bureaus may have demographic questions not worth including in the census but worth answering on a periodic basis for a less expensive sample. The U.S. Current Population Survey, a monthly series carried out by the Census Bureau since the 1940s, serves this, and other, functions. The same topics generally are covered at annual intervals. Indeed, the *Current Population Reports*, where these surveys are published, have become a major bibliographic source for current descriptions of the U.S. population, supplanting for many purposes the census itself.

Figure 2-4 Internet Access to Demographic Data and Major Data Resources

Sites	Internet Address
United States Census Bureau	http://www.census.gov
National Center for Health Statistics	http://www.cdc.gov/nchswww/nchshome.htm
Bureau of Labor Statistics	http://stats.bls.gov/blshome.html
Inter-University Consortium for Political and Social Research	http://www.icpsr.umich.edu
Immigration and Naturalization Service	http://www.ins.usdoj.gov/graphics/index.htm
Surveys	
Current Population Survey	http://www.census.gov/hhes/cpsdesc.html
American Housing Survey	http://www.census.gov/pub/hhes/www/ahs.html
Survey of Income Program and Participation	http://www.census.gov/hhes/sippdesc.html
National Health Interview Survey	http://www.cdc.gov/nchswww/nhis.htm
National Health and Nutrition Survey	http://ftp.cdc.gov/nchswww/nhanes.htm
Integrated Public Use Micro-Samples	http://www.hist.umn.edu/~ipums/

Source: Anderton et al., *Population of the United States,* 1997, ch. 2, appndx. 2–3.

There are a wide variety of demographic surveys that have been repeated over time and thus have come to serve as major sources of population data. While space prevents a discussion of all these resources, Figure 2-4 identifies some of the major U.S. demographic surveys and the Internet addresses for further information or data access. Also given in Figure 2-4 are the addresses for the Census Bureau, NCHS, the Bureau of Labor Statistics, and a large archive of social science data maintained by the Inter-University Consortium for Political and Social Research. Internet access to these data are constantly evolving and regular visits to the Internet sites identified are one way to keep abreast of demographic developments and data in the United States.

DEMOGRAPHIC ESTIMATION

Why Estimates Are Needed

In many of the graphs and tables presented in the following chapters, the reader will find the word "estimated" in the title. Why can't demographers stick to hard facts rather than making guesses? There are two main reasons: 1) ten years normally elapse between censuses and 2) not all population data are reliable.

The ten-year gap. Because there usually is a ten-year gap between censuses, there is a need for *intercensal* estimates, if one is interested in the past, and *postcensal* estimates, if one is interested in the present. Surveys can provide current estimates, but there is another, more traditional technique. This has been labeled "direct" estimation from census and registration data. Let us assume that we are making a postcensal (vs. intercensal) estimate. The basic process is to take the latest census count as the baseline. Then one subtracts people on the basis of registered deaths, adds people on the basis of registered births, and subtracts or adds on the basis of one's information about emigration and immigration. The process is very similar to that for making population projections. The difference lies in the source of one's input about mortality, fertility, and migration after the baseline count. In the case of projection, one employs assumptions; in the case of estimation, one optimally employs actual counts of events.

Unreliable data. The second reason for estimation is that trustworthy information may be lacking for one of the population processes, while being generally available for the others. Population size, growth, mortality, fertility, and migration form a closed system, described in the balancing equation already discussed in chapter 1:

crude growth rate = crude birth rate - crude death rate + crude rate of net migration

In the simplest case, when one term of that equation is missing (say, net migration), it can be inferred from one's knowledge of all other factors, i.e. growth, birth, and death rates. Unfortunately, data from less-developed countries often are not sufficient to allow this straightforward procedure. In many such countries, even those data that are available about population processes usually are suspect, incomplete, or in unconventional form. This situation arises, for instance, where sample surveys, using retrospective questions, are used instead of registration of births. To handle this complex estimation need, formal demographers have labored to describe in more detail the interrelationships among the various demographic variables, however measured. With that background, they have been able to gather a growing tool kit of very indirect estimation procedures. This is one of the methodological frontiers of demography (Arriaga, 1994; Brass, 1975; Bogue et al., 1993; Hill and Zlotnik, 1982; United Nations, 1983, 1967).

Estimation of Historical Population Size

Chapter 3 gives an account of world population growth from around 8000 or 10,000 B.C. to the present. But in the present chapter we have learned that modern population censuses, even in the more-developed countries, were a development mostly of the 1800s and that ancient censuses were taken rarely. If that is the case, how can we describe premodern worldwide population trends?

Part of the answer is that we cannot—not with any real confidence. Table 2-2 dramatizes the point. It shows the estimated population of the world from about 10,000 to 8000 B.C. to A.D. 1750, giving lower and upper estimates throughout. The estimates are the extremes of what Durand calls "indifference ranges, within which there seems little basis for preference" (1977, p. 284). We have computed the percentage difference between upper and lower estimates as a rough index of the degree of indecision. It decreases from 67% for the earliest period to 9% for the 1750 estimates.

The year 1750 can be considered to be late in the era before the development of modern demographic data. How do contemporary demographers estimate the populations of the 1700s? For the Western countries, demographers have to depend on unconventional data such as partial population listings (e.g. parish christening and burial records, tax rolls, military service rolls, etc.) or listings of habitable structures. For the rest of the world, demographers combine various clues, including counts for

Table 2-2
Range of World Population Estimates to 1750

Year	Estimate (millions)		Percentage Difference[a]
	Lower (1)	Upper (2)	(3)
10,000–8000 B.C.	5	10	67
A.D. 0–14	270	330	20
A.D. 1000	275	345	22
1250	350	450	12
1500	440	540	10
1750	735	805	9

[a]Percentages computed with denominator as mean of two estimates.
Source: Durand, "Historical Estimates of World Population," 1977, table 5.

particular cities and inference from area of cultivable land, strength of military forces, type of economy, and the nature of political organization (Durand, 1977).

Our presenting this humbling picture here has a purpose: it is to increase the reader's skepticism about sweeping descriptions of historical world population trends, including those in our next chapter. But, imprecise as they must be, those indirect historical estimates are all we have.

SUMMARY

Nations depend upon regular censuses as the foundation of their demographic data-gathering systems. Ideally, censuses are taken at even intervals (usually ten years) and list each of the people residing within a defined territory as of that moment. Censuses also ask fairly standard questions about individual traits, used for description of population composition. Almost all nations of the world now take censuses, but even the best censuses have some errors both of coverage and of content. Ideally, part of the census enterprise is to estimate errors.

The United States has the longest continuous series of modern censuses, which started in 1790. Recent innovations have included the use of mail in place of most personal interviews, the use of sampling for some of the questions, and the use of street surveys to enumerate transient populations. The modern Western practice has been to complement decennial censuses with registration of births and deaths. The administrative infrastructure for continuous and exhaustive registration has, however, proved difficult to maintain for less-developed countries.

Sample surveys have been used to supplement censuses or to substitute for registration. Particularly in the less-developed countries, retrospective questions about births often substitute for registration as a basis for estimating fertility. Surveys are used everywhere for evaluating censuses and providing intercensal estimates. Finally, supplementary surveys such as the U.S. Current Population Survey add regular detailed information that is too expensive or too current to be obtained by censuses.

Although most countries now take censuses, their other data are incomplete and questionable, especially in the less-developed regions. Complex procedures are continually being developed for inferring missing or doubtful data from the reliable data at hand. This effort is enhanced by the close interrelationships among the various demographic variables. Where no factors are known precisely, however, such as for prehistoric times, estimation becomes very indirect indeed.

▶ PROPOSITIONS FOR DEBATE

1. The sharp rise in coverage errors in the 1990 census reflected an increasing reluctance of citizens to provide census information.
2. In the next U.S. census, illegal immigrants should not be counted.
3. In countries that are completely mapped and where samples of subareas can be drawn, surveys can take the place of censuses.
4. Given coverage errors, U.S. courts should have the right to overturn U.S. census counts for localities, if they seem implausible.
5. The United States should maintain a national population register, as do many Scandinavian countries.
6. Little real information was lost by ending the U.S. national system of marriage and divorce registration in 1996.
7. I (name of reader) was missed in the last census of (name of country of residence).
8. The census will always undercount illegal immigrants, the homeless, and recluses in the United States.

▶ REFERENCES AND SUGGESTED READINGS

Anderton, Douglas L., Richard E. Barrett, and Donald J. Bogue. 1997. *The Population of the United States.* 3d ed. New York: Free Press.

Arriaga, Eduardo E. 1994. *Population Analysis with Microcomputers.* Vol. 1 & 2. Bureau of the Census International Programs Center/USAID/UNFPA. Washington, DC: Government Printing Office.

Bogue, Donald J., Eduardo E. Arriaga, and Douglas L. Anderton, eds. 1993. *Readings in Population Research Methodology.* Vol. 1–8. Chicago: UNFPA/Social Development Center.

Bos, Eduard, Mu T. Vu, Ernest Massiah, and Rodolfo A. Bulatao. 1994. *World Population Projections 1994–95 Edition: Estimates and Projections with Related Demographic Statistics.* World Bank. Baltimore: Johns Hopkins University Press.

Brass, William. 1975. *Methods of Estimating Fertility and Mortality from Limited and Defective Data.* Chapel Hill, NC: Laboratories for Population Statistics.

Broome, Claire V. 1995. "FR Response, Division of Vital Statistics." FR Doc. 95-30566, filed 12/14/95.

Durand, John D. 1977. "Historical Estimates of World Population: An Evaluation." *Population and Development Review* 3(3).

Edmonston, Barry. 1999. "The 2000 Census Challenge." *Population Reference Bureau Reports on America* 1(1).

Edmonston, Barry, and Charles Schultze, eds. *Modernizing the U.S. Census.* Panel on Census Requirements in the Year 2000 and Beyond, Committee on National Statistics, Commission on Behavioral and Social Sciences and Education, National Research Council. Washington, DC.

Eggerickx, Thierry, and Francois Begeot. 1993. "Les Recensements en Europe dans les Années 1990: De la divesité des pratiques nationales à la comprabilité internationale des résultats." *Population* 48(6).

Elo, I. T., and S. H. Preston. 1994. "Estimating African-American Mortality from Inaccurate Data." *Demography* 31(3).

Federal Register. 1995. "Change in Marriage and Divorce Data Available from the National Center for Health Statistics." *Federal Register* 60(241): 64437–64438.

Francese, Peter K. 1979. "The 1980 Census: The Counting of America." *Population Bulletin* 34(4). Washington, DC: Population Reference Bureau.

Hetzel, A. M. 1997. *U.S. Vital Statistics System: Major Activities and Developments, 1950–95.* National Center For Health Statistics. (PHS) 97-1003. Washington, DC: Government Printing Office.

Hill, Kenneth, and Hania Zlotnik. 1982. "Indirect Estimation of Fertility and Mortality." In John A. Ross, ed., *International Encyclopedia of Population.* Vol. 1. New York: The Free Press.

Iversen, Roberta Rehner, Frank E. Furstenberg, and Alisa L. Belzer. 1999. "How Much Do We Count? Interpretation and Error-Making in the Decennial Census." *Demography* 36(1).

Robinson, J. G., B. Ahmed, P. Das Gupta, and K. Woodrow. 1993. "Estimation of Population Coverage in the 1990 U.S. Census Based on Demographic Analysis." *Journal of the American Statistical Association* 88(423).

Roush, Wade. 1996. "A Census in Which All Americans Count." *Science* 274(1).

Seltzer, William. 1982. "Data Collection: National Systems." In John A. Ross, ed., *International Encyclopedia of Population.* Vol. 1. New York: The Free Press.

Shryock, Henry S. 1982. "Data Collection: United States Census." In John A. Ross, ed., *International Encyclopedia of Population.* Vol. 1. New York: The Free Press.

Shryock, Henry S., Jacob S. Siegel, and Associates. 1976. *The Methods and Materials of Demography.* Condensed edition by Edward G. Stockwell. New York: Academic Press.

Suharto, Sam. 1996. "Proposed Changes in the International Recommendations for Population and Housing Censuses." *United Nations Statistics Division, Technical Notes* (December).

Suliman, Sirageldin H. 1996. "Use of Administrative Records in Population Censuses and in Other Demographic and Social Statistics." *United Nations Statistics Division, Technical Notes* (December).

United Nations. 1967. *Manual IV: Methods of Estimating Basic Demographic Measures from Incomplete Data.* Population Studies no. 42. ST/SOA/Series A/42. New York: United Nations.

———. 1991. *Handbook on Vital Statistics Systems and Methods.* Vol. 1: *Legal, Organizational and Technical Aspects.* United Nations Department of International Economic and Social Affairs Statistical Office. Studies in Methods, Series F, no. 35. ST/ESA/STAT/SER.F/35. New York: United Nations.

———. 1996. Expert Working Group on International Statistical Programmes and Coordination, 18th session, Appendix. United Nations Economic and Social Council. E/CN.3/AC.1/1996/R.4. New York: United Nations.

United Nations. 1998. *Principles and Recommendations for Population and Housing Censuses.* Revision One. ST/ESA/STAT/SER.M/Rev.1. New York: United Nations.

———. 1999. *Concise Report on World Population Monitoring, 1999: Population Growth, Structure and Distribution.* Report of the Secretary-General. E/CN.9/1999/2. New York: United Nations.

United Nations Population Division and the National Academy of Sciences. 1983. *Manual X: Indirect Techniques for Demographic Estimation.* Population Studies no. 81. New York: United Nations.

United Nations Statistics Division. 1999. Population and Housing Census Dates 1900 and 2000 Round of Censuses (as of Feb. 15, 1999). www.un.org.

United States Bureau of the Census. 1992. *1990 Census of Population, General Population Characteristics, United States,* 1990 CP-1-1. Washington, DC: Government Printing Office.

———. 1999. *Census 2000 Operational Plan Using Traditional Census-Taking Methods.* Washington, DC: Government Printing Office.

Weed, J. A. 1995. "Vital Statistics in the United States: Preparing for the Next Century." *Population Index* 61(4).

Weeks, John R. 1996. *Population: An Introduction to Concepts and Issues.* 6th ed. Belmont, CA: Wadsworth.

Wright, Tommy. 1998. "Sampling and Census 2000: The Concepts." *American Scientist* 86.

3 ▶ Population Growth

This chapter begins presenting the facts of demography. It starts on what may be familiar ground for some readers, a description of world population growth in the past and projection into its future. With world population tripling from 2 billion to 6 billion over the past century there is no more obvious demographic trend than that of population growth. Our description of population growth distinguishes between the more-developed regions (MDRs) and the less-developed regions (LDRs), since the MDRs and LDRs have very different pasts and prospects. The chapter also distinguishes countries by their stage in the nearly universal fertility decline that has taken place over the past century. The chapter closes with analyses of the problems resulting from present and future growth in countries at different stages of development and fertility decline.

A HISTORY OF GLOBAL POPULATION GROWTH

Figure 3-1 is a familiar graph in demography. The line shows the size of the human population of the world from our earliest guesses to the present. The dates in this version of the graph range from between 2 and 5 million years before Christ to A.D. 2000. The time segment at the far left, the Old Stone Age and beginning of the New Stone Age with agrarian societies, cannot be drawn to scale, since it would extend way off the page. From 4000 B.C., a regular time scale allows us to see the pattern of increase in population size, or population growth.

It took millions of years before about 1650 for the global population to reach a *half billion* people, but by A.D. 2000 world population was over *6 billion*. In just the past one hundred years more than 4 billion people have been added; the world's population tripled in size! Since the birth of a now twenty-year-old college student, the world's population has increased by nearly as many people as were alive in the world in 1900.

Figure 3-1 Global Population Growth Through History

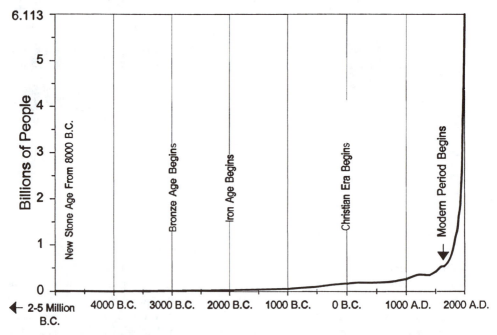

Source: Kremer, "Population Growth and Technological Change," 1993; Bos et al., *World Population Projections 1994–95 Edition*, 1994.

Clearly there was some dramatic change in the nature of population growth as the world reached modern times. To discuss the two very different patterns of population growth before and after about 1650, let us describe these two periods of growth separately, the "premodern" and then the "modern" period.

Premodern Growth, Before 1650

First, a warning is appropriate. To avoid distracting the reader with repeated cautions and qualifiers, we will write as though we really had a precise idea of how many people were alive in premodern times. In reality, our guesses are uncertain (see Cohen, 1995, appendix 2 for nine different recent estimates). This uncertainty is detailed in chapter 2, under "demographic estimation." Having said that, let us plunge boldly ahead.

In the premodern era from about 300,000 B.C. to roughly 1650, the harsh living conditions resulted in extremely high mortality rates and slow growth (Collins, 1982). After thousands of years of hunting and gathering, the development of agriculture at the beginning of the New Stone Age (i.e. 8000 B.C.) led to a more reliable food supply and more stable forms of social organization. Agricultural settlements in turn were followed by urban civilizations, first in Mesopotamia, then in Egypt, Crete, India, China, and Peru, wherein populations could flourish to a greater extent. With the emergence of agrarian societies, and despite continued high mortality, world population slowly increased, growing from an estimated 5 million to perhaps 170 million by A.D. 1.

During the early Christian era, while populations did slowly increase, growth was held in check, primarily by infectious disease and periodic decimating epidemics (McKeown, 1983; McNeill, 1976). However, disease was not alone among the hardships of life during this slow growth period. Unfavorable climatic changes (Wrigley, 1969), periodic severe famines (Meuvret, 1965), and even lower birth rates from malnutrition (Watkins and Van de Walle, 1983) were among the myriad hardships limiting population growth. With few exceptions, this era was characterized by high birth rates and high but fluctuating death rates, resulting in slow, frequently interrupted, population growth.

Modern Explosion, 1650 to the Present

Let us look more closely at the far right segment of Figure 3-1, from 1650 to 2000. One thing to notice, of course, is the large and soaring number of people in the modern world, compared with the premodern. The estimated 2000 population of over 6 billion (Bos et al., 1994) is more than eleven times as great as that in 1650, the end of the premodern era. Another feature to notice, one which needs explaining, is the rapidly increasing slope of the line.

For almost all of the modern era, there are two reasons for this increasing upward slope. First is that any sustained positive *rate* of growth will result in the increasing upward slope of such a line. If people normally are behaving in such a way that they are more than replacing themselves every generation, then every generation will have more people behaving that way, producing even larger increments. By analogy, annual crude rates of population growth are like interest rates on a savings account; the rates operate not only on the original principal but also on the interest that is being reinvested continuously. The higher the growth (or interest) rate, the greater the degree of the line's concave arching that is caused by compounding alone. (Exercises 1 and 2 at the end of the chapter allow the reader to demonstrate this phenomenon.)

There is an important second reason for the upward curve of this particular line: the population growth rate did not simply stay stable and positive; the growth rate itself grew through almost all of this period. Table 3-1 shows that the annual rate of global population growth doubled in the three centuries between 1650 and World War II, and the postwar era witnessed an even more dramatic explosion of growth rates.

Growth rates reached a plateau from around 1960 to 1975. They then fell slightly to 1.7% annually through the early 1990s, and by 1999 had dropped substantially to 1.3% annually. At this writing, they are projected to remain at about 1.3% for the coming quarter century. The recent drop in growth rates is due to declining births and the suddenly rising number of deaths from HIV/AIDS throughout the world. Note, however, that even this lower growth rate is higher than anything experienced by the world as a whole prior to World War II.

Table 3-1 also translates each of the annual growth rates into "years to double" at that rate. This is a device for dramatizing the implications of growth rates if extended over time. It is simple to make the conversion by using this formula:

$$\text{years to double} = \frac{70}{\text{\% annual growth rate}}$$

Table 3-1
Annual Growth Rates of World Population and Implied Years to Double, 1650 to 2000

Period	Annual Growth Rate (percent)	Years to Double
1650–1750	0.4	175
1750–1800	0.4	175
1800–1850	0.5	140
1850–1900	0.5	140
1900–1950	0.8	88
1950–1955	1.8	39
1955–1960	1.9	37
1960–1965	2.0	35
1965–1970	1.9	37
1970–1975	1.9	37
1975–1980	1.7	41
1980–1985	1.7	41
1985–1990	1.7	41
1990–1995	1.7	41
1995–2000	1.3	53

Source: United Nations, *The Determinants and Consequences of Population Trends*, 1973, table 2-1; *World Population Prospects as Assessed in 1980*, 1981, table 1; *World Resources 1990–91*, 1990, table 16-1; *World Resources 1994–95*, 1994, table 16-1; *Revision of the World Population Estimates and Projections*, 1999.

The reason why this formula works is explained mathematically in Box 3-1. The implication of this formula is that at the current annual growth rate (let us use the UN's estimate for 2000, 1.3%), the world's population would double in the following 53 years to just under *12 billion* by A.D. 2050; it would redouble to *24 billion* in the next 53 years (by A.D. 3003); and so on.

Such populations are unimaginable! But this exercise helps drive home an important point: as the size of the world population gets larger, the impact of *any* positive growth rate gets greater. Since the base population on which any growth rate works is now large, even a moderate rate of growth means many people are being added.

However, our example of doubling time assumed growth at the present rate over more than a century. Is that realistic? The consensus would seem to be "no." World mortality already is moderate or low, overall, but continues to decline for some groups while rising for others (see chapter 5). World fertility is declining and will likely continue to do so even more rapidly than mortality, thus causing further erosion of the world rate of natural increase (or growth).

But a cautionary note is appropriate: even if the world's growth rate has peaked, the world's population size certainly has not. Even if the world's growth rate were cut almost in half—say, to 0.7% per year—the population of the globe still would double in 100 years, then redouble, then redouble. . . . That is why demographers are not content with observing that the rate is no longer increasing; rather, they are trying to estimate when and how that rate will become *zero*, when the modern global population explosion will come to its end (Cohen, 1995).

Box 3-1   Why Does the "Doubling Time" Conversion Work?

Many readers will be willing simply to take our word for the legitimacy of the conversion of annual growth rates to "doubling time." This insert is for those who want a mathematical explanation.

Here are our variables. Let:

P_1 = the population at the beginning of an interval
P_2 = the population at the end of the interval
n = the number of years in the interval
r = the annual population growth rate during the interval

Now, let us take the simplest case, where the interval is one year (where $n = 1$). In that case,

$$P_2 = P_1 + rP_1$$

That is, the population at the end of the interval is equal to the population at the beginning of the interval plus the growth in between, that growth being calculated by multiplying the annual growth rate by the beginning population. This equation can also be stated as

$$P_2 = P_1(1 + r)$$

If we let n extend beyond one year, then the general formula would be

$$P_2 = P_1(1 + r)^n$$

This equation also can be stated as

$$\frac{P_2}{P_1} = (1 + r)^n$$

Taking logarithms of both sides of the equation and solving for n, the equation would be as follows:

$$n = \frac{\log P_2 - \log P_1}{\log (1 + r)}$$

Now let us see how many years it would take for the population to double under the conditions of an annual growth rate of 1.0%. That is, let us solve the above equation for n assuming first that the population will double, or,

$$P_2 = 2P_1$$

and, second, that the annual growth rate is 1%, or,

$$r = .01$$

Solving the formula with these values would produce the equation

$$n = \frac{\log 2}{\log (1 + 0.01)} = \frac{0.30103}{0.00432} = 69.68$$

In sum, the number of years required for a population to double at a 1% annual growth rate is precisely 69.68 years, usually rounded to 70 years.

Incidentally, if one chooses to use natural logarithms rather than common logarithms, then n would equal 69.32 rather than 69.68. Some texts will treat 69.3 (rounded to 69) as the number of years taken for a population to double at a 1% annual rate of growth. The difference is trivial for our purposes. We will use 70 as our "magic number."

The term "explosion" has a hysterical ring to it that annoys some demographers (e.g. Hartmann, 1995; Simon, 1986). Moreover, it may carry a negative connotation, implying a destructive and devastating event. Nevertheless, attempting to describe the dramatic population growth in Figure 3-1, we think the term is apt.

CLASSIFYING COUNTRIES

The Development Dichotomy: MDRs and LDRs

Regions of the world did not march lock-step from the 1600s to the present through those economic and demographic changes we call "modernization" or "development." Throughout, there have been the haves and the have-nots among nations. Earlier there were the colonial powers and their colonies. Later there were the imperial powers and their empires.

Most important for our discussion, there were those who started early in their agricultural, industrial, and demographic revolutions and then there were those who started late. One way in which that distinction is captured is by the familiar dichotomy between the countries of the more-developed regions (MDRs) and the less-developed regions (LDRs). In the past, economic development and demographic development have often gone hand in hand. (*Economic* development is measured by efficiency of productive technology while *demographic* development is measured by degree of control over death and birth.) As a result, the distinction between MDRs and LDRs has reflected many demographic, as well as economic, developmental differences between regions. The UN version of the classification has been widely accepted by demographers: the MDRs are North America, Europe, Japan, Australia, and New Zealand; the LDRs are Africa, Asia (less Japan), Oceania (less Australia and New Zealand), Latin America, and the Caribbean.

Recently, however, the lack of synchronization between economic development and demographic development in some countries has become troublesome for such a simple typology. Moreover, the United Nations version of the development dichotomy has classified entire world regions, rather than nations, since adjacent countries have tended to share similar economic histories. But not all regions are homogeneous: Oceania, for instance, is demographically dominated by Australia and New Zealand, but also contains Micronesia and Melanesia. East Asia includes Japan, clearly more-developed. Latin America, though not labeled as a mixed region, does include Temperate South America (Argentina, Chile, Uruguay), which stretches somewhat the label "less-developed." For both of these reasons, while employing the development dichotomy in the following discussion, we sometimes will supplement or even replace it with a more purely demographic classification of countries, described below.

The Demographic Taxonomy: Pre-Transition, Transitional, and Late-Transition Countries

As the category labels imply, the classification is on the basis of whether the country has made a transition to greater control over deaths and births. Unlike the development dichotomy, this taxonomy classifies individual countries, and not regions, into categories. Countries are distinguished as *pre-transition, transitional* (beginning to control births and deaths), or *late-transition* (controlled births and deaths). Countries in any one region may be in different transition categories.

Contrasts between Categories

Both classifications systems have their uses, as we shall see throughout this book. Table 3-2 gives the current United Nations classifications for both the development dichotomy and the demographic taxonomy. The top seven lines present data for regions of the world separately. These seven regions are ordered from the highest growth rate (Africa) to the lowest growth rate (Europe). In the next two lines of the table data is given for the more-developed and less-developed regions separately; the final three lines show data for pre-transition, transitional and late-transition categories of countries.

Table 3-2 also presents some demographic rates that dramatize the contrast between classes of countries. Let us compare the MDRs and LDRs. Demographically, although there is a difference between the crude death rates (column 2), that difference is small compared with the difference between the crude birth rates (column 1). The fertility of the LDRs collectively is nearly twice as high as that of the MDRs. The infant mortality rate (column 3), although strictly speaking a demographic measure, is often used as an index of overall well-being and of health care in nations; we see that

Table 3-2
Demographic Rates for Classes of Countries, 1995–2000[a]

	Crude Birth Rate	Crude Death Rate	Infant Morality Rate[c]	Annual Growth Rate (%)	Years to Double
	(1)	(2)	(3)	(4)	(5)
Regions[b]					
Africa	39.7	13.1	88.1	2.66	26
Latin America and Caribbean	22.5	6.5	39.3	1.52	46
Asia (excl. East and Southeast)	22.8	8.1	52.4	1.46	48
Oceania	18.5	7.8	19.8	1.32	53
East and Southeast Asia	18.5	7.6	33.1	1.08	65
Northern America	14.7	7.9	7.2	0.93	75
Europe	11.7	10.5	11.2	0.16	438
Less-Developed Regions	26.0	8.8	61.0	1.70	41
More-Developed Regions	13.1	9.3	11.7	0.45	156
Pre-transition Countries	43.4	14.2	94.7	2.92	24
Transitional Countries	20.2	7.1	38.0	1.33	53
Late-transition Countries	14.8	8.3	19.9	0.68	103

[a]Projected average annual rates.
[b]Ordered by annual growth rates.
[c]Infant deaths per thousand births
Source: Bos et al., *World Population Projections 1994–95 Edition,* 1994.

the infant mortality rate of the LDRs is more than five times as high as that of the MDRs. Column 4 contains the population's annual growth rate and column 5 contains the years to double calculated from that growth rate. The growth rate in LDRs is nearly four times greater than in MDRs. As a result, the population of the LDRs would double in only 41 years at their present rate of growth while the same doubling would require 156 years in MDRs. Not captured by these cold demographic statistics are the considerable differences in wealth and economic opportunity between MDRs and LDRs nor the vulnerability of the poorest LDRs to collective and personal economic disaster; famine and war being two dramatic examples of this.

If we use the demographic taxonomy to compare countries, the differences in demographic behavior are even more dramatic. Pre-transition countries as a class have a higher crude birth rate, crude death rate, infant mortality rate, and growth rate than any geographic region of the world. We would expect these results since pre-transition countries have little control over births or deaths. It is important to remember that these countries, spread throughout regions, are those whose people have the poorest health, lowest living standard, and whose future will be most heavily impacted by rapid population growth if birth control is slow to arrive. In contrast, late-transition countries have relatively low birth, death, infant mortality, and growth rates regardless of their region.

We should note, however, that not all of the countries in the late-transition category are necessarily alike on all measures. Those in Europe and North America, while clearly late-transition, have substantially lower infant mortality rates than does the late-transition class as a whole. There still are substantial differences in the health and well-being of even those countries with a substantial degree of control over births and deaths. Europe also is unique in its very low growth rate and relatively high crude death rate. As we will see in chapter 4, Europe is most typical of an aging population that has had a high degree of control over births and deaths for a long period of time.

Development and demographic categories in Table 3-2 not only have different *current* demographic traits but also had different demographic *histories* over the past two centuries. Starting in the late 1700s, one after another of the present MDRs began their "demographic transitions" from high to low death rates, and then from high to low birth rates. As regions experienced development many countries moved gradually from pre-transition to transitional categories. Early in this transition MDRs actually grew at more rapid rates than the LDRs, until about World War I at least. Starting with the period of the Great Depression, and especially since World War II, the transition to lower birth rates began to slow MDR growth, while the regions with the most rapid growth have been the less-developed ones. The postwar rates of growth in the LDRs generally surpassed anything previously experienced by the present MDRs. Many countries in the MDRs completed their transition during this time and became late-transition countries with low death, birth, and growth rates, and some even experienced negative growth rates. Some countries in the LDRs have since moved rapidly through similar demographic transitions. Others, however, are following new courses of transition with births leveling off after an early decline (India), showing little decline (Pakistan), or abrupt and sudden declines (Iran) (Gelbard et al., 1999).

Despite many variations, most countries of the world appear to have experienced or begun a basic demographic transition. Demographers study countries that are now in the later stages of transition both to understand the causes of the transition and as a historical precedent for what might happen demographically to present LDRs as they become more economically and demographically developed. This has been the underlying rationale for the study of the historic MDR demographic transitions.

THE PROTOTYPICAL EUROPEAN DEMOGRAPHIC TRANSITION

The time and place that provided the earliest model for the demographic transition was Western Europe between 1800 and the 1930s. This was the first world region to go through the sequence (Coale and Watkins, 1986). Economically, the Western European countries already had progressed in their agricultural revolutions before the 1800s. During the demographic transition period, they were going through that complex set of changes called the Industrial Revolution, with accompanying social changes such as urbanization, literacy, secularization, and growing consumerism.

Description

What happened to crude death and birth rates along with those economic changes is shown schematically in Figure 3-2. In pre-transition populations (left side of figure), both death rates and birth rates were high. Pestilence and famine were major causes of death. The transition generally began with a decline in epidemic mortality due to improved nutrition, sanitation, and so on. As death rates reached lower levels, remaining deaths were largely due to degenerative and man-made diseases; and as death rates reached lower levels, birth rates also fell. By the late transition (right side of figure), both birth and death rates were low. During the transitional phase, the model specifies that the death rate dropped before the birth rate, causing a period of very rapid natural increase, the classic population explosion. While death rates were more variable from year to year in the pre-transition phase, birth rates are more variable after the transition. The transition was not only from high to *low* rates, but also to *controlled* mortality and fertility.

Not all Western European nations went through their demographic transitions simultaneously (Coale and Watkins, 1986). Sustained declines in death began as early as 1750 in countries as different as France and Sweden. Births generally declined much later in the transition, from 1827 (France) to 1922 (Ireland and European Russia). The gap between rapidly falling death rates and a delayed decline in birth rates led to rising population growth, with the period of greatest natural increase between 1870 and 1910 for most Western European countries.

Aside from the timing of the transition, there were many other deviations from the general sequence given in Figure 3-2, even within Western Europe. Pre-transition fertility was not steady, nor completely uncontrolled, as the stylized demographic transition model implies (Coale and Watkins, 1986, pp. 429–430). Fertility sometimes fell simultaneous with mortality or even before (Coale, 1975, p. 351), and might even have risen at the outset of the transition, compounding the impact of mortality decline (Petersen, 1975, pp. 631–637). Figure 3-2 is not a theory of how mortality and fertility declines occurred or an exact model of any one country's experience. Nonetheless, the simplified model of Figure 3-2 is a useful device for understanding the general pattern

Figure 3-2 Simplified Diagram of the European Demographic Transition

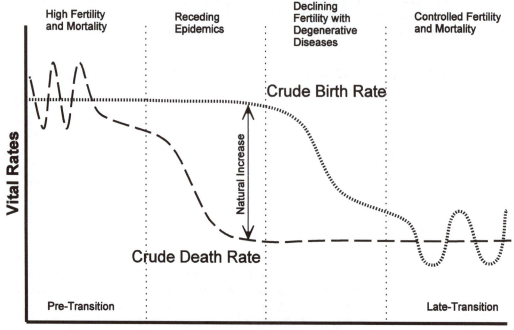

Stage of Demographic Transition

of demographic transition and why it often resulted in explosive population growth. Mortality and fertility declines did sweep across Europe, fertility declined steadily without reversal, and by 1930 few provinces of Europe remained untouched. With few exceptions, fertility declines lagged behind those in mortality and natural increase generated a population explosion within European countries.

Demographic Transition Theories

Let us suppose that the preceding description of the European demographic transition is true, generally. What does that tell us about the future of mortality and fertility in the developing countries? It tells us that if the current LDRs were to follow the Western model of modernization, they might eventually achieve low, stable mortality and low, variable fertility. But there are some important questions that such a simple descriptive model does not answer: *When* in the modernization and mortality-decline process will fertility decline? What *parts* of the modernization process are crucial for triggering such a fertility decline? And what are the prospects for a similar transition in LDRs in present times and circumstances?

To address such questions, one has to go beyond observing that trends coincide in time and investigate the causes of mortality and fertility declines in order to develop an analytical theory. There have been several provocative and plausible attempts to formulate such a general theory of demographic, and especially fertility, transition as well as harsh criticisms of each.

Following Mason (1997), we can identify six major transition theories. Classical demographic transition theory emphasizes fertility decline as following mortality decline and due to changes in social life accompanying industrialization and urbanization (Thompson, 1930; Notestein, 1945). Lesthaeghe (1983) adds to modernization the importance of a shift toward self-fulfillment of parents with rising affluence and modernization. Caldwell (1982) emphasized a shift in wealth flows, brought about by such changes as compulsory education and child labor laws, which made children a burden, not a net benefit, to the family. The neoclassical microeconomic approach (Becker, 1981) emphasizes both the rising cost of raising children and the desire for alternative uses of family resources (e.g. rising consumerism and alternative consumption goods). Easterlin and Crimmins (1985) expand this thinking to include the psychic or social costs of limiting fertility. And, the ideational theory (Cleland and Wilson, 1987) attributes declining fertility to the diffusion of contraceptive information and childbearing norms.

Most criticisms of these general demographic transition theories arise either from the simplicity with which transitions are characterized (Mason, 1997) or from exceedingly high expectations for prediction (Feeney, 1994). As Feeney notes, even the most satisfactory transition theory may not predict the beginning of fertility decline any better than we can predict earthquakes by knowing they are caused by the shifting of tectonic plates. Although transition theories are useful to understand changes in human behavior, there is no evidence they can predict the precise timing of demographic changes in a given set of circumstances.

Mason (1997) herself takes a different approach, summarizing what demographers have established, or have begun to establish, about the demographic transition:

1) mortality decline is usually a necessary, but not a sufficient, condition for fertility decline

2) fertility transitions occur in different circumstances when various *combinations* of conditions are sufficient to motivate or enable populations to adopt birth control

3) a transition caused by circumstances in a given population may influence, or *diffuse* to, other regions of different circumstance

4) such influences may travel at different speeds depending upon a variety of circumstances (e.g. state policy, information and transportation networks, etc.)

5) the number of children families can support varies across pre-transition populations

6) if families exceed their ability to support children, parents will resort to some form of fertility control

7) fertility control after pregnancy or birth depends upon available and acceptable forms of such control (e.g. whether abortion or infanticide are acceptable)

8) when conditions limit such controls after pregnancy, prenatal controls such as contraception or birth spacing will be encouraged (especially if aided by state policy or programs)

This summary emphasizes the variability in circumstances of demographic transition and highlights the difficulty in identifying a single cause, or a comprehensive list of causes, for transitions. Mortality and fertility declines may have different causes in different countries or periods. Moreover, transitions are not likely to proceed in LDRs exactly the same way they did in Western Europe.

Throughout this text we will treat demographic transition as consisting of two distinct, but interrelated, transitions, one in mortality and one in fertility. We will emphasize the variety of factors that have historically influenced mortality and fertility declines, rather than focus on a single example. We will revisit these in context throughout the text. In studying both mortality and fertility, later chapters of this text take European history as a point of departure. LDRs are contrasted and compared with the historical transitions in Europe and the MDRs. This is the strategy we follow in chapter 5, where we deal with the "mortality transition," and in chapter 7, where we discuss the "fertility transition" and spread of family planning in more detail. In these later chapters, we will find that the close links between economic and demographic development in industrializing Europe are far less direct in contemporary LDRs. We will also see that today's LDRs confront unique difficulties controlling both mortality and fertility.

DIFFERENTIAL GROWTH, 1950 TO 2035

Let us get back to the description of the modern world population explosion, seen at the right end of Figure 3-1. But let us now distinguish between the MDRs (who have largely completed their demographic transitions) and the LDRs (who have not).

Our coverage is divided into two time periods, from 1950 to 1995 and from 2000 to 2035. The first segment brings us almost up to the present, and for this period we can depend upon actual population counts or estimates from partial information. The second segment is in the future, and here we must depend upon projection. The source for both sets of figures is the United Nations (United Nations, 1994; Bos et al., 1994).

Counts and Estimates, 1950 to 1995

MDRs differ from LDRs not only in their current growth rates but also in the trends of those rates over time. The top half of Table 3-3 gives the growth rates for more-developed regions, less-developed regions, and the world as a whole, up to 1995.

In the MDRs the growth rate was fairly high in the 1950s and early 1960s, by the standards of industrialized countries, but has been declining steadily since. There has been a continuous gradual decline in mortality throughout the second half of the century. Fertility, on the other hand, has had wide swings, and so has the resulting natural increase. Most MDRs had postwar baby-booms (sustained, in the case of the United States) that kept natural increase higher than normal for MDRs. Fertility since the 1960s has been declining, even more rapidly than mortality, shrinking the rate of natural increase.

Even at the outset of the postwar era, LDR growth rates were about 70% higher than those for the MDRs. The gap widened for most of this period as LDR rates soared. But evidence now is accumulating that a peak rate was reached in the mid-

Table 3-3
Population Growth Rates for More-Developed and Less-Developed Regions, 1950–2035

Year	More-Developed Regions (1)	Less-Developed Regions (2)	World (3)
Estimated			
1950–55	1.20	2.05	1.78
1955–60	1.18	2.15	1.85
1960–65	1.10	2.36	1.99
1965–70	0.82	2.52	2.04
1970–75	0.81	2.37	1.96
1975–80	0.67	2.08	1.73
1980–85	0.56	2.09	1.73
1985–90	0.58	2.06	1.73
1990–95	0.50	1.87	1.56
Projected			
1995–2000	0.45	1.70	1.43
2000–05	0.36	1.56	1.31
2005–10	0.33	1.46	1.24
2010–15	0.28	1.32	1.13
2015–20	0.23	1.22	1.04
2020–25	0.18	1.12	0.96
2025–30	0.10	1.00	0.85
2030–35	0.04	0.87	0.74

Source: United Nations, *Demographic Yearbook, 1995,* 1997; Bos et al., *World Population Projections 1994–95 Edition,* 1994.

1960s, the rates gradually retreating since then (United Nations, 1994). Throughout the postwar period, overall mortality was declining substantially. True to demographic transition theory, fertility did not decline as early as mortality and generally stayed at high levels through the mid-1960s. Then it started to decline, in one country after another, eroding the overall high rate of natural increase.

There still is considerable variety among LDRs in their current growth rates. High mortality, especially from the HIV/AIDS virus, has contributed to lower growth rates in some LDR countries. Botswana's population over the next twenty-five years, for example, will grow to only three-fourths of what it would have without HIV/AIDS deaths. More important, late fertility declines in LDRs have resulted in a period of much higher natural increase for some countries than in historical European transitions. The greatest influence on variability in LDR growth rates is the timing of their fertility transitions.

What do these rates mean in terms of the size and distribution of world population? Larger and larger proportions of the world's population live in LDRs. Accordingly, what happens in the LDRs increasingly determines what happens in the world as a whole. This point is illustrated vividly in Figure 3-3, where we see that as the size of LDR populations soared from 1950 to 2000, so did the size of the world's population.

Figure 3-3 Population Growth of More-Developed and Less-Developed Regions, 1950–2035

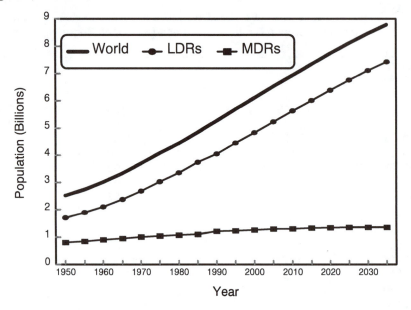

Source: United Nations, *Demographic Yearbook, 1995*, 1997; Bos et al., *World Population Projections 1994–95 Edition*, 1994.

Figure 3-4 diagrams the changing distribution of population by continental areas. All of the more-developed regions—especially Europe—witnessed a decline in their proportion of the world's population between 1950 and 1995. All of the less-developed regions increased their proportion.

Projections, 1995 to 2035

The United Nations, by itself and occasionally in collaboration with other agencies, provides regularly updated population growth projections. Most of the projections used in this text are from the 1994 or 1998 revised population forecasts. Because they boldly predict into the distant future, all projections are subject to such periodic revision. The method used in making these projections is the cohort-component method, described in more detail in chapter 4 of this text. For the moment, it is enough to say that in this method, separate projections are made for the population in each age category using assumptions about its future mortality, migration, and fertility experiences.

What are the assumptions for the recent United Nations projections? Mortality is assumed to continue a downward trend, fairly rapidly where it is still moderately high but gradually as it reaches low levels. Net migration is assumed to diminish progressively in its impact upon resident populations except in those particular nations where there is strong reason for suspecting otherwise. Finally, fertility assumptions are

Figure 3-4   Percentage Distributions of Population Among World Regions, 1950, 1995, and 2025

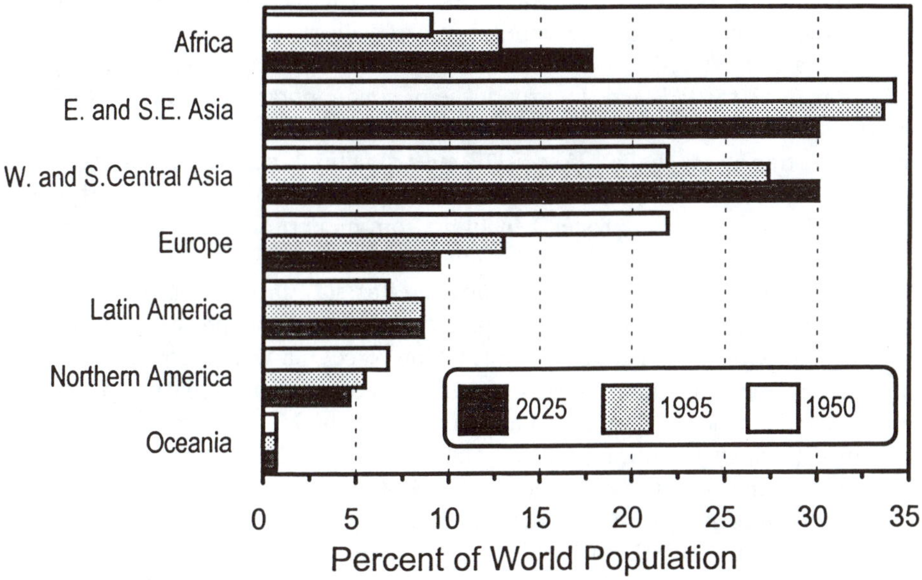

Source: United Nations, *Demographic Yearbook, 1995*, 1997; Bos et al., *World Population Projections 1994–95 Edition*, 1994.

more complex but are generally extrapolations of observed patterns of fertility decline within regions and countries (Bos et al., 1994; Lutz, 1994). In essence, these assumptions are based on the continuation of present trends.

If we accept these assumptions, what does the UN project will happen, in summary? The world's growth rate will fall to just above 1.0% by 2020. Table 3-3 tells us that the world rate will be kept at that level by the increasingly dominant LDRs, whose growth rate then will be 1.22%, compared with the MDRs' 0.23 percent. In the next fifteen years, from 2020 to 2035, MDR growth rates will fall to near zero. Despite their continuing decline, the growth rates of the LDRs will boost world population to over 8 billion people in 2028, and almost 7 billion of them will reside in the LDRs, as shown in Figures 3-3 and 3-4. Nearly all less-developed areas will increase in their proportion of the world population between 1980 and 2035, but some will increase faster than others. Africa, along with West and South Central Asia, will increase their share most dramatically, followed by Latin America. Europe will lose the greatest share of world population, along with East and South Asia (dominated by China and including Japan) and North America.

Projections as Predictions

As predictions, population projections can be no better than the mortality, fertility, and migration assumptions they employ. How much confidence can we have that the UN's current assumptions will turn out to be true over the next thirty-five years? As we have said, the projections essentially assume that present tends will continue. They also implicitly assume that mortality and fertility in the LDRs will follow some version of the sequence we call the demographic transition.

There are, however, many differences between the demographic history of MDRs from 1850 to 1900 and the experience of contemporary LDRs from 1950 to 2000, differences that affect the course of both the economic development and the demographic transitions in the LDRs. LDR rates of natural increase have surged earlier in the economic development process than they did in MDRs. LDR death rates dropped earlier and generally faster, benefiting from modern medical and sanitation technologies. LDRs probably will not be able to make use of emigration as a transitional population "safety valve" to the same degree as did Europe. Agrarian densities at the outset are higher in many LDRs, and the prospects for industrialization are quite different, with current LDR attempts taking place in a world economy already dominated by the industrialized MDRs. On the other hand, LDR prospects are affected by the potential for technical assistance from the MDRs, including fertility-reduction technology. Finally, LDRs have unique cultural influences on such things as the role of women in enterprise, the acceptability of fertility control measures, and so on. All of this gives one pause in assuming that LDR transitions will follow precisely the same track as did the MDR transitions.

Finally, past projections (by whomever) that simply assumed the continuation of present trends have proved abysmally wrong as long-term predictions. For instance, projections made in the 1930s did not assume the postwar Western baby-boom; most world projections made in the 1960s did not dare to assume the LDR fertility decline that even then must have been starting in some countries. Even recent assumptions understated the magnitude of LDR fertility declines and the dramatic rise of a worldwide HIV/AIDS epidemic. On the other hand, projections accurately reflect current information as a best collective guess of what will happen in the future. It is wise to view these projections not so much as scientific predictions but as statements about what would happen if current trends continue and LDRs do undergo Western-model demographic transitions.

PROBLEMS OF A CHANGING WORLD DISTRIBUTION

In chapter 1 we took the position that analysis of any population problem involves addressing a set of three questions: Who is concerned about the population trend in question? What do these concerned observers believe to be the consequences of the trend? Why do they dislike those consequences? Let us try to keep those questions in mind as we discuss the problems associated with world population growth.

There are three interrelated aspects of world population growth trends that seem to excite concern: the *size and density* of the world population, or of LDR national populations; the *rate of growth* of national populations; and the *changing distribution* of population around the world. Let us treat problems of distribution first, since we have just described relevant trends in Table 3-3 and Figures 3-3 and 3-4. The feature of these trends that arouses the most concern is the *changing distribution*, the progressive postwar tendency of LDR populations to outnumber MDR populations, a tendency projected to continue indefinitely.

Who seems to be worried about the changing world population distribution? Leaders of the LDRs may be concerned about the density or growth rates of their populations (discussed later), but apparently not about international distribution per se. There are few statements from Third World leaders decrying the increase in the proportion of the future world's population that live in less-developed countries. Rather, it is the MDRs to whom the changing distribution is a problem.

What unwanted consequences do the MDR publics anticipate? Interestingly, the rationale behind the concern seldom is stated. Rather, the facts of the changing distribution simply are presented and the unhappy consequences are assumed to be self-evident. The LDR publics, naturally, have their suspicions as to underlying motives behind the MDR concerns (Hartmann, 1995). Let us consider and analyze some of these possible MDR motives.

Can it be that MDRs fear a shifting population distribution will diminish their role in the global balance of power? The recognition that population is related to power lies behind some of the earliest demographic censuses, which tallied national populations available for industry and soldiering. If one defines power as being able to influence others' behavior, then (other things being equal) population probably still contributes to national power. For instance, nations treat mainland China with more care than they do Taiwan, even though the latter probably is at least as well developed, per capita. Given this, perhaps MDR publics are concerned that the changing world population distribution also means a changing world power distribution, to their disfavor.

Can it be that MDRs are worried about becoming an even smaller ethnic and racial minority? Ethnocentrism is universal. Are Westerners concerned about the submerging of Western culture? Or, do they worry about preserving their own socioeconomic privileges in the face of shifting population distributions? One clearly stated public concern in MDRs is a fear that immigration will rise as the share of population in LDRs continues to increase, eventually making many historically majority groups a minority in their "own" country. Clearly, MDR immigration policies are an expression of this concern, and we will treat them in detail in chapter 9.

It may also be that MDRs are concerned about being globally overwhelmed by the poverty or economic development of the LDRs. Do they see the rich countries as a shrinking, more embattled enclave in a poorer world? Or, do they fear that their higher standard of living and past economic dominance will no longer be tolerated under the new population circumstances? Such concerns appear reasonable given the resource consumption and waste production in MDRs. The United States contains only 5% of the world's population but accounts for 25% of fossil fuels, 20% of metals, and 33% of paper consumed, while producing 72% of the world's hazardous waste. LDRs, with 78% of the world's population, consume only 40% of fossil fuels, 20% of metals, and 25% of paper, while producing only 10% of hazardous waste (Population Reference Bureau, 1996). If LDRs tried to strictly emulate the United States, or other MDRs, resource constraints would likely require MDRs to reduce their privileged, and wasteful, use of world resources. This speculation about the basis of MDR concern over world *distribution* is not very flattering.

Speculations about the basis for MDR concern regarding LDR population *size* and *growth rates* are not so unflattering. They probably are as complicated and mixed as the motivation for LDR foreign aid. They could range from simple humanitarian desire to improve lives in LDRs, to a desire to cut down on the costs of international charity, to a desire to reduce LDR-to-MDR migration pressures.

Whatever the basis for the concern, the reasoning behind defining overpopulation and rapid growth as LDR problems is not as simple as it may seem. In an attempt to inject order into this discussion, let us separate our treatment of population size problems from that of population *growth* problems.

PROBLEMS OF POPULATION SIZE

Carrying Capacity and Density

The popular notion of "overpopulation" is vague. It suggests that the population of an area is too large. The closest demographic specification of that fear is in terms of *carrying capacity*. Cohen (1995, app. 4) provides twenty-six different definitions of carrying capacity published since 1975. For our purposes it is sufficient to define carrying capacity as the maximum population size within a given area which can sustain itself indefinitely without environmental degradation, given its technology and consumption patterns. Since at least 1679, there have been many estimates of the earth's carrying capacity for human populations, ranging from sizes below, to well above, the current world population (Cohen, 1995, app. 2).

Estimating carrying capacity is very precarious. First, one would have to be able to definitively measure environmental degradation. Current debates about the extent and significance of global warming illustrate how difficult it is to detect, or rule out, subtle environmental changes. Second, one would have to know the future course of both technology and consumption patterns. However, as we have said, long-range predictions generally presume that behaviors will stay the same or are at least easily extrapolated into the future. Such assumptions are foolhardy when predicting technologies. So, specific predictions of the point at which the human population might exceed or have exceeded carrying capacity are generally too speculative and controversial to be of specific use to demographers. Nonetheless, carrying capacity is an important concept. Moreover, thought-provoking discussions of carrying capacity often provide important warnings about continuing current behaviors into the distant future.

If we concentrate on the present, rather than speculate on long-term changes in technology and culture, a concept closely related to carrying capacity is *population density*, or the size of a population within a given area. Indeed, one notion of overpopulation is the idea that a population is too densely settled.

Chapter 1 defines density as the relationship between a population's size and the space it inhabits. Thus defined, density can be measured by this ratio:

$$\frac{\text{population size}}{\text{space (e.g. land area)}}$$

This is sometimes called the population per area.

But, in worrying about overpopulation, the concept of density is generalized far beyond this relationship to be something more nearly related to carrying capacity. Space is not the only thing that humanity needs for survival. One can generalize the ratio as follows:

$$\frac{\text{population size}}{\text{means for subsistence}}$$

Notice that carrying capacity is implicit in this more general ratio since the means for subsistence will depend upon both technology and consumption behavior. In the case of an agricultural economy, the "means for subsistence" may be primarily land, but the concept is meant to include all natural resources considered essential for human well-being and production (e.g. water, fresh air, a nonpolluted environment, energy sources). It also includes the other nonlabor determinants of productive capacity (e.g. investment capital, education, health services).

The judgment of overpopulation necessarily involves the idea of scarcity, too large a numerator and too small a denominator. Overpopulation can be eased either by decreasing the numerator or by increasing the denominator. Labeling a high ratio as overpopulation amounts to blaming the large numerator rather than the small denominator. Such a judgment often is made not only where the density is high but also where the denominator is difficult to expand given current technology and consumption behavior. The classic instance is an agricultural economy with no unused arable land to plow and not enough to go around among the potential farmers. In England at the end of the eighteenth century, for example, changes in agricultural technology came slowly at the same time grain had to be imported for sustenance. The tendency to blame the population size for shortages in the means for subsistence owes much to the theories of Thomas Malthus, which were formulated at just this time in English history.

From Malthus to Marx to the Neo-Malthusians

Thomas Malthus's publication of his first and second essays on the principles of population (in 1798 and 1803) were landmarks in the development of population theory. He was not the first to include demographic variables in economic and social analysis; in fact, his essays were partially in refutation of competitive theories by Godwin, Condorcet, and others. But the role of population size and growth was so prominent in Malthus's theory, and he spent so many years and later editions of his essays (seven in all) trying to test, polish, and defend his theory, that it could not be ignored.

Box 3-2 provides a summary of Malthus's central thoughts on the subject of overpopulation. Our main sources are William Petersen's summary in his textbook (1975), his volume titled, simply, *Malthus* (1979; see reviews by Dupâquier, 1980, and Keyfitz, 1980), and a volume of essays on *Malthus Past and Present* edited by Dupâquier (1983). We note these sources because many critics and fans of Malthus have responded to erroneous interpretations of what he said (Appleman, 1976). As someone wryly observed, few of us seem to have read Malthus "in the original English." Malthus's theory, as summarized, was simplistic and demonstrably wrong in many ways. Population does not increase geometrically. Nor does subsistence increase arithmetically. These erroneous simplifications by Malthus do not, however, alter the force of his central argument that, without checks, a population will tend to outgrow its means of subsistence (i.e. the numerator of density will increase more rapidly than the denominator).

Box 3-2 Thomas Malthus's Principle of Population

According to Malthus, populations tend to grow more rapidly than do the means for their subsistence; that is, unless checked in some way, populations tend to grow in a geometric progression (1, 2, 4, 8, etc.). On the other hand, there is no such tendency for the means for subsistence to expand by geometric progression; rather, they expand by arithmetic progression (1, 2, 3, 4, etc.). Moreover, where the means for subsistence are finite and limited, such as arable land in an already densely populated country, then a principle of diminishing returns will apply: the best land will be plowed first and each successive acre plowed will be of poorer land. By "means for subsistence," Malthus meant—ultimately—food supply, so this agricultural example is apt.

Population is kept within the limits of the means for subsistence mainly by "positive checks," those operating through the death rates. When the means for subsistence are not adequate to take care of a population at a given size, the death rate will go up until the population has shrunk to a supportable level.

By the same token, whenever a surplus might appear in the means for subsistence, this will tend temporarily to lower the death rate (and raise the rate of natural increase) until the population has grown to the limits of the new means for subsistence. This is the "Malthusian dilemma."

Hypothetically, the way out of the dilemma is through the application of "preventive checks" on population growth, operating through the birth rate. These fall into two categories: "moral restraint" and "vice." They are quite distinct in terms of how they correspond to the improvement of humanity (says the Reverend Malthus). Humanity differs from animals, at least potentially, in terms of its ability to foresee the consequences of its actions and to guide its current behavior accordingly.

"Moral restraint," as advocated by Malthus, consists of not marrying until one can support the resulting children and of remaining sexually chaste outside of such marriage. Clearly this appeals to the best in human nature, as Malthus saw it. Moreover, if marriage and sexual companionship must be earned, then people will work harder to win this prize, thereby increasing aggregate means of subsistence.

"Vice," according to Malthus, includes promiscuity, homosexuality, adultery, and birth control (including abortion). Undoubtedly Malthus did not foresee the degree to which the technology of contraception would develop over the next century and a half, nor the growing social acceptability of his other forms of "vice." His stated objection was on moral grounds. The use of any of these vices represented an indulgence in sexual appetites without an acceptance of the responsibility for the consequences of such indulgence. It was a rejection of individual responsibility, and Malthus saw acceptance of such responsibility as—in the long run—humanity's only hope for emerging from the dilemma. This pessimism seemed to soften over his seven consecutive editions of the essays.

Such a brief summary is clearly only a simplification of Malthus's life's work. What you have here is undiluted Malthusian thought, as it is preserved in demographic theoretical tradition.

Two important critics of Malthus, Karl Marx and Friedrich Engels, were both teenagers in Germany when Malthus died in England in 1834. Malthusian theory was dominant both in their native country and in England, to which they each moved (Weeks, 1996). Marx and Engels said what little they did about demography in rejection of Malthus. To the socialist theory that Marx and Engels were developing, the effect of population size on subsistence and wealth depended on the kind of social organization a society had. What were considered population problems by Malthus were actually results of an unwise and unjust social organization of production and distribution. Humanity is not universally trapped in the Malthusian dilemma. Marx and Engels believed we can escape the supposed negative consequences of population density by reordering society, specifically by socialist control over the means of production and distribution. Some classical Marxist scholars might go further and point out that the labor theory of value leads to the conclusion that "people are wealth," generally, and that population growth is never a root source of poverty. Some conservative "capitalist" economists have reached the same basic conclusion (e.g. Simon, 1986). The contribution of Malthus's critics, including Marx and Engels, was to remind us that population size is only half of the density, or carrying capacity, equation.

The tension between fears of overpopulation and the alternative of blaming current social organization of production and distribution, has been echoed in all subsequent discussions of population growth and development. In recent decades a *neo*-Malthusian perspective has used part of Malthus's theory as a justification for worldwide family-planning programs. *Neo*-Marxian perspectives, and economic development theory, have meanwhile promoted development policies such as improved agricultural technology, opportunities and access to credit for women and other marginalized social groups, and efficient social distribution systems, within LDRs. Not surprisingly, these two perspectives are complementary, reflecting the numerator, i.e. population size, and the denominator, i.e. means of subsistence, in our general formula for population density. Both clearly have a role in concerns over population growth. Malthus's contribution was to bring attention to the importance of population growth in this equation.

We can assume that Malthus would applaud the recognition that many countries have given to the importance of population growth. Even Communist China, the most populous socialist country, came to recognize its huge population and rapid growth as a cause of continued underdevelopment. And, despite the variety of opinions worldwide, officials in virtually all developing countries have respect for the possible negative consequences of entirely unchecked population growth.

Malthus would not, however, applaud the family-planning policies that many countries have implemented to address concerns with population growth. These policies are examples of neo-Malthusianism, which openly advocates the use of all the "preventive checks" to escape the Malthusian dilemma. That includes, prominently, birth control, which Malthus called "vice." In spite of this difference, neo-Malthusians and the modern family-planning movement are directly descended from Malthus and rely on a general notion of his "principle of population" as pointing to the need for family-planning programs.

Global Overpopulation

When talking about long time spans and speaking on a global level, Malthusian thinking is very attractive. It is easy to envision finite limits of arable land, water, clean air, any given natural resource, and ultimately living space itself. Thus on the global level, the people most sensitive to the problem of potential overpopulation are those most conscious of such limits, the environmentalists and human ecologists (Brown et al., 1999; Repetto, 1993; Falkenmark and Widstrand, 1992; Brown, 1981; Ehrlich and Ehrlich, 1979). However, not everyone who has studied the relationship between environment and global population is equally alarmed about potential scarcity. There are a variety of views about how global population size might respond to the earth's carrying capacity. Cohen (1995) identifies models for four views of population limits which are graphically depicted in Figure 3-5.

Figure 3-5   Global Population Size and Carrying Capacity: Four Models

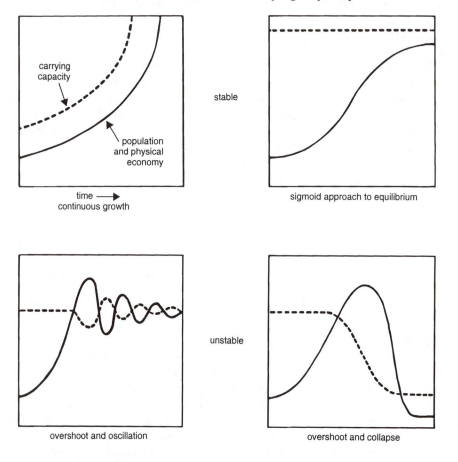

carrying capacity

population and physical economy

time ⟶
continuous growth

stable

sigmoid approach to equilibrium

unstable

overshoot and oscillation

overshoot and collapse

Source: Reprinted from *Beyond the Limits* copyright © 1992 by Meadows, Meadows and Randers. With permission from Chelsea Green Publishing Co.

The two models at the top of this figure are both stable, or *adaptive equilibrium*, models. In these models population growth responds to environmental conditions and grows up to, but not beyond, the carrying capacity. The models differ in whether carrying capacity increases as technology and culture develop (upper left) so that population can also continue to grow, or whether the carrying capacity is really an overall fixed limit which population size will approach as it grows (upper right). The central feature of both models is that population growth responds to limited carrying capacity before reaching limits to growth.

The two basic models at the bottom of this figure are unstable, or *overshoot*, models. In both of these cases population growth is not aware of, or at least not responsive to, limits to growth until it has already exceeded the carrying capacity. These two models differ in how population growth, and carrying capacity, respond to overpopulation once the carrying capacity of the population is exceeded. The first possibility (lower left) is that population drops off (i.e. negative growth) once it exceeds carrying capacity, perhaps with some damage to the environment, and oscillates above or below carrying capacity until, perhaps, an eventual equilibrium is reached. This model is often characterized as a population learning its carrying capacity by trial and error. It is also the model that is closest to what Malthus might have envisioned.

The second possibility (lower right) is the bleakest of all. In this model once the population exceeds its carrying capacity there is catastrophic damage to the environment. Once this happens both the carrying capacity and the population collapse in ruin or extinction. Some demographers, for example, worry about the biological possibilities for pandemic disease as global population density increases (Olshansky et al., 1997). Some scientists suggest that uncontrolled global warming might reach a threshold point which would trigger successive extinctions of basic life forms upon which the entire ecosystem of the planet rests, with just such catastrophic results. It should be remembered that this model is only the most pessimistic possibility. Yet, recent population growth has led demographers to at least envision the clear *possibility* of such a global demographic catastrophe.

A caution should also be noted. In reality, there is not one fixed carrying capacity or limit to a population's growth. Populations face many limits to growth—from finite water resources, limits to sustenance and food production, pollution, density and crowding, decreasing biodiversity, and so on. In terms of the models in Figure 3-5, that means a population must know how to live within many resource limitations to achieve a stable or adaptive growth model. In contrast, there are many limitations a population might inadvertently overshoot, potentially leading to catastrophic consequences. Human history has, at the least, provided examples of both such possibilities and does not yield any clear expectation for the future.

In a bit more optimistic view, those who believe that there are fixed limits to growth often point out that, with exceptions, humanity would not likely reach limits simultaneously all over the world. Depending upon both population and technology, some regions encounter limits earlier than others. If other regions with excess resources were willing to share them unselfishly, limits to growth, or possible overshoot, might be postponed and eventually avoided altogether. Can we have faith in such interregional altruism, and on the massive scale required as additional "overpopulated" regions are added, containing ever larger proportions of the world's population? Even if it is only a problem of distribution of resources, it is a massive and difficult one to resolve.

National Overpopulation

Countries vary greatly in their population densities, as Figure 3-6 dramatizes. The bars in the graph measure the population per area ratios for fourteen countries, from MDRs and LDRs, and selected for their widely varying densities. Australia, Canada, Brazil, and the United States, "frontier" nations, appear at the sparsely populated extreme. Bangladesh is at the other extreme, far outstripping even the Netherlands and Japan.

Are the more densely settled of these countries "overpopulated?" The debate over this issue is likely to be in terms of economics and health. For example, if country X had fewer people and a lower density, would that increase the wealth of the country and living standards of its citizens? Would lower density improve the available housing for the population? Would lower density improve health or lower death rates? Any number of such questions may be raised.

A large, densely settled population is deemed to both help and hurt the pursuit of national and personal wealth. On the benefit side, a large population, settled together in space, increases the possibility for division of labor and specialization of producing units; it also makes possible large enterprises that produce economies of scale. On the cost side, a large, densely settled population may limit the productivity

Figure 3-6 Population Density in Fourteen Selected Countries, 1999

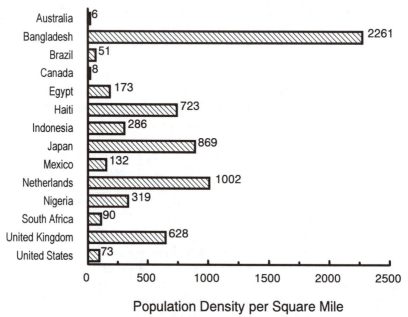

Population Density per Square Mile

Source: Population Reference Bureau, *1999 World Population Data Sheet*, 1999.

per worker by limiting the resources per worker. The balance between these pros and cons depends upon the basis of the economy. In MDRs, based on industry, the problem of undersupplying workers with the means for production may be less pressing because those means (capital equipment, skills, and energy) are expanded and relocated more flexibly. In LDRs, on the other hand, with extractive economies, the resources that make workers productive are less expandable and more easily outstripped in a given location. The classic example of a nonexpandable resource is agricultural land, but one also could mention mineral wealth, forests, and oil.

Aside from its effect on economic productivity, population density has complex effects on living standards and health. Local densities, such as those associated with urbanization, have their advantages as well as their disadvantages, as we will explore in chapter 10. And density has been historically related to mortality and health (chapters 5 and 6).

In all of these dimensions of overpopulation, the problem on a national level is either confined to, or much more acute in, the densely settled LDRs. In these countries, the benefits of size and density are outweighed by the detriments. Bangladesh is cited as the classic case of an overpopulated country, a country in the Malthusian dilemma. Not only is it densely populated but its economy is almost entirely agricultural. Living standards are marginal, public services are underdeveloped, and even climatological conditions aggravate public health concerns. The Netherlands and Japan, on the other hand, although fairly heavily settled, are not now thought of as "overpopulated" because their economies are not basically extractive. Even more dramatic cases of heavily populated but not "overpopulated" countries would be Singapore and Hong Kong, because of their commercial-industrial economies. Again, there are some negative costs of density in these countries, but they are limited compared to those in the LDRs' urban centers. There also are some LDRs that, though they have extractive economies, are not yet so densely populated that they would be considered as having an "overpopulation" problem; Nigeria might be one such example.

It is again important to remember that there are many costs and benefits of density. To have a particular problem that is aggravated by population density does not necessarily make a clear case for overpopulation. If that were so, then only hermits would not be overpopulated. As a result, demographers have gotten out of the habit of thinking in simple terms of overpopulation and underpopulation. This is more a layman's definition of the problem. It is difficult to arrive at a defensible all-purpose "optimum" population figure for any given area (Cohen, 1995). Instead, most demographers focus upon the specific effects of population growth rates.

PROBLEMS OF GROWTH RATES

Too-Rapid Growth

Who defines rapid growth as a problem for the less-developed countries? That belief is widespread in the American press, which is given to statements like this: "And to cap off the economic problems of impoverished (insert name of LDR country), it is burdened with a population growth rate of more than 2% per year. Thus every advance in its economy is gobbled up by its burgeoning masses." Many LDR governments, demographers, economists, and population policy planners share the fundamental similar belief that rapid population growth may limit or constrain economic development. While there are dissenting voices, the international influence of this perspective is sufficient for us to refer to it as the prevailing view.

How do development economists themselves feel about this conclusion? Most economists in the United States would likely agree that rapid population growth in LDRs can be detrimental for economic development, at least in the circumstances that prevail in many LDR countries. Most feel that poverty in LDRs, for example, is both worsened and made more difficult to redress by rapid population growth. At the same time, careful scholars recognize that, after decades of study, there is still little convincing empirical evidence and considerable controversy about the effects of population growth on economic development (McNicoll, 1998; Crenshaw et al., 1997). In fact, an alternative view, championed most recently by Julian Simon (1977, 1981, 1986), argues that the evidence (i.e. falling natural resource prices) shows that human ingenuity is "the ultimate resource" and the more people we have thinking about how to solve problems of production the greater will be the improvement of technology and economic development. As one might imagine, such joyously stated "revisionist" heresy has not met with much sympathy among the demographic establishment (see reviews by Anderton, 1988; Cutright, 1982; Timmer et al., 1982).

Like development economists, many LDR governments—presumably advised by their own economists—have also come to view population growth as a potential obstacle to economic development. These government concerns with population growth peaked in the early 1990s (United Nations, 1999b). Between the mid-1970s and the early 1990s, the percentage of governments concerned that growth rates were too high increased by nearly 60%. Since that time, however, as it became more apparent that nearly all nations have at least begun a demographic transition, concern among governments that population growth rates are too high has fallen by over 6%.

Such declining concern may be short lived, however. Recent slowing of LDR growth rates may not be a true measure of success in demographic transition. A substantial proportion of recently slowed LDR population growth is due to rising mortality rather than to falling fertility (see chapter 5), a setback to the transition. Paradoxically, if LDR countries opt to fight HIV/AIDS, for instance, they may thereby at least slow the decline in growth rates.

Again, acknowledging a diversity of views, the prevailing governmental view is that managing population growth must be a part of LDR strategies for economic development. Given this prevailing acceptance of the relationship between growth and development it is reasonable to ask how, theoretically, would rapid population growth rates result in slower economic development in the LDRs? Arguments seem to fall into two categories, one dealing with *youth dependency* and the other with the *productivity* of the workforce (Birdsall, 1977; Boserup, 1981; Coale and Hoover, 1958; Crenshaw et al., 1997; Lee, 1983, 1986; McNicoll, 1998).

Strictly speaking, the *youth dependency* problem results from high fertility rather than high growth rates. Rapid growth rates in the modern world are caused by high birth rates coupled with much lower death rates, as shown in the demographic transition in Figure 3-2. The number of new babies that are being added to the population every year is progressively larger. It is true, as Marx pointed out, that each of these babies comes equipped with not only one mouth but also with two hands. But, mouths become operative immediately (ask any mother) while the hands become productive after a long immaturity. Society has to treat these babies as consumers immediately and as producers only later in their life. First society has to bear the costs of their mothers' pre- and postnatal care, the babies' own infant care, and so on through their years of education and job training. It is only much later that children start to pay back the societal investment. In short, high-fertility populations tend to have large proportions of their people at young, dependent ages (see chapter 4, on age and sex structure).

In addition, if fertility can be brought under control, LDR economies may then actually get a one-time economic boost as these young dependents become adults, enter the productive labor force, and are replaced by smaller numbers of dependents in coming generations (Crenshaw et al., 1997). Theoretically, curtailing rapid population growth, then, may both reduce the immediate burdens of youth dependency and also provide a transition generation with extraordinarily low burdens of youth dependency. Both outcomes would, hypothetically, increase the capital and labor resources available for investment in economic development.

The second argument for how rapid growth rates inhibit development deals with the capacity of the economy to improve *worker productivity*. Theoretically, productivity per worker is related to how many workers share the means for production, the capital. This can be expressed as a version of the general density ratio encountered earlier:

$$\frac{\text{workforce}}{\text{capital}}$$

(Economists sometimes use the inverse of this ratio, capital available per worker, or the *capital-labor* ratio.) Economic development in the Western model results from expanding capital by providing better tools, better training, improving the transportation infrastructure, and so forth. But some argue that the more rapidly the population—and thus the workforce (in the numerator)—grows, the more rapidly the capital (in the denominator) has to grow in order to decrease the ratio between the two. This is less of a problem where capital is easily expandable, but the economic consensus seems to be that, by their very nature, technologically underdeveloped economies do not expand their capital flexibly; they are more extractive economies, relying upon agriculture, mining, forestry, and fishing. Indeed, most LDRs already suffer from problems of unemployment and underemployment, unable to keep their existing workforces supplied with capital for production. Controlling rapid population growth theoretically gives LDRs a greater amount of capital per worker, or *capital intensification*, which should allow greater economic development.

In simple form, the arguments of youth dependency and worker productivity seem convincing. Unfortunately, reality is much more complex and hard evidence supporting these theories is lacking (McNicoll, 1998; Crenshaw, 1997). Indeed, some demographers have even argued that the realities of population growth and various aspects of economic development are so complex as to defy any formal analysis (e.g. Rodgers, 1989). Even ardent supporters of these theories acknowledge that there is, as yet, little quantitative cross-national evidence for them. Yet, the lack of evidence is also, in large part, due to a lack of detailed longitudinal data and the result of seeking a single simple model which would apply across all LDR countries. Careful historical observation of individual countries does lend some support for these theories (McNicoll, 1998). Demographers have shown an increasing appreciation for how complex these relationships may be. However, as one demographer reminds us, "complexity does not imply inconsequence" (McNicoll, 1998, p. 4). And, despite recognizing the need for better data in less-developed countries and for continuing studies, the prevalent view remains that rapid population growth can be detrimental to development in the prevailing conditions of many LDRs.

Beyond these reactions, some scholars are skeptical about Western economic development theory generally, as it applies to contemporary LDRs as they modernize. Those theories were formulated domestically in countries whose economic development occurred in quite a different era, one ripe for industrialization and imperial exploits. In contrast, contemporary LDRs, so this criticism goes, are trying to scratch out a foothold in a world whose economic institutions are already shaped by the West. In particular, capital-intensive industrial production is dominated by the MDRs. Therefore, world economic development in the future might take quite a different form than has been true during Western modernization. It might involve an unprecedented pattern of economic development for the LDRs, one with more emphasis on labor-intensive production and the development of human capital (Sadik, 1991). Policies which promote women's economic development and provide agricultural education are examples of such human capital investments.

Too-Slow Growth

As Table 3-3 shows, the population growth rates of MDRs are low, relative to the LDRs, and getting lower. Between 1990 and 1995, the rates were 1% for North America and near zero for Europe as a whole. Eastern Europe had a negative growth rate. As one might expect, the definition of population growth problems is quite different in the MDRs than in the LDRs. The problem, where one is acknowledged, is "stagnation." Almost 15% (a proportion growing over time) of governments believe their population growth rates are too low (United Nations, 1999b, table 3). Thus, compared with the LDRs, the MDRs have the opposite concern about population growth, though the concern is less intense.

As Espenshade (1978, p. 645) points out, the MDRs have not always been so calm about slow population growth:

> When the Great Depression had plunged the Western world into a protracted period of sluggish economic growth and high unemployment, it was fashionable among academic economists in the United States and Western Europe to attribute these conditions partly if not wholly to the unprecedentedly low rates of population growth. This view, popularly known as the "stagnation thesis," held that population growth stimulated business investment in factories and machines; and by contributing to business optimism, in which investment misallocations were likely to be regarded less seriously than if population were to slow to nil.

The reaction to the current slow growth is calmer, informed by the Depression experience. The MDRs did live through the period of slow population growth in the 1930s without apparent damage. And, although critics of the prevailing views on population growth might take heart in such an explanation for the Great Depression, hindsight seems to blame factors other than slow population growth. And, economic growth of MDRs has not appeared to suffer inordinately from slowing population growth (Espenshade and Serow, 1978).

To the degree that slow growth still is seen as a source of social and economic problems, the path of its negative effect is largely through the age composition of the population. Contemporary slow growth is achieved by low birth rates, which generate a population whose average age is older. An aging population can create its own problems, which we will revisit at the end of chapter 4.

SUMMARY

After millennia of slow growth, the world's population took off at an unprecedented rate starting in the 1600s and probably peaking in the late 1960s. The continuing growth of the world's population may not necessarily remain within the carrying capacity of the planet. Environmentalists' concerns over global warming, the exhaustion of fisheries and fresh water resources, etc., are indications of these concerns. The modern population explosion also has not been equally intense worldwide. It started in what are now the more-developed countries. They have experienced, with their modernization, a sequence of declines in death and birth rates, described as the "demographic transition." After World War II the less-developed countries replaced the more-developed as those with exploding populations. Although all countries have experienced at least the beginnings of a demographic transition, rapid population growth will continue into the twenty-first century and will probably decline only slowly.

The explosive growth of many LDRs has theoretical consequences that are defined as potential problems. The fact that much of this growth is concentrated in LDRs means that the distribution of world population is changing. MDRs are becoming an ever smaller minority of the world's peoples, a fact which may strain the past privileged position and political dominance of MDRs. Some LDRs are densely settled, and are increasingly so. Population density places strains upon resources, living standards, and a population's health, especially in less-developed countries. The rapid natural increase (with accompanying high birth rates) in many LDRs means that economically immature, or dependent, segments of the population are large relative to the economically mature, or productive, segments. In addition, rapid population growth faced by these countries makes it difficult to supply growing workforces with capital, or the means for production. These economic concerns are largely based upon the historical experience of Western economies.

There is still much debate as to the causes of and solutions for these problems and even as to whether or not they really are "problems" for contemporary LDRs. Prevailing opinions are that rapid population growth in LDRs may limit economic development. Relationships between population growth and development are, however, complex, depending upon other characteristics of the specific population involved and requiring demographic policies suited to the unique challenges and resources of contemporary LDRs.

EXERCISES

1. Table E3-1 shows what would happen to the total population of the United States if it had started at 275,636,000 at the beginning of 2000 and increased 0.9% (i.e. 9 per thousand) every year until the beginning of 2005. Copy the same procedure and apply it to Mexico, filling in the blanks in the table. Assume an annual growth rate for Mexico of 1.8% (i.e. 18 per thousand). Figures are provided for the year 2000 to get you started. Round off the increment figure to the nearest thousand before adding it to the population as of the beginning of the succeeding year.

Table E3-1
Projected Population at Constant Growth Rates[a]

	Mexico		United States	
Year	Population at Beginning of Year (1)	Increment During Year (2)	Population at Beginning of Year (3)	Increment During Year (4)
2000	98,787	1,778	275,636	2,481
2001			278,117	2,503
2002			280,620	2,526
2003			283,146	2,548
2004			285,694	2,571
2005		—	288,265	—

[a]All figures in thousands.

2. Plot the projected population of Mexico for every year from 2000 to 2005 in Figure E3-1. Connect dots with a freehand curved line.

Figure E3-1   Graph of Projected Population of Mexico, 2000–2005

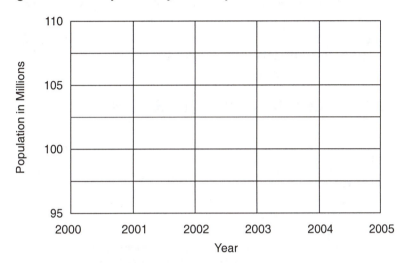

3. The implications of a constant growth rate can be expressed dramatically in terms of the years to double at that rate. The formula is:

$$\text{years to double} = \frac{70}{\%\ \text{annual growth rate}}$$

Suppose that the annual growth rates for the United States and Mexico are 0.9% and 1.8%, respectively. How many years would it take for the populations to double? Round to one decimal place.

U.S. doubling time_____
                                        (years)

Mexico doubling time_____
                                        (years)

▶ PROPOSITIONS FOR DEBATE

1. Thomas Malthus's principle of population is wrong.

2. World population is more likely to overshoot carrying capacity than stabilize below it, but it will not be too late to avoid a population collapse.

3. Those who view overpopulation and rapid population growth as problems lack sufficient faith in human ingenuity and technological development.

4. The motivation of MDR leaders in viewing LDR rapid growth as a source of problems is basically selfish, concerned only with the privileges and power of the MDRs.

5. It is not rapid population growth in the LDRs that is slowing development, it is domination of the world economy by the MDRs.

6. A rational policy for speeding the decline in LDR growth rates is to limit efforts to control the HIV/AIDS epidemic.

▶ REFERENCES AND SUGGESTED READINGS

Anderton, Douglas L. 1988. "Review of 'Theory of Population and Economic Growth, by Julian L. Simon,'" *Contemporary Sociology* 17(4).

Appleman, Philip, ed. 1976. *An Essay on "The Principles of Population" by Thomas Robert Malthus*. New York: Norton.

Becker, Gary S. 1981. *A Treatise of the Family*. Cambridge, MA: Harvard University Press.

Birdsall, Nancy. 1977. "Analytical Approaches to the Relationship of Population Growth and Development." *Population and Development Review* 3(1–2).

Bos, Eduard, Mu T. Vu, Ernest Massiah, and Rodolfo A. Bulatao. 1994. *World Population Projections 1994–95 Edition: Estimates and Projections with Related Demographic Statistics*. World Bank. Baltimore: Johns Hopkins University Press.

Boserup, Ester. 1981. *Population and Technological Change: A Study of Long-term Trends*. Chicago: University of Chicago Press; and Oxford, England: Basil Blackwell.

Brown, Lester R. 1981. "World Food Resources and Population: The Narrowing Margin." Population Bulletin 36(3). Washington, DC: Population Reference Bureau.

Brown, Lester R., Gary Gardner, and Brian Halweil. 1999. *Beyond Malthus: Nineteen Dimensions of the Population Challenge*. Washington, DC: Worldwatch Institute.

Caldwell, John C. 1982. *Theory of Fertility Decline*. London: Academic Press.

Cleland, J., and C. Wilson. 1987. "Demand Theories of the Fertility Transition: An Iconoclastic View." *Population Studies* 41(1).

Coale, Ansley J. 1974. "The History of Human Population." *Scientific American* 231(3).

———. 1975. "The Demographic Transition." In *United Nations, The Population Debate*, Vol. 1, pp. 347–355. Population Studies no. 57. New York: United Nations.

———. 1983. "Recent Trends in Fertility in Less Developed Countries." *Science* 221.

Coale, Ansley J., and Edgar M. Hoover. 1958. *Population Growth and Economic Development in Low-income Countries*. Princeton: Princeton University Press.

Coale, Ansley J., and Susan Cotts Watkins, eds. 1986. *The Decline of Fertility in Europe*. Princeton: Princeton University Press.

Cohen, Joel E. 1995. *How Many People Can the Earth Support?* New York: W. W. Norton and Co.

Collins, Lynn. 1982. "World Population." In John A. Ross, ed., *International Encyclopedia of Population*. New York: The Free Press.

Crenshaw, Edward M., Ansari Z. Ameen, and Matthew Christenson. 1997. "Population Dynamics and Economic Development: Age-Specific Population Growth Rates and Economic Growth in Developing Countries, 1965 to 1990." *American Sociological Review* 62(6).

Crosby, Alfred W. 1986. *Ecological Imperialism: The Biological Expansion of Europe, 900–1900*. Cambridge: Cambridge University Press.

Cutright, Phillips. 1982. "The Best of All Possible Worlds." A review of "The Ultimate Resource" by Julian L. Simon. *Contemporary Sociology* 11(6).

Davis, Kingsley. 1963. "The Theory of Change and Response in Demographic History." *Population Index* 29(4).

Dupâquier, Jacques. 1980. "Malthus Reconsidered." A review of "Malthus" by William Petersen. *Contemporary Sociology* 9(4).

Dupâquier, Jacques, ed. 1983. *Malthus Past and Present*. New York: Academic Press.

Easterlin, Richard A., and Eileen M. Crimmins. 1985. *The Fertility Revolution: A Supply-Demand Analysis*. Chicago: University of Chicago Press.

Ehrlich, Paul, and Anne H. Ehrlich. 1979. "The Population Bomb Revisited." *People* 6(2).

Espenshade, Thomas J. 1978. "Zero Population Growth and the Economics of Developed Nations." *Population and Development Review* 4(4).

Espenshade, Thomas J., and William Serow. 1978. *The Economic Consequences of Slowing Population Growth*. New York: Academic Press.

Falkenmark, Malin, and Carl Widstrand. 1992. "Population and Water Resources: A Delicate Balance." *Population Bulletin* 47(3). Washington, DC: Population Reference Bureau.

Feeney, Griffith M. 1994. "Fertility Decline in East Asia." *Science* 226(2).

Frejka, Tomas. 1981. "Long-term Prospects for World Population Growth." *Population and Development Review* 7(3).

Gelbard, Alene, Carl Haub, and Mary M. Kent. 1999. "World Population Beyond Six Billion." *Population Bulletin* 54(1).

Hartmann, Betsy. 1995. *Reproductive Rights and Wrongs: The Global Politics of Population Control*. Boston: South End Press.

Keyfitz, Nathan. 1980. "Petersen on Malthus." A review of "Malthus" by William Petersen. *Contemporary Sociology* 9(4).

Kremer, Michael. 1993. "Population Growth and Technological Change: One Million B.C. to 1990." *Quarterly Journal of Economics* 108(3).

Kuznets, Simon. 1979. *Growth, Population and Income Distribution*. New York: Norton.

Lee, Ronald. 1983. "Economic Consequences of Population Size, Structure, and Growth." *Newsletter of the International Union for the Scientific Study of Population* 17.

———. 1986. "Malthus and Boserup: A Dynamic Synthesis." In David Coleman and Roger Schoefield, eds., *The State of Population Theory: Forward From Malthus*. Oxford: Basil Blackwell.

Leontief, Wassily. 1983. "Technological Advance, Economic Growth, and Income Distribution." *Population and Development Review* 9(3).

Lesthaeghe, R. 1983. "A Century of Demographic and Cultural Change in Western Europe: An Exploration of Underlying Dimensions." *Population and Development Review* 6(4).

Lutz, Wolfgang. 1994. "The Future of World Population." *Population Bulletin* 49(1). Washington, DC: Population Reference Bureau.

Martin, Philip, and Elizabeth Midgley. 1995. "Immigration to the United States: Journey to an Uncertain Destination." *Population Bulletin* 50(3). Washington, DC: Population Reference Bureau.

Martin, Philip, and Jonas Widgren. 1996. "International Migration: A Global Challenge." *Population Bulletin* 51(1). Washington, DC: Population Reference Bureau.

Mason, Karen Oppenheim. 1997. "Explaining Fertility Transitions." Presidential Address to the Population Association of America, *Demography* 34(4).

McKeown, Thomas. 1983. "Food, Infection and Population." In Robert I. Roberg and Theodore K. Rabb, eds., *Hunger and History: The Impact of Changing Food Production and Consumption Patterns on Society*. Cambridge: Cambridge University Press.

McNamara, Regina. 1982. "Demographic Transition Theory." In John A. Ross, ed., *International Encyclopedia of Population*. New York: The Free Press.

McNeill, William H. 1976. *Plagues and Peoples*. Oxford: Blackwell.

McNicoll, Geoffrey. 1998. "Population and Poverty: The Poverty Issues, Parts I & II." Presented at the Workshop on Population, Poverty and Environment held at FAO, Rome, October.

Meuvret, Jean. 1965. "Demographic Crisis in France from the Sixteenth to the Eighteenth Century." In David V. Glass and David E. C. Eversley, eds., *Population in History*. London: Arnold.

Notestein, Frank W. 1945. "Population—The Long View." In Theodore W. Schultz, ed., *Food for the World*. Chicago: University of Chicago Press.

Olshansky, S. Jay, Bruce Carnes, Richard G. Rodgers, and Len Smith. 1997. "Infectious Diseases—New and Ancient Threats to World Health." *Population Bulletin* 52(2). Washington, DC: Population Reference Bureau.

Petersen, William. 1975. *Population*. 3d ed. New York: Macmillan.

———. 1979. *Malthus*. Cambridge: Harvard University Press.

———. 1980. "Further Comments on Malthus and 'Malthus'." *Contemporary Sociology* 9(4).

Population Reference Bureau. 1996. *World Population and Environment Data Sheet*. Washington, DC: Population Reference Bureau.

———. 1999. *1999 World Population Data Sheet*. Washington, DC: Population Reference Bureau.

Repetto, Robert. 1993. "Population, Resources, Environment: An Uncertain Future." *Population Bulletin* 42(2) (reprinting). Washington, DC: Population Reference Bureau.

Ridker, Ronald G., and Elizabeth W. Cecelski. 1982. "Resources and Population." In John A. Ross, ed., *International Encyclopedia of Population*. New York: The Free Press.

Rodgers, Gerry, ed. 1989. *Population Growth and Poverty in Rural South Asia*. New Delhi: Sage.

Sadik, Nafis, ed. 1991. *Population Policies and Programmes: Lessons Learned from Two Decades of Experience*. United Nations Population Fund. New York: New York University Press.

Schultz, T. Paul. 1981. *Economics of Population*. Reading, MA: Addison-Wesley.

Simon, Julian L. 1977. *The Economics of Population*. Princeton: Princeton University Press.

———. 1981. *The Ultimate Resource*. Princeton: Princeton University Press.

———. 1986. *Theory of Population and Economic Growth*. Oxford: Basil Blackwell.

Thompson, W. S. 1930. *Population Problems*. New York: McGraw Hill.

Timmer, C. Peter, Ismael Sirageldin, John F. Kantner, and Samuel H. Preston. 1982. "Review Symposium of Julian L. Simon, 'The Ultimate Resource'." *Population and Development Review* 8(1).

United Nations. 1973. *The Determinants and Consequences of Population Trends*. Vol. 1. ST/SOA/SER.A/50. New York: United Nations.

———. 1981. *World Population Prospects as Assessed in 1980*. Population Studies series, no. 78: ST/ESA/SER.A/78. New York: United Nations.

———. 1982. *World Population Trends and Policies: 1981 Monitoring Report*. Vol. I & II: Population Trends. Population Studies series, no. 79: ST/ESA.SER.A/79. New York: United Nations.

———. 1990. *World Resources 1990–91*. A Report by the World Resources Institute. Oxford: Oxford University Press.

———. 1994. *World Resources 1994–95*. A Report by the World Resources Institute. Oxford: Oxford University Press.

———. 1995. *World Population Prospects, the 1994 Revision*. Population Studies series, no. 145: ST/ESA/SER.A/145. New York: United Nations.

———. 1997. *Demographic Yearbook/Annuaire Démographique 1995*. E/F.97.XIII.1. New York: United Nations.

United Nations. 1998. *World Resources 1998–99.* A Report by the World Resources Institute. Oxford: Oxford University Press.

———. 1999a. *Revision of the World Population Estimates and Projections, 1998 briefing packet.* New York: United Nations.

———. 1999b. *Concise Report on World Population Monitoring, 1999: Population Growth, Structure and Distribution.* E/CN.9/1999/s. New York: United Nations.

United States Bureau of the Census. 1999. *World Population Profile: 1998.* Report WP/98. Washington, DC: Government Printing Office.

Visaria, Leela, and Pravin Visara. 1995. "India's Population in Transition." *Population Bulletin* 50(3). Washington, DC: Population Reference Bureau.

Watkins, Susan Cotts, and Etienne Van de Walle. 1983. "Nutrition, Mortality, and Population Size: Malthus' Court of Last Resort." In Robert I. Roberg and Theodore K. Rabb, eds., *Hunger and History: The Impact of Changing Food Production and Consumption Patterns on Society.* Cambridge: Cambridge University Press.

Weeks, John R. 1996. *Population: An Introduction to Concepts and Issues.* 6th ed. Belmont, CA: Wadsworth.

Wrigley, E. A. 1969. *Population and History.* New York: McGraw Hill.

Age and Sex Structure

Demography deals not only with population size and growth but also with population composition. The most important dimensions of composition, indisputably, are age and sex. Societies assign roles and statuses on the basis of age and sex more than on any other characteristics. Consequently, nations uniformly include questions on age and sex in their census questionnaires. So important is age-sex composition, many demographers give it a special label: population *structure*. We will use that term throughout this chapter.

The chapter proceeds from method to substance. We start with a review of census data on age and sex, noting some errors to be found there. Next we cover some of the simpler methods for describing population structure, ending with the familiar population (or age-sex) pyramid. We use these measures to describe the important contrasts between the structures of less-developed and more-developed countries, for, just as their structures differ, so do their resulting population problems. We close the chapter with an introduction to some of these problems.

DESCRIBING AGE-SEX STRUCTURE

Quality of Census Data

How, one might ask, could censuses make errors in recording something as simple as age and sex? Two kinds of errors can occur, which Shryock and Siegel call *underenumeration* and *misreporting* (1976, p. 115). Underenumeration of an age or sex class means failing to count somebody who would have fallen into that class. The errors arising from underenumeration are also called *coverage errors* or *undercounts*. Misreporting means counting somebody but misallocating him or her among the age-sex categories.

As one might expect, with respect to sex, underenumeration is more of a problem than is misreporting. There is not much ambiguity as to a person's sex or, more correctly, gender. But it is possible for someone's gender to influence whether his or her very existence will be reported. For instance, baby girls might be forgotten in household enumerations more than baby boys in a society where males are considered the important sex, or the existence of military-aged males might go unmentioned on purpose. Underenumeration of women was common, for example, in U.S. censuses of the southern states prior to the Civil War.

But generally the problems with sex data in contemporary censuses are trivial compared with those for age data. In addition to underenumeration, there is a serious problem of misreporting. Why is this a problem? Let us look at how age is determined by enumerators. The standard census definition is clear: "Age is the interval of time between the date of birth and the date of the census, expressed in complete solar years" (United Nations, 1978, p. 23). This is also called a person's *age in completed years* (Pressat, 1985). A census enumerator can find a respondent's age by either 1) asking the age directly or 2) asking the date of birth and letting the census office measure the difference. The United Nations recommends asking date of birth wherever circumstances permit, since it usually results in more precise reporting. Many censuses ask both to check on the reliability of each.

How could there be a problem in recording responses to these seemingly simple questions? Confusion and ignorance still enter in. Not everybody calibrates the *calendar* in exactly the same way, and there can be some confusion in translating from other modes to the Western one employed in much of demography. Not everybody counts age the same way, according to the Western system of describing people in terms of last anniversary of birth, the last completed year of age. Not every society shares the West's obsession for precise distinctions in age and time; many might settle for those distinctions that have meaning with respect to ascribed roles in their particular cultures, such as infant/prepubertal youth/postpubertal but unmarried youth/married young adult, and so on.

Lacking unambiguous evidence of precise age (in contrast with sex), it is tempting for respondents to bend the truth. They might intentionally report a youth of military age to be slightly too young or too old, report a middle-aged woman to be not quite middle-aged, report a sixty-four-year-old to be of retirement age (where that is sixty-five), report a ninety-eight-year-old to be a centenarian.

Or they might carelessly round off reports, resulting in what demographers call "age heaping." There is an almost universal tendency to report age, or date of birth, as years ending in zero, five or in even numbers, sometimes especially avoiding other numbers that are culturally tabooed (Myers, 1940; Shryock and Siegel, 1976; Ewbank, 1981).

Although misreporting and underenumeration in age and sex data cannot be eliminated totally, they have the advantage of being detectable. One way to estimate census errors is through *intercensal reconciliation*. This springs from the fact that people change their sex only with great difficulty and change their age only according to a fixed and knowable schedule. This allows us to trace age-sex classes of people from one census to the next, thereby detecting implausibilities. For instance, women aged fifteen to nineteen in the 1980 U.S. census should bear some correspondence to women aged twenty-five to twenty-nine in the 1990 U.S. census, taking into account the effects of intervening mortality and migration (Robinson et al., 1993; Shryock and Siegel, 1976). We also can estimate census errors using supplemental *post-enumeration samples* of the population. Intensive efforts are made to collect highly accurate data for a small statistical sample of the population. These data are then compared to the census to estimate coverage and reporting errors for various groups (Hogan, 1993; Hill, 1987; Wolter, 1986). Using both of these methods, estimates of coverage errors for the 1990 census are available by age and sex as well as for special groups such as urban minorities and the homeless. Largely due to the importance of coverage errors in the 1990 census, post-enumeration samples are an integral part of the year 2000 U.S. census (Edmonston and Shultze, 1995).

Describing Age Structure

Some of the techniques that demographers use for describing age and sex structure may be familiar. Frequency distributions, percentage distributions, ratios, and bar graphs are standard descriptive statistics. Seeing their application here will be a simple review for some readers.

The first step in constructing a frequency distribution is categorization or grouping of cases. Conventionally, census tabulations dealing with age alone, or with age and sex together, use five-year intervals or *age groups*, as illustrated in Table 4-1. At the youngest end, the under-five category is sometimes divided into under-one and one-through-four years of age because of the importance of separate figures on the first year of life, infancy. At the oldest end, because there are so few survivors in the very old categories, demographers conventionally use an open-ended category, such as the one for eighty-five years and over in Table 4-1.

The first three columns of Table 4-1 present the estimated *frequency distributions* by age class, according to the 1990 U.S. census, first for both sexes together and then separately for males and for females. One could look down one of those columns, note the relative size of the figures, and get some notion of the shape of the age distribution. However, if one wanted to compare the same age class in two columns, for instance males versus females aged five to nine, one would have to correct for differences in the total size of the population being distributed. That is the purpose of *percentage distributions*, shown in columns 4 and 5.

To compute the percentages, one multiplies the entry in each age-sex category by one hundred, then divides every such product by the total of the population in that same sex category. The formula would be

$$\frac{(\text{population in age and sex class}) \times 100}{\text{population in all age classes of same sex}}$$

Columns 4 and 5 of Table 4-1 are percentage distributions of males and of females. It is legitimate to compare male with female percentages for any given age class in those columns. We see, for instance, that in the contemporary United States, relatively larger percentages of males are in the younger categories and larger percentages of females are in the older categories.

Table 4-1
Age-Sex Distribution of U.S. Population, 1990

Age[a]	In Thousands			Percentages		
	Both Sexes	Males	Females	Males	Females	Sex Ratio
	(1)	(2)	(3)	(4)	(5)	(6)
All Ages	248,710	121,239	127,470	100.00	100.00	95.1
Under 5	18,354	9392	8962	7.75	7.03	104.8
5–9	18,099	9263	8837	7.64	6.93	104.8
10–14	17,114	8767	8347	7.23	6.55	105.0
15–19	17,754	9103	8651	7.51	6.79	105.2
20–24	19,020	9676	9345	7.98	7.33	103.5
25–29	21,313	10,696	10,617	8.82	8.33	100.7
30–34	21,863	10,877	10,986	8.97	8.62	99.0
35–39	19,963	9902	10,061	8.17	7.89	98.4
40–44	17,616	8692	8924	7.17	7.00	97.4
45–49	13,873	6811	7062	5.62	5.54	96.4
50–54	11,351	5515	5836	4.55	4.58	94.5
55–59	10,532	5034	5497	4.15	4.31	91.6
60–64	10,616	4947	5669	4.08	4.45	87.3
65–69	10,112	4532	5579	3.74	4.38	81.2
70–74	7995	3409	4586	2.81	3.60	74.3
75–79	6121	2400	3722	1.98	2.92	64.5
80–84	3934	1366	2568	1.13	2.01	53.2
85 and over	3080	858	2222	0.71	1.74	38.6
Under 15	53,568	(21.5%)				
15–64	163,900	(65.9%)				
65 and over	31,242	(12.6%)				

Median ages: Male = 31.7; Female = 34.1

$$\text{Age-dependency ratio} = \frac{53,568 + 31,242}{163,900} \times 100 = 51.7$$

[a]Since entries for particular age categories are rounded to thousands, they may not add up to precisely the subtotals and totals presented.
Source: U.S. Bureau of the Census, *Census of Population, 1990,* 1990.

There are eighteen categories, however, in each of the distributions of Table 4-1. For many purposes, that is so much detail that it leads to confusion. Demographers often combine age categories to make certain comparisons more salient, using certain cutoff points in the age continuum that are more important than others. For example, age fifteen has become an arbitrary cutoff point for eligibility for adult economic roles. Age sixty-five has come to mean the eligibility for retirement. So a conventional way to describe what proportion of the total population is "young" is the percentage aged fifteen or less; this is 21.5% in Table 4-1. At the other extreme, the proportion that is "old" is measured by the percentage aged sixty-five and over; this is 12.6% in the table.

Such percentages in broad categories, however, do not give an overall picture of the age distribution; for that we need some summary measures. It is conventional to use the median to summarize age distributions. Although the computation of the median is too complex to show here, the meaning of the measure is straightforward: the median is the age above which and below which precisely half of the population falls. (The average, or arithmetic mean, would be misleading in this context because of the generally skewed shape of age distributions.) Table 4-1 shows that the 1990 U. S. male median age (31.7 years) was slightly less than the female median (34.1 years). This confirms our impression from scanning the percentage distributions.

A convenient way to compare the relative size of any two numbers is by constructing a *ratio*, dividing one number by the other. When applied to age distributions, the most frequently used is the *age-dependency* ratio. In the numerator are all those people who are supposedly dependents in that they are either too young (conventionally, under fifteen) or too old (sixty-five and over) to be fully economically productive (Shryock and Siegel, 1976). In the denominator are all of the rest of the population of working ages, i.e. those aged fifteen through sixty-four. The formula is

$$\frac{P_{0\text{-}14} + P_{65+}}{P_{15\text{-}64}} \times 100$$

where

$P_{0\text{-}14}$ = population aged under fifteen years
P_{65+} = population aged sixty-five or more years
$P_{15\text{-}64}$ = population aged fifteen through sixty-four

The age-dependency ratio in Table 4-1 shows that there were 51.7 dependents for every 100 persons of working age.

Describing Sex Structure

Demographers often describe the sex composition of populations by comparing the number of persons of each sex with a ratio. The *sex ratio* is the number of males divided by the number of females multiplied by a constant of one hundred:

$$\frac{\text{Males}}{\text{Females}} \times 100$$

The sex ratio sometimes is called the "masculinity ratio," which should remind you that the number of men is arbitrarily divided by the number of women in the ratio. In column 6 of Table 4-1, one sees that the sex ratio for the total U. S. population in 1990 was 95.1, meaning that there were about 95 men for every 100 women in the population.

Sex ratios can be computed not only for total populations but also for classes within those populations. Demographers frequently find it helpful to pay attention to sex composition at different age levels. Column 6 of Table 4-1 dramatizes how the sex ratio varied by age class in the United States in 1990. This decreasing sex ratio with aging is a reflection of the slightly younger overall age of the U.S. male population in contrast with the female. (The relative youth of the male population, in turn, is explained primarily by differential mortality risks, described in chapter 5.)

Population Pyramids

By far the most familiar way of depicting age and sex structure together is with population pyramids, which are composed of bar graphs. Bar graphs make it possible for one to compare visually the sizes of a series of classes. They can be used to compare the classes in any frequency distribution or percentage distribution.

A population pyramid consists of a bar graph showing the age distribution of both males and females, presented together in a particular way. The age categories proceed from the bottom to the top. The male bars conventionally proceed from a vertical center line leftward; the female bars proceed from a vertical center line rightward. The term "pyramid" comes from the fact that in times past there were more young people than old people in national populations, and thus the younger (lower) bars were longer than the older (upper) ones (more about that later).

Pyramids can be constructed from either *frequency* distributions or from *percentage* distributions. One could, for instance, construct a population pyramid directly from columns 2 and 3 of Table 4-1. The length of each bar would be proportional to the number of thousands in each age-sex class. Such absolute-number pyramids are particularly useful for registering changes in the sizes of age-sex classes over time.

More frequently, however, one sees population pyramids representing percentage distributions. Note, however, that the percentages are not of age distributions for males separately and for females separately; they represent age-sex percentage distributions for the population of both sexes together. For instance, it would be incorrect for us to construct a percentage population pyramid from Table 4-1 by juxtaposing a bar graph for column 4 with a bar graph for column 5. Rather, we would have to construct a new percentage distribution by dividing each figure in columns 2 and 3 by the total population (248,710) and multiplying it by one hundred. Then the length of any bar would be proportional to this percentage.

Percentage pyramids have the advantage of not being influenced by the total size of the population. The area of all percentage pyramids is the same if they are all drawn on the same scale. The feature to notice is the *shape* of the pyramid, which registers only the relative sizes of the age-sex classes in that pyramid. Percentage pyramids are particularly useful in comparing populations of considerably different size. The population pyramids shown in Figure 4-1 are good examples.

The best way to make sure that you understand these measures is to compute examples. Exercises at the end of the chapter offer practice in all of the measures in this section, including population pyramids.

CONTRASTS BETWEEN MORE-DEVELOPED AND LESS-DEVELOPED COUNTRIES

The Recent Past, Up to 1990

Age structure. Table 4-2 presents dramatic evidence of world contrasts in age structure. Each column gives one measure of age structure introduced in the preceding section. The first seven rows present age measurement for the world regions. We have ordered them according to the percentages of their populations "young," from high to low percentage. The next two rows give age measurements for the two categories of world regions, less-developed (LDRs) and more-developed (MDRs). The final three rows are for *pre-transition* countries which have not yet had a major decline in fertility, *transitional* countries in the middle of declining fertility, and *late-transition* countries (such as the United States) which have already had major fertility declines. To some degree, these two classification schemes run parallel, but the United Nations finds both to be useful, as will we. (See chapter 3 for details.)

The first thing to notice is how similar to each other the various more-developed regions and the various less-developed regions are. Regarding their young populations, under age fifteen, the MDRs (North America, Europe) show 21.6% and 20.5% respectively. In contrast, the less-developed regions of Africa, the balance of Asia, and Latin America (and the Caribbean) have 44.9, 38.2, and 35.7% of their population under the age of fifteen. (Note, however, that only Africa as a whole region has a percentage under fifteen similar to "pre-transitional," i.e., very high fertility.) In mixed regions such as East and Southeast Asia and Oceania, the percentage under fifteen is between the extremes (28.8 and 26.3%, respectively). The MDRs and LDRs show similar homogeneity with respect to percentage aged sixty-five and over. However, with respect to this older population, the MDRs (Northern America, Europe) are in extreme contrast with all other regions.

Given the similarity among more-developed and among less-developed countries, we can treat the MDRs and LDRs as homogeneous categories, and we can summarize the differences between them. The less-developed regions have a much higher

Table 4-2
Summary Measures of Age Structure, World Regions, 1990

Regions[a]	Less Than 15 Years Old (%) (1)	15 to 64 Years Old (%) (2)	65 Years Old or More (%) (3)	Age-Dependency Ratio (4)
Africa	44.9	52.0	3.0	92.2
Asia (excl. East and Southeast)	38.2	57.6	4.2	73.6
Latin America and Caribbean	35.7	59.5	4.8	68.0
East and Southeast Asia	28.8	65.4	5.7	52.9
Oceania	26.3	64.7	8.9	54.5
Northern America	21.6	66.1	12.4	51.4
Europe	20.5	66.8	12.7	49.8
LDR	35.5	60.0	4.5	66.6
MDR	21.4	66.4	12.1	50.6
Pre-trans	45.8	51.3	2.8	94.8
Transitional	37.9	57.9	4.2	72.6
Late-trans	24.1	67.0	8.9	49.3

[a]Ordered by percentage less than 15 years old.
Source: Bos et al., *World Population Projections 1994–95 Edition,* 1994.

proportion of their population under fifteen years of age. On the other hand, the more-developed regions have almost three times as high a proportion aged sixty-five and over. These proportions translate into a much higher age-dependency ratio for the less-developed regions, 66.6, versus the 50.6 for the more-developed regions.

Figure 4-1 contrasts these age structures graphically in population pyramids for more- and less-developed regions. The population pyramids are given for actual 1990 populations in each region and for projected populations in 2020 and 2050. Look first at the graphs for 1990; we will discuss the projections later. The graph for the less-developed regions is indeed pyramidal, rising regularly from a broad base to a sharp peak. This is the classic shape of age structures before national demographic transitions. The shape that has emerged with development, however, might better be described as columnar.

Sex structure. Figure 4-1 also allows one to see the nature of sex-structure contrasts between the less-developed and more-developed regions. For the less-developed regions, the pyramid is almost symmetrical, while the one for the more-developed regions has a marked rightward, or female, lean as it rises to the older age categories. In both cases, in the earliest ages males are slightly more predominant. As one reaches the higher ages, females tend to outnumber the males more and more. But the degree to which this is true varies greatly with the level of development of the region. Female predominance in the elder age categories is a feature of more-developed countries where aging of the population emphasizes the greater longevity of females. This feature was demonstrated for the United States in Table 4-1, showing sex ratios by age.

Projected Changes, 1990 to 2050

Modern methods of population projection specify not only future population sizes but future population structures. The most widely accepted method for making projections, the cohort-component method, is explained in Box 4-1. Any projection, of course, depends upon the fertility, mortality, and migration assumptions employed. The projections shown in Figure 4-1 are based on the assumptions that the World Bank considers most likely as of 1994, generally a continued slow decline in worldwide mortality and in the fertility of less-developed regions (Bos et al., 1994, p. 3).

As one can see, the pyramids for the less-developed and more-developed regions are projected to change in the same direction (see Figure 4-1), but at each date they are caught at different points in that change. To simplify a little, the more-developed regions will evolve from a tall bell shape to an even more columnar shape as the average age of the population gets older. The growing percentage of the population over seventy-five years of age is evident in the apparent "T" or "anvil" shape of future population pyramids in the developed regions. The less-developed regions will move from their triangular or pyramidal shape to one which is very similar to the current pyramid of the developed regions. These trends, of course, are apparent only in projections which reach far into the future. (A later section of this chapter analyzes the theoretical impact of changes in fertility, mortality, and migration on age-sex structure.)

Figure 4-1 Population Pyramids for More-Developed and Less-Developed Regions, 1990, 2020, 2050

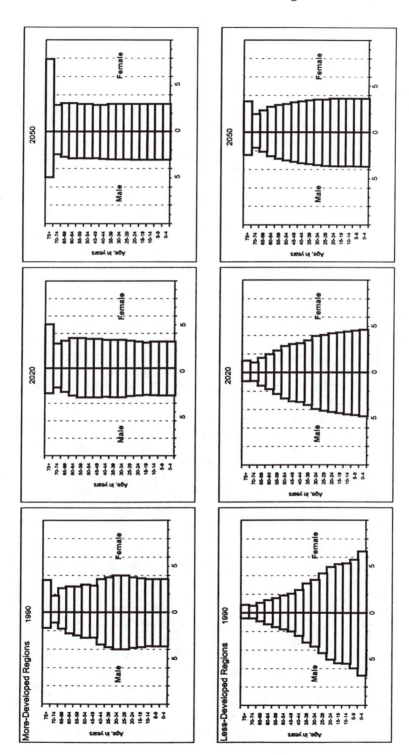

Source: Bos et al., *World Population Projections 1994–95 Edition*, 1994.

Box 4-1 Projecting Age-Sex Structure

The most generally accepted modern method for projecting national populations is the *cohort-component method*. It has the advantage of providing figures not only on total size but also on age-sex structure.

A *cohort* is a set of people identified on the basis of having experienced a specified demographic event in the same short interval of time. Thus a *birth cohort* is a set of people born in the same short interval and, of course, having similar present ages. One also could identify marriage cohorts, immigration cohorts, and so on. But when demographers use the word "cohort" unmodified, they mean birth cohort.

Each cohort is projected forward separately. Specific assumptions about future mortality, fertility, and migration are applied to each cohort, and these determine its projected size at points in the future. That is, separate assumptions are made about the *components of growth* (or population processes) for each cohort.

Although the actual production of a projection can be technically complex, the underlying strategy is simple. It can be summarized in a series of five steps. An actual projection of the population of Mexico from 1990 to 2015, shown in Table 4-3, serves as a concrete example. Let us confine our attention to the female population in that example, for simplicity.

1. *Make a baseline estimate of the population and its age-sex distribution.* Estimate the number of people in each age-sex class for the most recent date possible. If your baseline date happens to be the date of a census count, then no further estimation is required; you use the count. But if you want to start with some post-censal date, then you have to estimate by taking into account information about deaths, births, and migrations since the census. In our illustrative table, the baseline figures are derived from the 1990 Mexican census.

2. *For each existing birth cohort, add and subtract members according to migration and mortality assumptions.* Let us illustrate with the youngest existing birth cohort in the baseline year, 1990, that aged zero through four years (<5). *Fertility* can no longer influence this cohort (or any older one) since its members are born already. *Mortality* is usually the major factor influencing the future size of existing national cohorts. On the basis of assumed sequences of *age-sex-specific death rates* (see Box 4-2 for details), demographers estimate how many of the children aged zero through four in 1990 would survive to be five through nine in 1995, ten through fourteen in 2000, and so on. However, regarding *migration*, some of those surviving to older ages will emigrate out of the region's population while others will immigrate into the region's population. The difference between those moving in and out of the population as the cohort is projected forward is the net migration. Migration data are often difficult to obtain and projections make simplified assumptions about *age-sex-specific net migration rates*. Applying these rates to the cohort gives an estimate of the number of net migrants which will be added or subtracted from the surviving population while moving that cohort through the time intervals. You can follow the combined influence of mortality and migration on this (initially <5) cohort just below the stepped line in Table 4-3. Each existing birth cohort is followed forward through the series of five-year steps in the same manner.

3. *For cohorts yet unborn in the baseline year, project births by sex of child.* The cohorts yet unborn in 1990 are those above the stepped line in Table 4-3. The future fertility assumptions are stated in terms of the *age-specific fertility (birth) rates* (see Box 4-2 for details) for each five-year age interval of women from fifteen to forty-five

years of age. The assumed specific birth rates are multiplied by the number of women projected to be in each of the age categories (i.e. for ages at which women are assumed fecund), after which the number of births to all women are totaled. How many of these projected total births will be boys and how many girls is estimated by applying an assumed sex ratio at birth, normally something like 105 males per 100 females.

4. *Add and subtract members from the new cohorts on the basis of migration and mortality assumptions.* Not all of the birth cohorts projected in step three will survive to be counted at the end of the projection interval into which they are born. Each birth cohort will be depleted by mortality during its first interval of life, just as in all the later ones. Thus we subtract members of these new cohorts on the basis of assumptions about infant mortality (death before age one) and early childhood mortality (death at ages one through four). Children and infants also migrate, as do all age groups, and the numbers carried forward to the next interval of life are thus also modified by net migration rates in these early years of life.

5. *Carry out step two for each of the new cohorts.* For example, those 5,651 (thousand) members of the 1990–1994 birth cohort surviving to 1995 are projected forward to 2015. Their path is seen just above the stepped line in Table 4-3. The cohort survivors are depleted according to assumed age-sex-specific death rates and either depleted or increased by assumed age-sex-specific migration rates.

For further details, see Bogue, Arriaga, and Anderton, 1993, chapter 17; or Shryock and Siegel, 1976, chapter 23.

Table 4-3
Illustrative Cohort-Component Projection, Mexican Females, 1990–2015

Age	1990	1995	2000	2005	2010	2015
Total	41,004	45,476	49,744	53,807	57,550	61,210
< 5	5423	5651	5500	5305	5016	5030
5–9	5119	5339	5575	5438	5255	4977
10–14	4750	5074	5296	5539	5409	5233
15–19	4883	4705	5030	5259	5508	5385
20–24	4160	4807	4631	4967	5207	5467
25–29	3434	4075	4720	4558	4906	5159
30–34	2796	3365	4004	4658	4507	4865
35–39	2263	2743	3310	3954	4614	4471
40–44	1873	2223	2702	3270	3916	4577
45–49	1500	1840	2187	2664	3232	3876
50–54	1195	1467	1802	2148	2622	3185
55–59	1099	1158	1425	1756	2099	2566
60–64	818	1049	1108	1369	1695	2030
65–69	622	757	976	1038	1293	1606
70–74	439	544	669	872	940	1178
75 +	628	679	809	1011	1331	1605

[a]Since entries for particular age categories are rounded to thousands, they may not add up to precisely the subtotals and totals presented.
Source: Bos et al., *World Population Projections 1994-95 Edition*, 1994.

Evolution of the U.S. Structure

Figure 4-2 presents six successive percentage pyramids for the United States, from 1900 to 2030. The last two, obviously, are projections. Together this sequence shows the structural changes already experienced in one Western country as it developed economically and demographically, along with future expectations.

Here is how to read this kind of sequence. Each of the bars in a given pyramid refers to a *birth cohort*, a set of people born about the same time. In later pyramids, the same birth cohort climbs up the pyramid because it is caught at a later age. Figure 4-2 illustrates this by identifying the cohort of 1955 to 1959 as it climbs the last four pyramids. The number of survivors of the birth cohort who will remain to be included in a pyramid depends on how many it had at birth (fertility), how many died off since birth (mortality), and how many moved in or out of the country since birth (net migration). The shape of the pyramid in any given year is determined by the relative sizes of all surviving cohorts.

What happened in the United States during the past century? The U. S. population pyramid of 1900 is more like the contemporary LDR pyramid shown in Figure 4-1 than the contemporary MDR one. Fertility was still relatively high, considerably higher than mortality. Net immigration was heavy and favored young people. The first major departure from that pyramidal shape came during the Great Depression. Both fertility and migration declined drastically. The cohorts of 1930 through 1939, aged zero through nine in 1940, are markedly slimmer than the preceding ones. These Depression cohorts were aged thirty to thirty-nine in the 1970 pyramid. In spite of the small proportion of the population at reproductive ages, as these cohorts moved through childbearing they managed to create a baby-boom (Bouvier, 1980). Childbearing that had been delayed during World War II by these Depression cohorts, combined with early marriage and rapid fertility of younger cohorts entering reproductive ages in the prosperous postwar decades, contributed to the baby-boom seen in the large cohort of infants and children in the 1970 pyramid. By 1990, both the slim Depression cohorts and the fat baby-boom cohorts marched up the pyramid but had less pronounced effects on the composition of the entire population. Recent cohorts in the youngest ages of the 1990 pyramid reflect both the baby-bust of the late 1960s and 1970s (i.e. those aged ten to twenty-four) and the slight baby-boom echo of the 1980s (i.e. those born to baby-boomers and aged zero to nine).

These projections for the years 2010 and 2030 assume a constant set of age-specific fertility rates, just high enough for replacement, resulting in about 2.1 children born per woman in her lifetime. Mortality is assumed to decline slightly with the typical age of death (i.e. life expectancy) rising from about seventy-six to just under eighty-three years old. Legal immigration is presumed to stay near its recent level of 880,000 immigrants per year. The main new feature in these projected pyramids is the change from a youthful one to an aged one. The broad base of the 1900 pyramid has shrunk to a narrow band. The pyramidal shape of 1900 has changed to a more columnar one, and the population at older ages has increased. In 2010, the baby-boom population will still be of working age. However, by 2030 the baby-boom will reach retirement age. Children were clearly the majority of dependents in 1900, while the elderly will be a growing proportion of

Figure 4-2 Population Pyramids for the United States, 1900–2030

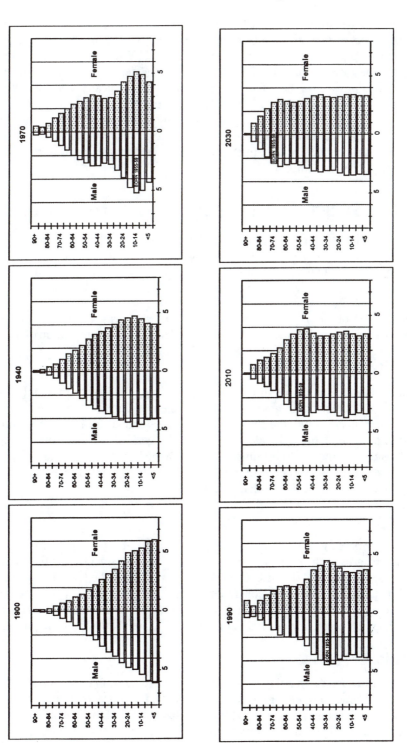

Source: U.S. Bureau of the Census, *Current Population Reports P-25 1130*, table 2, 1996, p. 52; Anderton et al., *Population of the United States*, 1997.

dependents in the future. While the baby-boom is still of working age, e.g. the 2010 pyramid, the impact of an aging population on dependency will be minimized, giving rise to what demographers have called the "false good times." When the baby-boom exits the workforce, the growing contribution of the elderly to age-dependency ratios will be felt by programs that provide for the elderly (e.g. pension funds, Medicare, social security, etc.).

In this descriptive account of the changing structure of the U.S. population, we have made passing reference to the proximate causes of the changes—swings in U.S. migration, fertility, and mortality rates. Those three population processes are the only forces that can change population structure. Now is the time for a more theoretical treatment of how they impact.

How Structure Affects the Population Processes

The likelihood of dying, giving birth, or migrating varies with age and sex. Thus all of the crude rates are affected by the age-sex structure of the population. Structure is not the only determinant of mortality, fertility, and migration, but it is an important one.

Figure 4-3 graphs the age pattern of mortality, by sex, and of fertility in the United States in 1997. Each line connects age-sex-specific rates for one of the sexes. (This important kind of rate is explained in Box 4-2.) These rates register the probability of dying and of giving birth at each of the ages specified on the bottom margin of the graph.

Mortality

For each sex, moderate mortality during infancy declines to minimal mortality during youth, climbs again gradually through the middle years, and then rises more rapidly thereafter. Though the shape of that curve is similar for both sexes, mortality for males is higher than for females, at all ages. The general "J" shape of these age distributions of mortality is almost universal, though the lean of the "J" may vary. Everywhere, sex influences mortality, although not always in precisely the pattern shown in Figure 4-3. (More about this in chapter 5.)

Fertility

Only women give birth, and only over about a thirty-year span. Moreover, the tendency to give birth, even within that span, varies considerably with female age. One can see in Figure 4-3 that U.S. fertility rises rapidly in the teens to a peak in the twenties, then declines to negligible levels in the mid-forties. The general shape of this curve, as well, is universal; but again there are variations with overall fertility level and the number of women having births at later ages. (More about this in chapter 7.)

Migration

One can suppose that the ways in which age and sex influence mortality and fertility are fundamentally biological. It may come as a surprise, then, that age and sex also strongly affect migration and that there is a biological link, although not so obvious or direct. Universally, contemporary mobility is at its peak ages between the late teens

Figure 4-3
Age-Sex-Specific Death Rates and Age-Specific Birth (Fertility) Rates for the United States, 1997

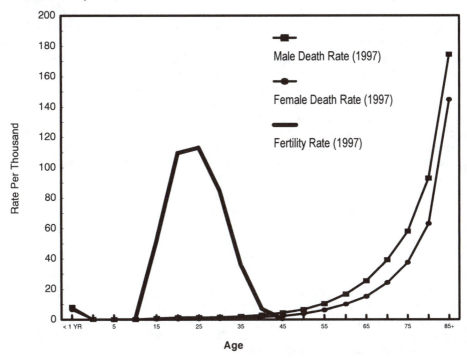

Source: National Center for Health Statistics, *Vital Statistics of the United States, 1997*, 2000, table 1-13; *Deaths: Final Data for 1997*, 1999, table 2; U. S. Bureau of the Census, Resident Population Estimates of the United States, Internet Release, April 11, 2000.

and the mid-thirties. This corresponds to the life-cycle phases where men and women are taking on adult roles, finding their places in the workforce, and forming new households. Mobility also differs by sex, but here the nature of the difference varies, apparently influenced by cultural variations in female roles. (More about this in chapter 9.)

How the Population Processes Determine Structure

Assessing the hypothetical impacts of mortality, fertility, and migration changes on age-sex structure requires imagination. One takes a given population pyramid and imagines what it would look like at some specific future date if certain assumed things were to happen to its population processes during the interval (Bogue, 1993; Coale, 1972; Stolnitz, 1956). The projection can be done either precisely, with numbers, or approximately, in the head, as we ask you to do here.

What kind of assumptions should we make? Remember that only the three components of growth (mortality, fertility, and migration) can influence the size of either the total population or any age cohort within it; therefore, if you are trying to imagine

---

Box 4-2 Age-Sex-Specific Rates

Age-sex-specific rates are used for two main purposes. One is to describe the impact of age and sex upon the population process in question. The second purpose is to discount, or "control" for, the influence of age-sex structure while measuring some other population process.

Demographers use rates in general to discount the influence of specified factors on measures of the population process (Ross, 1982). In the case of *crude* rates, treated in chapter 1, the factor being discounted was the size of the total population. When one compares two crude rates, one knows that whatever may be causing them to differ, it cannot be the sizes of the total populations producing the events in question. In the case of *age-sex-specific* rates, the factor being discounted is the structure of the population. When one compares two specific rates for the same age-sex category, one knows that whatever may be causing them to differ, it cannot be the proportion of the total population that falls into the age-sex category.

For either of these purposes, specific, separate rates are computed for each pertinent age class in the population, that is, for each bar of the population pyramid. Rates normally are constructed for one sex at a time. For each age category, the general formula is

$$_n r_x = \frac{_n E_x}{_n P_x} \times 1{,}000$$

where x is the initial age, n is the number of years in the age category, E is the number of events (e.g. births or deaths) occurring to persons in the age category, and P is the number of persons in the age category (Shryock and Siegel, 1976). For example, the age-specific birth rate for women aged 20–24 in the United States in 1990 would be obtained by solving the following formula:

$$_5 r_{20} = \frac{_5 B_{20}}{_5 P_{20}} \times 1{,}000$$

where B is the number of children born in 1990 to women aged 20–24 and P is the number of women aged 20–24 in the 1990 population. Exercises at the end of the chapter illustrate these computations with real data and provide the reader a chance to construct some rates.

Figure 4-3 is a graph of age-sex-specific rates. Death rates are computed for each sex and age interval. In the case of births, however, rates do not have to be constructed for all age-sex classes. Although it certainly can be argued that both sexes participate in the production of children, the number of women available is the more limiting factor (so far). Moreover, female fertility is so low as to be negligible before age fifteen and after age forty-five (so far). Therefore, conventionally, age-specific birth rates are computed only for females, one each for the six five-year age intervals between ages fifteen and forty-five. Conventionally such rates are called fertility rates rather than birth rates, for no apparent reason (IUSSP, 1982).

the separate influence of any one component on the future age structure, the simplest strategy is to assume that the other two components will not change, or at least not change in such a way as to alter the shape of the projected pyramid. Then you specify an assumed change in the one remaining population process and imagine the results of that assumed change.

The following examples start by assuming changes that actually do occur normally in the demographic transition accompanying economic development: mortality decline and fertility decline. So what you are getting here is also a formal demographic explanation of the main changes in MDR population pyramids as they went through their transitions, the kind of change presented in Figure 4-2 for the United States. Of course, it also is an explanation of the current difference between MDR and LDR pyramids, summarized in Figure 4-1.

Mortality Decline

Effect on age. Suppose that we have an absolute-number population pyramid for an imaginary country in 2000. The length of each of the bars in the pyramid represents the number of people in a five-year age category as of 2000.

Now, let us make some simplifying assumptions about migration and fertility. Let us assume that there is no net migration for any of the cohorts during the five-year span from 2000 to 2005. Fertility changes between 2000 and 2005 could affect the size of only the youngest age category in 2005, that is, those aged zero to five in 2005. Therefore, the length of the bar for each of the 2000 already-born cohorts (or age categories over five years old) as of 2005 will be determined solely by the death toll during the five-year time span.

Now let us try to imagine what that pyramid would look like in 2005 if overall mortality were to decline between 2000 and 2005, rather than stay at prior levels. The impact of the decline would depend upon the *relative* shrinkage of the specific death rates for the various ages.

Let us first suppose that mortality declined so as to improve life chances *equally*, across the board. For instance, try to imagine what would happen if age-specific death rates declined in such a way that survivorship between 2000 and 2005 doubled for every cohort. Each cohort would be larger in 2005 than it would have been under stable mortality conditions, larger in proportion to its original size. The size of the absolute-number pyramid would be larger, but that pyramid would have grown proportionally in each cohort or age group. The shape of the 2005 population pyramid would be the same under both stable mortality and equally declining-mortality assumptions; the *percentage* population pyramids would be *identical*.

In general words, an equal increase in survivorship rates for all age categories would have no impact on the relative age composition of the population. Incidentally, an equal decrease in survivorship for all age categories also would have no impact.

But what if survivorship does not change equally at all age levels? Then, indeed, mortality change can have an impact on age structure. In fact, during demographic transitions to lower mortality, survivorship generally improves more at the youngest ages. What would be the impact of such a disproportionate improvement of infant and early childhood survivorship? It would mean that younger birth cohorts would swell by a greater percentage than would the older cohorts during a specified interval; thus the shape of the pyramid would be made broader at the bottom after the mortality decline.

Historically, the declines in mortality that have accompanied demographic transitions have had a greater impact on previously high levels of infant and child mortality than on adult mortality. As a result, mortality declines have *not* been a major cause of the aging of MDR populations. Indeed, if transitional mortality declines have had any impact on percentage pyramids, it probably has been to make them slightly *younger* than they would have been.

These are not trivial facts, nor are they widely understood by laypeople. The popular wisdom still is that the historical aging of the U.S. population, for instance, has been due to mortality decline. Not so, but it is easy to understand from where the misconception arose. Mortality decline obviously does improve the life expectancy of *individuals*, but it does not necessarily affect the age structure of *collectives*. Population aging is not the same as individual aging.

Recently, however, things have changed in late-transitional, MDR populations. They have had a disproportionate decline in mortality among the elderly. As Treas and Torrecilha note, in recent decades, the percentage gain in survivorship at age 60 and above exceeded the gains for younger people, whose already low death rates left less room for improvement (1995, p. 62). Moreover, this imbalance is likely to continue into the future. If youthful and middle-age death rates in the MDRs are already irreducibly low, then future decreases are likely to focus on older-age rates. Declines in those rates will improve survivorship disproportionately at the top of the population pyramid (Friedlander and Malul, 1983; Stolnitz, 1982).

In sum, then, we can say that during the main demographic transition, mortality changes theoretically made little contribution to the aging of populations. However, in late-transitional countries, recent disproportionate mortality declines have indeed contributed to population aging, and will do so in the future (see chapter 5).

Effect on sex. Table 4-4 dramatizes the gradual shift from male to female majority throughout the life span. In column 1, that for the whole world, we see that a sex ratio of 104 in the zero-to-four age category gradually declines to a sex ratio of only 62 in the seventy-five-and-over category. Worldwide, there are roughly three females for every two males in these older ages.

What could be the explanation of this depletion of the world's males relative to its females with age? Again, we can proceed by process of elimination. Fertility could not be a factor, since males universally outnumber females at birth. Interworld migration cannot be an explanation (yet). That leaves higher male mortality as an explanation for the greater depletion of males at higher ages. For the world as a whole, throughout the life span, females tend to survive better than do males.

The degree to which this is true, however, varies internationally. True, the same general pattern of declining sex ratios at higher ages characterizes more- and less-developed regions (columns 2 and 3) as well as countries which are pre-transition, transitional, and late-transition populations (in columns 4–6). And Table 4-4 shows that the sex ratio for the MDRs and LDRs is about the same in age groups from zero

Table 4-4
Sex Ratios by Age Category, Worldwide and in Regions, 1990

	World (1)	More-Developed Regions (2)	Less-Developed Regions (3)	Pre-Transition Countries (4)	Transitional Countries (5)	Late-Transition Countries (6)
Total, all ages	102	95	104	100	103	100
0–4	104	105	104	102	105	105
5–9	105	105	105	102	105	106
10–14	105	105	105	102	106	106
15–19	105	105	105	101	106	106
20–24	105	104	105	100	104	106
25–29	104	102	105	100	104	106
30–34	104	101	105	99	104	104
35–39	104	101	105	98	105	104
40–44	103	100	104	97	102	104
45–49	102	98	104	97	100	104
50–54	100	95	103	95	99	102
55–59	98	92	102	93	98	99
60–64	94	85	100	90	98	93
65–69	86	72	96	86	95	81
70–74	80	65	91	83	91	74
75 +	62	50	79	76	84	56

Source: Bos et al., *World Population Projections 1994–95 Edition,* 1994.

to twenty-four. However, sex ratios in these regions differ dramatically past age sixty, with ratios of only 50 past age seventy-five in MDRs compared to 79 in LDRs. With a faster depletion of males in adulthood, females become a majority by their mid-forties in the MDRs but not until their late sixties in the LDRs.

How can we explain this difference between more- and less-developed regions? Again, international migration is not likely to be a contributing factor; indeed, it would work in the reverse direction if at all. The balance of modern international migration is from LDRs to MDRs, and long-distance international migration of adults tends to select males, not females (see chapter 9). Such migration, therefore, would tend to increase the adult sex ratios in MDRs, the opposite of what Table 4-4 shows.

Eliminating the effect of fertility is more complicated. Higher fertility in LDRs could possibly increase maternal mortality, lowering the number of surviving females nearer to that of surviving males and thus keeping sex ratios more equitable into older ages. That would be consistent with higher sex ratios in LDRs. Yet, other evidence in Table 4-4 suggests the opposite is true of high-fertility countries. If we compare countries before, during, and after declining fertility, pre-transition countries have a lower, rather than higher, sex ratio from infancy through adult reproductive years.

We are left with differences in mortality as an explanation. Mortality in MDRs is clearly more sex-selective, higher for males, at older ages. This is especially true after age sixty-five, where there are less than three males for every four females in

MDRs. MDRs and late-transition countries both have sex ratios showing nearly twice as many females as males in those over seventy-five years of age.

What aspects of development are responsible for the lower female, and relatively higher male, mortality at older ages? Let us leave that question for chapter 5.

Fertility Decline

Figure 4-4 shows schematically how fertility affects an absolute-number population pyramid. In it, a broad arrow arises from that segment of the pyramid representing the women of reproductive age and extends around to the base of the pyramid, where it splits into boys and girls before entering the base of the pyramid. This is meant to symbolize that final delivery of babies is confined to women (almost entirely to those aged fifteen to forty-five), that they produce babies of both sexes in almost equal numbers, and that all babies enter the pyramid at the bottom, at age zero.

The figure also dramatizes that two factors determine the number of babies that will be produced. The first is the number of women in the childbearing ages, fifteen through forty-five. The other is the level of the age-specific birth (fertility) rates being experienced by those women—the higher the rates, the more the births.

Figure 4-4 How Fertility Influences the Age Structure

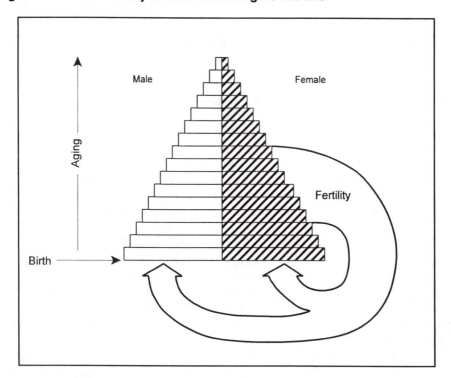

Source: Bos et al., World Population Projections 1994-95 Edition, 1994.

Effect on age.   Just as we did in the case of mortality, let us try to imagine the changes in age composition that would result from a *decline* in age-specific fertility rates. Unlike the case of mortality, there is both a short-term and a long-term effect of any such change in rates. So let us proceed one stage at a time.

For the first fifteen years, a decline in age-specific fertility rates would lead to a proportional decline in the number of births entering the bottom of the population pyramid. Since the younger cohorts would be small relative to the previously born cohorts, the pyramid would become slimmer at its base than it would have if the older (higher) fertility rates had continued to prevail. That is, the *percentage* pyramid would look something like that for the United States in 1940, seen in Figure 4-2. That figure shows the impact of the fertility declines that reached their nadir during the 1930s (exaggerated in this particular case by the decline in immigration as well).

Remember, however, that the number of births produced is a factor not only of age-specific rates but also of the number of women in the childbearing ages. It is that second factor that leads to the delayed, "echo" effect of a decline in rates. This begins some fifteen years after the initial decline in rates. At this point, daughters born over the initial fifteen years are beginning to enter their childbearing years. There are fewer of them, however, so their reduced numbers combine with the already reduced rates to produce even smaller birth cohorts.

The same kind of complementary short-term and long-term effects could occur if there were a sustained increase of age-specific birth rates. First there would be an increase in the base of the pyramid with the entry of the first, larger birth cohorts. Then, some fifteen years later, there would begin to be a compounding of this swelling at the base as the baby-boom cohorts reached their reproductive ages. Together, there would be more women of reproductive age and higher fertility rates resulting in a squatter population pyramid.

However, the two factors also can work to oppose rather than complement each other. Generally speaking, this is the recent experience of the United States. The baby-boom in the United States resulted in the population bulge at ages five to nineteen in the population pyramid for 1970, shown in Figure 4-2. That is, the baby-boom began roughly twenty years earlier as the depleted birth cohorts of the Depression years were entering their childbearing ages during the 1950s. How can this be? The age-specific birth rates were raised enough during the 1950s to overwhelm the impact of there being relatively few women to experience those high rates. The baby-bust of the 1970s illustrates a converse situation. The population pyramid for 1970 shows large numbers of women from the baby-boom entering peak childbearing years in their late teens and early twenties. But the baby-bust is already evident in the small number of infants under five years of age. This baby-bust is a case of lower age-specific fertility rates off-setting an increase in the number of potential mothers. The U.S. crude birth rate would be even lower than it is at this writing were it not for the "momentum" created by the girl babies of the postwar boom still being in the childbearing ages (see chapter 7).

Effect on sex.   The impact of fertility on the sex composition of cohorts is quite insignificant under present medical conditions. In order for the level of fertility to influence the sex composition of birth cohorts, level of fertility somehow would have to influence the sex ratio at birth. Any sex selection practices that are potentially associated with fertility decisions are insubstantial. At present there is very little variation among countries in the sex ratios at birth.

Migration

The potential impact of migration on age-sex structure varies with the size of the geographic area being considered. That is because the relative size of the migrant population in comparison with the resident population tends to vary with the size of the area. The closer together the borders of an area are, the greater will be the proportion of residential movements by people who will cross these borders and thus constitute migrations.

A college town exemplifies how migration can create bizarre population pyramids for small geographic units. The age structure of such a town is massively transformed every fall as the student body arrives and settles in. For the academic year, youth dominates the scene. Then, toward the end of the spring, the student body scatters to its summer life, leaving the relatively middle-aged or old, permanent resident population to catch its breath. Many readers of this text are familiar with the cycle from personal experience.

Figure 4-5 illustrates what may be an extreme case by using the population pyramid of Amherst, Massachusetts, according to the 1990 federal census. Amherst is at the center of the "five colleges" area. Most students of Amherst College, Hampshire College, and the University of Massachusetts-Amherst, as well as a few from Mount Holyoke and Smith Colleges, were included in this population.

Whatever impact migration has on population structure operates both directly and indirectly. It has a *direct impact* upon age-sex structure only to the degree that *net* migration is *selective* with respect to sex and age. Remember that, potentially, both immigration and emigration may go on during any specified period. It is imbalance between the two processes that might affect structure. The simplest case where there is no age-sex selectivity in net migration is that in which each immigrant is matched by one emigrant of the same sex and age: since there is no net migration, then there can be no selective net migration. A more complicated case of having no age-sex selectivity might occur where there was positive net migration—having more immigrants than emigrants—but where the net migration population gained through the interchange had precisely the same proportionate age-sex structure as did the resident population. In this latter case, the age-sex classes in the resident population would be enlarged in equal proportions. The same noneffect would result with a negative net migration if it were proportional across age-sex classes.

The age structure of a net migrant population, however, seldom matches the age structure of a resident population. We will describe the patterns of selectivity in migration in much greater detail in chapter 9. But it is generally true that long-distance migration, and especially that to sparsely settled areas, tends to be dominated by the young, and initially by young working-age males. Thus the broad-based population pyramid for the United States in 1900, shown in Figure 4-2, is a result not only of high fertility but also of selective immigration of young adults and their children. The narrowing of the base in 1940 is a result not only of declines in fertility but also of the decline in immigration after World War I.

Figure 4-5   Percentage Population Pyramid of a College Town: Amherst, Massachusetts, 1990

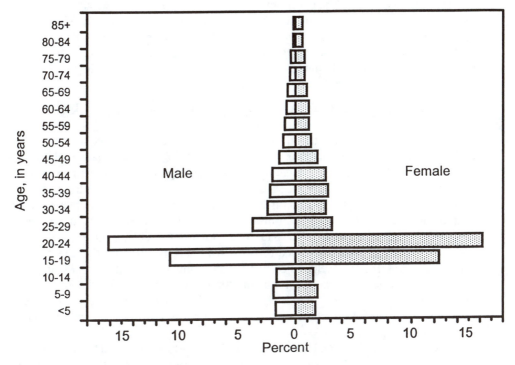

Source: State Center for Massachusetts Data, University of Massachusetts at Amherst.

Indirect effects occur when selective net migration has a direct impact on population composition which, in turn, influences fertility, which then has its own effect on the age-sex structure. Suppose that migration is age and sex selective in such a way that it increases the proportion of the total population that are females in the childbearing years. If there is no compensating decline in the age-specific fertility rates, the result will be an increase in the crude birth rate. This in turn will create larger birth cohorts.

Thus if a country experiences heavy net immigration of young couples, that will create a bulge on the pyramid in the young adult ages (direct effect) and, in subsequent years, will produce larger birth cohorts at the base of the pyramid (indirect effect). This is precisely what happened in the United States during its years of heaviest immigration. In contrast, one would expect the European countries of origin of these emigrants to have their young-adult categories depleted by the direct effect of emigration and their birth cohorts depleted as an indirect effect. Aging of some European countries' populations was then amplified by both direct and indirect effects of substantial emigration.

Migration effects continue to be substantial for some countries. International migration is at an all-time high, with nearly 2% of the world's population living outside their country of birth or origin in the mid-1990s (Martin and Widgren, 1996). Net international migration accounted for 120% of Germany's population growth between 1985 and 1995. That is, all of Germany's demographic growth, including compensation for natural decrease (the reason more than 100% of growth is accounted for) was due to migration over this period (United Nations, 1995). In Austria and Greece, 86% of growth over the same period was due to net international migration. With new population growth being almost exclusively due to immigration, it is clear that age-sex selectivity of migration will impact population structure in such countries.

PROBLEMS OF YOUNG POPULATIONS IN THE LDRs

The definition of a population pattern as being a social problem requires two mental steps: 1) believing some theory of cause and effect and 2) passing negative value judgment on the supposed effect. Therefore, to understand public definitions of problems blamed on age and sex structure, we should ask such questions as these: What aspects of present and future population structures are seen as sources of social problems? What consequences are believed to flow from these structural characteristics? Why are these supposed consequences judged to be bad? Who defines the problems thus?

We have seen that more-developed countries have populations that are old and getting older, while less-developed countries have populations that are still young. As one might expect, the perceived problems for the two categories of countries are almost opposite. For LDRs, "youth dependency" is the overwhelming concern; very seldom is any other feature of the age-sex structure of these countries mentioned as an equally pressing problem.

We have just seen evidence of the striking youthfulness of LDR populations. Table 4-2 tells us that 35.5% of LDR populations in 1990 were less than fifteen years old. In pre-transition countries almost half, 45.8%, of the population was less than fifteen. Figure 4-1 shows that such a situation is projected to change only well into the present century, and only on the assumption that LDR fertility continues to decline. This implies that more than one out of every three people in LDRs are and will be "youth dependents" as this century begins.

Development Concerns

Youth dependency is by itself simply a structural population characteristic; but it is also seen as a source of social problems. Youth dependency is seen as a constant drain on per capita wealth in LDRs. The larger the cohorts that are too young to work in comparison with the cohorts that are of working age, the greater the number of consumers there are relative to producers (Coale and Hoover, 1958). But is it realistic to assume that being less than fifteen years old means being economically unproductive everywhere? While that may be true in industrialized economies, in LDRs, and especially in rural regions, children are put to economic use much earlier and kept out of school (e.g. Visaria and Visaria, 1995, p. 25). On the other hand, economic development, at least according to the Western model, will involve precisely such changes as taking the children out of the fields and putting them into schools. Youth has thus been increasingly defined as an age of dependence.

There is nothing new about LDR populations being youthful; what is relatively new is the definition of that youthfulness as a problem. As we saw in the previous section, the dominant cause of a young population structure is high fertility. LDRs generally have had high fertility, by current standards. It is only recently that many countries within the LDRs have experienced the beginnings of a fertility transition. But during the latter half of the twentieth century a new kind of social and economic change was proposed for, or even imposed upon, these countries—capital-intensive modernization after the Western model. The youthfulness of many LDR populations, and the resulting need to invest in human capital and education of a growing labor force, can limit capital-intensive industrial modernization, and fertility declines can boost economic growth (Crenshaw et al., 1997). Defining a youthful population as a social problem has certainly been, in large part, due to the implicit problems dependency presents for prevailing models of industrial development.

Social and Health Concerns

A younger population generally has a high percentage of persons in young, initially sexually active ages. A young high-fertility population creates a number of social and health concerns (Noble et al., 1996). In West Africa, for example, more than half of young women have a child before age twenty, where the risk of dying from pregnancy-related causes is twice as high as for those between twenty and twenty-four years of age. The risk of low birth weight, infant mortality, and childhood death are all greater for the offspring of such young women. In addition, unsafe abortion is a closely related concern. In Benin, Nigeria, for example, almost three of four deaths among women under age nineteen are due to complications following unsafe abortions. With a large reproductive-age population, these concerns comprise a greater share of health problems in LDRs and the need to address such reproductive health concerns is more pronounced.

Sexually transmitted diseases also are more frequent in a young population, with the highest infection rates among twenty to twenty-four-year-olds followed by those fifteen to nineteen (Noble et al., 1996). HIV is spreading rapidly among young women of these ages. Young people under age twenty-five account for one-half of all HIV infections, many of whom were infected in their teens.

Other problems (in both MDRs and LDRs) may be more frequent in younger populations. In many countries, for example, crime rates are highest among the young. Crime rates in the United States increased when the baby-boomers were in the younger ages and have declined as they have aged. Targets of sexual violence are also primarily children and young women. With a younger population such concerns loom larger in LDRs (United Nations, 2000). These, and other social problems associated with youth, generate additional social and health concerns in LDRs.

PROBLEMS OF OLD POPULATIONS IN THE MDRS

The problems resulting from age structure in the MDRs are just about the opposite of those in the LDRs. As seen in Figure 4-1, MDR population pyramids are almost columnar in shape and are projected to be even more so in the future. This means that increasingly larger proportions of their populations are "old"—however that may be defined.

This overall aging of MDR populations itself seems to raise vague alarms from Western commentators. When one tries to find explanations for such alarm, two distinct aspects of the overall aging process are singled out for attention. First is the supposedly changing age structure of the workforce, and second is the increasing size and visibility of the "elderly" population.

Let us discuss the two aspects separately, but first, a reminder: there is a difference between the aging of individuals and the aging of populations (Friedlander and Malul, 1983). It is true that, in the MDRs, individuals on the average live longer and presumably will live even longer in the future; however, individual longevity is not what we are talking about in this section. Instead, we are talking about the changing age structure of the population, that is, the increasing proportion of the population that is—at a given moment—in the older ages and the decreasing proportion that is in the younger ages. You may remember from our previous discussion that these two distinct phenomena have different causes: increasing individual longevity is caused by declines in death rates, but increasing age of populations has historically been more influenced by declines in birth rates.

Productivity of the Workforce

One trend seen to be problematic by many is the increasing average age of those who are within the supposed workforce ages, fifteen to sixty-five. Let us divide these fifty years into three segments: fifteen to twenty-nine, thirty to forty-four, and forty-five to sixty-four. In MDRs, the proportion of the population in each working age group is nearly identical (i.e. just over a fifth of the population). In LDRs, the proportion of the population in the youngest working-age category is over twice that of the oldest and nearly a third of the entire population (United Nations, 1995). From Figure 4-1 we can see that it is projected to be mid-century before LDRs have a labor force structure similar to the MDRs.

In MDRs there is an aging in the population, or potential workforce, aged fifteen to sixty-five. If we can assume changes in the age composition of the *total population* will result in changes in the age composition of the *workforce* (defined as people having jobs or looking for them) between the ages of fifteen and sixty-five, the MDR workforce is aging. That is, we are assuming for the moment that changes in workforce participation rates at the various ages will not counteract the impact of aging within the population aged fifteen to sixty-five.

Who is concerned about the consequences of an aging workforce? Those who publish theoretical statements on the subject are predominantly Western economists. One can guess, however, that an equally—though perhaps less publicly—interested set of people are employers, eager to get maximum productivity from their workers.

What negative consequences do they see? The first fear deals with *worker productivity*. As Espenshade noted, "It is frequently imagined that an older labor force will be less productive because the advantages of experience are more than outweighed by the relative reduction of the number of more youthful and energetic workers whose formal education has only recently been completed. . . . It has also been hypothesized that rates of innovation and technological progress will be slower with an older workforce on the grounds that, beyond some point, age and creativity are inversely related" (1978, p. 651). Reviewing available studies, Espenshade found little empirical support for either hypothesis.

Nevertheless, the belief that worker productivity and innovation diminish with age is still widespread and is reflected in recent population policy discussions. Bell, for example, suggests "It would seem permissible to anticipate that over the next few decades major sources of intellectual initiative and innovation are likely to come from what are now relatively poor countries. The numbers of young, well-educated, creative persons in industrialized countries is likely to stabilize or decline; the numbers of such persons in developing countries will steadily rise" (1986, p. 227).

A second concern is *labor mobility*, the likelihood of people moving from jobs in one organization to jobs in another. Economists seem to agree that older workers are less inclined to change jobs this way. At a time of industrial restructuring when the occupational structure is changing rapidly, an aging workforce could lead to higher "structural unemployment" and demands for retraining of the workforce (Wetzel, 1995). Industrial restructuring has, of course, led to even greater problems in the inter- and intraregional imbalances or "spatial mismatch" between the socially disadvantaged labor force and employment opportunities in the United States (Kasarda, 1995).

A related concern is individual *mobility within organizations*. The type and number of occupations within the organization tend to fall into a pyramid, with a few bosses over many workers. If changes in the age structure of the workforce as a whole are mirrored *within* organizations, then old-timers will hang on to their higher status jobs, while the workers may find they have to wait longer to become bosses (Easterlin, 1980). Such a consequence is conjecture; nevertheless, belief in this outcome could reinforce concerns about the aging workforce.

Now let us relax our assumption that change in the age structure within the working ages will be faithfully reflected by a change in the age structure of the workforce. Is there evidence that there may be changes in workforce participation patterns that will blunt this effect?

In the United States, workforce participation rates have been changing in such a way as to offset partially the changing age structure of the working-age population. There has been a marked increase in workforce participation by women, almost entirely in the adult and older age categories. Age-specific participation rates, especially for males, dropped for both the young and the older ends of the working ages, reflecting an extension of higher education on the young end and earlier retirement (voluntary and involuntary) on the older end (Siegel, 1978). Although the older population in the United States increased markedly from 1950 to 1990, the proportion of men sixty-five and over in the workforce declined by over one-half as Social Security provided pension plans and an early retirement option (Wise, 1997). Some decline in the older-age labor force participation rate may also be involuntary as companies have "downsized" in the face of competition. Employers have low levels of commitment to retain older workers since they view them as expensive and slow to adapt to changing technologies (Bouvier and De Vita, 1991; AARP, 1989). All of these changes in labor force participation rates combine to counteract the supposed aging of the workforce in MDRs. Aging of the population and aging of the workforce are only tenuously linked and depend heavily on prevailing labor force participation patterns.

Increasing Size and Visibility of the Elderly Population

Let us start with some statistical elaboration about the proportionate size of the elderly population. Then, we will discuss other trends that have increased the visibility of the elderly over the past half-century and specific concerns that have been voiced about the aging of the U.S. population.

Table 4-2 tells us that the proportion of the population aged sixty-five and over in 1990 was greater in MDRs than in LDRs, and greatest for the regions of Europe and Northern America. Figure 4-6 deals with the United States in particular. The increasing proportion of elderly through the last century registered the effects of declining fertility. While the proportion aged sixty-five and over more than tripled over the century, the proportion aged eighty-five and over increased seven-fold, so the population achieving extremely old ages, or *grandevity*, is increasing.

The right half of Figure 4-6 gives projections into the distant future, until mid-century (middle series Census Bureau projections). The proportion aged sixty-five and over is projected to peak in about forty years, while the percentage aged eighty-five and over will continue to increase slightly past mid-century. The percentage aged eighty-five and over will have doubled between 1995 and 2020 (De Vita, 1996).

Figure 4-6   Percent of the Total U.S. Population in the Older Ages, 1900–2050

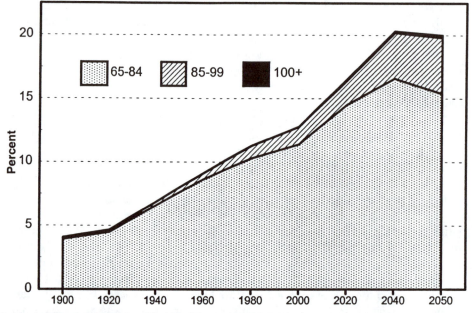

Source: Anderton et al., *Population of the United States*, 1997; U.S. Bureau of the Census, *Current Population Reports P-25 1130*, 1996, table G.

Several other factors contribute to the visibility of the elderly population in the United States. One is that they are heavily concentrated in selected geographic regions of the country. Despite the fact that the percentage of elderly increased in all states during the past several decades, selected areas saw a more extreme increase in the proportion of elderly residents. In terms of absolute number, California, Texas, Florida, New York, and Pennsylvania all had over 1.5 million elderly residents in 1994 and, taken together, contained half of the country's elderly population. Paradoxically, areas of the country with the highest *proportion* of elderly are not those sought out by retirees, but are the areas left by younger migrants, especially the Midwest (Treas, 1995).

Another reason for the increasing visibility of the elderly is that retirees, often equated with the elderly in popular culture, are increasing even more rapidly than are the elderly. Over the last half-century the proportion of males over sixty-five who remain in the labor force has declined from nearly half to around one-sixth (Anderton et al., 1997). As more of the elderly retire at younger ages they are more visible as a segment of society.

The elderly in the United States are a rapidly changing social group. Among many other trends, the elderly are increasingly likely to live in independent households, to return to schooling, to be childless, to be more ethnically diverse, and to have greater disposable income (Treas, 1995; Anderton et al., 1997). In a variety of ways, each of these trends contributes to a cultural increase in the visibility of the elderly population that is even greater than their already substantial demographic increase.

Another significant change has been the increasing feminization of the elderly population. Especially in MDRs, females tend to outnumber males; the older the age category, the more the female dominance. Figure 4-7 graphs this trend in U.S. history and projects its continuation into the future. The United States has changed from near parity between the sexes in the elderly population at the turn of the last century to a present situation where females outnumber males by more than two to one in the eighty-five-and-over category. Recent gains against mortality have been greater for males than females and have reversed this trend in those over sixty-five years of age (Treas, 1995). These gains are projected to somewhat reverse sex imbalances among the elderly at older ages and then level off toward mid-century. In the meantime, elderly women are especially prominent in those achieving grandevity.

So what is *wrong* with these trends of increasing size and visibility of the elderly population? Who is worried about them? What negative consequences are anticipated? A number of policy-related issues have dominated discussions about the elderly. Visiting a selected few of these important issues will convey the variety and range of concerns expressed about the aging of the U.S. population.

Old-Age Dependency

MDRs vary in the severity of their old-age dependency problems. Baby-booms and busts have not exactly coincided internationally, so the pattern of imbalances between succeeding generations is not entirely uniform. Moreover, countries differ in their systems for providing economically for their elderly. At present, North America has a slightly smaller proportion of people aged sixty-five and over than Europe (see

Figure 4-7   Sex Ratios at Older Ages, United States, 1900–2050

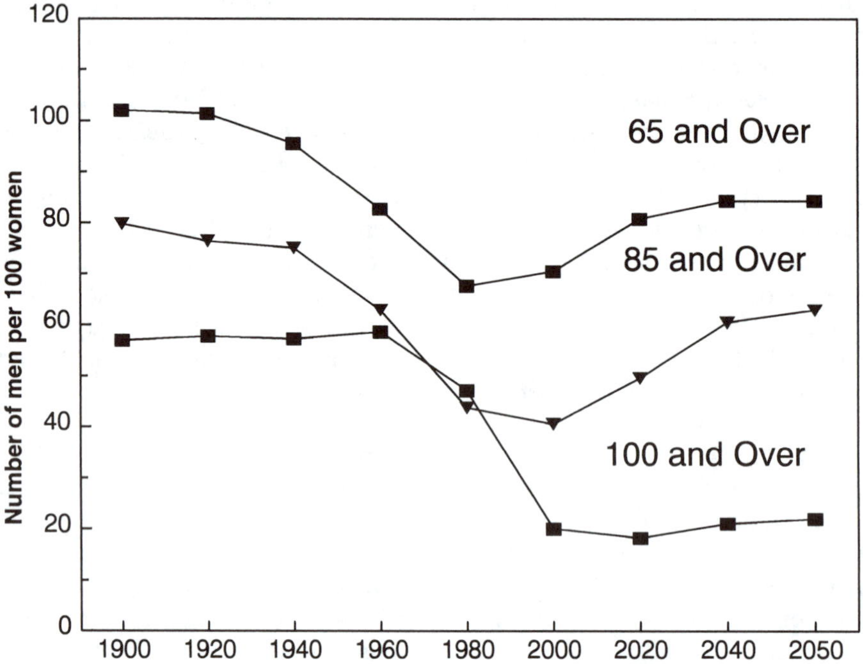

Source: Anderton et al., *Population of the United States*, 1997; U.S. Bureau of the Census, *Current Population Reports* P-25 1130, 1996, table 2.

Table 4–2). In part this reflects a longer duration baby-boom in the United States which has not yet aged to the same extent as in Europe.

We should remind ourselves, however, that old age is not the only source of age dependency. There is youth dependency as well, and it often counteracts old-age dependency. Treas (1995) examined the trends of age-dependency ratios (young and old together) in the United States from 1900 to the present, and projected to mid-century. In 1900, the ratio for the United States was about 80 dependents for every 100 persons aged eighteen to sixty-four. This ratio dropped to a low of around 60 per 100 following the low-fertility Great Depression years only to return to a peak of around 82 per 100 during the 1960s' baby-boom. Since then the ratio has fallen back near the low point of the 1940s. The ratio is projected to remain low through 2010 and then to begin rising as the baby-boom enters old age. Despite this projected rise, the ratio is forecast to level off around 2030 slightly below levels at the turn of the last century or at the peak of the baby-boom. That is, the age-dependency ratio is, at present, near the low point of the past century and even given the maturation of the baby-boom, will not likely exceed its high point of the last century.

Although levels of dependency are not historically atypical, the composition of dependency has changed significantly. What has happened, and is projected to continue throughout the next half-century, is an aging of the dependent population and a rise of grandevity.

It is time to introduce a special modification of the measure we have called the age-dependency ratio. You will remember that the numerator of that ratio combined the youth-dependent and the old-age-dependent populations; the denominator was the population in the normal working ages, conventionally fifteen through sixty-four. When analyzing the composition of age dependency, Treas (1995) uses a modification we will call the old-age-dependency ratio. The numerator consists of the population sixty-five and older; the denominator consists of the population age eighteen through sixty-four.

The old-age dependency ratio in 1900 was only 7 per 100 persons aged eighteen to sixty-four. Old-age dependency increased steadily over the century and by 2000 this ratio had tripled to 21 per 100. Old-age dependency is projected to remain stable for a short while, dubbed the *false good times* by those who worry about old-age dependency, and then increase again between 2010 and 2030, as baby-boomers retire, to nearly 36 per 100, where it will stabilize through mid-century.

Those who are alarmed about prospective old-age dependency in the United States point to this period when the baby-boom cohorts finally reach elderly ages. These elderly cohorts are supposedly to be supported by the small, low-fertility cohorts that followed them. However, an important implicit assumption lurks behind the whole idea of old-age dependency. It is that, in any given year, those who have completed their working lives are to be supported by those who have not yet done so. The belief is that supporting the elderly has to be done on a pay-as-you-go basis, by intergenerational transfer of wealth (Barberis, 1981).

There are a number of reasons that elderly dependency in the United States may not reflect the economic dependency implicit in dependency ratios. First, elderly poverty has been dramatically reduced as Social Security has proven a remarkably effective social program of collective support. Second, during the so-called *false good times* of the present there are considerable resources and interest devoted to preparing for the coming retirement of the baby-boom. Third, wealth holdings and assets available to the elderly population for self-support have increased in recent generations (Anderton et al., 1997). And fourth, labor force participation rates have proven remarkably flexible and adaptive in the younger elderly ages. Despite an increase in early retirement, the elderly constitute around 3% of the labor force (Treas, 1995). With effective social programs in place, the resources and foresight to prepare in advance, and their individual resources of wealth and marketable skills, elderly dependents differ markedly from the young dependents who characterized the historically high peaks of dependency in the United States.

The Future of Social Security

The predominant concern over aging in the United States has been the fear that the Social Security system will be bankrupted by the burden of payments to retiring baby-boomers. The U.S. Social Security system is theoretically operated on a pay-as-you-go basis. Contrary to what might be assumed, payments to the system by the baby-boomers have not been invested to pay for their retirement. Payments currently being made by workers and their employers are used to support the retirement of those who already have aged out of the workforce. And, glancing forward, the implications of continuing such a system are alarming indeed. Smaller cohorts would be strained to provide for bulging ones entering retirement if no alternative were adopted. According to a number of recent surveys, younger people do not even anticipate the Social Security system will survive to provide for their retirement.

However, other support strategies are possible and the system will continue to be modified over the coming decades. Each cohort could be made responsible, and helped to be responsible, for saving for its own retirement. This principle would eliminate the problem of irregularities in relative cohort sizes; large cohorts would have accumulated large savings. To implement such a system would likely require a gradual transition. It would leave a generation stranded between the current pay-as-you-go system and those beginning a genuine retirement savings program. Cohort savings programs also rely upon the value of savings and investments, which depend upon market forces. Even with cohort savings there is no guarantee that savings will provide for retirement many years into the future. The most likely course of action, then, is a more gradual move in the direction of cohort investment and savings. In the short run there will almost certainly be a continued reliance on current contributions and a guarantee through the full credit of the government.

Whatever changes are made to Social Security, it is clear that both the imminent retirement of the baby-boom cohort and the increase in life expectancy will require some revision to retirement systems. Yet, it is also worth remembering that the elderly are not as dependent upon support from the working-age population as in past generations. An increase in health, life span, personal wealth, education, and other personal assets means the elderly are in a position to, and now do, contribute to their own retirement support. It is likely that modifications to Social Security might eventually include increases in the mandatory retirement age, adjustments for personal wealth and alternative income sources, and many changes reflecting the evolving meaning of "old" in the United States.

Health and Capacity

Another prominent concern with rising old-age-dependency ratios is the unique health concerns and health care needs in a growing elderly population. According to the National Center for Health Statistics (1994), nearly half of the elderly suffer from arthritis. Roughly a third of the elderly suffer from hypertension, heart disease, and hearing loss. And, most of the elderly report at least one chronic health problem (Treas, 1995). In short, older people require more health services because they are more likely to suffer from health problems. As a result, health care burdens upon the elderly and society have reached record levels as the number and proportion of elderly have increased. Just as Social Security has demanded adjustment, Medicare and the health care system in general are struggling to adapt to changes in population composition. If the hospital insurance program is to remain solvent over the next seventy-five years, payroll taxes for this program would have to be raised by 175% or Medicare costs cut by 65% (Treas, 1995). Reassessment of health care services and delivery will be a continual process as the population ages.

Functional impairments also increase dramatically with aging. Mobility or self-care disabilities double among those aged sixty-five to seventy-four and then double again for those over seventy-five (Anderton et al., 1997). Beyond age seventy-five, nearly a fourth of all males and over a third of all females have such a disability and require living assistance. These disabilities can be expected to increase as grandevity increases. Most elderly caregiving is not within institutions but is provided through informal assistance or family members, and the burdens of such caregiving will continue to increase in the coming years. The percentage of elderly living in institutions or assisted-living centers can also be anticipated to increase after remaining relatively steady in recent years. These changes will be among many that are a part of the adapting social milieu that is arising from the aging of America. While it is easy to emphasize the potential needs of the elderly it should be remembered that the elderly also increasingly report themselves to be in better health over time (Anderton et al., 1997). Once again, the elderly are not simply dependent upon younger generations. They will, in large part, determine the nature of changes in their own individual lifestyles and politically shape the way in which society adapts to their health care needs.

The Intergenerational Distribution of Wealth

A very different concern over the rising elderly population is that of an intergenerational shift in personal wealth. The concern here is not with increasing dependence of the elderly but with the increasing share of wealth held by the elderly. This viewpoint largely takes a zero-sum view of social resources in that those held by one generation are not available to another.

These concerns are exemplified by the fact that in 1991 the median net worth of elderly married couple householders was nearly $150,000 while that of female householders under age thirty-five was just over $1,000 (Anderton et al., 1997). Moreover, as the poverty level among the elderly has fallen almost steadily since the mid-1960s, the poverty rate among children has correspondingly increased. Over the same period, female-headed families have increased from around a fifth to more than half of all poor families. As wealth has been accumulated and held longer by those reaching older ages, and as social resources have succeeded in reducing poverty among the elderly, less wealth is held by younger generations and specifically by those who are most truly societal dependents and in the greatest need.

It is especially unfortunate that social programs addressing young women and children in poverty have been dramatically reduced just as an increasing share of social wealth is held by older generations. The declining share of dependency that is due to youth might, in contrast, signal a unique opportunity to address the needs of the young dependent population just as it decreases in relative size. Unlike the growing elderly population there is relatively little the young dependents can do to contribute to their own support. One can hope that concerns over the aging baby-boom do not overwhelm commitments to address the severe needs of dependent children and young mothers in poverty.

Intergenerational Perceptions and Structural Relations

An implicit conflict about the distribution of resources among generations can be seen in each of the concerns just discussed. The conflict in intergenerational distribution of resources, whether real or a zero-sum fiction, can also be seen in real cultural expressions at both ends of the age distribution. In defeating property tax initiatives to support education, for example, the elderly face a conflict between their fixed incomes and rising property taxes. If they vote to stabilize property taxes they risk being viewed as miserly toward society's youth. But old age also means confronting a limited resource horizon and great financial, as well as physical, uncertainties. Being conservative with finances appears a reasonable and prudent course of action. Meanwhile, young post-baby-boomers fear they will bear the burdens of caring for the elderly and be overshadowed by, or confined to, a baby-boomer dominated culture. More importantly, they are one of the first American generations to anticipate a lower lifestyle standard than their parents. Many believe they are saddled with social and environmental problems created by an earlier generation that has reaped all of the benefits and left behind the burdens.

From a sociological standpoint these sentiments may have more to do with increasing social distance between the young and elderly than any real inherent conflicts over social resources. What can be seen if we compare the population pyramid of 1900 in Figure 4-2 with that of 2030? At the beginning of the twentieth century the vast majority of adults were still of working age and from a relatively narrow range of birth cohorts. That is, the adult population was relatively similar to one another in age and cohort experiences with only a scattering of older generations. However, by 2030 adults will be relatively evenly distributed from ages twenty through seventy-five and there will be a substantial group of the "old-old" beyond age seventy-five. Over the past century the population, with minor fluctuations, has increasingly become one in which individuals are less similar to each other in terms of age and cohort experiences. Or, as sociologists might say, society has become more differentiated with respect to age.

Other historical changes may amplify the increasing social distance between cohorts. Rapid development and dissemination of technology, for example, has meant that the experiences and skills of one cohort are rapidly replaced by those of the next. Mid-career retraining for employment is a notion that would have seemed foreign in times past. Yet, without retraining, a demographer trained in 1970 with a "slide rule" would have been left behind by those using personal computers just a decade later. The faster pace of social, technological, and historical change in recent generations has potentially amplified the structural effects of increasing social distances between cohorts. While some events and experiences may unify generations, these are less easily identified and more likely are exceptions to the rule.

PROBLEMS OF FLUCTUATIONS IN COHORT SIZE IN THE MDRS

MDRs may experience significant fluctuations in cohort size. As we saw in chapter 1, having completed the "demographic transition" means that a country will have brought its fertility under individual voluntary control. Individually controlled fertility, however, is collectively quite variable, swinging upward and downward on the basis of whatever it is that makes masses of couples decide to have many or few children early or late in their own lives. Because birth rates are the major determinant of the size of birth cohorts, swings in the rates are reflected as bulges and bottlenecks in the population pyramid.

That this not only can happen but does happen is well illustrated by the example of the United States in Figure 4-2, where the population pyramid for 1990 clearly identifies the baby-boom generation that peaked with the 1955–1959 birth cohort and the baby-boom echo of the 1980s. Identifiable in the pyramid as bottlenecks are two other extreme generations. Those aged fifty-five through fifty-nine in 1990 were the birth cohorts of 1930 through 1934, the Depression generation. Those aged ten through nineteen in the 1990 pyramid, born between 1970 and 1980, are the baby-bust or self-labeled "generation X," reflecting anonymity in the wake of the baby-boom.

Institutional Problems

Those who are in charge of planning for the future, of preparing institutions to provide for society, are repeatedly undone by having either too many or too few facilities. This is particularly true when the facilities involved are inflexible. The U.S. baby-boom provides a familiar example. Educational institutions, for example, strained to meet the load of the baby-boom, expanding physical facilities and welcoming new teachers into the fold. As the baby-bust moved through the school years there was pressure to curtail educational expenditures. Yet, right after the bust bottomed out in elementary schools, secondary schools, and colleges (roughly 1985, 1990, and 1995, respectively) these same institutions that had cut back now faced increasing numbers of baby-boom echo students. The same experience may be faced by health care institutions as these cohorts reach older ages and, eventually, the end of their lives.

There are other examples of wrenching adjustments in the economy. Both the size and age composition of the workforce can take wild swings. As large and small cohorts enter and leave the workforce, periods of job opportunity can alternate with periods of stagnation. Housing prices inflated wildly as the baby-boom generation bought housing only to stagnate, and even lose value, as the baby-bust generation arrived at the usual home-buying ages of twenty to thirty. Prices will likely be affected as baby-boomers relocate to retirement housing and as the baby-boom echo enters the housing market. Finally, we already have discussed the potential problems of providing Social Security to the retiring baby-boom generation on the basis of the payments made by smaller subsequent generations.

Cohort Problems

So far we have discussed the problems of varying cohort size as defined by the society at large and its institutions. Do these variations also cause special problems for the members within each cohort? Easterlin (1980), among others, stresses that the relative size of a cohort has a lot to do with the fate of its members.

Again, the most dramatic and familiar illustration in recent U.S. history is the baby-boom cohort. It was big, much bigger than the especially small Depression cohort that preceded it. It was the cohort that personally experienced, and still is experiencing, many of the institutional problems we have just described. First, it had to cope with overcrowded classrooms and teacher shortages. Yet, as a large and young generation it felt uniquely empowered to end the Vietnam War and change the world. When it entered the workforce in search of first employment, labor was in oversupply. Baby-boomers faced housing shortages as they entered the housing market. And, as they matured in working ages, many boomers fell victim to corporate pressures to "downsize" them from higher paying jobs and replace them with younger, and cheaper, workers. Eventually, baby-boomers can look forward to retiring under circumstances in which their support from the rest of society seems still questionable and grudgingly given.

The baby-bust and the younger baby-boom echo are each living through unique demographically influenced cohort experiences. The baby-bust is entering an already crowded labor force and housing market. The baby-boom echo is being educated in overcrowded schools as was the baby-boom. However, this smaller boom will face less competition for jobs and housing than those slightly older despite being a larger cohort. The baby-bust cohorts will be in more direct competition with the immediately preceding baby-boomers than those of the more distant baby-boom echo. In many ways, both of these younger cohorts have grown up in the shadow of the baby-boom. As the discussion above suggests, the sheer size of the baby-boom has structurally impacted both groups. In addition, the baby-boom has exerted a disproportionate influence on the culture in which younger cohorts have lived. As the largest pool of consumers the baby-boom dominates commercial culture and the marketing of products.

Another, potentially problematic, aspect of fluctuations in cohort size comes from the sense of identity a cohort can form. A shared unique history tends to create in any cohort a sense of identity and perhaps a shared definition of the cause of its problems (Riley, 1979; Ryder, 1968). Differing cohort identities can amplify the sense of conflicts between generations over resources, ideology, and so forth. Just as rapid technological change may amplify the increasing social distance between cohorts as MDR populations age, fluctuations in cohort size may further emphasize unique cohort identities and further strain intergenerational relations. Baby-boomers proudly identified with their uniqueness and proclaimed a "generation gap." Generational or cohort identities are clearly associated with the baby-boom, bust, and echo cohorts. Each group has a sense of cohort identity that is frequently defined in relation, or opposition, to the others.

SUMMARY

The age-sex composition of a population is so important that many demographers simply refer to it as a population's "structure." In describing age or sex structure separately, demographers use familiar statistical techniques, such as frequency distributions, percentages, and ratios. A particular kind of bar graph that handles age and sex simultaneously is the population pyramid.

Age and sex strongly influence the demographic processes. Demographers use age-sex-specific rates to describe age and sex differences in mortality, fertility, and migration. They also use specific rates to control the influence of age and sex while comparing the fertility or mortality of populations with different structures.

Countries of less-developed and more-developed regions have dramatically different structures. Because of their sustained high fertility, LDRs continue to have young populations and broad-based population pyramids. Fertility declines in the MDRs, and to a lesser degree declining elderly mortality, have aged their populations and resulted in more columnar population pyramids. Large variations in MDR population composition are usually due to intergenerational swings in fertility that show up as bulges or troughs working their way through population pyramids. Until very recently, mortality improvements for females have been more extreme than those for males and have resulted in an increased feminizing of sex ratios throughout the life span, especially for MDRs.

Just as MDRs and LDRs differ with respect to their population structures, so do they differ in the resulting problems. For LDRs the overriding problem is that of youth dependency. For MDRs the converse is true: they are concerned about the future productivity of a workforce whose average age supposedly will increase along with that of the rest of the population. They also worry about the problem of old-age dependency and issues arising from the allocation of societal resources across an increasing variety of generations and cohort needs. Finally, because of fertility booms and busts, some MDRs also worry about providing for successive cohorts that vary greatly in size. Social resources such as schools or health care facilities face the strains of adapting to changing cohort sizes.

On the individual level, members of a boom or bust cohort may face unique opportunities or shortages. The growing age diversity of MDRs and cohort identities formed from unique cohort experiences have simultaneously reinforced the cultural meaning and impact of age structures.

EXERCISES

1. Table E4–1 presents age frequency distributions for the projected 2000 population of Mexico, for males, females, and for both sexes together. Using these data, complete exercises a, b, and c by filling in the cells in the "Mexico" column of Table E4–2. Use the "United States" column of that table as a model.

   a. Compute the percentages of both sexes combined under fifteen years of age, fifteen through sixty-four, and sixty-five years and over. Round the percentages to two decimal places and enter these percentages in the spaces provided in Table E4–2.

   b. Compute the sex ratios for each of the three age categories, round to two decimal places, and enter in the spaces provided in Table E4–2. The formula for the sex ratio is

$$\frac{\text{Males}}{\text{Females}} \times 100$$

Table E4-1
Estimated Age-Sex Distribution of Mexican Population, 2000 (in thousands)

Ages	Males (1)	Females (2)	Both Sexes (3)
All Ages[a]	49,043	49,744	98,787
0–4	5722	5500	11,222
5–9	5784	5575	11,359
10–14	5466	5296	10,762
Subtotal, 0–14	16,972	16,371	33,343
15–19	5168	5030	10,198
20–24	4709	4631	9340
25–29	4728	4720	9448
30–34	3933	4004	7937
35–39	3184	3310	6494
40–44	2547	2702	5249
45–49	2047	2187	4234
50–54	1689	1802	3491
55–59	1299	1425	2724
60–64	952	1108	2060
Subtotal, 15–64	30,256	30,919	61,175
65–69	792	976	1768
70–74	506	669	1175
75 & over	514	809	1323
Subtotal, 65 +	1812	2454	4266

[a]Since entries for particular age categories are rounded to thousands, they may not add up to precisely the subtotals and totals presented.
Source: Bos et al., *World Population Projections 1994-95 Edition,* 1994.

c. Compute the age-dependency ratio for both sexes together, round to one decimal place, and enter in the space provided in Table E4–2. The formula for the age-dependency ratio is

$$\frac{P_{0-14} + P_{65+}}{P_{15-64}} \times 100$$

2. Table E4-3 classifies the projected population of Mexico for A.D. 2020 by age and sex. Construct a population pyramid from these data, taking the following steps:

a. In the columns provided, enter the missing percents. Remember that these percents have as their denominators the total population of *both sexes.*

b. In the graph paper provided, draw a population pyramid, using the percentages in columns 3 and 4. Shade the area within the pyramid.

Table E4-2
Estimated Age-Sex Structure of the United States and Mexico, 2000

Measure	United States	Mexico
Percent of Total Population Under 15	21.47	
15–64	65.89	
65 and over	12.64	
Age Dependency Ratio	51.76	
Sex Ratio at Ages Under 15	104.87	
15–64	98.19	
65 and over	70.45	

Source: U.S. Bureau of the Census, *Current Population Reports*
P-25 1130, 1996, table 2, p. 52.

Table E4-3
Estimated Age-Sex Distribution of the Mexican Population, 2020
(in thousands)

	In Thousands		Percentages	
Age	Males (1)	Females (2)	Males (3)	Females (4)
All Ages	63,531	64,924	49.46	50.54
0–4	5436	5207	4.23	4.05
5–9	5211	5001		3.89
10–14	5162	4961	4.02	
15–19	5412	5215		4.06
20–24	5530	5355	4.31	4.17
25–29	5570	5431	4.34	4.23
30–34	5199	5127	4.05	3.99
35–39	4849	4835	3.77	3.76
40–44	4381	4440		
45–49	4394	4535	3.42	3.53
50–54	3597	3823	2.80	2.98
55–59	2824	3121		2.43
60–64	2139	2488	1.67	
65–69	1571	1931	1.22	1.50
70–74	1116	1473	0.87	1.15
75 & over	1140	1981		1.54

Source: Bos et al., *World Population Projections 1994–95 Edition*, 1994.

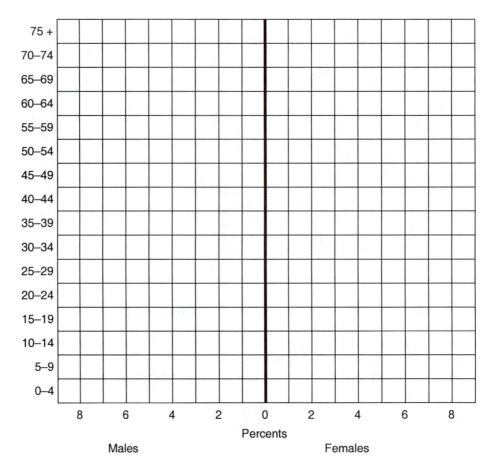

3. How would the Mexican population pyramid for A.D. 2020 have differed from the one you just did, if the assumptions employed had differed in the following ways?

a. If fertility had remained higher from 2000 to 2020, the average age of the population would have been

_____ younger

_____ older

_____ the same

b. If mortality had declined to even lower levels and in equal proportion at all ages, the average age of the population would have been

_____ younger

_____ older

_____ the same

4. Practice constructing age-sex-specific rates for death. Table E4–4 presents the necessary data for U.S. females in 1995. For each age category, column 1 tells how many females of that age died in 1995, column 2 tells the estimated number of females of that age there were to die in 1995, and column 3 tells the age-sex-specific death rate (per thousand females). Thus, to get the rate for the "under 1 year" row, the 12,892 deaths were divided by the 1,882 (thousand) existing females, producing a death rate of 6.85 per thousand females. Compute rates for the three rows where rates have been omitted. (Refer to Box 4-2 for an explanation of age-sex-specific rates.)

5. Calculate the implications of age-sex-specific death rates found in Table E4-4. Where the number of deaths have been omitted from column 1, multiply the death rate by the population to estimate the number of deaths which would have produced the given death rate.

Table E4-4
Computing Age-Sex-Specific Death Rates for U.S. Females, 1995

Ages	Deaths (1)	Population in Thousands (2)	Rate per Thousand (3)
Under 1 yr	12,892	1882	6.85
1–4	2767	7685	
5–14	3349	18,605	0.18
15–24		17,605	0.48
25–34		20,438	0.77
35–44	32,144	21,429	1.50
45–54	51,850	15,905	
55–64	93,403	11,093	8.42
65–74	207,482	10,421	19.91
75–84	333,606	6825	
85 & over	379,545	2619	144.92

Source: U.S. Bureau of the Census, *Current Population Reports P-25 1130,* 1996, table 2, p. 42; U.S. Bureau of the Census, *Statistical Abstract of the United States, 1997,* 1997, table 121, p. 90.

PROPOSITIONS FOR DEBATE

1. The "problem" of youth dependency in the LDRs is an illusion, based on an ethnocentric Western view of the proper roles for children.

2. The main reason for the aging of the U.S. population since 1900 has been the overall decline in mortality.

3. Given a choice, it would be nicer to belong to a small cohort than to a large cohort.

4. The U.S. view of "the elderly" as a troublesome minority will change as the baby-boom generation reaches retirement age.

5. If one is concerned about youth dependency in the LDRs and old-age dependency in the MDRs, a rational policy would be to encourage more international migration from the former to the latter.

6. If one recent cause of aging in the U.S. population has been reduction of death rates at the older ages, then a rational solution would be to stop spending scarce medical resources on old-age diseases.

▶ ## REFERENCES AND SUGGESTED READINGS

AARP. 1989. "Business and Older Workers: Current Perceptions and New Directions for the 1990s." Report issued by the American Association of Retired Persons, Washington, DC.

Alba, Francisco. 1982. "Mexico." In John A. Ross, ed., *International Encyclopedia of Population.* New York: Free Press.

Anderton, Douglas L., Richard E. Barrett, and Donald J. Bogue. 1997. *The Population of the United States.* 3rd ed. New York: Free Press.

Banister, Judith. 1987. *China's Changing Population.* Stanford, CA: Stanford University Press.

Barberis, Mary. 1981. "America's Elderly: Policy Implications." *Population Bulletin* 35(4 suppl.). Washington, DC: Population Reference Bureau.

Bell, David E. 1986. "Population Policy: Choices for the United States." In Jane Menken, ed., *World Population & U.S. Policy.* New York: W. W. Norton.

Bennet, Neil G., and S. Jay Olshansky. 1996. "Forecasting U.S. Age Structure and the Future of Social Security: The Impact of Adjustments of Official Mortality Schedules." *Population and Development Review* 22(4).

Binstock, Robert H., Wing-Sun Chow, and James H. Schulz, eds. 1982. *International Perspectives on Aging: Population and Policy Changes.* New York: United Nations Fund for Population Activities.

Bogue, Donald. 1993. "The Components Method of Forecasting: Rationale." In Bogue, Arriaga, and Anderton, eds., *Readings in Population Research Methodology.* United Nations Fund for Population Activities, Chicago: Social Development Center.

Bogue, Donald, Eduardo Arriaga, and Douglas L. Anderton, eds. 1993. *Readings in Population Research Methodology.* United Nations Fund for Population Activities, Chicago: Social Development Center.

Bos, Eduard, Mu T. Vu, Ernest Massiah, and Rodolfo A. Bulatao. 1994. *World Population Projections 1994–95 Edition: Estimates and Projections with Related Demographic Statistics.* World Bank, Baltimore: Johns Hopkins University Press.

Bouvier, Leon F. 1980. "America's Baby Boom Generation: The Fateful Bulge." *Population Bulletin* 35(1). Washington, DC: Population Reference Bureau.

Bouvier, Leon F., and Carol J. De Vita. 1991. "The Baby Boom—Entering Midlife." *Population Bulletin* 46(3). Washington, DC: Population Reference Bureau.

Centers for Disease Control. 1996. *Atlas of United States Mortality.* PHS-97-1015. Hyattsville, MD: Public Health Service.

Clark, Robert L., Juanita Kreps, and Joseph J. Spengler. 1982. "Aging Population: The United States." In John A. Ross, ed., *International Encyclopedia of Population.* New York: Free Press.

Coale, Ansley J. 1972. *The Growth of Human Populations: A Mathematical Investigation.* Princeton, NJ: Princeton University Press.

Coale, Ansley J. 1996. "Age Patterns and Time Sequence of Mortality in National Populations with the Highest Expectation of Life at Birth." *Population and Development Review* 22(1).

Coale, Ansley J., and Edgar Hoover. 1958. *Population Growth and Economic Development in Low Income Countries: A Case Study of India's Prospects.* Princeton, NJ: Princeton University Press.

Coleman, David A. 1993. "Contrasting Age Structures of Western Europe and of Eastern Europe and the Former Soviet Union: Demographic Curiosity or Labor Resource?" *Population and Development Review* 19(3).

Crenshaw, Edward M., Ansari Z. Ameen, and Matthew Christenson. 1997. "Population Dynamics and Economic Development: Age-Specific Population Growth Rates and Economic Growth in Developing Countries, 1965 to 1990." *American Sociological Review* 62(6).

Davis, Kingsley, and Pietronella van den Oever. 1981. "Age Relations and Public Policy in Industrial Societies." *Population and Development Review* 7(1).

De Vita, Carol J. 1996. "The United States at Mid-Decade." *Population Bulletin* 50(4).

Easterlin, Richard. 1980. *Birth and Fortune: The Impact of Numbers on Personal Welfare.* New York: Basic Books.

Edmonston, Barry, and Charles Schultze, eds. 1995. *Modernizing the U.S. Census.* Washington, DC: National Academy Press.

Elder, Glen H. 1974. *Children of the Great Depression: Social Change in Life Experience.* Chicago: Chicago University Press.

Espenshade, Thomas J. 1978. "Zero Population Growth and the Economics of Developed Nations." *Population and Development Review* 4(4).

Ewbank, Douglas C. 1981. "Typical Patterns of Distortion in Reported Age Distributions." In *Age Misreporting and Age Selective Under-enumeration: Sources, Patterns and Consequences for Demographic Analysis.* Washington, DC: National Academy Press.

Friedlander, Dov, and Ruth Klinov Malul. 1983. "The Aging Society and Economic Burden." *Intercom* 11(1–2).

Higgins, Matthew, and Jeffrey G. Williamson. 1997. "Age Structure Dynamics in Asia and Dependence on Foreign Capital." *Population Development Review* 32(2).

Hill, Kenneth H. 1987. "Estimating Census and Death Registration Completeness." *Asian and Pacific Population Forum* 1(3).

Hogan, Howard. 1993. "The 1990 Post-Enumeration Survey: Operations and Results." *Journal of the American Statistical Association* 88(423).

International Union for the Scientific Study of Population (IUSSP). 1982. *Multilingual Demographic Dictionary.* English Section. Liege, Belgium: Ordina Editions.

Kasarda, John D. 1995. "Industrial Restructuring and the Changing Location of Jobs." In Reynolds Farley, ed., *State of the Union: America in the 1990s.* Vol. I. New York: Russell Sage Foundation.

Keyfitz, Nathan. 1973. "Individual Mobility in a Stationary Population." *Population Studies* 27(2).

Lutz, Wolfgang. 1994. "The Future of World Population." *Population Bulletin* 49(1).

Manton, K. G., and B. Soldo. 1985. "Dynamics of Health Changes in the Oldest Old: New Perspectives and Evidence." *Milbank Memorial Fund Quarterly/Health and Society* 63.

Martin, Philip, and James Widgren. 1996. "International Migration: A Global Challenge." *Population Bulletin* 51(1).

Mueller, Eva. 1976. "The Economic Value of Children in Peasant Agriculture." In Ronald G. Ridker, ed., *Population and Development.* Baltimore: Johns Hopkins University Press.

Myers, Robert J. 1940. "Errors and Bias in the Reporting of Ages in Census Data." *Transactions of the Actuarial Society of America* XLI(2):104.

National Center for Health Statistics. 1994. *Vital and Health Statistics Series 10*, no. 189.

———. 1996. *Vital Statistics of the United States, 1992*. Vol. II, Sec. 6, Life Tables. Washington, DC: Public Health Service.

———. 1999. *Deaths: Final Data for 1997*. Vol. 49, no. 19: 99–1120. Washington, DC: Public Health Service.

———. 2000. *Vital Statistics of the United States, 1997*. Part I, Natality—First Internet Release of Files. Washington, DC: Public Health Service.

Noble, Jeanne, Jane Cover, and Machiko Yanagishita. 1996. "The World's Youth 1996." Washington, DC: Population Reference Bureau.

Olshansky, S. Jay, and Bruce A. Carnes. 1997. "Ever Since Gompertz." *Demography* 34(1).

Population Reference Bureau. 1982. "U.S. Population: Where We Are, Where We're Going." *Population Bulletin* 37(2). Washington, DC: Population Reference Bureau.

———. 1999. *1999 World Population Data Sheet*. Washington, DC: Population Reference Bureau.

Pressat, Roland. 1985. *The Dictionary of Demography* (Christopher Wilson, ed.). New York: Basil Blackwell Ltd.

Riley, Matilda W. 1979. "Introduction: Life Course Perspectives." In Matilda W. Riley, ed., *Aging from Birth to Death: Interdisciplinary Perspectives*. AAAS Selected Symposium Series, no. 30. Boulder, CO: Westview Press.

Robinson, J. G., P. D. Gupta, and R. A. Woodrow. 1993. "Estimation of Population Coverage in the 1990 United States Census based on Demographic Analysis." *Journal of the American Statistical Association* 88(423).

Ross, John A. 1982. "Rates and Ratios." In John A. Ross, ed., *International Encyclopedia of Population*. New York: Free Press.

Ryder, Norman B. 1968. "Cohort Analysis." In David L. Sills, ed., *International Encyclopedia of the Social Sciences*. Vol. 2. New York: Macmillan.

Shryock, Henry S., Jacob S. Siegel, and Associates. 1976. *The Methods and Materials of Demography*. Condensed edition by Edward Stockwell. New York: Academic Press.

Siegel, Jacob S. 1978. "Demographic Aspects of Aging and the Older Population in the United States." *Current Population Reports*, Special Studies Series P-23, no. 59 (rev.). Washington, DC: U.S. Bureau of the Census.

Smith, James P., and Raynard Kington. 1997. "Demographic and Economic Correlates of Health in Old Age." *Demography* 34(1).

Soldo, Beth. 1980. "America's Elderly in the 1980s." *Population Bulletin* 35(4). Washington, DC: Population Reference Bureau.

Spengler, Joseph J. 1978. *Facing Zero Population Growth: Reactions and Interpretations, Past and Present*. Durham, NC: Duke University Press.

Stillman, Jeanne Betsock. 1982. "Aging Population: Overview." In John A. Ross, ed., *International Encyclopedia of Population*. New York: Free Press.

Stolnitz, George J. 1956. "Mortality Declines and Age Distribution." *Milbank Memorial Fund Quarterly* 34(2).

———. 1982. "Mortality: Post-World War II Trends." In John A. Ross, ed., *International Encyclopedia of Population*. New York: The Free Press.

Treas, Judith. 1995. "Older Americans in the 1990s and Beyond." *Population Bulletin* 50(2).

Treas, Judith, and Ramon Torrecilha. 1995. "The Older Population." In Reynolds Farley, ed., *State of the Union: America in the 1990s*. Vol. II. New York: Russell Sage Foundation.

Turke, Paul W. 1991. "Theory and Evidence on Wealth Flows and Old-Age Security—A reply to Fricke." *Population and Development Review* 17(4).

United Nations. 1978. *Draft Principles and Recommendations for Population and Housing Censuses*. Part 2. E/CN.3/515/Add.2. New York: United Nations.

United Nations. 1995. *World Population Prospects: The 1994 Revision.* New York: United Nations.

United States Bureau of the Census. 1990. *Census of Population, 1990. CP-1-1: General Population Characteristics, United States.* Washington, DC: Government Printing Office.

———. 1996. *Current Population Reports: Population Projections of the United States by Age, Sex, Race and Hispanic Origin: 1995 to 2050.* P-25 1130. Washington, DC: Government Printing Office.

———. 1997. *Statistical Abstract of the United States, 1997.* Washington, DC: Government Printing Office.

Visaria, Leela, and Pravin Visaria. 1995. "India's Population in Transition." *Population Bulletin* 50(3).

Wetzel, James R. 1995. "Labor Force, Unemployment, and Earnings." In Reynolds Farley, ed., *State of the Union: America in the 1990s.* Vol. I. New York: Russell Sage Foundation.

Wise, David A. 1997. "Retirement Against the Demographic Trend: More Older People Living Longer, Working Less and Saving Less." *Demography* 34(1).

Wolter, Kirk M. 1986. "Some Coverage Error Models for Census Data." *Journal of the American Statistical Association* 81(394).

5

Mortality

In chapter 3 (on population growth), we were introduced to the "demographic transition" that has swept through the more-developed countries and is sweeping through the less-developed. According to that model, demographic transitions are heralded by gradual, then rapid, declines in mortality, followed by declines in fertility. Thus it is the drop in national mortality, not a rise in fertility, that is blamed for the national population explosions. This chapter focuses on describing and analyzing such "mortality transitions."

First we will take some time to acquaint the reader with two measures of mortality: average life expectancy and infant mortality rates. These are the ones now used most in international comparisons. Any mortality measure—these included—requires a count of deaths.

MEASURING MORTALITY VIA LIFE EXPECTANCY

Mortality, as we have said before, is one of the three processes that determine the pace of population growth, the others being fertility and migration. Demographers sometimes call them, collectively, the "components of growth." The pace of each of these processes is determined by the frequency of its relevant *event*. The event determining fertility is birth; for migration it is change of residence; for mortality it is death (not including fetal death). Mortality, then, refers to the frequency with which deaths occur.

Counting Deaths

In Western countries, civil registration has been the dominant system for counting deaths (see chapter 2). Each event supposedly is recorded as it occurs, along with certain characteristics of the deceased (e.g., age, sex) and of the death itself (e.g., cause). This information is funneled to statistical centers for tallying. As a result, there are often delays in obtaining mortality data. And even in more-developed countries civil registration of vital events has been less complete than counting people in censuses; therefore, MDR demographers normally use census data to estimate the degree of underenumeration of deaths. LDR civil registration is even less complete (Bogue et al., 1993, vol. 2; Shryock and Siegel, 1976).

What kinds of errors occur? One kind is not counting a death at all. Infant deaths, especially, get ignored. If the infant lives a very short time, there is a strong tendency to register neither the birth nor the death, to forget the whole tragic affair.

Even if all deaths do get registered, they can be misallocated in place and time. In urbanized countries especially, there is a tendency to register a death at the location of the hospital where it took place rather than the residence of the victim, or to register sudden deaths that occurred away from home at the place of occurrence rather than the place of residence. Where administrative systems are not well developed and the death isn't registered until after some delay, there may be a temptation to record the time of the death as the time of registration rather than the time of occurrence.

Because of the extreme difficulty of running a civil death registration system well, many LDR countries rely on other data services. One involves registration but confines it to a sample of areas in the nation. Another source is sample surveys, usually asking retrospectively about all deaths that occurred within a specified, short time interval, or a combination of a sample registration system and sample surveys such that one can estimate the degree of undercounting and reporting errors resulting from either source alone (Vallin et al., 1990, part I; Krotki, 1978).

Computing and Interpreting Life Expectancy

Let us be optimistic and suppose, for the moment, that we have ideal death data for a country; that is, let us suppose that we not only have a complete count of deaths by year, but also that we know the age and sex of each person at death. Let us also assume that we have a good estimate of the total population by year as well as the age-sex breakdown of that total. If we had all this, then we would be in a position to compute not only the crude death rates (see chapter 1) but also the age-sex-specific death rates (see chapter 4).

Both of these rates have their uses; both have their limitations. Although a crude death rate summarizes the mortality of an entire population in a single figure, it is influenced by the age-sex structure of the population. The strengths and weaknesses of age-sex-specific death rates are just the opposite: they are not influenced by the structure of the population, but it takes many of them to describe the population's mortality.

Wouldn't it be convenient if we had a measure of a population's mortality that avoided both of these limitations, that presented a single figure not influenced by the age-sex structure of the population? Life expectancy at birth is such a measure.

To comprehend it, however, one needs to consider not only the concept of mortality but also two related concepts: survival and longevity. A death rate measures mortality, the risk of dying in a given year. The opposite of death is *survival*. Demographers can, and sometimes do, construct survival rates, telling the probability of avoiding death through a given year. Closely related to the idea of survival is the idea of *longevity*, the age at which one dies. Individually, one's longevity is determined by how many years one escapes (survives) death. Collectively, the average age at which a cohort of people dies is determined by its rate of death or survival from age to age through its collective lifetime.

Most of us, apparently, intuitively grasp this connection between a sequence of annual risks of death and average longevity. Therefore, we are prepared to use longevity itself as a way of summarizing complex information about age-specific mortality. This is what we do when we combine information contained in age-specific death rates into a measure of average life expectancy.

Life expectancy is a hypothetical figure. The mental game involved in computing it is as follows: Start with a given set of age-specific death rates for one of the sexes (life expectancy figures normally are computed separately for the two sexes). Then conjure up an imaginary set of people and put them through a lifetime of mortality risks and resulting attrition as described by that series (or "schedule") of age-specific death rates. That is, construct an imaginary or *synthetic birth cohort* and trace how it would shrink if it were to have the mortality history described in some particular schedule of age-specific death rates. Finally, note the average age at which cohort members are likely to have died. This is their (average) life expectancy at birth.

Demographers use *life tables* for tracing such imaginary mortality histories. Table 5–1 gives an illustration. The life expectancy figures are those found in column 7, and the life expectancy at birth (that is, at age zero) is the topmost figure in that column, 79.1 years. This means that, if a cohort of women actually experienced the sequence of age-specific (female) mortality rates listed in column 2, the mean age at which they would have died would be 79.1 years.

There are some important features of life tables and the life expectancy figures that result from them. First, everything in the table is generated from the schedule of age-specific death rates. Column 2 expresses these rates in terms of risks of dying, by age; all subsequent columns are derived solely from column 2. No additional information is used to arrive at column 7, life expectancy by age; meaning nothing else has influenced the figures in column 7. That is why we can say that life expectancy figures are not influenced by age structures of populations. That is also why we say that life tables assume no net migration; migration (normally) is not allowed to add or subtract from age categories as the synthetic cohort passes through.

Second, the mortality assumptions employed in constructing any given life table are hypothetical—and probably unrealistic. There probably never will be a birth cohort that will experience precisely the schedule of age-specific death rates employed in the table. The purpose is to describe the implications of mortality during a given year, not to describe a real cohort's life experiences.

Third, life expectancy statements can be made for any age. Expectancy at birth, or at age zero (e_0), is influenced by the entire series of age-specific death rates following birth and therefore is the most frequently used. On the other hand, sometimes one needs to focus on mortality at later stages in life. It may be of interest to a life insurance company, for instance, that according to the U.S. female life table (Table 5–1), women aged sixty-five still had 22.9 more years of life expectancy, on the average.

Table 5–1
Female Life Table, United States, 1996

Age Interval[a]	Proportion Dying[b]	Number Living at Beginning of Age Interval (of 100,000 born alive)	Number Dying During Age Interval (of 100,000 born alive)	Person Years Lived		Average Remaining Lifetime[c]
				In the Age Interval	In this and all Subsequent Age Intervals	
x to x+n	$_nq_x$	l_x	$_nd_x$	$_nL_x$	T_x	e_x
(1)	(2)	(3)	(4)	(5)	(6)	(7)
0–1	0.00659	100,000	659	99,435	7,907,507	79.1
1–5	0.00135	99,341	134	397,043	7,808,072	78.6
5–10	0.00083	99,207	82	495,812	7,411,029	74.7
10–15	0.00093	99,125	92	495,426	6,915,217	69.8
15–20	0.00220	99,033	218	494,654	6,419,791	64.8
20–25	0.00242	98,815	239	493,488	5,925,137	60.0
25–30	0.00311	98,576	307	492,128	5,431,649	55.1
30–35	0.00430	98,269	423	490,336	4,939,521	50.3
35–40	0.00608	97,846	595	487,848	4,449,185	45.5
40–45	0.00858	97,251	834	484,325	3,961,337	40.7
45–50	0.01269	96,417	1,224	479,247	3,477,012	36.1
50–55	0.02036	95,193	1,938	471,421	2,997,765	31.5
55–60	0.03150	93,255	2,938	459,363	2,526,344	27.1
60–65	0.05068	90,317	4,577	440,808	2,066,981	22.9
65–70	0.07484	85,740	6,417	413,497	1,626,173	19.0
70–75	0.11607	79,323	9,207	374,780	1,212,676	15.3
75–80	0.17495	70,116	12,267	321,360	837,896	12.0
80–85	0.27721	57,849	16,036	250,275	516,536	8.9
85 and over	1.0000	41,813	41,813	266,261	266,261	6.4

[a]Period of life between two exact ages, stated in years.
[b]Proportion of persons alive at beginning of age interval who die during interval.
[c]Average number of years of life remaining at beginning of age interval.
Source: National Center for Health Statistics, "U. S. Abridged Life Tables, 1996," 1998, table 1.

(Incidentally, it was from life insurance actuaries that demographers borrowed the life table model and the resulting measure of life expectancy by age.)

Becoming comfortable with the use of life tables depends upon understanding how they are built. That, in turn, is best learned by building them. For that reason, we have included an exercise at the end of this chapter that first describes the steps in constructing a life table and then gives the reader practice in filling in blank spaces in such a table. Resist the temptation to skip over this exercise; you will find us referring back to it.

One drawback of life expectancy as a mortality measure is that it requires ideal data; that is, it requires full reporting of deaths by age and sex of person dying. Few LDR countries have such data. This means that demographers have to develop sophisticated estimation procedures to fill the gap. Some of these procedures are described in Box 5–1.

Box 5–1   Estimating Life Expectancy

Most MDR countries gather the data necessary for constructing life tables and estimating life expectancy. But what about the LDRs? These countries are unlikely to have any comprehensive death registration system, much less one that records age or cause of death precisely. But they may have one or more censuses and even a sample survey, perhaps including a marital and family-building history (Vallin et al., 1990, part I; Shryock and Siegel, 1976). How can such limited data be used to estimate the age-sex-specific mortality information needed for a life table? Formal demography has developed techniques to do just this (Arriaga, 1994; Ewbank, 1990; Hill and Zlotnik, 1982). It would be confusing for us to attempt a detailed summary of these techniques here, but a few examples might illustrate the basic strategies involved.

The simplest situation arises when a country has a sequence of decennial censuses, each classifying the population by age and sex. In this circumstance, one can follow a birth cohort from the earlier census to the later one and measure its shrinkage. That shrinkage can have been caused only by age-sex-specific migration or mortality. If one knows enough about the migration pattern during the intercensal interval, one can infer what the age-sex-specific mortality must have been. We can call this *direct* estimation.

A more complex situation arises when one has a single census or sample survey with incomplete information. In these data-deficient cases, one has to rely upon *indirect* estimates of population characteristics. If some information about the population is available, and if we assume basic relationships among demographic measures are similar to some other populations around the world which we have observed, it may be possible to make very good guesses about other unobserved population characteristics.

An illustration is a technique developed by Brass (1975) and since modified by several others (see Arriaga, 1994). Suppose, as is frequently the case in censuses and/or surveys, women are asked a) their own age, b) how many children they have ever borne, and c) how many of those children are still living. There is a logical relationship between these three factors and rates of infant and early childhood mortality. Obviously, a young woman who has borne many children but has few surviving has experienced high infant and childhood mortality among her offspring. The detailed pattern of these relationships already has been studied for countries where all factors are known; therefore, one can infer infant and child mortality rates from a few known factors.

Similar methods can use survey data about orphanhood and widowhood to estimate adult mortality (see Arriaga, 1994) and about sisterhood to estimate maternal mortality (see Simons et al., 1996). Still, any one of these indirect techniques is likely to provide death rates for only a few of the age categories. How do demographers fill in the figures for other categories?

Empirical life tables have been accumulated for many countries over the years. These life tables demonstrate that age-specific mortality is highly predictable if one knows the overall level of mortality in a population. These observed patterns have been generalized to serve as *model life tables* likely to be found at various levels of overall mortality (Coale and Demeny, 1966). One can use what one does know about the mortality of a country—perhaps infant mortality or crude death rate—to determine which model table to use, then read off other estimates from that table. We have made this sound much simpler than it is in practice, but the strategy is straightforward and model life tables are available in the form of computer programs (Arriaga, 1994).

HISTORICAL MORTALITY TRANSITIONS

Increases in Life Expectancy

In the more-developed regions. Chapter 3 described, in broad strokes, the demographic transition that accompanied the modernization of the countries we now call "more-developed." Let us call the changes in MDR mortality and life expectancy during that era the *mortality transition* (sometimes called the epidemiological transition). We can divide it into three segments: a pretransitional segment of high mortality (before 1850), a transitional segment characterized by a decline in epidemic and infectious diseases (from 1850 to 1950), and a late transition segment characterized by degenerative and human-made diseases (from 1950 to the present).

Demographic transition theory says that pretransitional mortality was high and variable from year to year. How high? Fragmentary data imply that, from the thirteenth to seventeenth centuries, life expectancy among Europeans ranged from twenty to forty years. In Western Europe, there seems to have been a gradual improvement in the mid-1700s, resulting in life expectancies of thirty-five to forty years (Coale, 1986, figure 1.2), and over the next century a further increase of about ten years, to between forty and forty-five years in the mid-1800s (Anderson, 1996, p. 272). Thus, overall mortality had been edging gradually downward for a century or more, even before the rapid transition started in the later 1800s.

Now let us look at the second, transitional segment. Once mortality started to fall in a given country, it fell at an increasing pace for several decades, and life expectancy soared accordingly. Figure 5–1 shows the increasing improvements in life expectancy from 1840 to 1940 for six Western European countries (plus the state of Massachusetts) on which we have reliable data. One can see that the improvement increased decade by decade in these countries, peaking in 1910–1920, and then tapering off slightly.

Not all more-developed regions entered their mortality transitions at the same moment. Generally speaking, Northern and Western Europe, what one might call the "frontier areas" of Northern America, and Oceania seemed to have started earliest. Western European mortality experienced a sustained decline in the late eighteenth century (Anderson, 1996); in the United States, this mortality decline began in the 1870s (Preston and Haines, 1991). Eastern and Southern Europe lagged behind (Schofield et al., 1991; United Nations, 1973). As a result of this staggered start, in the peak decade of improvement in life expectancy (1910–1920), it ranged from forty to sixty years of age across Europe (Vallin, 1991, table 3.1).

By 1950 life expectancy in Europe had increased to more than sixty-five years of age (see Table 5-2). During the late transition (third) segment, improvement in life expectancy among the leading countries continued, but at a slower pace. Since 1950 there has been an improvement of just over seven more years in life expectancy in both Europe and Northern America. Although the timing of MDR mortality declines varied, there has been considerable convergence among MDRs in the last few decades. As seen in Table 5-2, the difference in life expectancy between Northern America, Europe, and Oceania is only 3.6 years (less than half what it was in 1950). But such national averages mask continuing socioeconomic and racial/ethnic differentials.

Figure 5–1
Life Expectancy in Europe,[a] 1840–2000

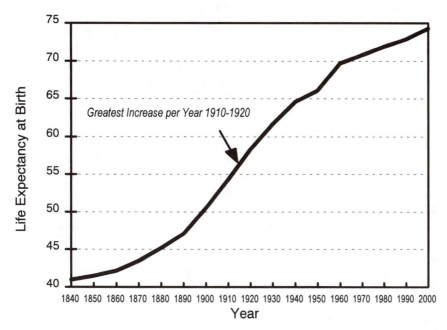

[a]Data for 1840–1940 includes six Western European countries and the state of Massachusetts; 1950–2000 includes all Europe.
Source: United Nations, *Determinants and Consequences of Population Trends*, 1973, table V.2; United Nations, *World Population Prospects, 1994 Revision*, 1995, table A.27.

Table 5-2
Life Expectancy by World Region, 1950–2000

Region[a]	1950–1955 (1)	1955–1960 (2)	1960–1965 (3)	1965–1970 (4)	1970–1975 (5)	1975–1980 (6)	1980–1985 (7)	1985–1990 (8)	1990–1995 (9)	1995–2000 (10)
World	46.4	49.5	52.3	55.9	57.9	59.7	61.3	63.0	64.4	65.8
MDRs	66.5	68.5	69.8	70.5	71.2	72.1	73.0	74.0	74.4	74.4
LDRs	40.9	44.4	47.7	52.2	54.6	56.7	58.5	60.5	62.3	63.8
Northern America	69.0	69.8	70.1	70.5	71.5	73.3	74.7	75.2	76.1	76.9
Oceania	60.8	62.9	64.6	65.3	66.6	68.2	70.1	71.2	72.8	73.8
Europe	66.1	68.2	69.7	70.4	70.8	71.3	71.9	73.0	72.9	73.3
Latin America & Caribbean	51.4	54.4	56.9	58.9	61.1	63.2	65.1	66.9	68.5	69.8
Asia	41.3	44.9	48.4	53.6	56.3	58.4	60.4	62.5	64.5	66.2
Africa	37.8	39.9	42.0	44.0	46.0	47.9	49.4	51.7	53.0	54.2

[a]Regions listed in order of decreasing 1995–2000 life expectancy.
Source: United Nations, *World Population Prospects, 1994 Revision*, 1995, table A.27.

The main point is that during the rapid MDR mortality transition—taking little more than a century—life expectancy at birth grew by more than 50%. Such a demographic event was unprecedented in world history.

In the less-developed regions. The LDRs also have begun such a mortality transition, at least. Looking at Table 5-2 we see that over the past fifty years LDRs have lengthened life expectancy by almost twenty-three years, to levels approaching those of the MDRs in 1950. The LDRs, with much later mortality transitions, have gained some ground in catching up with the MDRs. The difference between MDRs and LDRs is still over ten years of life expectancy; but back in 1950 this difference was even greater—over 25 years of life.

The LDRs are even more different from one another than were the MDRs during their epidemiological transitions. Public health and modern medicine are not being newly discovered, as in Europe during its transition, but are known technologies that can be used when resources are available. Thus, LDR mortality declines are more likely to vary directly with level of economic development across, and within, countries.

Theoretically, mortality in the LDRs should achieve life expectancies similar to those of the MDRs. Unfortunately, new mortality threats such as HIV/AIDS have, as we shall see, heavily impacted some less-developed countries and will mean significant delay in LDR mortality declines. Nonetheless, the epidemiological transition is at least now in progress worldwide.

Proximate Causes of Death

One can think of the causes of death as falling into two categories, based on how immediate their contribution to the death was. Thus the most immediate—or *proximate*—causes of death would be the ones that finally brought about the event: cancer, heart disease, murder, or whatever. Less immediate (nonproximate) causes would be a whole host of factors that contributed to the death only in the sense that they increased the likelihood of experiencing one of the proximate causes. For instance, chemical pollution might increase the risk of cancer, smoking might increase the risk of heart disease, or living in a rough part of town might increase the risk of being murdered. When responsible authorities register the cause of death for medical and legal purposes, they are recording what we call the proximate cause of death. Some readers may prefer to think of these two categories as the biological (proximate) versus the cultural (nonproximate) causes of death.

Our strategy in this section is to deal first with the proximate and then the nonproximate causes; that is, we first describe the changes in the proximate causes of death that accompanied the mortality transitions, noting which proximate causes have been brought under control in the MDRs and those LDRs that are in an advanced stage of mortality decline. Then we address the question of what cultural (including medical) changes allowed these reduced proximate causes to be brought under control.

Ideally, civil registration of deaths includes registering the proximate causes of deaths; that is, whoever registers the death (such as a coroner) not only records the event of the death and the sex and age of the deceased, but also what that person died of. In reality, historical records of causes of deaths are extremely hard to come by.

Usually we are limited, even in the MDRs, to a few local long-time series (such as the State of Massachusetts or the City of New York in the United States). Even then we are plagued by shifts in diagnostic terminology over time that threaten to invalidate many historical comparisons (Kunitz, 1991) or require reclassifying causes of death to a consistent standard (Vallin and Meslé, 1990).

Omran (1982) studied the incomplete evidence to find the general pattern of change in the causes-of-death profiles that have accompanied mortality transitions throughout the world. He identified three models of change: the *Western*, the *accelerated*, and the *delayed*. Most MDRs would be described by his Western model, in which mortality started to decline early and gradually. The accelerated model describes many countries in which rapid mortality declines began later, such as the remaining MDRs (e.g., Japan, Eastern Europe, or the USSR) and now those LDR countries already advanced in their mortality decline (e.g., Argentina, Brazil, Costa Rica, Cuba, Cyprus, Mauritus, Thailand, or Uruguay). The delayed model refers to most LDRs, still at the very early stages of mortality decline (e.g., much of Africa, Asia, and Latin America). The Western and accelerated models differ primarily in the speed with which they have gone through the transition and only secondarily in terms of the shifts in the causes of deaths.

Omran says that the "epidemiologic transition" for the Western-model countries consisted of three stages. Indeed, his labels for those stages summarize the dominant causes of death in each (Omran, 1977, p. 9):

1. The age of *pestilence* and *famine*. This precedes the mortality transition. Annual life expectancy at birth vacillates between twenty and forty years.

2. The age of *receding pandemics*. A pandemic is an outbreak of disease that involves large proportions of the population, devastating it briefly. The resulting peaks in the mortality curve become less lofty and less frequent as pandemics recede. Life expectancy increases steadily from about thirty to about fifty years and varies less from year to year.

3. The age of *degenerative* or *human-made* diseases. Life expectancy approaches stability at more than seventy years.

Figure 5–2 illustrates a particular example that follows the Western model: New York City from about the early 1800s to 1970. Through the mid-1800s, the crude death rate line is exceedingly jagged and each peak seems clearly identifiable with a specific outbreak of yellow fever, smallpox, or cholera. Through the later 1800s and the 1900s, the line both declines and becomes less jagged. People are being spared from these proximate causes of death, these infectious diseases, to succumb later to other less sporadic killers. During the early part of the period depicted, New York City probably had higher death rates than did much of the rest of the country, especially the rural areas. Cities were not the best places to survive early in the demographic transition (see chapter 10).

Caselli (1991) estimated the gains in life expectancy won from the decline of infectious diseases during the MDR mortality transition. Table 5-3 shows the estimated years added to life expectancy of males and females due to declines in several specific causes of death during the mortality transitions of England and Wales, and of

Italy. The last row of the table gives the total increase in life expectancy from changes in all causes of death. Column 1, for example, shows that male life expectancy in England and Wales increased by over twenty-six years between 1871 and 1951. The first row of the table shows the increase in life expectancy from declines in infectious disease. Looking again at the first column we can see that nearly half of the increase in male life expectancy in England and Wales, or 11.5 years, was due to declining infectious diseases. The decline of tuberculosis alone accounts for nearly four years of this added life (Caselli, 1991). The first four rows of the table are for epidemic or infectious diseases, which show a significant decline over the mortality transition. By the end of World War II, the mortality transition had created a new pattern of *degenerative* or *human-made* diseases in MDRs that has remained relatively unchanged despite continuing increases in life expectancy (Caselli, 1991).

The decline of epidemic and infectious diseases over the mortality transition also can be seen by comparing causes-of-death profiles for the MDRs with those of the LDRs. In less-developed regions, with most countries at the early stages of transition, the greatest percentage of deaths is, not surprisingly, due to infectious and parasitic diseases (see Figure 5–3). A substantial percentage is also due to perinatal and maternal deaths associated with less adequate health care and high fertility. All these causes of death are a very small percentage of MDR mortality. In contrast, MDR mortality is largely due to degenerative diseases. Diseases of the circulatory system, followed by cancers and then diseases of the respiratory system, are all more substantial causes of death in MDRs than in LDRs.

Figure 5–2 Epidemiological Transition in New York City, 1800–1970

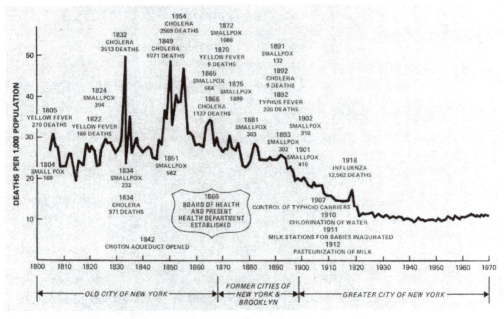

Source: Omran, "Epidemiological Transition in the U.S.," 1977, figure 3. Used with permission.

Some demographers have argued that the more-developed regions possibly are entering a fourth stage of mortality transition, where degenerative diseases will slowly decline, or even a fifth stage of mortality transition, where new infectious diseases will re-emerge (Olshansky et al., 1997, p. 11). These arguments are, however, speculative.

Table 5-3
Increased Life Expectancy Due to Declines in Selected Causes of Death, England and Wales (1871–1951) and Italy (1881–1951)

| Cause of Death | England and Wales | | Italy | |
	Males (1)	Females (2)	Males (3)	Females (4)
Infectious diseases	11.51	12.13	12.08	13.29
Bronchitis, pneumonia and influenza	3.47	3.78	4.74	4.64
Diarrhea and enteritis	2.01	2.01	3.13	3.72
Diseases of infancy and early childhood	1.82	1.77	2.47	2.16
Diseases of the circulatory system	0.36	0.86	0.52	1.07
Accidents	1.08	0.31	0.58	0.39
Neoplasms (incl. cancers)	-1.06	-0.46	-0.17	-0.21
Other causes	7.43	8.07	6.97	8.08
Total from all causes	26.62	28.47	30.32	33.14

Source: Caselli, "Health Transition and Cause-Specific Mortality," 1991, table 4.4.

Figure 5–3 Comparative Percentage Cause-of-Death Distributions in More-Developed and Less-Developed Regions, 1997

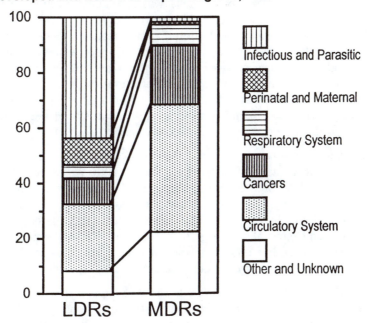

Source: WHO, *World Health Report 1998*, 1998, figure 6.

The past is more certain. What is clear is that the infectious and parasitic diseases which dominated the world before the mortality transition have been largely replaced by degenerative diseases in MDRs, with a tremendous rise in life expectancy.

How Certain Proximate Causes of Death Were Avoided

Bringing infectious, parasitic, and respiratory diseases under control in the MDRs required profound social, economic, and medical changes. What follows is a generalized description of those changes as they occurred in the countries of Northern and Western Europe and in frontier countries such as the United States (see, for example, Corsini and Viazzo, 1997; McKeown, 1976; Preston, 1976; and Schofield et al., 1991). We treat these changes in the order in which they began to impact mortality.

Economic development and rising income levels. Remember that Western mortality was declining gradually for a century or more prior to the more rapid decline we call the mortality transition. This early decline in mortality resulted mainly from reduction in the frequency and extent of periodic crises, such as famines and epidemics. Such escapes from mortal catastrophes were largely due to improvements in general living conditions.

For one thing, the food supply and people's diets gradually improved. The agricultural revolution brought the possibility of surpluses and thus the avoidance of periodic famines. Methods of storing food were improved. Centralization of authority on a wider, national level made it likely that food surpluses could and would be moved from localities of current surplus to localities of current shortage. The reduction in outright starvation due to famines probably was secondary in importance to the reduction of malnutrition and lowered resistance to other killers.

For another thing, people could afford better personal hygiene as their living standards rose. While the use of soap, the wearing of undergarments, and the shift from wool to cotton clothing may have been motivated on aesthetic grounds, they also discouraged lice, the carriers of typhus, and relapsing fever.

People also were able to afford better housing. Brick housing helped to thwart disease-carrying rats. Good ventilation, access to sunshine, and the reduction of crowding all probably raised general resistance to disease.

Institutionalized sanitary reforms and public health measures. Increasingly after the 1850s, the state intervened on behalf of the public's health. We are not talking about the medical advances that followed the establishment of the germ (or microbial) theory of disease causation. Rather, we are talking about government-sponsored changes in environmental conditions based on a yet-incomplete understanding of the causes of disease. This included the removal of garbage, the building of covered sewers, and the purification of drinking water that limited cholera and water-borne diseases. Prior to these reforms, cities were stinking, filthy, difficult places in which to live.

Social reforms. This category refers to those changes, sometimes instituted by governments, which were not directly aimed at improving longevity but did so as a by-product. Working conditions were improved by reducing child labor, shortening the length of the working day, and improving the workplace. Housing legislation set minimum standards. Social security schemes started providing such benefits as old-age pensions, health insurance, medical care, unemployment insurance, and payments to the indigent.

Advances in medicine. The impact of medical advances came later than for the other three categories, probably mostly in the early 1900s. Immunization against disease was, of course, a major factor. Smallpox vaccination spread before the turn of the century, and other immunizations came into use after that. Antiseptic surgery became more common. Later, in the 1930s, there were great strides in chemotherapy, the use of drugs to cure or halt the progress of an infectious disease. There were further improvements in the use of antibiotics and wonder drugs during and immediately after World War II. Finally, the development of effective insecticides greatly reduced insect-borne diseases such as typhus and malaria.

In conclusion, the popular belief that improvements in medical science played a heroic role in European and American mortality transitions is generally incorrect. In fact, the contribution of medicine came relatively late in the mortality transition. Before that, there had been important social and economic changes that already had set mortality plummeting.

MORTALITY DECLINES IN THE LESS-DEVELOPED REGIONS

Increases in Life Expectancy

We have seen, in Table 5-2, that the LDRs have also experienced some mortality decline over the past half-century as they have begun mortality transitions. How does declining LDR mortality compare to the historical mortality transitions in the MDRs?

LDRs include a wide variety of countries, cultures, and environments. Despite these differences, LDR countries had in common the high and fluctuating epidemic mortality that characterized most populations before mortality transition. LDR mortality did not experience any sustained decline until the twentieth century. Indeed, life expectancy in 1935–1939 in the LDRs as a class was still estimated at thirty years, not very different from what it had been in the MDRs in the early 1800s.

But in the 1950s, after World War II, life expectancy started to soar, reflecting a mortality transition that extends to the present. Dramatic life expectancy gains of twenty to thirty years took place rapidly in such countries as Trinidad, Sri Lanka, and Taiwan (Heer and Grigsby, 1992). In the past half-century, life expectancy has risen by over twenty years for LDRs as a class (see Table 5-2). More than half of this increase occurred between 1950 and 1970, just two decades. Stolnitz contrasts this with the prior European mortality transition:

> Within a decade in numerous instances and no more than two decades in most, many of the world's low-income nations have passed through successions of longevity stages that today's highest-income nations . . . needed generations or even half-centuries to reach and leave behind. It is safe to say that nothing in world history would have prepared a pre-World War II or even a 1950 observer for the mortality trends that soon emerged. (1982, p. 465)

Because of this steep mortality drop in the LDRs, there has been a gradual and partial convergence between LDR and MDR longevity. A difference of more than twenty-five years in life expectancy in 1950 shrank to just over ten years at the turn of the century (see Table 5-2).

LDRs still vary much more with respect to mortality than do MDRs. Africans have the shortest life expectancy. The current difference between sub-Saharan Africa (with a life expectancy of fifty-one) at one extreme, and Central America (with a life expectancy of seventy-one) at the other, is twenty years of life expectancy. There seems little tendency for convergence among the regions. Countries with the highest mortality rates are not catching up with the others. Some countries and regions, especially within Africa, still find themselves with brutally short life expectancies for their people, virtually the same as what present MDRs experienced a century ago. On an even grimmer note, there is evidence of a recent setback of improvement in survivorship in some LDRs. Africa, for example, is experiencing the brunt of world mortality from newly emergent diseases.

Decreases in Infant Mortality

Why infant mortality is considered so important. In the study of mortality transitions, deaths during the first year—*infant* mortality—tend to be of greater interest than mortality at any other age. There are several reasons for this.

One is that such a large proportion of all deaths in high-mortality countries involve infants. Age-specific mortality rates are generally highest at the very youngest and oldest ages in a population. If infant mortality is lowered, children surviving the early years will likely survive until much older ages, thereby contributing substantial years to life expectancy in the population. Interventions that lower infant mortality are especially effective in extending longevity.

Figure 5–4 dramatizes this relationship. In this figure, world regions are ordered from lowest to highest infant mortality as one reads from left to right across the page. As a general pattern, life expectancy decreases significantly as infant mortality increases, especially for the four LDRs on the right half of the graph.

Another reason we focus on infant mortality is its sensitivity. For instance, deaths in the first year are particularly responsive to intervention through medicine. Indeed, infant mortality often is used as an index of the general medical and public health conditions in a country. It even is used as a general indicator of socioeconomic well-being and development.

A final reason for special interest in infant mortality is the plausible relationship (or relationships) between infant death and fertility. In one direction, the chances of a couple's offspring surviving infancy have been hypothesized to influence their likelihood of choosing to have more children (e.g. Preston, 1978). We will review the evidence for this in chapter 6. In the opposite direction, closely spaced births do increase infant mortality (Palloni, 1989). Family-planning programs thus provide another possible intervention to reduce infant mortality.

Measuring infant mortality. One measure of infant mortality would be, of course, that available in the first row of a life table. For instance, in Table 5-1, the first

Figure 5–4   Infant Mortality and Life Expectancy in World Regions, 1995–2000

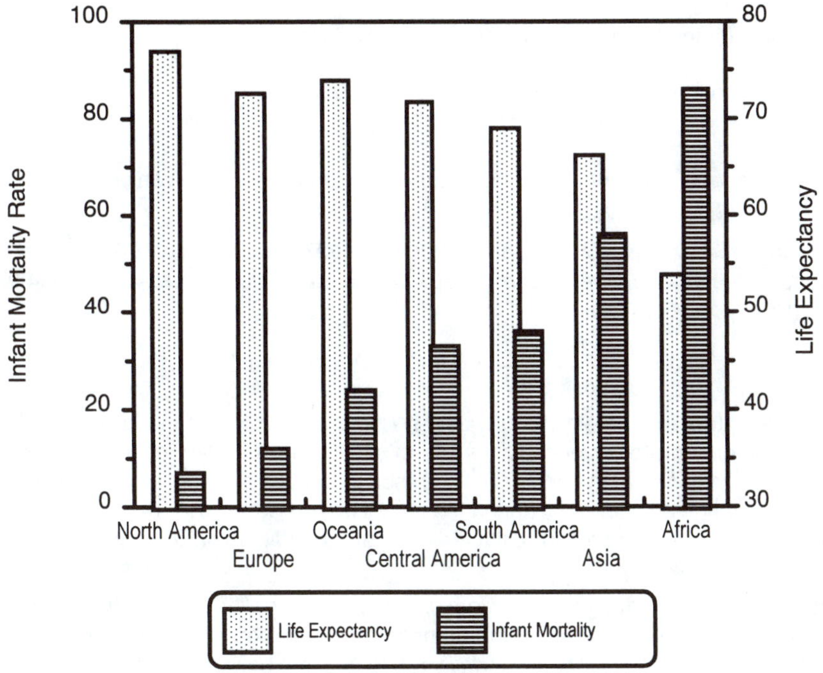

Source: United Nations, *World Resources 1998–99*, 1998, table 7.2.

entry in column 2 tells us that, per hundred females starting their lives, 0.659 U.S. females would die as infants, according to 1996 U.S. mortality risks. But, as we have stressed, such life tables require death reporting by age for all ages, complex data infrequently available in LDRs and usually estimated. An independent measure, based partially on other more reliable data, has become the standard: the "infant mortality rate." It is simply the total deaths to infants in a given year divided by the total births in that same year, multiplied by 1,000. Box 5–2 describes the computation of and rationale behind the infant mortality rate.

Regional differences in infant mortality. Figure 5–5 presents estimated infant mortality rates for world regions for the periods 1950–1955 and 1990–1995. (It also presents projections for the distant future; more on that later.) The regions are ordered from highest to lowest by infant mortality rate as of 1990–1995.

The results can be interpreted in more than one way. It is true that in all regions shown there has been a marked decrease in infant mortality rates over the period represented; the black bars are much longer than the gray bars. But it is also the case that the percentage decline in the rate was not generally most precipitous where the rate had been highest. In other words, infant mortality may be declining across the board, but gaps in infant mortality among the LDRs are not necessarily closing. The percentage decrease in Africa, for instance, was not as great as for the other regions.

Box 5–2   Infant Mortality Rates

The formula for the infant mortality rate (IMR) is as follows:

$$IMR = \frac{D_0}{B} \times 1{,}000$$

where

D_0 = deaths to infants (children under one year of age) in a given year

B = births in the given year

Let us take the example of the United States in 1997. There were 27,691 deaths to persons less than one year of age in 1997. In that same year, there were 3,894,970 births (NCHS, 1998c). Thus:

$$IMR = \frac{27{,}691}{3{,}894{,}970} \times 1{,}000 = (.00711) \times 1{,}000 = 7.11$$

There is an interesting difference between the logic of an IMR and the logic of an age-sex-specific death rate (or mortality rate from column two of a life table). Death rates (and mortality rates) use the population exposed to the risk of dying, i.e. the number of people in that age-sex category during the period of the deaths, as a denominator. The infant mortality rate, in contrast, *estimates* the "at-risk" denominator by the number of births during the same period.

Let us distinguish infant mortality from other early mortality. *Fetal mortality* is not included in infant mortality, nor in the demographic definition of mortality generally; it occurs before live birth. *Neonatal mortality* refers to death between birth and the end of the first twenty-eight days of life. *Post-neonatal mortality* is that which occurs during the rest of the first year. The separation between neonatal and post-neonatal mortality has been made because the causes of death very soon after birth are seen to differ from those later in infancy.

Where registration is reliable, both infant-death and birth data can come from the civil registration system. More frequently in the LDRs they come from sample surveys or censuses. Sometimes surveys involve direct questions about births and infant deaths during the preceding year. Many surveys ask the number of children ever born, the survivors by age, and the age of the mother. From these, one can estimate infant mortality rates indirectly (e.g., Box 5–1).

For each region represented in Figure 5–5, the bottom bar is a projection about a quarter-century into the future. Remember that such predictions are speculative, and the future of LDR mortality trends (including infant mortality trends) remains uncertain. To make intelligent guesses, it helps to study the changing profile of the proximate causes of death that has accompanied the LDR "mortality transition" thus far.

Proximate Causes of Death and Their Control

What former immediate causes of death were brought under control in order to reduce so drastically LDR mortality? Superficially, the postwar cause-of-death transition for LDRs was similar to the one experienced earlier by the MDRs. Infectious and

Figure 5–5   Estimated and Projected Infant Mortality Rates for 1950–1955, 1990–1995, and 2020–2025, by World Region

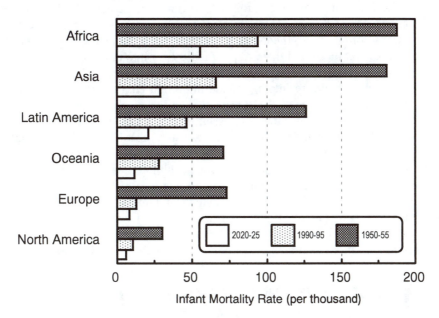

Infant Mortality Rate (per thousand)

Source: United Nations, *World Population Prospects, 1994 Revision*, 1995, table 65; Bos et al., *World Population Projections 1994–95 Edition*, 1994.

parasitic diseases—in particular, respiratory tuberculosis, bronchitis, and pneumonia—have been brought under control (Frenk et al., 1996; Preston and Nelson, 1974).

However, there also seem to be some interesting differences from the MDR transitions. LDR mortality declines have owed more to programs targeted at particular killers, such as smallpox, yaws, plague, relapsing fever, polio, malaria, measles, trachoma, etc. (WHO, 1998a). LDR mortality declines resulted less from control of diarrhetic diseases than was true in previous MDR declines (Olshansky et al., 1997). In addition, the transition has been less uniformly widespread than in the MDR declines, with much greater variation from one disease to another. Some infectious diseases remain persistent or even have increased recently in LDRs. Newly emergent diseases such as dengue and dengue hemorrhagic fever, hepatitis C, leischmaniasis, and especially HIV/AIDS have had a dramatic increase and impact on populations of the LDRs (WHO, 1998a; Olshansky et al., 1997). Cases of sleeping sickness have doubled in Central Africa over the past few years. Cholera, schistosomiasis, tetanus, tuberculosis, meningitis, and many other diseases either remain endemic or are increasing in many less-developed countries. Also, chronic diseases have appeared early in the LDR transition (Lopez, 1993). In short, LDRs are not experiencing the steady and broadly uniform epidemiological transition that characterized the MDRs.

An underlying contrast between the MDR and LDR transitions has been the role of medicine. During the slow and fitful LDR mortality declines of the early 1900s, survival increases probably were won by gradual improvements in living conditions. Soon after World War II, however, there was a massive infusion of Western medical and public health technology for controlling infectious disease in the LDRs. Not only was the knowledge of disease control in place (unlike at the beginning of the MDR mortality transition), but also there was a foreign aid commitment on the part of the MDR countries that motivated them to put their theory into practice. Thus a striking contrast between the LDR and MDR mortality transitions has been the point at which medical and public health technology made important contributions (Olshansky et al., 1997). It was very early in the LDR transition and relatively late in the MDR.

Rapid LDR mortality declines, and resulting population growth, have outpaced economic development in many countries. As a result, most less-developed countries have not had the broadly rising standard of living which accompanied slower-paced MDR transitions. Western medicine and public health have made great contributions to some early LDR declines, bringing mortality down to moderate levels (Phillips, 1991). However, without improvements in living standards, lowering LDR mortality further may be difficult (Tabah, 1980). Diarrheal diseases, for example, have been particularly resistant to control in LDRs, a failure clearly related to continued low living standards, malnutrition, ignorance, and undeveloped public administration.

SEX DIFFERENCES IN MORTALITY IN THE MORE-DEVELOPED REGIONS

As modernization has reduced MDR mortality, it has not been evenhanded in its distribution of additional survivorship. Female survivorship has improved more than has male, and the improvements in age-specific rates have been greater for those under fifty than for those over fifty. In short, the category that has benefited *least* from increases in remaining survivorship has been older males.

Let us start by documenting the current sex differentials in the MDRs contrasted with the LDRs. Then we will analyze how MDR patterns arose and how persistent they might be.

Current Contrasts between More-Developed and Less-Developed Regions

Table 5–4 presents estimated sex differences in life expectancy by world region, 1995–2000. Columns 1 and 2 show estimates for males and for females; column 3 shows the difference, or the years by which life expectancy of females exceeds that of males. Females outlast males for the world as a whole and for all regions. But the *degree* to which that is true varies by the development level of the region. In the LDRs as a class, females survive males by 2.9 years only; in the MDRs that difference is 7.4 years. Europe is the extreme example of this MDR disparity: women outlive men by 8.0 years.

Since, worldwide, females outlive males, that has a cumulative impact on the sex composition in older ages. The femininity ratio (females per 100 males—see chapter

Table 5–4
Sex Differences in Estimated Life Expectancy at Birth for World Regions, 1995–2000

Region[a]	Male (1)	Female (2)	Female minus Male (3)
World	63.7	67.8	4.1
MDRs	71.2	78.6	7.4
LDRs	62.4	65.3	2.9
Europe	69.3	77.3	8.0
Northern America	73.5	80.2	6.7
Latin America	67.1	72.4	5.3
Oceania	71.3	76.4	5.1
Africa	52.7	55.7	3.0
Asia	64.9	67.7	2.8

[a]Regions listed in order of femininity in life expectancy.
Source: United Nations, World Population Prospects, 1994 Revision, 1995, table A.27.

4) is only 103 at ages fifty-five to fifty-nine, but rises to 181 at ages eighty to eighty-nine, to 287 at ages ninety to ninety-nine, and to 386 among centenarians (United Nations, 1999).

Life expectancy figures, however, are averages, representing the whole life cycle. Let us take a longitudinal view of that cycle. The literature tells us that in the MDRs female survivorship is superior at all ages. In the LDRs the picture is not so simple. Female survivorship through the first year of life (infancy) is superior to male. During the early childhood years (ages one through four) the gap not only closes but in some countries male survivorship surpasses female. This implies (at the least) inferior allocation of scarce survival resources to female children. Later, during the female reproductive ages, the female survivorship superiority again narrows and even reverses in some LDR countries (United Nations, 1995a). Thus in the LDRs there remain life periods during which females are in greater jeopardy relative to males than they would be in the MDRs.

To what degree is current female survivorship superiority in more-developed regions the result of reducing mortality in periods of former special female jeopardy? The answer to that calls for a historical review of changes in mortality by sex in the MDRs.

Explaining Superior Female Longevity in the More-Developed Regions

Not only is life expectancy universally higher for females than for males in the MDRs, but that gender gap has been growing until the very recent past. The difference in MDR male and female life expectancies in 1950 was 5.1 years; by 1990–1995 it was 7.5 years (United Nations, 1995a).

Before the mortality transition, the situation in the MDRs was quite different from the present, with generally higher mortality for females. At least two changes lowered female mortality relative to male mortality during the course of the epidemiological transition. First, in the younger ages, improvements were made in economic, social, and health conditions, which had been responsible for higher female mortality among children and adolescents. Homes, for example, where girls spent more time than did boys, became more habitable and less overcrowded. At the same time, with urbanization the external environment became more and more hazardous for the boys, who spent relatively more time in it (Pinnelli and Mancini, 1997). In early adulthood, the most important trend for improving female survivorship has been the decline in maternal mortality. (Maternal mortality means female deaths associated with pregnancy, labor, and the *puerperium*, the period immediately following childbirth.) It is usually measured by the maternal mortality "rate," the number of maternal deaths per 100,000 live births in a specified year.

Figure 5–6 shows the dramatic drop in U.S. maternal mortality rates from the end of World War I. The immediate reasons for this impressive decline are several: expectant mothers have better nutrition because of an improved standard of living. Mothers are getting better medical care before and after childbirth. And the great majority of diseases responsible for maternal mortality happen to be preventable and controllable with proper medical care.

In addition, maternal mortality was cut by reduced childbearing. Generally speaking, the fewer children a mother has, the larger the proportion of her children born at low parities (e.g. first or second children) and born at prime maternal ages (e.g. in the mother's twenties versus her teens or late thirties). High parity and very early or late maternal age influence the risk per childbirth to which mothers are exposed. Moreover, the fewer times that women subject themselves to any risk—the fewer children they have—the fewer the women who will die of childbearing.

Figure 5–6   U.S. Maternal Mortality Rates, 1915–1991

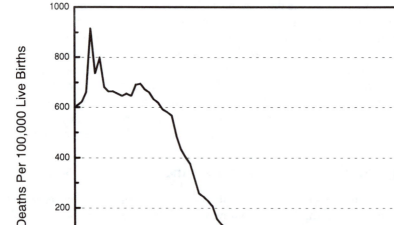

Source: Anderton et al., *Population of the United States*, 1997, table 4-15; U. S. Bureau of the Census, *Historical Statistics of the United States*, 1960, Series B 101–112.

Beyond maternal mortality, there has been a change in the dominant immediate causes of death in the MDRs, and that has affected the sexes differently. Figure 5–3 shows that cancers and diseases of the circulatory system have become more dominant in the MDRs; both of these causes have not only increased in importance, but seem to have turned first upon males. Before the mortality transition, infectious and parasitic diseases had a higher impact on females, so their decline especially benefited women (see Table 5–3). Overall, the shift in causes of death over the transition has benefited survivorship of females in the MDRs.

But this dramatic closing of the MDR gender gap in survivorship may be ending. Male life expectancy actually is improving at a faster rate than female. The difference in life expectancy has likely just passed its peak and stabilized. By 2015–2020 the difference between female and male life expectancy is projected to be down to 6.4 years, with little change into the mid-century mark (United Nations, 1995a). But beware of projecting present trends far into the future!

What are some plausible changes affecting present trends? Anybody can join in the conjecture. Female smoking is on the increase and will likely be the biggest influence on their relative mortality in the future (Lopez et al., 1995). Females also have entered the labor force, and participate in hazardous, traditionally male sports and occupations, etc. Increasing gender equity in the MDRs may have the unfortunate side effect of subjecting women to the same, higher, risks of mortality as males. Many of the new major health threats cut across gender groups or are even more likely to impact women, like AIDS/HIV contagion.

PROBLEMS OF MORTALITY

Defining Mortality Problems

How can the worldwide plunge in mortality be a problem? As we have seen (chapter 3), the mortality decline contributed to rapid population growth in the LDRs, which may present a variety of problems for their economic development and the provision of social services. We also have seen that the mortality decline has contributed, although clearly less than declining fertility, to the growing percentage of the "oldest old" in the MDRs (chapter 4), which may strain their ability to provide adequate social services (see chapter 6). All of these potential problems are *indirect* effects of mortality decline and not directly mortality problems. They also are discussed in other places throughout this text. So, let us confine our attention here to the more *direct*, and dramatic, mortality problems worldwide.

There are two categories of concern with respect to mortality declines which we address in this section. First, mortality decline is not as certain to continue as one might think. Mortality improvements of the past half-century already are facing major setbacks in some MDRs and LDRs, from both newly emergent diseases and tobacco-related mortality. Second, across world regions and within countries, not all groups have benefited equally from mortality decline. Persistent yet preventable mortality differentials and particularly vulnerable groups remain even in the MDRs.

Let us again go through the mental exercise of asking how these phenomena get defined as "problems." Who is concerned? What consequences are believed to follow? Why are those consequences perceived to be bad?

These questions seem almost silly when they refer to concerns about slowing or reversing declines in mortality. Nearly all of us wish for long lives, not only for ourselves but also for all members of humanity. And we all subscribe to the belief that the consequences of long life are happier than those of short life, at least so far. If this be so, then we almost automatically define any interruption of the mortality transition as a problem.

How do our questions apply to the problem of differentials in mortality? Let us assume, from the preceding paragraph, that long life is favored over short life. Who is concerned about vast differences among nations, among classes, among gender or age or ethnic categories in life expectancy? What consequences are supposed to flow from persistence of these inequalities? Why are these consequences supposed to be bad? These questions are seldom asked, yet are thought-provoking. (See "Propositions for Debate" at the end of the chapter.)

Problems of Stalled Mortality Transitions

However likely, the continuing decline of mortality is not a certainty. Demographers often have failed to anticipate changes in population trends by assuming that things will continue more or less as they have in the past. But how safe are such assumptions? We focus here upon two reasons for skepticism: the slowing and even reversal of European mortality declines, and the emergence of new pandemics, especially HIV/AIDS and tobacco-related illnesses. (A third potential reason for skepticism, the apparent intractability of higher mortality in socially underprivileged classes, is treated in the following section.)

Recent reversals in Europe. In 1997 the World Health Organization reported that mortality crises in the newly independent states of Europe, and continuing premature death in the lower social classes of almost every European country, actually led to a decline in European life expectancy for the first time since World War II (WHO, 1998b). European life expectancy fell from 73.1 years in 1991 to 72.4 years in 1994. Life expectancy in the newly independent states was eleven years less than in the rest of Europe, and Russian male life expectancy dropped to fifty-six years of age.

Programs to address the social determinants of health (e.g. poverty, homelessness, alcoholism, tobacco consumption, and unemployment) will likely be required to address the fall in European life expectancy. More ominously, infectious diseases unknown in Europe for decades have also reemerged to play a part in shifting mortality trends, including diphtheria, cholera, influenza, sexually transmitted diseases, and drug-resistant strains of tuberculosis, pneumonia, and malaria (WHO, 1998b). Lifestyle-related mortality also is cited as a cause of decreasing life expectancy, with high mortality from cardiovascular diseases and tobacco-related deaths. The setback in European life expectancy may be a temporary result of dramatic economic and social restructuring in Europe. But new infectious diseases such as HIV/AIDS, antibiotic-resistant disease strains, and tobacco-related deaths are neither unique to Europe nor most severe in the MDRs. Trends in Europe and elsewhere may suggest more than temporary mortality problems.

HIV/AIDS and Other Emergent Diseases

Perhaps the most obvious, and universally recognized, mortality problem is the worldwide HIV/AIDS pandemic. Estimated years of life lost to HIV/AIDS increased fifteen-fold in New York City between 1983 and 1994 (Obiri et al., 1998). But the populations in many LDRs, especially in sub-Saharan Africa, are being truly devastated by this disease. In Botswana, the hardest hit country, one of every four adults is infected by HIV and life expectancy at birth is projected to fall from sixty-one years of age in 1990–1995 to forty-one years of age in 2000–2005 (United Nations, 1999). Figure 5–7 shows the projected life expectancy at birth with and without HIV/AIDS mortality for twenty-nine African countries that have been hardest hit by the pandemic. By 2010–2015, sixteen years of average life expectancy will have been lost to AIDS in these countries. Population will most likely continue to increase due to high fertility, but natural increase will be affected as, for example, in Botswana, where the population in 2015 is projected to be 20% smaller than it would have been without HIV/AIDS (United Nations, 1999). HIV/AIDS also is increasing rapidly in Southeast Asia, India, and the newly independent states of the former Soviet Union.

Figure 5–7 Life Expectancy at Birth in 29 African Countries with and without AIDS, 1985–2015

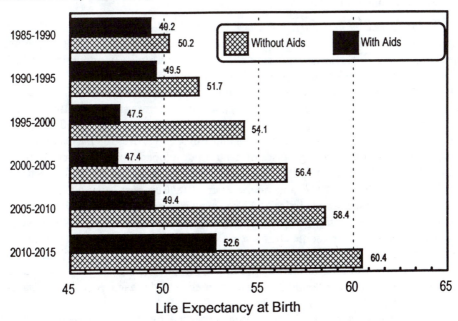

Source: United Nations, *Revision of the World Population Estimates and Projections, 1998,* 1999.

The World Health Organization projects that the worldwide impact of HIV/AIDS will peak somewhere around 2005–2010 (Murray and Lopez, 1996). Of course, even if the pandemic declines worldwide it will continue to impact some countries significantly, and potentially could resurge with any lapse in prevention efforts.

As Europe's experience suggests, HIV/AIDS is not the only emergent or newly identified disease. Since 1973 WHO has recognized over thirty new disease-causing microbes or infectious diseases. Some of these may be familiar to the reader, such as ebola (1977), Legionnaires' disease (1977), Hantaan hemorrhagic fever (1977), toxic shock syndrome (1981), HIV/AIDS (1983), hepatitis C (1989), HHV-8 associated with AIDS (1995), avian flu H5N1 (1997), and others (Olshansky et al., 1997, table 2; WHO, 1998a). Although HIV/AIDS has had the largest impact, the importance of other emergent diseases should not be discounted. Over 3% of the world's population is, for example, infected with the hepatitis C virus.

In part because of population growth and increasing density, infectious diseases are being provided ever more opportunities to mutate new strains and disperse through human hosts (Olshansky et al., 1997). Older diseases also have experienced some resurgence. Africa and Central America, for example, recently have seen a dramatic resurgence of yellow fever, a doubling of reported cases of sleeping sickness, and epidemic levels of meningitis. Whether human populations can continue to adopt and provide successful public health and medical measures as rapidly as diseases can adapt or reassert themselves is an open question. The twentieth century began with an influenza pandemic and has ended in the midst of the HIV/AIDS pandemic, sobering reminders that Malthus's *positive* checks on population growth (see Box 3–2) are not necessarily a thing of the past.

Tobacco-related mortality. A second pandemic, less obvious than HIV/AIDS but rivaling it in impact, is the dramatically rising mortality attributed to tobacco use. Smoking is the single largest preventable cause of mortality worldwide. By 2020 tobacco is expected to kill more people than any single disease, surpassing even HIV/AIDS (Murray and Lopez, 1996); and, unlike projected trends in HIV/AIDS, this trend will likely continue to increase through at least the next quarter-century.

Tobacco-related mortality is a relatively recent problem. In the 1930s lung cancer was a rare disease in the United States and Europe. Yet over the past sixty years it has become one of the leading causes of death in developed countries, accounting for about 5% of all deaths (Lopez, 1995). One of every five deaths in the United States is smoking-related (CDC, 1997) and one of every five European men aged thirty-five will die from a tobacco-related disease before age sixty-nine (WHO, 1998b).

Smoking is becoming an equal opportunity killer. In the MDRs, smoking began first with men and then, some thirty years later, became popular with women. In France, one survey shows that young girls are now smoking more than young boys. Women are now smoking in increasing numbers in developing countries as well. By the year 2020, more than 1 million adult women will die each year from tobacco-related mortality (United Nations, 1995b).

In the LDRs, the percentage of deaths caused by tobacco is rising as other causes are brought under control, as survivorship into older ages increases, and as tobacco consumption continues to increase. Over the next thirty years, tobacco-related mortality is projected to more than double (United Nations, 1995b) and to be an increasing cause of death in developing countries (WHO, 1998a).

Tobacco-related mortality tells a sobering story. It seems astounding that a clearly self-made threat to human life could loom even larger than the past century's greatest pandemic. Faced with a clearly preventable cause of death, MDR and LDR countries alike have failed to stop their tobacco epidemics. In large part this is because controlling a tobacco epidemic requires either modification of individual behavior or unpopular substance-abuse regulations. Widespread obesity and sedentary lifestyles, unhealthy diets, alcohol and substance abuse, and so forth all suggest that longevity is not always an overwhelming individual priority.

Inequality of Persistent High Mortality

Another major group of mortality problems concerns classes of people whose mortality has not declined as much as others'. Social class differences are found for most causes of death (Marmot, 1995) and high mortality persists in many disadvantaged nations.

International inequality. Let us review some disturbing aspects of present LDR mortality shown in Table 5–2. While the gap in life expectancy between MDRs and LDRs has narrowed, MDR populations overall still expect to live twelve years longer. Moreover, the large gap among the LDRs seems to be persisting. Africa, in particular, is falling even further behind the other LDRs. Within all of these less-developed regions, the mortality improvements have been least for the poorest of the countries and the poorest subgroups within those countries.

The narrowing gap in life expectancy between less- and more-developed countries, and between the rich and the poor within LDR countries has been largely due to declines in infant mortality among poor people and poor nations (Guzman, 1989). Further improvements in combating infectious diseases could further close the gap between rich and poor mortality (Arriaga, 1989).

Mortality transitions have, themselves, led to some reasons for persistent and increasing international inequalities. In many less-developed countries the increasing population resulting from the decline of communicable diseases has not met with increased economic opportunities. Instead, population increases have fueled a rapidly growing lower class with persistently higher mortality (Taucher et al., 1996). In other LDR countries, increased life expectancy and economic development have led to "premature" increases in chronic and degenerative diseases among the more well-to-do population (Gwatkin, 1993). These countries face a dual burden of mortality, with rising health care needs among the wealthy contesting for resources needed to combat persistent communicable diseases among the poor.

Socioeconomic class inequality. In the MDRs, as well, social class differences in mortality persist in all countries for which statistics are available. However, these differences vary widely depending upon the specific cause considered (Marmot, 1995), and the specific groups that suffer from higher mortality vary from country to country. For example, huge differences in infant and maternal mortality between socioeconomic classes in the United States have declined over time but still persist (National Center for Health Statistics, 1998b). In other cases, such as tobacco-related deaths in Sweden, social class differences have played a major role in widening mortality gaps (Vågerö and Lundberg, 1995). Regardless of the trend, differences in mortality by socioeconomic status are persistent in MDRs as well as LDRs.

There also are reasons to be concerned about possible widening of socioeconomic differences in mortality in the MDRs. Even these countries, with their privileged share of world resources, confront rising health costs that present difficult choices. The aging of MDR populations, in particular, places strains on resources. The MDR population over age seventy-five consumes many times more medical and social services than those under seventy-five, and some European countries already have foreseen that they will not be able to meet the needs of their aging populations (WHO, 1998a). As populations continue to age, MDR countries will likely have to make difficult choices between a) allocating resources to help socially disadvantaged groups who lag behind in life expectancy and b) providing for the rising chronic conditions and health care demands of an aging population.

Vulnerable groups. Across national and regional boundaries, and across socioeconomic classes, certain segments of the population suffer disproportionately from mortality that is premature and largely preventable. The United Nations has placed particular emphasis on identifying and protecting the basic health of such vulnerable groups. Not surprisingly, these vulnerable groups are also economically disadvantaged ones with higher unemployment, lack of housing, poverty, and poor health (United Nations, 1992).

In both the more-developed and the less-developed regions, *infants and children* suffer disproportionately from poverty and preventable mortality. In the LDRs poverty-related causes of death such as diarrheal and communicable diseases (Chackiel and Plaut, 1996), cholera (Brandling-Bennett et al., 1996), and pneumonia (WHO, 1998a) are major causes of child death. Children in LDRs also face risks from malnutrition, HIV/AIDS, adolescent pregnancy, and rising effects of neglect, abuse, and violence, especially among growing numbers of street children (WHO, 1998a). Nonetheless, spectacular progress has been made in reducing child mortality, and that trend is projected to continue or even accelerate. Most deaths under five years of age are preventable—at least 2 million per year could be prevented by existing vaccines (WHO, 1998a).

Child and adolescent deaths in the MDRs also are largely due to preventable causes. In the United States, for example, 73% of all deaths to school-age youth and young adults are due to four preventable causes: motor vehicle crashes, other unintentional injuries, homicide, and suicide (CDC, 1997). Sexually transmitted diseases and unintended pregnancies also contribute to adolescent mortality risks in the MDRs. Reducing these largely preventable deaths at young ages would contribute substantially to increased life expectancy.

Concern has grown over the mortality and health of *LDR women* in the past few decades. Since the early 1980s, there has been a decline in the standard of health and nutrition of women in parts of every developing region due, inter alia, to a decline in per capita expenditure on health. This is a particularly alarming situation since maternal and neonatal health are crucial to infant survival. Infant and child mortality rates have been rising in a number of countries after having declined for decades (United Nations, 1995, recommendation XII).

Social and biological conditions contribute to preventable women's mortality. Malnutrition rates, for example, are higher for females than for males in regions of South Asia where food is distributed within the household according to a member's status rather than to nutritional needs (United Nations, 1995b). In these regions there is a higher risk that girls, as compared to boys, will die before age five despite their natural biological mortality advantages. Reproductive biology also burdens women. Well over half a million women die each year during childbirth and these risks rise where the number of pregnancies is greater and health care is less adequate—maternal mortality is 1 in 1400 in Europe but 1 in 16 in Africa (UNFPA, 1999; WHO, 1998a).

Much of the premature mortality among women is associated with lower status. In past decades programs addressing women's health have focused upon reproductive health. More recent initiatives also have focused on development initiatives, recognizing that women's educational attainment, work patterns, social roles, and access to resources all have considerable impact upon their health and mortality (Sadik, 1991).

Women and children, however, are not the only groups vulnerable to premature and preventable mortality. There are, in fact, other clearly vulnerable groups whose health needs have been neglected or are largely unknown. One such group are *indigenous peoples*, for whom demographic data are sadly lacking. It is clear that many indigenous peoples are both disproportionately in poverty and in poor health. Small-scale studies clearly demonstrate the need for basic health services. Moreover, in many countries indigenous peoples are growing faster than the general population, meriting special attention (United Nations, 1995b).

SUMMARY

In today's more-developed countries, the "mortality transition" resulted in a near-doubling of life expectancy at birth in a little over a century. Such a sustained improvement in survivorship was unprecedented in human history. Its immediate cause was the control of infectious, parasitic, and respiratory diseases. The control of these killers was initiated by economic development and improving living standards, sanitary reforms, and public health measures. Advances in medicine, such as mass immunization against disease, made their contribution relatively late in the MDR mortality transition.

In today's less-developed countries, in contrast, Western medical technology made an early and significant contribution to their mortality transitions. Although there had been a gradual, fitful decline in LDR mortality in the early 1900s, the exporting of Western medicine soon after World War II was largely responsible for the universal and rapid decline in LDR mortality during the following decades.

There continues to be considerable variety among LDR countries regarding mortality. The poorest still have life expectancies that are distressingly short by modern standards. Continuing substantial improvements in LDR mortality cannot likely be achieved by waving the medical wand; improvement in living standards may be a prerequisite. The LDRs also have suffered some setbacks in their mortality transitions. Foremost among these have been the HIV/AIDS pandemic and resurgences of other infectious diseases. The consequences have been dramatic, as life expectancy in some African countries has fallen by nearly twenty years due to these diseases.

Even within nations, vast differentials in preventable mortality persist, related to socioeconomic status, age, and sex, among other social distinctions. Most infant and child mortality and many persistent causes of mortality among women are preventable. Regarding sex, female survivorship has improved more with development than has male, largely due to declines in maternal mortality. But this pattern of longer lives for females has not been uniformly achieved in LDRs, where women continue to face a number of status-related mortality disadvantages and higher maternal mortality. These differentials to some degree reflect internal competition for scarce health resources, a competition that is likely to continue.

The mortality transition has been an unprecedented worldwide historical event that continues to unfold. Epidemic mortality will not necessarily disappear from the face of the earth as this transition continues. The threats of Malthus's *positive* checks on population remain with us at the start of this century. Continuing mortality differences between rich and poor nations, and peoples, are equally clear within LDRs and MDRs. Speculating from recent history, it is most likely that the mortality transition will continue to progress throughout the world and that socioeconomic differences in mortality will generally decline as it does. Yet, new threats to mortality will almost certainly be encountered, and societies may shift their allocations of scarce health resources; the course of future mortality decline is not certain.

► EXERCISES

1. Table E5–1 is a male life table for the United States according to the age-sex-specific death rates of 1996. Some blanks have been left intentionally in columns 3, 4, 6, and 7 of the table. Your task is to fill in those blanks, copying the computations used for determining the other entries for the same columns. What follows is an explanation of each of the columns, from left to right:

   Column 1 simply lists the age intervals. With two exceptions, we have used five-year intervals rather than single-year ones; thus, this is an "abridged" life table. The exceptions are at either end of the age range. Infant mortality (age zero to one) is separated from early childhood mortality (age one to five). The terminal category (eighty-five and over in this table) is open-ended.

   Column 2 $(_nq_x)$ presents the assumed risk of dying over the n years beginning at age x for each of the age intervals. Each such "mortality rate" is based on an age-sex-specific death rate. The entire rest of the table is generated from column 2.

   Column 3 (l_x) and column 4 $(_nd_x)$ are best explained together. We start at the top of column 3 with an arbitrary, large, hypothetical cohort (or "radix"); this table follows the convention of using 100,000. Then we trace what the fate of this hypothetical cohort would be if it experienced the probabilities of death listed in column 2. For instance, the 100,000 males born experienced a probability of death of 0.00802 until their first birthday. This would result in 802 deaths by the first birthday. This is the entry for column 4 for the first age interval. How many males would start their second year of life? We subtract the deaths (802) from those who started the first interval (100,000) and get 99,198, the next entry in column 3. Multiplying these 99,198 survivors by the probability of dying over the next four years to age five, or 0.00167, we find that 166 of them will die, the next entry in column 4, and so on, back and forth between columns 3 and 4. Algebraically stated,

$$_nd_x = (_nq_x)(l_x)$$

and

$$l_{x+n} = l_x - {_nd_x}$$

where

x = exact age at the beginning of the age interval

n = number of years in the age interval

Column 5 ($_nL_x$) is the number of person years lived in the age interval by the survivors of the hypothetical cohort. In the first row, if there were 100,000 babies born and 99,198 survived the whole first year, how many person years did they collectively live during that one-year age interval? It depends on when during the year death occurred. Because of the unusual pattern of death during infancy, demographers use a complex procedure to arrive at an estimate for the top entry in column 5. For subsequent age intervals, however, deaths are more evenly spread throughout the interval. Thus, for most of the age intervals beyond infancy, the entry will be very close to the average of 1) the number of people alive at the beginning of the interval and 2) the number alive at the end of the interval. You are not required to make such a complex interpolation here.

Column 6 (T_x) is derived entirely from column 5 ($_nL_x$). It tells how many *person years* will be lived by the survivors of the hypothetical cohort from any specified age until all are dead. Thus, the entry 7,305,955 at the top of column 6 indicates this hypothetical cohort collectively will have that many years of life among them before the last one dies. Arithmetically, the column is constructed by summing the number of years lived in each interval from the bottom row upwards to the top in column 5. Stated algebraically,

$$T_x = \sum_{x=85+}^{0} {_nL_x}$$

Column 7 (e_x) tells the life expectancy remaining after each specified birthday. Take the top entry as an illustration, the life expectancy at birth (e_0). If there were 7,305,955 person years of life to be shared among the 100,000 males who were born into the hypothetical cohort (see column 3), then there were about 73.06 years per male. Algebraically stated,

$$e_x = \frac{T_x}{l_x}$$

It can be thought of as the average number of years men in the hypothetical cohort would live, according to the death rates assumed in column 2. Life expectancies can be computed for later ages as well, and they frequently are. The exercise requests that you do so for ages five and fifty-five.

2. Consult Table E5–1 to arrive at the following figures:

a. From the $_nq_x$ column, find the percentage of the cohort reaching their sixty-fifth birthday that would survive to their seventieth birthday: _____.

b. From the l_x column, find the percentage of the cohort who would reach their sixty-fifth birthday: _____.

c. From the $_nd_x$ column (or the l_x column), find the number of cohort members who would die between their sixty-fifth and seventieth birthdays: _____.

Table E5–1
Male Life Table, United States, 1996

Age Interval[a]	Proportion Dying[b]	Number Living at Beginning of Age Interval (of 100,000 born alive)	Number Dying During Age Age Interval (of 100,000 born alive)	Person Years Lived In the Age Interval	Person Years Lived In This and All Subsequent Age Intervals	Average Remaining Lifetime[c]
x to x+n (1)	$_nq_x$ (2)	l_x (3)	$_nd_x$ (4)	$_nL_x$ (5)	T_x (6)	e_x (7)
0–1	0.00802	100,000	802	99,307	7,305,955	73.1
1–5	0.00167	99,198	166	396,407		72.6
5–10	0.00111	99,032	110	494,860	6,810,241	
10–15	0.00142		140	494,355	6,315,381	63.8
15–20	0.00552	98,782	545	492,690	5,821,026	58.9
20–25	0.00755	98,237	742	489,370	5,328,336	54.2
25–30	0.00774	97,495		485,567	4,838,966	49.6
30–35	0.00994	96,740	962	481,323	4,353,399	45.0
35–40	0.01281	95,778	1,227	475,977	3,872,076	40.4
40–45	0.01714	94,551	1,621	468,983	3,396,099	35.9
45–50	0.02348	92,930	2,182	459,601		31.5
50–55	0.03465	90,748	3,144	446,380	2,467,515	27.2
55–60	0.05276	87,604	4,622	427,115	2,021,135	
60–65	0.08395		6,966	398,394	1,594,020	19.2
65–70	0.12205	76,016	9,278	357,755	1,195,626	15.7
70–75	0.18255	66,738	12,183	303,928	837,871	12.6
75–80	0.25936	54,555		237,528	533,943	9.8
80–85	0.38255	40,406	15,457	162,498	296,415	7.3
85 and over	1.00000	24,949	24,949	133,917	133,917	5.4

[a]Period of life between two exact ages, stated in years.
[b]Proportion of persons alive at beginning of age interval who die during interval.
[c]Average number of years of life remaining at beginning of age interval.
Source: National Center for Health Statistics, "U. S. Abridged Life Tables, 1996," 1998, table 1.

d. From the $_nL_x$ column, find the number of person years lived by the cohort between ages sixty-five and seventy: _____.

e. From the e_x column, find the life expectancy at age sixty-five: _____.

PROPOSITIONS FOR DEBATE

1. In a life table, the life expectancy at age one (e_1) logically can never exceed the life expectancy at age zero (e_0).

2. LDR life expectancy will continue to increase rapidly until it is about the same as MDR life expectancy.

3. Medical science is eliminating communicable diseases worldwide as major proximate causes of death and they will never be as important on the national level again.

4. Glaring international and socioeconomic differentials in mortality both could be eliminated by redistributing resources from the rich to the poor.

5. Less attention should be paid in the MDRs to reducing women's mortality since they are now living longer than men anyway.

6. As U.S. life expectancy increases and its population ages (see chapter 4), efforts to decrease mortality rates in the senior years will diminish.

7. The competition for national health resources will decline, both within MDR and LDR countries.

REFERENCES AND SUGGESTED READINGS

Anderson, Michael. 1996. *British Population History from the Black Death to the Present Day*. Cambridge: Cambridge University Press.

Antonovsky, Aaron. 1967. "Social Class, Life Expectancy and Overall Mortality." *Milbank Memorial Fund Quarterly* 45(2).

Arriaga, Eduardo E. 1989. "Changing Trends in Mortality Decline during the Last Decades." In Lado Ruzicka, Guillame Wusch, and Penny Kane, eds., *Differential Mortality: Methodological Issues and Biosocial Factors*. Oxford: Clarendon Press.

———. 1994. *Population Analysis with Microcomputers*. Vol. I. Washington, DC: International Programs Center, Population Division, Bureau of the Census.

Bogue, Donald J., Eduardo E. Arriaga, and Douglas L. Anderton, eds. 1993. *Readings in Population Research Methodology*. Vol. 1–8. Chicago: UNFPA/Social Development Center.

Bos, Edward, Mu T. Vu, Ernest Massiah, and Rodolfo A. Bulatao. 1994. *World Population Projections 1994–95 Edition: Estimates and Projections with Related Demographic Statistics*. World Bank, Baltimore: Johns Hopkins University Press.

Brandling-Bennett, David A., Marlo Libel, and Américo Migliónico. 1996. "Cholera in the Americas in 1991." In Ian M. Timæs, Juan Chackiel, and Lado Ruzicka, eds., *Adult Mortality in Latin America*. Oxford: Clarendon Press.

Brass, William. 1975. *Methods of Estimating Fertility and Mortality from Limited and Defective Data.* Chapel Hill, NC: Laboratories for Population Statistics.

Caselli, Graziella. 1991. "Health Transition and Cause-Specific Mortality." In Roger Schofield, David Reher, and Alain Bideau, eds., *The Decline of Mortality in Europe.* Oxford: Clarendon Press.

Centers for Disease Control (CDC). 1997. *Facts about Cigarette Mortality.* Fact Sheet from the Division of Media Relations. Washington, DC: Centers for Disease Control and Prevention.

Chackiel, Juan, and Renate Plaut. 1996. "Demographic Trends with an Emphasis on Mortality." In Ian M. Timæs, Juan Chackiel, and Lado Ruzicka, eds., *Adult Mortality in Latin America.* Oxford: Clarendon Press.

Coale, Ansley J. 1986. "The Decline of Fertility in Europe since the Eighteenth Century as a Chapter in Human Demographic History." In Ansley J. Coale and Susan Cotts Watkins, eds., *The Decline of Fertility in Europe.* Princeton: Princeton University Press.

Coale, Ansley J., and Paul Demeny. 1966. *Regional Model Life Tables and Stable Populations.* Princeton, NJ: Princeton University Press.

Committee on Population and Demography. 1981. *Collecting Data for the Estimation of Fertility and Mortality.* Report no. 6. Washington, DC: National Academy Press.

Corsini, Carlo A., and Pier Paolo Viazzo, eds. 1997. *The Decline of Infant and Child Mortality— The European Experience: 1750–1990.* Dordrecht, The Netherlands: Martinus Nijhoff Publishers.

Ewbank, Douglas C. 1990. "Evaluation of Model Life Tables for East Africa." In Jacques Vallin, Stan D'Souza, and Alberto Palloni, eds., *Measurement and Analysis of Mortality: New Approaches.* Oxford: Clarendon Press.

Frenk, Julio, José Luis Bobadilla, and Rafael Loranzo. 1996. "The Epidemiological Transition in Latin America." In Ian M. Timæs, Juan Chackiel, and Lado Ruzicka, eds., *Adult Mortality in Latin America.* Oxford: Clarendon Press.

Guzman, José Miguel. 1989. "Trends in Socio-economic Differentials in Infant Mortality in Selected Latin American Countries." In Lado Ruzicka, Guillame Wusch, and Penny Kane, eds., *Differential Mortality: Methodological Issues and Biosocial Factors.* Oxford: Clarendon Press.

Gwatkin, Davidson R. 1993. "Distributional Implications of Alternative Strategic Responses to the Demographic-Epidemiological Transition—an Initial Inquiry." In James N. Gribble and Samuel H. Preston, eds., *The Epidemiological Transition: Policy Planning and Implications for Developing Countries.* Washington, DC: National Academy Press.

Heer, David M., and Jill S. Grigsby. 1992. *Society and Population.* 3d ed. Englewood Cliffs, NJ: Prentice Hall.

Hill, Kenneth, and Hania Zlotnik. 1982. "Indirect Estimation of Fertility and Mortality." In John A. Ross, ed., *International Encyclopedia of Population.* Vol. 1. New York: The Free Press.

Krotki, Karol J., ed. 1978. *Developments in Dual System Estimation of Population Size and Growth.* Edmonton, Alberta: University of Alberta Press.

Kunitz, Stephen J. 1991. "The Personal Physician and the Decline of Mortality." In Roger Schofield, David Reher, and Alain Bideau, eds., *The Decline of Mortality in Europe.* Oxford: Clarendon Press.

Lopez, Alan D. 1993. "Causes of Death in Industrial and Developing Countries: Estimates for 1985–1990." In Dean T. Jamison et al., eds., *Disease Control Priorities in Developing Countries.* Oxford: Oxford University Press.

———. 1995. "The Lung Cancer Epidemic in Developed Countries." In Alan D. Lopez et al., eds., *Adult Mortality in Developed Countries: From Description to Explanation.* Oxford: Clarendon Press.

Lopez, Alan D., Graziella Caselli, and Tapani Valkonen, eds. 1995. *Adult Mortality in Developed Countries: From Description to Explanation*. Oxford: Clarendon Press.

Marmot, Michael. 1995. "Social Differentials in Mortality: The Whitehall Studies." In Alan D. Lopez et al., eds., *Adult Mortality in Developed Countries: From Description to Explanation*. Oxford: Clarendon Press.

McKeown, Thomas. 1976. *The Modern Rise in Population*. New York: The Academic Press.

McNamara, Regina. 1982a. "Infant and Child Mortality." In John A. Ross, ed., *International Encyclopedia of Population*. New York: The Free Press.

———. 1982b. "Mortality Trends: Historical Trends." In John A. Ross, ed., *International Encyclopedia of Population*. New York: The Free Press.

Murray, Christopher J. L., and Alan D. Lopez, eds. 1996. *The Global Burden of Disease: A Comprehensive Assessment of Mortality and Disability from Diseases, Injuries and Risk Factors in 1990 and Projected to 2020*. Published by Harvard School of Public Health on behalf of the World Health Organization and World Bank. Cambridge, MA: Harvard University Press.

National Center for Health Statistics (NCHS). 1998a. "Births and Deaths: Preliminary Data for 1997." *Monthly Vital Statistics Report* 47(4).

———. 1998b. "Deaths: Final Data for 1996." *Monthly Vital Statistics Report* 47(9).

———. 1998c. "United States Abridged Life Tables, 1996." *Monthly Vital Statistics Report* 47(13).

Obiri, G. U., E. J. Fordyce, T. P. Singh, and S. Forlenza. 1998. "Effect of HIV/AIDS Versus other Causes of Death on Premature Mortality in New York City, 1983–1994." *American Journal of Epidemiology* 147(9).

Olshansky, S. Jay, Bruce Carnes, Richard G. Rodgers, and Len Smith. 1997. "Infectious Diseases—New and Ancient Threats to World Health." Population Bulletin 52(2). Washington, DC: Population Reference Bureau.

Omran, Abdel R. 1977. "Epidemiological Transition in the U.S." *Population Bulletin* 32(2). Washington, DC: Population Reference Bureau.

———. 1982. "Epidemiological Transition." In John A. Ross, ed., *International Encyclopedia of Population*. New York: The Free Press.

Palloni, Alberto. 1989. "Effects of Inter-birth Intervals on Infant and Early Childhood Mortality." In Lado Ruzicka, Guillame Wusch, and Penny Kane, eds., *Differential Mortality: Methodological Issues and Biosocial Factors*. Oxford: Clarendon Press.

Phillips, D. R. 1991. "Problems and Potential of Researching Epidemiological Transition: Examples from Southeast Asia." *Social Science and Medicine* 33(4).

Pinnelli, Antonella, and Paola Mancini. 1997. "Gender Mortality Differences from Birth to Puberty." In Carlo A. Corsini and Pier Paolo Viazzo, eds., *The Decline of Infant and Child Mortality—The European Experience: 1750–1990*. Dordrecht, The Netherlands: Martinus Nijhoff Publishers.

Pollard, John H. 1990. "Cause of Death and Expectation of Life: Some International Comparisons." In Jacques Vallin, Stan D'Souza, and Alberto Palloni, eds., *Measurement and Analysis of Mortality: New Approaches*. Oxford: Clarendon Press.

Population Reference Bureau. 1999. *1999 World Population Data Sheet*. Washington, DC: Population Reference Bureau.

Preston, Samuel H. 1976. *Mortality Patterns in National Populations, with Special Reference to Causes of Death*. New York: Academic Press.

Preston, Samuel H., ed. 1978. *The Effects of Infant and Childhood Mortality on Fertility*. New York: Academic Press.

Preston, Samuel H., and Michael R. Haines. 1991. *Fatal Years: Child Mortality in Late Nineteenth-Century America*. Princeton, NJ: Princeton University Press.

Preston, Samuel H., and Verne E. Nelson. 1974. "Structure and Change in Causes of Death: An International Summary." *Population Studies* 28(1).

Ross, John A. 1982. "Life Tables." In John A. Ross, ed., *International Encyclopedia of Population*. New York: The Free Press.

Ruzicka, Lado T. 1983. "Mortality Transition in the Third World Countries: Issues for Research." IUSSP *Newsletter* 17.

Ruzicka, Lado T., and Harold Hansluwka. 1982. "Mortality Transition in South and East Asia: Technology Confronts Poverty." *Population and Development Review* 8(3).

Ruzicka, Lado, Guillame Wusch, and Penny Kane, eds. 1989. *Differential Mortality: Methodological Issues and Biosocial Factors*. Oxford: Clarendon Press.

Sadik, Nafis, ed. 1991. *Population Policies and Programmes: Lessons Learned from Two Decades of Experience*. United Nations Population Fund. New York: New York University Press.

Schofield, Roger, David Reher, and Alan Bideau. 1991. *The Decline of Mortality in Europe*. Oxford: Clarendon Press.

Shane, Barbara. 1997. *Family Planning Saves Lives*. 3d ed. Washington, DC: Population Reference Bureau.

Shryock, Henry S., and Jacob S. Siegel. 1976. *The Methods and Materials of Demography*. Condensed edition by Edward G. Stockwell. New York: Academic Press.

Simons, Harmen, Laura Wong, Wendy Graham, and Susan Schkolnik. 1996. "Experience with the Sisterhood Method for Estimating Maternal Mortality." In Ian M. Timæs, Juan Chackiel, and Lado Ruzicka, eds., *Adult Mortality in Latin America*. Oxford: Clarendon Press.

Stolnitz, George J. 1982. "Mortality: Post-World War II Trends." In John A. Ross, ed., *International Encyclopedia of Population*. New York: The Free Press.

Tabah, Leon. 1980. "World Population Trends: A Stocktaking." *Population and Development Review* 6(3).

Taucher, Erica, Cecilia Albala, and Gloria Icaza. 1996. "Adult Mortality from Chronic Diseases in Chile, 1968–90." In Ian M. Timæs, Juan Chackiel, and Lado Ruzicka, eds., *Adult Mortality in Latin America*. Oxford: Clarendon Press.

UNFPA. 1999. "Women's Rights, Human Rights." *Populi* 26(1).

United Nations. 1973. *The Determinants and Consequences of Population Trends: New Summary of Findings on Interaction of Demographic, Economic and Social Factors*. Vol. 1. Population Studies series, no. 50. ST/SOA/SER.A/50. New York: United Nations.

———. 1992. "Chapter 6: Protecting and Promoting Human Health." In *Report on the United Nations Conference on Environment and Development*. A/CONF.151/26 (Vol. I). New York: United Nations.

———. 1995a. *World Population Prospects, 1994 Revision*. Population Studies series, no. 145: ST/ESA/SER.A/145. New York: United Nations.

———. 1995b. *Preparations for the Fourth World Conference on Women*. Commission on the Status of Women E/CN.6/1995/3/add.3. New York: United Nations.

———. 1998. *World Resources 1998–99*. A Report by the World Resources Institute. Oxford: Oxford University Press.

———. 1999. *Revision of the World Population Estimates and Projections, 1998 Briefing Packet*. New York: United Nations.

United States Bureau of the Census. 1960. *Historical Statistics of the United States, Colonial Times to 1957*. Washington, DC: Government Printing Office.

Vågerö, Denny, and Olle Lundberg. 1995. "Socio-economic Mortality Differentials among Adults in Sweden." In Alan D. Lopez et al., eds., *Adult Mortality in Developed Countries: From Description to Explanation*. Oxford: Clarendon Press.

Vallin, Jacques. 1991. "Mortality in Europe from 1720 to 1914: Long Term Trends and Changes in Patterns by Age and Sex." In Roger Schofield, David Reher, and Alain Bideau, eds., *The Decline of Mortality in Europe.* Oxford: Clarendon Press.

Vallin, Jacques, Stan D'Souza, and Alberto Palloni, eds. 1990. *Measurement and Analysis of Mortality: New Approaches.* Oxford: Clarendon Press.

Vallin, Jacques, and France Meslé. 1990. "The Causes of Death in France, 1925–1978: Reclassification according to the Eighth Revision of the International Classification of Diseases." In Jacques Vallin, Stan D'Souza, and Alberto Palloni, eds., *Measurement and Analysis of Mortality: New Approaches.* Oxford: Clarendon Press.

van de Walle, Francine. 1986. "Infant Mortality and the European Demographic Transition." In Ansley J. Coale and Susan Cotts Watkins, eds., *The Decline of Fertility in Europe.* Princeton, NJ: Princeton University Press.

WHO. 1998a. *World Health Report 1998: Executive Summary.* Geneva: World Health Organization.

———. 1998b. *Health in Europe 1997: Report on the Third Evaluation of Progress Towards Health for all in the European Region of WHO (1996–1997).* WHO Regional Publications, European Series, no. 83. Copenhagen: World Health Organization.

6

Morbidity and Health

"Morbidity" probably is not so familiar a term to most readers as are "fertility" or "mortality." Therefore, let us start with a tentative definition: *morbidity* refers to the prevailing condition of disease in a population. In this context, *disease* is being defined broadly, to include *disability* and *illness*. More specifically, morbidity refers to the *frequency* of disease, both its *incidence* (how diseases spread through a population over time) and its *prevalence* (how much disease is encountered in a population at a given moment). One can think of morbidity as the opposite of *health* in a living population.

Morbidity is closely related to mortality, but it is not the same. Disease and disability often do hasten death, but not always. Death often follows disease and disability, but sometimes occurs without them.

WHY DEMOGRAPHERS STUDY MORBIDITY

Let us recall the guiding questions for demography, introduced in chapter 1: How many people, of *what kind*, are where. . .? That is, demography is charged with studying not only population size, but also population *composition*. We already have treated two dimensions of composition in chapter 4: age and sex. These take priority in our text because they have such immediate impact on the population growth processes we are explaining. But what about morbidity; why does it enjoy prominence?

We begin with the most obvious reason: disease is universally abhorred. Any incidence or prevalence of disease in a society is a "problem," almost by definition. The societal stake in knowing the incidence and prevalence of undesired disease conditions is self-evident. In fact, the fields of demography and public health developed largely in tandem during Western modernization, motivated by a common purpose of improving the human condition, as that became more possible.

A second reason is the relation between morbidity and the population processes. The close relation between morbidity and mortality (and thus population growth) is only the most obvious. Disease and disability also affect the likelihood of successful childbearing, as well as marriage, divorce and widowhood, migration, and indeed most of the processes treated in this text.

MORBIDITY AND MORTALITY IN THE EPIDEMIOLOGICAL TRANSITION

Let us adopt, somewhat arbitrarily, the following terminology. *Epidemiology* is a branch of medical science that deals with the incidence, distribution, and control of disease in a population. The *epidemiological transition*, as that term is used by demographers, consists of both the familiar Western *mortality transition* described in chapter 5 and the parallel *morbidity transition* described here.

Sources of Data

Where do we get data on the morbidity transition? Since mortality data are more commonly available for historical populations than are data on health and morbidity, much of what we know about disease in past times comes from mortality trends and causes of death. Yet, as we have cautioned, it is a mistake to equate rates of mortality and morbidity. Mortality measures often understate the health impact of disease. Morbidity was as high as 55% during the 1720–1722 plague in France, while mortality was as low as 8% (Benedictow, 1987). Morbidity and mortality trends also can follow different paths: Alter and Riley (1988) found that morbidity in England increased during the period from 1840 to 1890 as mortality rates were falling. When nineteenth-century urban conditions in the United States improved, mortality declined but morbidity from infectious diseases, such as tuberculosis, continued long after (Preston and Haines, 1991).

Fortunately, mortality data are not our only sources to study historical health. Human populations leave behind many pieces of evidence regarding historical morbidity, including skeletal remains (e.g. Armelagos, 1990; Vargas, 1990), institutional records of health condition and physical stature (e.g. Fogel and Costa, 1997), diaries and personal accounts (e.g. Porter, 1993), records of physicians and clinics (Morel, 1977; Alter and Riley, 1988), newspapers and public health records (Rosenberg, 1987), and so on. From such sources we can derive measures of health (e.g. physical stature, frequency of epidemics, etc.) and often find accounts of morbidity and its causes (e.g. health behaviors, public works initiatives, diagnoses and treatments, etc.).

Historical evidence also reveals popular misconceptions and limitations in medical knowledge. Figure 6-1, for example, highlights the medical advice distributed in all New York City newspapers during the cholera epidemic of 1832. This advice reflects prevailing morality and mythology, but little real knowledge of the underlying causes of cholera. When reading historical accounts or using historical data one should bear in mind the limitations of knowledge and cultural biases of the time.

Figure 6-1   Cholera Advice of the New York City Medical Council, 1832

> ✣ *Notice* ✣
>
> *Be temperate* in eating and drinking,
>
> avoid crude *vegetables and fruits;*
>
> abstain from *cold water*, when heated;
>
> and above all from *ardent spirits* and
>
> if habit have rendered it indispensable, take much less than usual.
>
> *Sleep and clothe warm*
>
> Avoid labor in the heat of day.
>
> Do not sleep or sit in a draught of air when heated.
>
> *Avoid getting wet*
>
> Take no medicines without advice.

Source: Rosenberg, *The Cholera Years*, 1987, pg. 30.

Two Underlying Causes

From these scattered pieces of evidence it often is possible to gain a broad picture of historical health and morbidity. Recounting all we know would be an encyclopedic task. Instead, we will briefly mention two important historical morbidity issues that played a major role in the mortality decline and are of special interest to contemporary demographers: a) malnutrition and b) environmental hazards, especially contagion.

Malnutrition posed a major threat to the health of pretransition and transitional populations. Even where famine mortality was not apparent, health and behavior were affected in the years after food shortages (Outhwaite, 1991; Wrigley and Schofield, 1981). By some estimates, beggars constituted nearly a fifth of the population in premodern times (e.g. Cipolla, 1980; Laslett, 1983). More than a quarter of the English population of 1900 suffered the effects of poverty and hunger (Bowley and Burnett-Hurst, 1915). Physiological measurements, such as the height of military recruits, suggest that European populations at the beginning of the nineteenth century were chronically malnourished, and that risk of chronic disease may have been related to malnutrition among U.S. Civil War recruits half a century later (see Fogel and Costa, 1997). Nutritional deficiencies could, in turn, reduce resistance to infection and contributed to the frailty and poor health of historical populations (Swedlund and Armelagos, 1990; Rotberg and Rabb, 1985).

Contagion played a dominant role in the urbanizing societies. Infectious diseases had a greater chance of passing from one individual to the next in densely settled urban areas (Preston and Haines, 1991). Tuberculosis, for example, is spread by respiratory contact (e.g. sneezing, coughing) and was one of the top two urban causes of death in the nineteenth century (Olshansky et al., 1997). Dense urban areas with inadequate sanitation and clean water also generated breeding grounds for waterborne diseases such as cholera, typhoid, or diphtheria.

Cholera, virtually nonexistent in rural areas, was a major disease in nineteenth-century urban centers (Olshansky et al., 1997; Rosenberg, 1987). In a pioneering urban health study of 1855, John Snow (1965) mapped cases of a cholera epidemic in London only to discover a single contaminated well was responsible for nearly 500 deaths (see Figure 6-2). Removing the pump handle ended the epidemic and proved a turning point in understanding urban infectious disease.

Contagion was not the only environmental threat to health in crowded and rapidly growing urban areas. By the middle of the nineteenth century, demographers were studying the connections between poverty, urban life, and health (Cassedy, 1986). Despite the growing awareness of urban health issues, conditions in emerging cities and towns often did not improve until population growth and rapid development slowed, allowing public health services to keep pace with urban growth (Hautaniemi et al., 1999; Szreter, 1997).

Figure 6-2 Cholera Fatalities and Water Sources in London, 1854

Note: The pump causing the epidemic is marked just below the "D" in Broad Street.
Source: Snow, *Snow on Cholera*, 1965 reprint.

Infant and Child Health

Just as demographers have a particular interest in infant mortality (see chapter 5), so do they in infant and child morbidity. Again, we find that the earliest years of life are particularly vulnerable, not only to death but also to disease. By the same token, morbidity in these years is most susceptible to transitional change with modernization.

The causes of improving infant and child health from the late eighteenth to the early twentieth century are still hotly contested. Nutrition likely played a major role and has been argued to be the major influence on improving health (McKeown, 1976). More recent studies, however, have suggested that improved nutrition and access to other material resources were not major influences, or improved health only where conditions had been very unhealthy (Preston and Haines, 1991; Reid, 1997). As we have seen, eighteenth- and nineteenth-century cities were such harsh environments, with elevated levels of respiratory and summer diarrheal diseases among children (Schofield and Reher, 1991; Preston and Haines, 1991; Woods, 1993).

Preston and Haines (1991) among others (e.g. Corsini and Viazzo, 1997; Schofield et al., 1991) argue that health knowledge and practices played a major role in improved urban infant and child health. Specific practices reduced specific diseases. Hygiene in the home, such as breast-feeding infants or heating often-contaminated milk before bottle feeding, eventually reduced summer diarrheal diseases. New medical developments such as diphtheria antitoxin limited other diseases.

Historical health studies from the now more-developed countries have greatly influenced contemporary policies in less-developed countries (Corsini and Viazzo, 1997). As we shall learn, less-developed countries face many of the same health problems pre-transition MDRs did, even as they confront ominous new health threats.

MODERN MORBIDITY DATA

Even in the more-developed regions, morbidity data-gathering is difficult to standardize. This springs partially from the difficulty in defining morbid conditions. Whereas the major demographic processes are defined by specific events—births, deaths, moves across borders—such clarity does not attend the onset and departure of disease. Moreover, the very identification of a health condition (e.g. arthritis) as a "disease" is often ambiguous, even changing over time in the same country. Finally, the extreme variety in the time sequence followed by the various diseases makes it difficult to settle on a single monitoring system.

Nevertheless, the public concern over health that has accompanied economic development is generating a growing body of morbidity data. These data, however, are varied in source and difficult to interpret, relative to other demographic data. Three categories of sources are described in the following sections: 1) surveillance systems and registries, 2) health surveys, and 3) cause-of-death reports.

Surveillance Systems and Registries

When a particular disease becomes widespread or otherwise alarming to the medical community, it can be defined a *reportable disease* and trigger a surveillance effort. *Surveillance systems* are established to estimate the size of a health problem, detect epidemic outbreaks, characterize disease trends, and determine the necessary public health measures to respond. Local authorities are typically charged with collecting data on new cases of disease and reporting these to a central, or national, organization that monitors, reports, and reacts to epidemic outbreaks or health threats.

The World Health Organization maintains several disease surveillance systems for reporting countries. These systems include the 142 WHO country offices, 110 national influenza centers forming FLUNET, a network of national rabies reference centers forming RABNET, and more than 60 HIV sentinel surveillance sites, among others. WHO chronicles weekly outbreaks and reported cases of specific diseases in the *Weekly Epidemiological Record*.

In the United States, most surveillance systems are overseen by the Centers for Disease Control. CDC maintains surveillance systems for such conditions as birth defects, HIV/AIDS, sexually transmitted diseases, tuberculosis, waterborne disease outbreaks, and so on. The CDC reports weekly outbreaks and the occurrence of reportable diseases in the *Morbidity and Mortality Weekly Report*.

Some health conditions are chronic or terminal, lasting either for long periods or until death. In such cases, disease *registries* may be set up to monitor the progress of known cases, demographic and diagnostic details, treatments, and so forth. Registries often are maintained at a local or state level with support from central governments. Since registries are expensive and difficult to maintain, they usually are established only for diseases of great medical research concern.

In the United States, the best example of a disease registry program is that for cancer, maintained by state and territorial health departments. The National Cancer Institute's Surveillance, Epidemiology and End Results (SEER) program maintains registers of cancer occurrence, treatment, and survival in five states and six metropolitan areas of the United States. The CDC provides support and standards for registries in the forty-five states and territories not covered by the SEER program. Together, these registries provide morbidity data on all cases undergoing treatment.

Health Surveys

Surveillance systems and registries, however, track only diseases prominent enough to be defined as "reportable." A far more inclusive source of morbidity data is a health survey (Gray, 1989). Since 1984 the U.S. Agency for International Development has funded a series of *Demographic and Health Surveys* (DHS+) for samples of residents in over 100 countries throughout the world. These surveys collect information on family planning, maternal and child health, AIDS/STDs, and the like. Additional surveys are often circulated by national and local governments. In the United States, the *National Health Interview Survey, National Survey of Maternal and Infant Health*, and *National Survey of Family Growth* are just a few of the many quality surveys that provide detailed demographic and health information (see chapter 2, Figure 2-4). Repetitive health surveys have the potential for generating surveillance systems; such systems, of course, can monitor a broad array of health conditions, not just a few prominent reportable diseases.

Cause-of-Death Reports

As we said in chapter 5, vital statistics systems normally report not only the fact of death and facts about the victim, but also the cause of death. The value of cause-of-death reports for the study of morbidity was enhanced greatly by enriching the reporting of *multiple causes* of death. In 1949 the sixth revision of the *International Statistical Classification of Diseases, Injuries and Causes of Death* was modified to recommend recording of the immediate cause of death, intervening or intermediate causes, the underlying cause of death, and a list of other unrelated but contributing causes (Hetzel, 1997). Tabulations by underlying causes of death were adopted the same year internationally and in the United States. Underlying causes reveal the initial health problem that started the chain of events eventually leading to death, rather than the "final straw" or immediate cause. Analyses of the multiple causes recorded in death certificates can provide a fairly detailed picture of the morbidity events leading up to mortality. Methods for analyzing such complex data are, however, in need of further development and the quality of this detailed data varies widely (Nam, 1990).

Morbidity data have improved dramatically. However, the quality of data still varies greatly between more-developed and less-developed countries, and by the severity of the specific medical conditions involved. In all countries, many individuals suffer from illness or poor health that goes unreported or unrecorded; many suffer from health impairments such as arthritis or malnourishment, but regard these as normal conditions of life rather than ill health. Because of the uneven development of national health monitoring systems, much of the data reported in this chapter for less-developed countries are only estimates from surveys or sample reporting areas.

MEASURING MORBIDITY

With adequate data from surveillance systems, there are a variety of measures that can be used to assess morbidity, defined as the frequency of disease. In earlier chapters we've discussed crude rates and age-sex-specific birth and death rates. Such rates measure the frequency of *events* in a population at risk of the event. Disease, however, is not simply an event nor as clearly defined as birth and death. A person can become ill suddenly or gradually. The illness may be reported or may never be reported. One disease may kill suddenly while another may last over a considerable period of time without mortality.

Morbidity Rates

First, let us consider how to compute simple rates for the occurrence or incidence of morbidity. Since the onset of morbidity is not always observed, the best we can do is to consider a *reported diagnosis*, which may occur well after the onset, of the event we wish to measure. With this provision, a similar approach to birth and death rates can be used in measuring the levels of morbidity in a population; we can compute a rate at which people are diagnosed with the illness. The numerator of this rate would be the number of *newly reported cases* of the condition in a given period (usually a year). The denominator would be the *population at risk* of getting the illness during the same time period. This measure is called the *incidence rate*, that is:

$$\text{Incidence Rate} = \frac{\text{Number of New Cases}}{\text{Population at Risk}}$$

Once persons are diagnosed with a condition they are no longer at risk of being *newly* diagnosed cases (until they have a full recovery and reenter the population at risk), but they may live for any number of years afterward with the condition. Thus in the incidence rate, the *population at risk* of new incidence is not simply the population remaining alive, but those who have not been previously diagnosed with the condition. That is, the incidence rate measures the new incidence of a condition among the population not previously diagnosed with the condition. Since incidence rates measure new cases of morbidity, they are especially useful in detecting epidemic outbreaks and changes over time in the occurrence of morbidity. However, they do not tell us how prevalent the morbidity condition is at any given time.

To measure prevalence, we use a more familiar sort of rate, the *prevalence rate*, which is simply the number of people with a morbidity condition divided by the total population.

$$\text{Prevalence Rate} = \frac{\text{Number of All Cases}}{\text{Total Population}}$$

Both incidence and prevalence rates may be computed for age-sex-specific groups to reveal the age and sex patterns of morbidity. Both rates are often multiplied by 1,000 to express the rate per 1,000 people (at risk or total), but the denomination chosen can vary with the size of the numerator.

Because we have two common measures of morbidity frequency, it is important to remember that they measure two very different things. Since the incidence rate measures new cases, instead of all cases, it will usually understate the prevalence or level of morbidity in a population. Conversely, a prevalence rate will generally overstate the incidence in the population because it includes all cases rather than only new cases. There are exceptions to these expectations. If diseases have a short duration and commonly occur, such as diarrheal diseases, they will not remain prevalent in a population but might have a very high incidence. Incidence and prevalence rates provide different information, and it is important not to confuse them.

Incidence and Prevalence of Leading Morbidity Causes

Incidence and prevalence rates for the twelve leading worldwide causes of morbidity, and for selected other infectious diseases, in 1997 are presented in columns 2 and 3 of Table 6-1. Death rates for the same causes are given in column 1. These rates are estimates from countries reporting to the World Health Organization and WHO sample reporting areas (see chapter 2). The "leading causes of morbidity" are chosen and ranked on the basis of incidence rate.

Aside from the substantive morbidity information it provides, Table 6-1 allows us to contrast the various rates. For instance, diarrhea is the leading cause of global morbidity, with an incidence rate of nearly seven episodes for every ten persons. How-

Table 6-1
Incidence, Prevalence, and Deaths from Leading Morbidity Causes and Other Infectious Diseases, World, 1997

	Rates Per 100,000		
	Deaths (1)	Incidence (2)	Prevalence (3)
Leading Causes of Morbidity			
Diarrhea	42.1	68,575.3	...
Malaria	36.0	6857.5	...
Acute Lower Respiratory Infection	64.2	6771.8	...
Occupational Injuries	5.7	4286.0	428.6
Occupational Diseases	...	3720.2	342.9
Trichomoniasis	...	2914.5	1937.3
Mood (Affective) Disorders	...	2106.4	5828.9
Chlamydia	...	1525.8	1457.2
Hepatitis B	10.4	1161.2	...
Gonococcus	...	1062.9	394.3
Amoebiasis	1.2	822.9	...
Whooping Cough (Pertussis)	7.0	772.3	...
Selected Other Infectious Diseases			
Tuberculosis	49.9	124.3	279.4
HIV/AIDS	39.4	99.4	524.6
Measles	16.5	532.7	...
Tetanus	4.7	7.1	...
Dengue Hemorrhagic Fever	2.4	53.1	...

Notes: Data are for WHO reporting countries and sample areas. Midrange values are reported for interval estimates, and prevalence of occupational injuries and diseases includes only persons with severe activity limitation.
... means not applicable or not available.
Source: WHO, World Health Report 1998, 1998, tables 3, 4, and B.

ever, since this disease can be very short-lived, individuals could have had more than one episode during the year. The incidence rate does not imply that seven of every ten *persons* had an episode. Moreover, given the tremendous incidence of diarrheal diseases, the death rate is relatively low, showing that diarrhea, although a major cause of morbidity, is not as lethal per episode as are many other leading causes of morbidity. Malaria, for instance, has a much lower incidence rate, but the death rate from malaria is nearly as high as that for diarrhea.

Other morbidity causes may last a very long time yet not directly cause death, resulting in high rates of prevalence but low rates of either death or incidence. Mood disorders, for example, usually are neither readily cured nor lethal. As a result, the prevalence rate for mood disorders is much higher than their incidence rate. In contrast, gonococcus is often cured in a short span of time, resulting in a much higher incidence than prevalence.

Let us turn briefly from methodology to the substantive implications of the table. An obvious conclusion is the continued importance of infectious diseases on a worldwide level. The three leading causes of global morbidity, ranked by incidence rates (diarrhea, malaria, and acute lower respiratory infections) all are infectious diseases. In fact, only two of the leading causes listed (i.e. occupational injuries and mood disorders) are not infectious or parasitic diseases. Moreover, there are other infectious diseases shown at the bottom of the table which, while having lower incidence rates, have substantial prevalence or death rates. Tuberculosis and HIV/AIDS, for example, have mortality impacts about as great as the three leading causes of morbidity, but these deaths came from a much lower incidence of new cases. That is, tuberculosis and HIV/AIDS are more lethal than the leading causes of morbidity but are contracted by fewer people.

Age and Sex Patterns of Morbidity

In the less-developed countries, before their epidemiological transitions, epidemic diseases dominate as the ultimate cause of death. Generally speaking, these diseases are particularly dangerous for women and children, although age and sex patterns of morbidity differ from one disease to the next. This may be partially due to the unequal distribution of those underlying conditions that allow infectious diseases, e.g. poor nutrition and contagious conditions. Whatever the reason, examples of the imbalance abound: incidence and prevalence rates of both leading causes of world morbidity, i.e. diarrheal diseases and malaria, are more than six times higher among children under four years of age than at any older age (Murray and Lopez, 1996b). The incidence of acute lower respiratory infections is limited to children under four and slightly higher for female children.

The more-developed regions, where degenerative diseases predominate, generally have the opposite age and sex pattern. Ischaemic heart disease, one of the leading causes of worldwide mortality, for example, has an incidence rate over age sixty that is more than six times higher, and a prevalence rate more than three times higher, than in any younger age group (Murray and Lopez, 1996b). Cerebrovascular disease occurs only at older ages, with a prevalence rate for those aged sixty or older that is more than three times higher than for those between forty-five and sixty years of age. Males have much higher incidence and prevalence rates for these causes, with the male prevalence rate for cerebrovascular disease nearly twice that of females.

The obvious inference is that, over the course of the epidemiological transition, incidence and prevalence of morbidity have generally declined among women and children and have increased among men and older ages. The evidence supports this as a generalization, although age and sex patterns of morbidity do differ from one disease to the next.

The general shift in age and sex morbidity patterns over the course of the transition does not, however, mean that older people spend more time ill than younger people. A lower respiratory infection in a child may lead to a lifetime of illness while an older person with ischaemic heart disease could have a very short period of morbidity before death. Comparisons of mortality, incidence, and prevalence rates provide a great deal of information, but there are important questions these rates do not directly answer.

MORBIDITY PROBLEMS: COSTS OF LOST LIFE AND HEALTH

Our self-imposed exercise when defining population "problems" is to ask: Who is alarmed? What effects do these people see springing from the problematic trend or condition? What do they judge to be wrong with those effects? When dealing with morbidity problems, however, such questions seem superfluous. The negative evaluation of disease and disability seems universal, not requiring rational elaboration or justification. So demographers quickly turn to the problem of measuring the *degree* of the negative impact. Many of these costs, such as anguish, lost opportunities, or suffering, are difficult or impossible to measure. We all know what it is to feel *pain*, for example, but there is no scientific way to measure it. Demographers can, however, provide some answers to more limited questions concerning the personal and social costs of ill health.

Years of Life Lost

Using a life table, for example, we can estimate how many more years people might have lived if they had not died from a particular illness or cause (see chapter 5). When a person dies at age x he or she fails to live out the average remaining lifetime, e_x, for other persons of that same age. If we sum all these years of life lost to those who died from a specific cause we would have the *total cause-specific years of life lost*, or YLL, to deaths from that cause:

$$YLL = \text{Sum of } e_x \text{ for all Deaths From a Cause}$$

The total YLL gives us a picture of the cost to society in lost years-lived from deaths due to a given cause. If we divide this total by the number of people dying from the cause, we would get the *average cause-specific years of life lost* to deaths from that cause. The average YLL tells us the average personal cost in lost years-lived for those who die from the cause.

Variations on the strategy are possible. Where data are limited, we might simplify the calculation of YLL by assuming all individuals are expected to live an average life expectancy at birth, e_o, or by setting some arbitrarily high potential life expectancy (Murray and Lopez, 1996a). To emphasize *productive* years of life lost we might count only years of life lost up to an expected retirement age, e.g. sixty-five years old (Anderton et al., 1997).

Reliable data to compute YLL are difficult to obtain in many parts of the world. As part of a path-finding and ambitious effort by the World Health Organization and the World Bank to study the *Global Burden of Disease*, Murray and Lopez (1996) used statistical models to estimate years of life lost to specific causes throughout the world. Figure 6-3 gives these estimates for the percentage of years of life lost due to twelve leading causes of death and premature death in the world. The causes are listed in order of the percentage of deaths they are responsible for, also shown in the graph.

Comparing deaths to years of life lost from these leading causes shows a basic fact of morbidity. Infectious diseases, accidents, and conditions that occur early in life account for a far greater percentage of YLL than of deaths. Conversely, those conditions which cause high mortality concentrated in the older population, e.g. heart, cerebrovascular, and chronic obstructive pulmonary diseases, account for a far greater

Figure 6-3   Percentage of Deaths and Years of Life Lost to Leading Causes, World, 1990

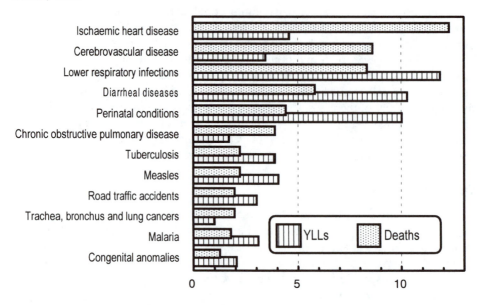

Source: Murray and Lopez, *The Global Burden of Disease*, 1996a, figure 10.

percentage of deaths than years of life lost. In developing countries a young population structure (see chapter 4) with a high prevalence of infectious disease deaths (see chapter 5) results in a very high number of life-years lost.

Years of Health Lost

Years of life lost tell us how much life is lost due to premature death. But, strictly speaking, that is a measure of the cost of mortality, not morbidity. Where detailed survey data can be had, we can ask how long a person has suffered from ill health due to a particular cause, what medical resources he or she required, how disabled he or she was during the illness, and so on. The *National Health Interview Survey* collects this sort of data for the population of the United States. But in areas without detailed surveys, as in many developing countries, we have to estimate morbidity impacts indirectly. Some of these complex estimation procedures are described below.

Episodes of ill health differ in their *duration* and also in their degree of *disability*, i.e. the severity of limits they place on going about our normal lives. Missing a day of school from a nasty cold, something we've probably all experienced, is an example of short duration with minimal disability. In other cases, which we hope not to experience, morbidity is long-term, very disabling, and life-threatening.

Let us deal with duration first. Suppose, for example, that we have medical data telling us the average incident of tuberculosis lasts for 2.1 years (Murray and Lopez,

1996b, table 10). If we multiply the reported occurrences of tuberculosis by this average duration, we get a crude estimate of how many years will be spent with this disability.

But to what extent were those people disabled during this time? If we knew a particular disease let a person do only half of his or her normal activities, we might estimate that for each year that person had the disease, half of a healthy year was lost to ill health. A person who was completely disabled would have lost the entire year to ill health. This sort of calculation is called—perhaps gracelessly—*quality adjusted life-years*, or QALY.

Using a basically similar but more complex calculation, the *Global Burden of Disease* project estimated years of life lived with, and lost to, health disabilities of known severity and duration (Murray and Lopez, 1996a). This measure is called the *years lived with disability*, or YLD. Stated as a general formula,

$$YLD = \text{occurrences} \times \text{duration} \times \text{disability}$$

Given a much higher morbidity in less-developed regions of the world, it is not surprising that those regions account for most of the world's years lived with disability (i.e. 84.1%). The estimated percentage distribution of YLD by region and age group are shown in Figure 6-4. This figure shows that nearly half of the years lived with dis-

Figure 6-4   Percentage Distribution of Years Lived With Disability, by World Development Region and Age, 1990

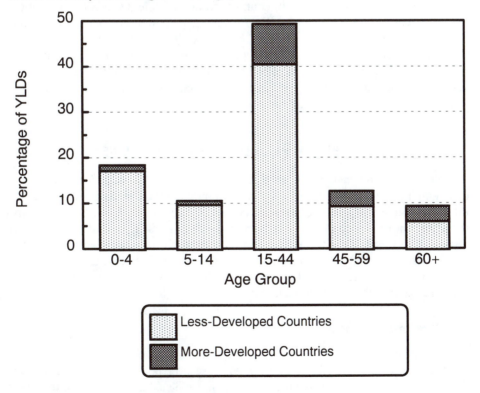

Source: Murray and Lopez, *The Global Burden of Disease*, 1996a, table 4.11.

ability are within the highly productive working ages of fifteen to forty-four. Yet morbidity of infants and children under age fifteen in less-developed countries causes more than a quarter of worldwide YLD, almost double the total years lived with disability in more-developed countries.

Years of Life and Health Lost

To measure the total loss of healthy life from disability during morbidity episodes and from resulting mortality, we can add together the YLD and YLL for a given cause. Murray and Lopez (1996a) labeled this sum of all years lost to morbidity causes the *disability adjusted life-years lost*, or DALY.

$$DALY = YLD + YLL$$

Disability adjusted life-years lost gives a total picture of morbidity and mortality impacts due to specific causes. That is, one DALY represents one lost year of healthy living whether from disability or from death. (The statistical procedures Murray and Lopez used to *estimate* DALY worldwide were considerably more complex.)

Not surprisingly, in the more-developed countries, noncommunicable and degenerative diseases cause the greatest loss of healthy life (see Table 6-2, column 1). Over half of the DALYs are due to psychiatric, cardiovascular, and cancer morbidity in the more-developed countries. In contrast, communicable diseases and conditions related to children or childbearing (i.e. maternal, perinatal, and nutritional conditions) cause the greatest loss of healthy life in less-developed countries (column 2). Over a fourth of all DALYs in less-developed countries are due to infectious and parasitic diseases. The biggest differences between the MDRs and LDRs in terms of loss of healthy life are explained by the major shift from infectious diseases to degenerative diseases over the epidemiological transition.

MORBIDITY PROBLEMS: RISK FACTORS

It is our habit in this text to define "problems" as unwanted *consequences* of demographic facts. In this chapter, we wish to broaden the discussion to include the immediate underlying *causes* of those facts, that is, morbidity *risk factors*. Partially this is because morbidity conditions are themselves so universally devalued that we can assume a universal desire to minimize them. Partially it is because such risk factors are so closely associated with unwanted morbidity conditions that the factors themselves share the negative social evaluation; malnutrition, for instance, is considered bad, irrespective of its morbidity consequences.

Relative Importance

To compare the worldwide importance of major categories of risk factors, let us employ the measures introduced in the previous section: percent of deaths, of years of life lost, of years lived with disability, and disability adjusted life-years lost to the factor. These measures are presented for the ten major categories of risk factor in Table 6-3.

Table 6-2

Percentage of Disability Adjusted Life-Years Lost Due to Specific Morbidity Causes by World Region, 1990

Morbidity Cause	More-Developed Countries (1)	Less-Developed Countries (2)	World (3)
Communicable, maternal, perinatal and nutritional	7.8	48.7	43.9
Infectious and parasitic diseases	2.7	25.6	22.9
Respiratory infections	1.6	9.4	8.5
Perinatal period conditions	1.9	7.3	6.7
Nutritional deficiencies	0.9	4.1	3.7
Maternal conditions	0.6	2.4	2.2
Noncommunicable diseases	77.7	36.1	40.9
Neuro-psychiatric conditions	22.0	9.0	10.5
Cardiovascular diseases	20.4	8.3	9.7
Malignant neoplasms	13.7	4.0	5.1
Respiratory diseases	4.8	4.3	4.4
Digestive diseases	4.4	3.3	3.4
Congenital anomalies	2.2	2.4	2.4
Musculo-skeletal diseases	4.3	1.0	1.4
Genito-urinary diseases	1.3	1.1	1.1
Sense organ diseases	0.1	0.8	0.8
Diabetes mellitus	1.9	0.7	0.8
Oral conditions	0.8	0.5	0.5
Other neoplasms	0.8	0.2	0.3
Injuries	14.5	15.2	15.1
Unintentional	10.3	11.1	11.0
Intentional	4.2	4.1	4.1
All Causes	100.0	100.0	100.0

Source: Murray and Lopez, *The Global Burden of Disease*, 1996a, table 5.1.

The leading cause of lost healthy life in the world remains malnutrition, followed by environmental hazards such as poor water supply and sanitation. Malnutrition is responsible for the greatest percentage of disability adjusted life-years lost (DALYs). The lost healthy life malnutrition causes is largely due to years of life lost (YLLs), or deaths caused. The same is true for environmental hazards. Both of these causes disproportionately affect children and infants of less-developed countries.

Of the remaining risk factors in Table 6-3, many reflect unhealthy lifestyles, such as unsafe sex, tobacco and alcohol consumption, inactivity, drug use, etc. These risks weigh heavily on adults and young adults in more-developed countries, but some also are major threats in less-developed countries. Unsafe sex and tobacco use, for example, are major health problems in MDRs but cause a much greater loss of life in LDRs (see chapter 5). The same is true of injuries, intentional and unintentional (see Table

Table 6-3
Morbidity and Mortality Attributable to Major Risk Factors, World, 1990

Risk Factor	Percent of Deaths Caused (1)	Percent of Years of Life Lost (YLL) (2)	Percent of Years Lived Disabled (YLD) (3)	Percent of Disability Adjusted Life-Years Lost (DALY) (4)
Malnutrition	11.7	22.0	4.2	15.9
Poor Water, Sanitation, and Hygiene	5.3	9.4	1.7	6.8
Unsafe Sex	2.2	3.0	4.5	3.5
Tobacco	6.0	2.9	2.1	2.6
Alcohol	1.5	2.1	6.0	3.5
Occupation	2.2	2.5	3.3	2.7
Hypertension	5.8	1.9	0.3	1.4
Physical Inactivity	3.9	1.3	0.5	1.0
Illicit Drugs	0.2	0.3	1.2	0.6
Air Pollution	1.1	0.6	0.3	0.5

Source: Murray and Lopez, *The Global Burden of Disease,* 1996, table 5.

6-2). These lifestyle risk factors are the major problems in more-developed regions because morbidity from infectious and parasitic diseases, malnutrition, and unhealthy environments has been reduced.

Because many morbidity causes and health risks are shared by MDRs and LDRs, we will not, as in most other chapters, sharply divide our discussion of health problems by the development dichotomy. Instead, we will discuss health problems in a sort of general progression, from those which are most concentrated and severe in LDRs, to those which are shared health concerns, ending with those which are most concentrated in MDRs. This progression also roughly parallels the historical importance of morbidity problems over the epidemiological transition experienced by MDRs.

Malnutrition

Nutritional morbidity is best identified by its universal consequence, physical growth deficiencies in children (Onis et al., 1999). Figure 6-5 shows the prevalence of children in less-developed countries who suffer from malnutrition, as evidenced by being underweight, stunted, or wasting. Malnutrition is worst in Asia, where more than four of every ten children are underweight and nearly half of all children are stunted. Combining the less-developed regions, roughly four of every ten children are underweight, more than four of every ten are stunted, and nearly one of every ten are wasting. LDRs have yet to experience the broadly improved nutrition that characterized the epidemiological transition in the MDRs.

Figure 6-5 Prevalence of Malnutrition Morbidity, Less-Developed Regions, 1992

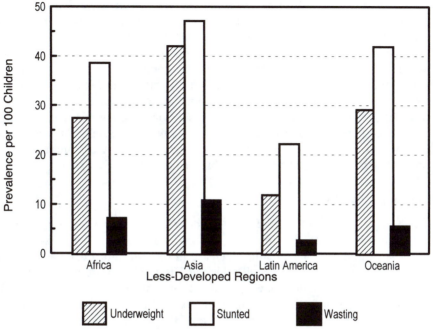

Source: WHO, *The Worldwide Magnitude of Protein-Energy Malnutrition*, 1992, table 3.

Environmental Health

Table 6-3 tells us that poor water, sanitation, and hygiene combined are second only to malnutrition as morbidity risk factors. Population density historically has contributed to all of these environmental deficits and, through them, to more immediate causes of death. Infectious diseases continue to plague densely settled areas with inadequate public health services. Cholera, for example, is an ongoing threat in developing countries, especially in times of crisis or natural disaster, where sanitation and fresh water supplies are inadequate. Olshansky et al. (1997) also point out that new or emergent diseases, such as dengue hemorrhagic fever in the 1980s, and sexually transmitted diseases such as HIV/AIDS, chlamydia, and gonorrhea, also flourish in LDR areas of population density.

Environmental health concerns associated with density are again, generally, worst in rapidly growing urban centers of the LDRs (see chapter 10). Over half of the urban population in less-developed countries live in extreme conditions of deprivation, with 2.9 billion people lacking access to adequate sanitation and 1.1 billion lacking access to safe water supplies (WHO, 1997). Less-developed countries have not had the same broad improvements in urban environments that characterized many MDRs during their epidemiological transitions (WHO, 1997).

Infant and Child Morbidity

Malnutrition and unhealthy environments are especially burdensome to the health of infants and children in the LDRs (see chapter 5). However, the past two decades have seen some considerable improvements. Two public health campaigns played major roles in reducing morbidity among children: First, immunization against six major diseases (measles, tuberculosis, diphtheria, whooping cough, tetanus, and polio) increased from 20% of the world's children in 1981 to 80% in 1995 (Gelbard et al., 1999). Second, a treatment for diarrheal disease—oral rehydration therapy—has been used in about 80% of episodes over the past decade, preventing millions of additional deaths (Gelbard et al., 1999). Nevertheless, these diseases remain major health threats—and the rising threat of HIV/AIDS among children threatens to negate the gains from these public health campaigns.

Unhealthy Lifestyles

The major sources of morbidity in more-developed countries are degenerative diseases and other health risks that are artifacts of human activity; less-developed countries also have seen a premature increase in these health threats as they have begun their mortality declines. Specifically, the HIV/AIDS and tobacco pandemics clearly are related to lifestyle behaviors—unsafe sex or illicit drug use (the major, but not the only, sources of HIV infection) and smoking. Both epidemics cause not only death but significant morbidity. Morbidity from HIV/AIDS is currently projected to reach a global peak around 2005 while tobacco morbidity is projected to increase into the foreseeable future, causing more disability adjusted life-years lost than any other single disease worldwide by the year 2010.

Obesity is another example of lifestyle-related health risks in MDRs (WHO, 1998). It is also a problem in some less-developed countries with aging populations. One of every two people in the Russian Federation and the United Kingdom, for example, is overweight (i.e. body mass index greater than 25), as is more than one of every four persons in Sweden and Colombia and more than one of every three persons in Brazil and Costa Rica (WHO, 1998). Obesity is a direct cause of disability and, more importantly, is a major contributing factor for heart disease and other degenerative diseases.

Injuries

Injuries result from human activities such as automobile accidents, dangerous occupations, and firearm use and abuse. Resulting morbidity is considered a major health problem, especially in MDRs, for two reasons: First, many of these risks are clearly preventable. Second, younger people are particularly at risk, so the years of life lost are magnified.

The significance of injuries is apparent in Figure 6-6, which shows the years of life lost (YLL) per 100,000 population due to injury, compared with cancer and heart disease, in several more-developed countries (Rockett, 1998). In the United States, injuries are responsible for more years of life lost than cancer or heart disease com-

Figure 6-6   Years of Life Lost (Before Age 65) Due to Injuries, Cancer, and Heart Disease in Six More-Developed Countries, 1993

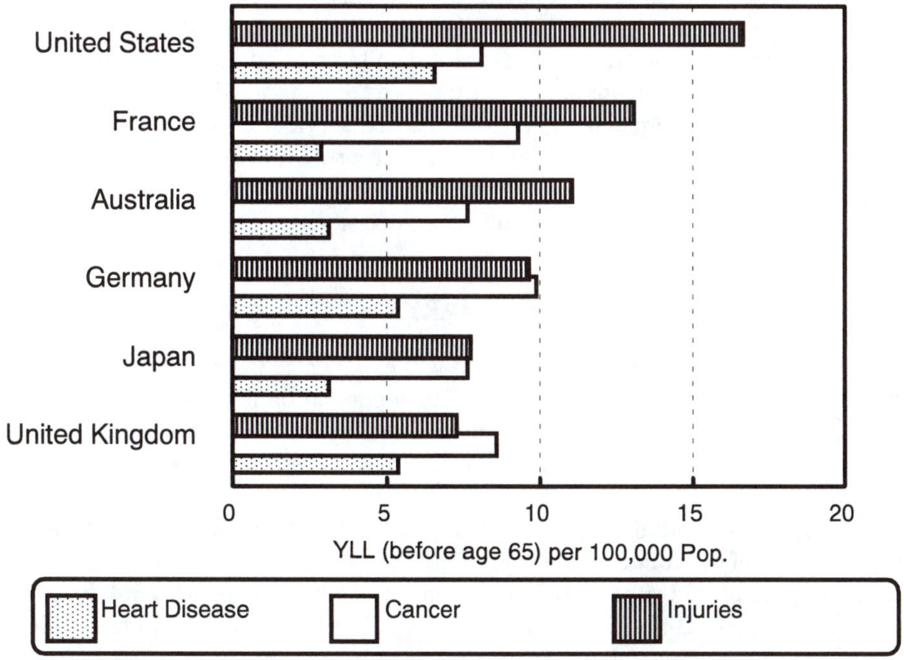

YLL (before age 65) per 100,000 Pop.

Heart Disease   Cancer   Injuries

Source: Rockett, *Injury and Violence*, 1998, adapted from p. 13.

bined, even though the mortality rate from injuries is only one-fifth that of heart disease and one-third that of cancer. Eliminating only injury mortality in the United States would add more than two years to male life expectancy at birth (Rockett, 1998). Injuries result in morbidity losses similar to those for the leading causes of death in all the more-developed countries listed in Figure 6-6.

Frail Old Age

We have seen (in chapter 4) that populations age as fertility and old-age mortality decline. As we suggested in the last chapter, it is difficult to call increasing life expectancy a "problem." However, the growing percentage of the world's population that is very old (sometimes called "grandevity") does raise morbidity concerns. According to United Nations projections, the number of people over eighty years of age will increase by more than 560% by 2050. Nonagenarians (90–99 years of age) are projected to increase by about 780%, and the number of centenarians (100 plus years old) will increase by about 220% (1999).

These growing groups of oldsters also are the most likely to experience degenerative diseases and disability. A third of the U.S. population over age seventy-five, for example, reported they were not in good health, and over a fifth of those over age eighty-five required nursing home care in 1992 (Anderton et al., 1997). Grandevity also can mean that an individual is more likely to require medical services. For example, in the United States in 1992, residents over seventy-five years of age spent more than four times as many days (per 1,000 people) in hospitals as did those of working age and more than ten times as many days as did children (Anderton et al., 1997).

The morbidity and attendant health care needs that come with very old age are largely responsible for the much higher cost of social services for those over age seventy-five in the MDRs (chapter 5). Many MDRs have said they soon will not be able to meet these needs (WHO, 1998). Morbidity among those who achieve grandevity will force, and has already forced, difficult policy decisions.

SUMMARY

Almost everyone has experienced, and will experience, the personal costs of ill health and morbidity during his or her life. Every population bears significant social costs from morbidity, and ill health can affect virtually all other demographic behaviors. Not surprisingly, then, morbidity historically has been of considerable interest to demographers.

Key aspects of morbidity include the *severity* of disabilities caused by the condition, the *duration* of the condition, the age of morbidity incidence, and the chances the condition will result in death. These dimensions of ill health suggest several different ways to measure morbidity, each of which captures different aspects of morbidity. *Incidence rates* tell us how frequently new cases are reported among those at risk of developing or contracting the condition in a given period of time. *Prevalence rates* measure what proportion of a population currently has the morbid condition.

Other measures estimate the costs of morbidity. *Years of life lost* (YLL) reflects the effects of a condition on life expectancy, the number of years we might have expected persons to live if they had not experienced the condition. *Years lived with disability* (YLD) is a measurement that combines the effects of severity, duration, and incidence to measure the loss of healthy life to morbidity during a person's lifetime. The sum of life-years lost to mortality and years lived with disability is called the *disability adjusted life-years lost* (DALY).

The three leading causes of worldwide morbidity incidence are diarrhea, malaria, and acute lower respiratory infections. These are all infectious diseases such as those which characterized MDRs prior to their epidemiological transitions. Infectious diseases, accidents, and other conditions which occur early in life account for a far greater percentage of years of life lost to morbidity than they do of all deaths. Noncommunicable diseases that are concentrated in the older population, on the other hand, account for a far greater percentage of deaths than of years of life lost.

The major causes of morbidity in more-developed and in less-developed countries reflect the extent of their epidemiological transition and the decline of infectious diseases. Communicable diseases and conditions related to infancy or childbearing are responsible for the greatest loss of healthy life, or DALYs, in less-developed countries. Noncommunicable and degenerative diseases cause the greatest loss of healthy life in more-developed countries and are rapidly increasing in many less-developed countries. Over the course of the epidemiological transition, as infectious diseases decline and degenerative ones rise, the age-sex incidence of morbidity also changes, with morbidity among women and children generally falling as morbidity among older males increases.

Prior to the epidemiological transition, the greatest *underlying* influences on levels of MDR morbidity were nutrition and hazardous urban environments. These two factors are still the greatest underlying causes of worldwide morbidity and ill health. Moreover, as in the MDRs prior to their transition, these morbidity threats bear especially hard upon women, infants, and children. The experience of the MDRs may provide greater knowledge of health and hygienic practices that might help speed the epidemiological transitions in some less-developed countries. For example, widespread vaccination and specific medical training programs have given LDRs advantages that MDRs did not have. The HIV/AIDS and tobacco pandemics are, however, significant challenges to transitions underway in many less-developed countries.

In MDRs, and increasingly in LDRs, unhealthy lifestyles are a major underlying cause of morbidity. Injuries arising from human activities also are major underlying causes of morbidity, especially in more-developed countries. Most of the morbidity from lifestyle and injury is regarded as preventable. In contrast, much of the morbidity among those who achieve extreme old age is difficult to prevent and is increasing in MDRs. The health care needs of aging MDR populations will require difficult choices to be made in the allocation of scarce social resources.

As premature mortality has declined throughout much of the world, concerns over morbidity have risen. Ill health has both personal and social costs that often can exceed even those of mortality. And morbidity can affect every other aspect of life, including all demographic behaviors. Although the past few decades have seen dramatic successes in combating morbidity, e.g. vaccination programs and oral rehydration therapy, the rise of degenerative diseases and emerging infectious diseases may challenge this progress in the future. If recent advances against infectious diseases, in providing adequate nutrition, and in public health continue, aging of the world's population and lifestyle choices will likely continue to shape morbidity trends into the foreseeable future.

EXERCISES

1. Table E6-1 shows the estimated prevalence and incidence of HIV/AIDS in the United States during 1998. Dividing the prevalence of AIDS in row 2 by the population (in 100,000s) of row 1 gives us the prevalence rate per 100,000 population shown in row 3 of the table. Looking at column 1, for example, 117.9 of every 100,000 adults and adolescents lived with AIDS in 1998.

    Dividing the prevalence of HIV infection in row 4 by the population in row 1 gives the prevalence of HIV (without AIDS) in row 5.

    Finally, row 6 estimates the population at risk of contracting a new HIV infection (again in 100,000s) during the year and row 7 reports the new HIV cases reported during 1998. Dividing these new cases by the population at risk gives the incidence rates reported in row 8 of the table.

Your exercise is to fill in the three blank cells of this table.

Table E6-1
HIV/AIDS Incidence and Prevalence Estimates, United States, 1998

Population and Rate Estimates	Adults and Adolescents (1)	Children Under 13 (2)	Total (3)
1. 1998 Population (100,000s)	2227	515	2742
2. Living with AIDS	262,554	3325	265,879
3. AIDS Prevalence Rate (per 100,000)	117.9	6.5	
4. Living with HIV	96,223	1727	97,950
5. HIV Prevalence Rate (per 100,000)		3.4	35.7
6. Estimated Population at Risk (100,000s)	2224	514	2738
7. HIV Cases Reported in 1998	102,592	1819	104,411
8. HIV Incidence Rate		3.5	38.1

Source: CDC, HIV/AIDS Surveillance Report, 1998, tables 1, 2, 3, and 19.

2. On February 12th, 1999 the *Morbidity and Mortality Weekly Report* carried this story:

Human Rabies—Virginia, 1998
On December 31, 1998, a 29-year-old man in Richmond, Virginia, died from rabies encephalitis caused by a rabies virus variant associated with insectivorous bats.

From the most recent life table (use Table E5-1 of the previous chapter), how many years of life were lost due to this single death?

YLL = _____

3. On April 30th, 1999 the *Morbidity and Mortality Weekly Report* carried this story:

Outbreak of Poliomyelitis—Angola, 1999
On March 23, 1999 the Pediatric Hospital in Luanda, Angola, reported 21 cases (three deaths) of acute flaccid paralysis (AFP) . . . By April 25, 635 AFP cases (39 deaths) were reported.

Further investigation determined that these cases occurred primarily among children under five not fully vaccinated for polio.

a. For the 596 cases that did not result in death, the estimated duration of poliomyelitis would be up to 58.9 years (Murray and Lopez, 1996a). (Let's assume survivors lived this long.) Using a severity, or disability, of 0.24 (24% disabled), compute how many years lived with disability could have been caused by this outbreak.

YLD = _____

b. If the 39 cases resulting in death had an average remaining life expectancy of 58.9 years, how many years of life were lost due to their deaths?

YLL = _____

c. If those surviving experienced no years of life lost (YLL) and those dying experienced no years lived with disability (YLD), how many total disability adjusted life-years lost (DALY) could have been caused by this outbreak?

DALY = YLL + YLD = _____

▶ PROPOSITIONS FOR DEBATE

1. As the incidence of a lifelong disease declines, the prevalence also will decline.

2. The *best* measure of morbidity is the prevalence rate.

3. Saving individuals from death from one cause leaves them at risk of death from other causes, rather than insuring that they live through average remaining life expectancy. Therefore, computing years of life lost (YLL) always overstates the consequences of an illness.

4. It would be better for less-developed countries to ignore recently rising morbidity from degenerative diseases and concentrate on lowering morbidity from infectious diseases, because morbidity among the young will always cause more disability adjusted life-years lost (DALY).

5. Morbidity is under individual control in the MDRs to a greater extent than in the LDRs.

6. The likelihood of morbidity increases with extreme old age; therefore old age itself should be considered a disease.

▶ REFERENCES AND SUGGESTED READINGS

Alter, George, and James C. Riley. 1988. "Frailty, Sickness, and Death: Models of Morbidity and Mortality in Historical Populations." *Population Association of America Meetings*, New Orleans, LA.

Anderton, Douglas L., Richard E. Barrett, and Donald J. Bogue. 1997. *The Population of the United States.* 3rd ed. New York: The Free Press.

Armelagos, George J. 1990. "Health and Disease in Prehistoric Populations in Transition." In Alan C. Swedlund and George J. Armelagos, eds., *Disease in Populations in Transition.* New York: Bergin and Garvey.

Benedictow, O. J. 1987. "Morbidity in Historical Plague Epidemics." *Population Studies* 41(3).

Bowley, A. L., and A. R. Burnett-Hurst. 1915. *Livelihood and Poverty.* London: Ratan Tata Foundation. (cf. Fogel and Costa, 1997)

Cassedy, James H. 1986. *Medicine and American Growth, 1800–1860.* Madison: University of Wisconsin Press.

Centers for Disease Control (CDC). 1998. *HIV/AIDS Surveillance Report*, 10(2).

———. 1999. "Provisional Cases of Selected Notifiable Diseases." *Morbidity and Mortality Weekly Report* 48(15).

Cipolla, C. M. 1980. *Before the Industrial Revolution: European Society and Economy, 1000–1700.* 2nd ed. New York: Norton.

Corsini, Carlo A., and Pier Paolo Viazzo, eds. 1997. *The Decline of Infant and Child Mortality.* Dordrecht, The Netherlands: Martinas Nijhoff Publishers.

Department of Health and Human Services. 1999. *Healthy People 2000 Review (1998–1999).* Office of Disease Prevention and Health Promotion. Washington, DC: DHHS.

Fogel, Robert W., and Dora L. Costa. 1997. "A Theory of Technophysio Evolution, with some Implications for Forecasting Population, Health Care Costs, and Pension Costs." *Demography* 34(1).

Foster, Kenneth R., David E. Bernstein, and Peter W. Huber, eds. 1993. *Phantom Risk.* Cambridge: MIT Press.

Gelbard, Alene, Carl Haub, and Mary M. Kent. 1999. "World Population Beyond Six Billion." *Population Bulletin* 54(1).

Gray, Ronald H. 1989. "The Integration of Demographic and Epidemiologic Approaches to Studies of Health in Developing Countries." In Lado Ruzicka, Guillame Wusch, and Penny Kane, eds., *Differential Mortality: Methodological Issues and Biosocial Factors.* Oxford: Clarendon Press.

Hautaniemi, Susan I., Alan Swedlund, and Douglas L. Anderton. 1999. "Mill Town Mortality: Consequences of Industrial Growth in Two 19th Century New England Towns." *Social History* 23(1): 1–39.

Hetzel, A. M. 1997. *U.S. Vital Statistics System: Major Activities and Developments, 1950–95.* National Center For Health Statistics. (PHS) 97-1003. Washington, DC: Government Printing Office.

Krug, Etienne G., Linda L. Dahlberg, and Kenneth E. Powell. 1996. "Childhood Homicide, Suicide, and Firearm Deaths: An International Comparison." *World Health Statistics Quarterly* 49:230–35.

Laslett, Peter. 1983. *The World We Have Lost: England Before the Industrial Age.* 3rd ed. New York: Scribner.

Manton, Kenneth G., Eric Stallard, and Larry Corder. 1997. "Changes in the Age Dependence of Mortality and Disability: Cohort and Other Determinants." *Demography* 34(1).

McKeown, T. H. 1976. *The Modern Rise of Population.* New York: Academic Press.

Morel, Marie-France. 1977. "City and Country in Eighteenth-Century Medical Discussions about Early Childhood." *Annales E. S. C.* 32.

Murray, Christopher J. L., and Alan D. Lopez, eds. 1996a. *The Global Burden of Disease: A Comprehensive Assessment of Mortality and Disability from Diseases, Injuries and Risk Factors in 1990 and Projected to 2020* (with executive summary). Published by Harvard School of Public Health on behalf of the World Health Organization and World Bank. Cambridge, MA: Harvard University Press.

———. 1996b. *Global Health Statistics.* Published by Harvard School of Public Health on behalf of the World Health Organization and World Bank. Cambridge, MA: Harvard University Press.

Nam, Charles B. 1990. "Mortality Differentials from a Multiple-Cause-of-Death Perspective." In Jacques Vallin, Stan D'Souza, and Alberto Palloni, eds., *Measurement and Analysis of Mortality: New Approaches.* Oxford: Clarendon Press.

National Center for Health Statistics. 1998. "Births and Deaths: Preliminary Data for 1997." *Monthly Vital Statistics Report* 47(4).

Olshansky, S. Jay, Bruce Carnes, Richard G. Rodgers, and Len Smith. 1997. "Infectious Diseases—New and Ancient Threats to World Health." *Population Bulletin* 52(2). Washington, DC: Population Reference Bureau.

Onis, M. de, C. Monteiro, J. Akré, and G. Clugston. 1999. "The Worldwide Magnitude of Protein-Energy Malnutrition: An Overview from the WHO Global Database on Child Growth." *WHOSIS Electronic Bulletin.*

Outhwaite, R. B. 1991. *Dearth, Public Policy and Social Disturbance in England, 1550–1800.* Cambridge: Cambridge University Press.

Porter, Roy. 1993. *Disease, Medicine and Society in England, 1550–1860.* 2nd ed. Cambridge: Cambridge University Press.

Preston, Samuel H., and Michael R. Haines. 1991. *Fatal Years: Child Mortality in Late Nineteenth-Century America.* Princeton, NJ: Princeton University Press.

Reid, Alice. 1997. "Locality or Class? Spatial and Social Differentials in Infant and Child Mortality in England and Wales, 1895–1911." In Corsini and Viazzo, eds., *The Decline of Infant and Child Mortality: The European Experience, 1750–1990.* New York: UNICEF.

Rockett, Ian R. H. 1994. "Population and Health: An Introduction to Epidemiology." *Population Bulletin* 49(3).

———. 1998. "Injury and Violence: A Public Health Perspective." *Population Bulletin* 53(4).

Rosenberg, Charles E. 1987. *The Cholera Years: The United States in 1832, 1849, and 1866.* Chicago: University of Chicago Press.

Rotberg, Robert I., and T. K. Rabb, eds. 1985. *Hunger and History.* Cambridge: Cambridge University Press.

Schofield, Roger, D. Reher, and A. Bideau, eds. 1991. *The Decline of Mortality in Europe.* Oxford: Clarendon Press.

Snow, John. 1965. *Snow on Cholera.* New York: Hafner.

Swedlund, Alan C., and George J. Armelagos, eds. 1990. *Disease in Populations in Transition.* New York: Bergin and Garvey.

Szreter, S. 1997. "Economic Growth, Disruption, Deprivation, Diseases and Death: On the Importance of the Politics of Public Health for Development." *Population and Development Review* 23(4).

United Nations. 1999. *Revision of the World Population Estimates and Projections, 1998 Briefing Packet.* New York: United Nations.

Vargas, Luis A. 1990. "Old and New Transitions and Nutrition in Mexico." In Alan C. Swedlund and George J. Armelagos, eds., *Disease in Populations in Transition.* New York: Bergin and Garvey.

WHO. 1992. "The Worldwide Magnitude of Protein-Energy Malnutrition: An Overview from the WHO Global Database on Child Growth." *World Health Organization - Bulletin.* Geneva: World Health Organization.

———. 1997. "Health and Environment in Sustainable Development." *World Health Organization Information Fact Sheet no. 170.*

———. 1998. *World Health Report 1998: Executive Summary.* Geneva: World Health Organization.

———. 1999. "Diseases Subject to the Regulations." *World Health Organization - Weekly Epidemiological Record* no. 15.

Woods, Robert. 1993. "On the Historical Relationship between Infant and Adult Mortality." *Population Studies* 47:195–219.

Wrigley, E. A., and Roger Schofield. 1981. *The Population History of England, 1541–1871.* London: Edward Arnold.

7 Fertility

Childbearing, or *fertility*, of populations has received more attention from demographers than any other topic. There are several reasons for this. First, as we discussed in chapter 4, fertility largely determines a population's age structure: high fertility is responsible for youth dependency in less-developed regions; declining fertility is responsible for aging of populations in more-developed regions; variable fertility has created major fluctuations in cohort size, such as the baby-boom, in many more-developed countries. A second reason for interest in fertility is its contribution to population growth: continuing high fertility, after mortality began to decline, has produced the most explosive population growth episodes of modern times. A final reason is that the biological potential for childbearing, or *fecundity*, has increasingly come under voluntary control over the past century. As a result, people can plan their childbearing, and policy makers can reasonably attempt to influence these choices.

While fertility remains the driving force of world population growth, world fertility probably never has been as low as it is today (U.S. Bureau of the Census, 1999). Over a third of all nations, and practically all of the more-developed countries, have fertility levels below those which would replace their existing populations. Moreover, fertility decline has spread to many less-developed countries (United Nations, 1999a). The causes, consequences, and likely future course of this worldwide fertility transition are among the most compelling demographic questions of the past century.

In this chapter, we look first at the earliest fertility transitions of the now more-developed countries and then at fertility transitions underway in the less-developed. We then introduce methods to measure fertility, and discuss how both biology and culture impact fertility. As in previous chapters, we then discuss perceived problems associated with trends in this demographic process. Finally, we describe family-planning programs and the debate surrounding them.

European Fertility Transitions

The European demographic transition had both mortality and fertility components. We covered the earlier drop in mortality in chapter 5. In this section we treat the downward transition in fertility.

With few exceptions, the really steep drops in fertility in European countries started in the four decades bracketing 1900, but the beginning of this steep drop often was foreshadowed many decades earlier by more gradual declines. Conventional European demographic data do not go back far enough to cover the whole sweep of the fertility transition in some countries. By "conventional data" we mean regular censuses and continuous civil registration of vital events (see chapter 2). Both of these practices spread through Europe mostly during the 1800s (van de Walle and Knodel, 1980). In many localities, fertility started to edge downward well before that.

Historical Demography

Recently, demographers have developed methods to infer demographic behavior and population structure of earlier times from other historical data. These data and methods have come to be known as *historical demography.* One major data source for Europe is parish registers of baptisms, weddings, and burials by Catholic and Protestant clergymen. These registers record not only the event and its date, but also the crucial information of the participants' *names.*

Figure 7-1 gives a (typically, barely legible) example. This 1803 register was made in a parish northeast of Manchester, England. The column headings indicate, from left to right, infant's name and seniority; father's name, abode, and profession;

Figure 7-1 Baptismal Register, Wigan Parish, England, 1803

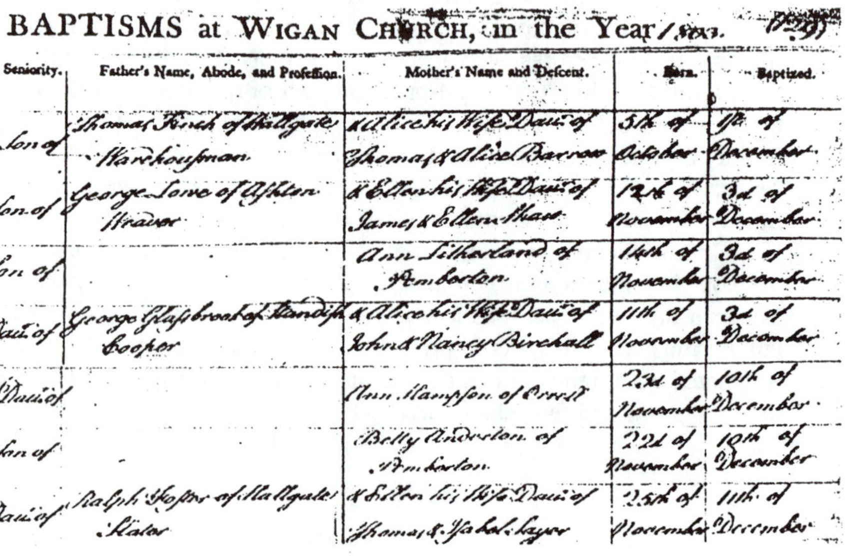

BAPTISMS at WIGAN CHURCH, in the Year 1803.

Infant's Name and Seniority.	Father's Name, Abode, and Profession.	Mother's Name and Descent.	Born.	Baptized.
Jonathan third Son of	Thomas Finch of Wallgate Warehouseman	& Alice his Wife Daur. of Thomas & Alice Barrow	5th of October	4th of December
George third Son of	George Lowe of Ashton Weaver	& Ellen his Wife Daur. of James & Ellen Shaw	12th of November	3d of December
Benj. (Base) Son of		Ann Sutherland of Pemberton	14th of November	3d of December
Elizab. first Daur. of	George Glassbrook of Standish Cooper	& Alice his Wife Daur. of John & Nancy Birchall	11th of November	3d of December
Betty (Base) Daur. of		Ann Hampson of Orrell	23d of November	10th of December
John (Base) Son of		Betty Anderton of Pemberton	22d of November	10th of December
Nancy fifth Daur. of	Ralph Foster of Wallgate Slater	& Ellen his Wife Daur. of Thomas & Isabel Layer	25th of November	11th of December

mother's name and descent; dates of birth and baptism. In the first line, for example, Jonathan was born on the 5th of October 1803 as the third son of Thomas Finch of Wallgate, a warehouseman, and Alice his wife who was the daughter of Thomas and Alice Barrow. Note the illegitimate births without a record of father and designated by "Base" in the infant's name. John, the sixth listed infant and an illegitimate birth to Betty Anderton, is the great-great-grandfather of one of the text's authors.

One fruitful method for analyzing such parish registers is "family reconstitution." It "links the birth, marriage, and death dates of each married couple and their children into a chronology of vital events. . . . [From] this chronology, many important demographic variables, such as birth intervals, family size, people's age at marriage, age of mother at each birth, infant mortality, and marital fertility can be readily calculated" (van de Walle and Knodel, 1980, p. 8). The construction of individual life histories from such old records, somewhat incomplete and always difficult to read, is a tedious and time-consuming undertaking, but it is essential and rewarding.

Historical demography also applies a variety of other methods to various data sources such as wills, genealogies, hearth and household enumerations, organizational records, etc., all of which contain valuable demographic data on populations in the past (Reher and Schofield, 1993; Willigan and Lynch, 1982). And, in good historical tradition, demographers also rely upon observations written by persons living in the period being described. They find them in such diverse sources as letters and novels of the time and reports by trained contemporary observers (such as statisticians evaluating their own data in introductions to their reports) and by doctors reporting on their patients and on general health conditions (van de Walle and Knodel, 1980).

Much of what we know about the role of marriage and fertility limitation within marriage during the early European fertility decline comes from these historical demographic studies. The most notable collection of such studies, although far from the only one, is that of the Princeton Fertility Project (for a summary see Coale and Watkins, 1986).

The Malthusian Transition

When fertility declined in Europe, there were two components of the decline. One was delay and/or curtailment of marriage. Coale (1973) labels this the *Malthusian transition*, after Thomas Malthus. (You will remember that Malthus hoped that delayed marriage would act as a preventive check on population growth.) The other component was the declining childbearing of married couples. Coale labels this the *neo-Malthusian transition* (described in our next section).

The Malthusian transition in Europe spread what Hajnal (1965) has called the *European marriage pattern*. That pattern combines late female age at first marriage (say, until the middle or late twenties) with many women never marrying (say, 10% or more). The pattern from which the affected European provinces moved probably was similar to what we now observe in the less-developed countries, early and universal marriage of females.

When did this unique European marriage pattern begin? We know that its start antedated the introduction of conventional demographic data gathering, such as regular censuses and civil registration of vital events. From available data, about all we can say for sure is that the change-over in marriage patterns started after the Middle Ages and had swept through Western Europe before industrialization (Coale and Treadway, 1986). The timing was later for Eastern Europe; therefore, the degree to which the pattern had been adopted by 1900 was quite different between Eastern and Western Europe. Hajnal (1965) suggests that one could draw a north-south line between Trieste (on the Adriatic) and Leningrad (on the tip of the Baltic) as a border between the two patterns in 1900.

This gap in European marriage behavior narrowed after the 1930s as Western Europe experienced somewhat of a resurgence in early and universal marriage while Eastern Europe (most notably Russia) experienced a Malthusian decline in marriage (Coale and Treadway, 1986). Despite continuing regional variations, all of the more-developed countries now have completed the Malthusian component of the fertility transition. Their women marry later, and more end up never marrying (more about this in chapter 8).

As the European marriage pattern spread, overall fertility declined. Being unmarried must have limited the sexual contact of young women, although illegitimacy was often high during this period (Shorter et al., 1971). In contrast, the resurgence of marriage after the 1930s did not substantially increase fertility. By that time, efficacious contraception allowed control of fertility within marriage to limit childbearing even as marriage became more common (Coale and Treadway, 1986).

The Neo-Malthusian Transition

The neo-Malthusian transition was a decline in *marital* fertility—childbearing among married women. This transition represented mainly a change from what Louis Henry (1961) has called *natural fertility* behavior.

Natural fertility, according to Henry's definition, results when couples do not attempt to terminate childbearing before the end of their biological reproductive span. This does not mean that natural-fertility populations have as many children as possible. Most populations produce far fewer births than they could if everyone was working at biological capacity (Henry, 1961). The Hutterites, a religious sect living in the Dakotas, Montana, and Canada, are considered to have the maximum fertility for a large group, an average family size of 10.9 children in 1950, and even that was considered a couple of children below capacity (Eaton and Mayer, 1954). Natural fertility simply means that couples do not try to stop having children after a given number of births or completed family size.

Parity-specific fertility limitation, in contrast, means stopping childbearing after enough children have been had. (Parity is simply the number of children already born.) Demographers distinguish attempts to stop at a specific number of children born from behavior that may space births but does not intentionally stop childbearing. Either stopping or spacing births can reduce the overall fertility in a population and it can be difficult to distinguish these behaviors in the early stages of fertility decline (Guinnane et al., 1994; Anderton and Bean, 1985). Some long intervals between births, for example, may reflect failed attempts to stop childbearing and long birth intervals at older ages can mistakenly appear to be stopping behavior (Anderton, 1989). Once fertility transitions were underway, however, there is little doubt that efforts to stop childbearing at smaller family sizes was responsible for the dramatic fertility declines in Europe (Coale and Treadway, 1986; van de Walle and Knodel, 1980).

The timing of the Malthusian and neo-Malthusian components of fertility transition relative to each other varied among European countries, notably between Western and Eastern Europe. In Eastern Europe, the two generally overlapped, tending simultaneously to push total fertility down rapidly during the early 1900s. In Western Europe, in contrast, the Malthusian transition had an early start and tended to antedate the neo-Malthusian. Let us focus here on the decline in marital fertility in Western European countries.

Western European marital fertility before the neo-Malthusian transition had two important features: 1) it was high, by modern standards and 2) it varied considerably around that high average, both among nations and among localities within nations.

Figure 7-2 illustrates the differences among European nations from the mid-1800s up to 1980. The "index of marital fertility" used in the graph is too complex to explain in detail in an introductory textbook; however, it is sufficient for one to know that it compares the total marital fertility of the countries described with that of the most fertile population on which we have complete records, the Hutterites (Shorter et al., 1971). If a European country had age-specific marital fertility on a par with the Hutterites, its index of marital fertility would be 1.0. One can see that, by 1860, France had an index of about 0.5, while the Netherlands and Belgium were above 0.8. Moreover, the Princeton University team that provided these figures also carefully studied data from localities and found considerable variation among them as well (Coale and Treadway, 1986).

How did these early fertility differences come about? Most local differences were due to variations in the "frequency and duration of breast-feeding, periods of separation due to seasonal migration of one of the spouses, variation in frequency of intercourse, customs prohibiting resumption of intercourse for some period following a birth, and nutritional levels of the population" (van de Walle and Knodel, 1980, p. 12). For our purposes, the most important observation is that these early nineteenth-century differentials in marital fertility were caused only to a minor degree by voluntary family size limitation.

Figure 7-2 also describes the national transitions in marital fertility during the period from 1860 to 1980. For any given country, fertility first edges gradually downward, typically drops into a steep dive, and ends at levels of marital fertility less than half what they were at the beginning of this transition (with the notable exception of Ireland). There was national variation, with France and Ireland representing the early and late extremes. Among the rest, there was a tendency for Western European countries to decline earlier and Eastern and Southern European countries to decline later. For most of the Western European nations, fertility lines converge as they reach modern times. Regardless of prior national variations, a similar change swept rapidly through all the region in the late 1800s and early 1900s.

With the exceptions of France and Ireland, the steep national declines all started within less than a forty-year period. This point is made more graphically in Figure 7-3, which shows the timing of the fertility drops for local European *provinces* within nations. The early peak in this figure is entirely composed of local populations within France. For the rest of Western Europe the decline is concentrated in a narrow time period. Nearly 60% of provinces within these nations have their first sustained decline in marital fertility between 1890 and 1920.

Not all the people in each of these localities responded with equal promptness. During the transition, fertility differentials increased temporarily. The already lower

Figure 7-2 Levels and Changes in Marital Fertility, Selected European Countries, 1860–1980

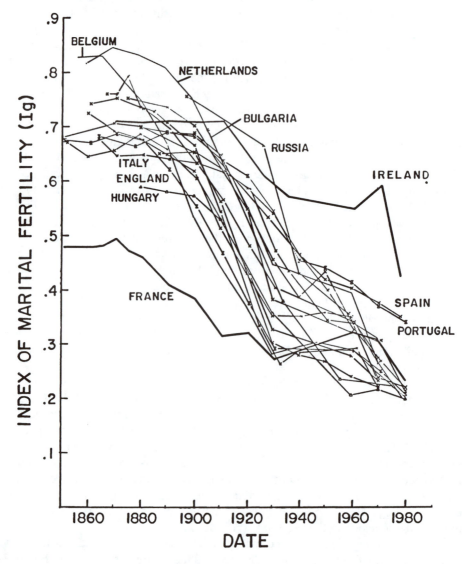

Source: Coale and Watkins, eds., *The Decline of Fertility in Europe*, 1986, fig. 2.3. Used with permission.

Figure 7-3   Starting Dates of Fertility Transitions in Selected European Provinces, 1780–1960

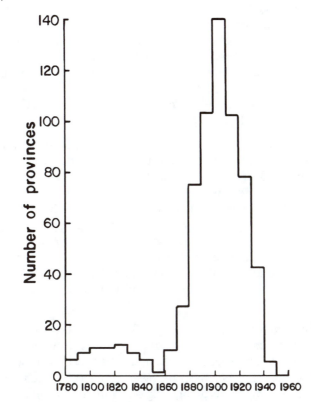

Date of beginning of decade

Source: Coale and Watkins, eds., *The Decline of Fertility in Europe*, 1986, fig. 2.2. Used with permission.

urban fertility dropped before the rural, widening that gap. The middle and upper classes restricted their fertility before the lower class did. Those involved in the new economic order—the educated and those in nonagricultural occupations—lowered their fertility first. Ethnic, religious, and racial groups in the population participated differentially in modernization and also in family size limitation. Just as the transition widened these differentials, its end has meant a convergence (Coale and Watkins, 1986; Ryder, 1959).

Causes of the Neo-Malthusian Transition: Some Theories

What social and cultural changes made these populations start to employ birth control so suddenly? Demographers still disagree over which causes deserve the most emphasis, mainly because so many possibly important changes happened about the same time. There was a change from rural to urban living, from agricultural to industrial occupations and economies. There was modernization of social institutions, and there evolved broader acceptance of the Western conjugal family model. There was a mortality decline, apparently preceding the fertility decline on the national level. Which of these changes caused the increase in family size limitation?

Mason (1997) provides a review of the six leading theories of fertility decline, in Europe and subsequently elsewhere. We will rely here on a summary of her review but extend her critical comments in some cases. The reader is forewarned that the presentation that follows may seem abstract, sophisticated, and intimidating to beginning students. The summaries are presented to demonstrate the earnest attempts by demographers to explain the facets of fertility decline rather than to finally answer the question.

Classic demographic transition theory. This theory attributes fertility decline to changes in social life associated with industrialization and urbanization (Thompson, 1930; Notestein, 1953). These changes first increased the survival of children and then created a modern lifestyle in which large families became increasingly expensive. Although the classic theory is heavily used by demographers as a general framework, it has critical flaws as a specific theory. First, the theory is so general that it does not provide sufficient detail to constitute a testable hypothesis in any one specific instance of fertility decline. Second, the classic theory is left unsupported by the relatively weak correlations between fertility and urbanization or industrialization, either in historical MDR transitions (Coale and Watkins, 1986) or in LDR transitions (Bongaarts and Watkins, 1996).

Modernization and secularization theory. This line of thinking extends the classic theory by emphasizing the rising values of individualism and self-fulfillment that are associated with increasing affluence and secularization (Lesthaeghe, 1983; 1995). This modification of classic theory provides insight into the historical European fertility transitions where declining religious authority, alternative life-course possibilities, etc., were associated with fertility decline. It does not, however, fare as well in LDR countries where fertility declines have occurred with less evidence of an erosion in traditional values.

Wealth flow theory. This view argues that a key turning point in modernization occurs when changes in child labor, compulsory education, extended family structures, old age security, and so on, shift the economic benefits of family life from the parents to the offspring (Caldwell, 1982). As children become more of a burden than benefit to parents, fertility is limited. Again, this theory works well in some countries such as sub-Saharan Africa, but less well in others where fertility has declined with little change in extended family structures (Thornton and Fricke, 1987) or in European settings where extended families were not significant even before fertility declines.

Neoclassical microeconomic theory. This approach emphasizes a rational choice model where decisions to limit fertility are contingent upon fertility desires, childbearing and rearing costs, budget or income constraints, and the substitutability of children for other available goods (Becker, 1960). As with most highly generalized microeconomic approaches, one flaw of the theory is its failure to explain the historical changes in these decision-making conditions which led to fertility transitions in

specific cases. The ahistorical nature of the model tends to make its application tauto-
logical and uninformative (Robinson, 1997).

Regulatory microeconomic theory. This theory extends the neoclassical model
by emphasizing more sociological interpretations of the supply, demand, and costs of
children (Easterlin and Crimmins, 1985). In Easterlin's theory, the supply of children
is a theoretical one, or natural fertility in the absence of deliberate decisions to limit
childbearing. Demand for children is a desired surviving family size and only one
proximate determinant of fertility. The costs of fertility regulation are extended to
include psychic and social, as well as monetary, costs. The theory has encouraged
innovative thinking about fertility decisions and provides a better explanation of fertility fluctuations than other transition theories (Abernethy, 1995). But the theory still
suffers from a similar ahistoricism as does the neoclassical microeconomic theory.

Ideational theory. This perspective attributes fertility declines to the diffusion of
innovations in birth control technologies and social norms, perhaps after mortality
declines have created an excess supply of children (Cleland and Wilson, 1987). Diffusion
of such information is clearly important to many fertility transitions, especially those
reliant upon modern technological innovations (Bongaarts and Watkins, 1996). The diffusion of norms and technologies may affect attempts both to stop fertility at a desired
number of children or to space children even where desired levels have not yet been
reached (Caldwell et al., 1992). Like other theories reviewed, however, the ideational
theory is incomplete and neither identifies when diffused innovations will be adopted
nor elaborates the institutional factors underlying the origin of such ideational changes.

It is not surprising for academics to have different theories for such complex and
widespread events as fertility transitions—and the controversy among learned demographic scholars undoubtedly will continue. It may be of some relief to recognize that
one does not have to choose. Some of the theories above emphasize a single underlying social change which may be very important in one setting and less so in another.
Some of these theories provide insight into one aspect of fertility decisions but are
incomplete, neglecting social changes that may drive these fertility decisions. Being
realistic, all of the relationships put forward by these transition theories may have
been important to a different degree in different fertility transitions. This perspective
does not contradict the idea that worldwide fertility transitions have been part of a
common historical experience and are broadly similar (Caldwell, 1997b). It does,
however, suggest we should not expect any one narrow model to provide great insight
to fertility declines that have taken place across vastly different times and cultures.

MEASURING PERIOD FERTILITY

When we turn to contemporary times we have much more, and more reliable,
data available to study fertility transitions. And, as with mortality and morbidity, there
are a number of different measures that can illuminate different aspects of fertility.

Do not be confused by use of the word "period" here to modify fertility. Period
rates, such as those in earlier chapters of this book (e.g. crude birth and death rates

and age-sex-specific death rates), all refer to events (such as births or deaths) that occur within a specified short period, usually a single year.

However, in studying fertility, we will also use measures that view fertility longitudinally, as childbearing accumulates in the history of an age group. For instance, we might want to measure fertility by the average number of children that women of a given cohort, such as baby-boomers, bear in their lifetimes. This measure is not for a specific period but rather measures "cohort" fertility. We will pursue cohort fertility later in this chapter. For the moment we are simply introducing the phrase "period fertility" to be clear which type of measure we are referring to.

Getting Information about Births

The vital event defining fertility is *live birth* (not conception) and to measure fertility one first needs to record births. In the Western tradition, records of live births come mostly from the civil registration system, just as do the records of deaths (see chapter 2). Designated people likely to witness the birth are held responsible for recording its occurrence, time, and location. They normally also are responsible for recording some information about the mother, such as her age and marital status, how many children she already has (that is, the parity of this child), and even her education and/or ethnic identity.

However, as chapter 2 details, civil registration of births is incomplete, at least in the less-developed regions. The task is so difficult that many LDRs do not seriously attempt nationwide birth registration. A more manageable procedure is to select a representative sample of geographic areas within the nation for more intensive registration efforts.

Demographers also use censuses, either to check on the completeness of birth registration or to supply independent *estimates* of births by date (see chapter 2 and Box 5-1). The children found at the various ages below ten in a given decennial census must have been born during the preceding ten years; more precisely, they are the survivors of those born. If one has enough information about infant and childhood mortality in the population, as well as migration, one can estimate how many births must have occurred in order to leave the number of survivors found in the census.

The major technical trend in counting births in the LDRs, however, has been the introduction of retrospective sample surveys. Aside from counting births in lieu of effective civil registration systems, these surveys have been charged with gathering information on the potential determinants of fertility. Thus they conventionally get from responding women not only a complete history of conceptions and births, but also a marital history, a contraceptive and abortion history, and information on relevant parental characteristics (such as education and ethnic status and rural or urban residence). The two most widely administered sets of surveys with detailed fertility information are the World Fertility Surveys (WFS) and the more recent Demographic and Health Surveys (DHS+). Both groups of surveys receive support from the United Nations and the U.S. Agency for International Development. The WFS program started in 1972; DHS+ surveys were begun in 1984.

Both surveys are available for a large number of developing countries and have sufficient numbers of respondents for detailed fertility analyses. The basic strategy for maintaining international comparability of results has been to standardize survey questionnaires to the extent possible. While optional survey items vary across countries, a common core of information generally includes the respondent's and spouse's background, maternity history, contraceptive knowledge and practices, marriage history, fertility regulation, work history, and possible determinants of fertility including socioeconomic factors and more immediate influences. One important caution regarding such surveys is that much of the fertility data collected are retrospective; that is, respondents are asked to recollect their family and fertility events and (sometimes remote) dates.

Fertility Rates

Given records of live births, how does one measure the fertility of a population in a given year? The simplest approach is to divide the number of births by the total population. The result is the *crude birth rate*, still one of the most useful annual measures of fertility; but people in the population contribute unequally in the production of births. In an ultimate sense, giving birth is limited to females, though males obviously made earlier contributions. Moreover, it is limited to females of reproductive age, normally considered to be ages fifteen through forty-nine. Even within those childbearing years, a female's fecundity characteristically peaks in her twenties. Therefore, the age-sex structure of a population partially determines how many births it will produce.

Demographers conventionally call rates applying to women *fertility* rates rather than *birth* rates, which apply to the total population. The rate of births to all women of childbearing age (usually assumed to be women aged fifteen to forty-nine years of age) is simply called the *fertility rate*. But, as we have seen, one way of discounting the influence of age-sex structure upon fertility is to deal in *age-sex-specific fertility rates* (see Box 4-2). One can, for instance, classify the female reproductive cycle into seven five-year age categories and compute a separate age-sex-specific rate for each population category. This is illustrated in Table 7-1. The population counts in column 2 are estimated from censuses. Column 3 records births by age of mother, information ideally obtained from the civil registration system but often necessarily estimated from other data. Column 4 records the annual specific fertility rates, that is, the number of births per thousand women in the age category.

Age-specific fertility rates are not affected by population structure. One can compare the rate for United States women aged fifteen to nineteen with that for the same-aged women in Mexico, for instance. Any resulting difference would be due to something other than the differences in their population structures.

Total Fertility Rates

In order to compare the *overall* fertility of different populations with age-sex-specific rates, one would have to make seven comparisons, one for each of the age classes of women. A more convenient approach would be to combine these age-sex-specific rates into a *single* summary measure that was not influenced by population structure. The *total fertility rate* (TFR) is such a measure.

Table 7-1
Illustrative Computation of Total Fertility Rate, United States, 1997

Age	Female Population (midyear, in thousands) (1)	Births (2)	Births per 1,000 Women per Year (col. 2 ÷ col. 1) (3)	Projected Resulting Births during Age Interval (5 x col. 3) (4)
15–19	9,248	489,211	52.9	265
20–24	8,533	946,357	110.9	555
25–29	9,401	1,074,559	114.3	572
30–34	10,397	887,892	85.4	427
35–39	11,336	408,111	36.0	180
40–44	10,837	74,778	6.9	35
45–49	10,697	3,209	0.3	2
Total	70,450	3,884,117	406.7	2,034

$$\text{Total Fertility Rate} = \frac{2,034}{1,000} = 2.03$$

Source: NCHS, "Births and Deaths: Preliminary Data for 1997," 1998a, table 1.

The reasoning behind the TFR is very similar to the reasoning behind life expectancy measures (see chapter 5). It involves establishing a hypothetical cohort and then following it through a specific schedule of hypothetical events to see what the end result would be. In this case, the hypothetical cohort starts out as 1,000 women, all of whom reach age fifteen simultaneously. We can trace their experience in Table 7-1 as an illustration. As they progress through the ages fifteen through nineteen, they experience *each year* the specified age-specific fertility rate (52.9 per thousand, shown in column 3), and thereby, during the five-year age interval, produce 265 births. Similarly, for each successive age category, one computes the number of births that would result during five years to this hypothetical cohort by multiplying the age-specific rate by five. When one has carried the cohort through the end of its fecund years (age forty-nine), one can total column 4 to obtain the number of births they collectively would have produced (in this case, 2,034 babies to the 1,000 women or 2.03 births per woman).

Formally defined, the total fertility rate (TFR) is "the average number of children that would be born alive to a woman (or a group of women) during her lifetime if she were to pass through all her childbearing years conforming to the age-specific fertility rates of a given year" (Haupt and Kane, 1978, p. 19).

A computational shortcut for determining the TFR is first to total the age-specific fertility rates and then multiply the total by five (if using five-year age groups). In our Table 7-1 illustration, that would mean totaling column 3 and then multiplying that total (406.7) by five, giving us the same 2,034 babies, and the same TFR of 2.03.

Demographers have studied enough cases so they know fairly precisely the relationships among 1) the total number of births in a population, 2) the number of women in each of the age categories of the childbearing years, and 3) the total fertility rate. Therefore, if they are supplied the first two facts, they can estimate the third (Shryock and Siegel, 1976, p. 287).

A very similar fertility measure is the *gross reproduction rate* (GRR). The GRR is identical to the TFR except that it counts only female babies. That makes the GRR a measure of the average number of daughters a woman would bear; that is, a measure of women's reproduction of themselves across generations. It is constructed by multiplying the TFR by the proportion of all births that are daughters, usually about 48%. Therefore, the GRR is about half the TFR for the same population and year.

General Fertility Rates

But what if one does not have all the precise data necessary for the computation of age-specific fertility rates and, thus, total fertility rates? What if one does not have for each birth a record of the age of the mother?

It is quite normal in the less-developed regions to be missing this detail and yet to have some other useful information, such as 1) the age-sex structure of the population (obtained from censuses) and 2) the *total* number of births, irrespective of age of mother. Censuses are better developed in most LDRs than are civil registration systems. Registration systems are more likely to contain complete records of the number of births alone than information about the age of the mothers. Even failing that, total births by calendar year of occurrence can be inferred after the fact, from subsequent censuses.

Given those data, one has two options: either *estimate* indirectly what the TFR might have been (as described above) or compute a *general fertility rate* (GFR, sometimes called simply the "fertility rate"). The formula for the GFR, according to Shryock and Siegel (1976, p. 178), is

$$GFR = \frac{B}{P_{15-49}} \times 1,000$$

where B is the total births for the year and P_{15-49} is the women aged fifteen through forty-nine in the year. We can illustrate its computation from data contained in Table 7-1:

$$GFR = \frac{3,884,117}{70,450} \times 1,000 = 55.1$$

The GFR *partially* controls for the influence of age-sex structure on fertility; that is, it does control for differences in the proportion of the total population that consists of women in the childbearing years. But it does not control for variations from one population to another in terms of the age distribution of women between the ages of fifteen and forty-nine.

(Incidentally, there is an annoying lack of demographic consensus about whether the end of the female childbearing years should be put at the forty-fifth or the fiftieth birthday. One sees GFRs and TFRs using either upper limit.)

RECENT FERTILITY DECLINES

In the past century, fertility decline has become a nearly universal trend. In fact, demographers generally have been surprised at the rapid spread and strength of fertility declines in recent decades. In response, the United Nations revised downward its worldwide fertility estimates in the 1998 *Revision of the World Population Estimates and Projections* (United Nations, 1999a).

In Less-Developed and More-Developed Regions

In the less-developed regions, fertility has declined steadily in most of Asia, Latin America, and North Africa during the last forty or so years. In the developing countries other than China, fertility has fallen by more than half since the 1950s. As for China, with a TFR of 1.8 in 1998, fertility has now fallen below that of the United States (with a TFR of 1.99)!

As for the more-developed regions, fertility has reached dramatically lower levels than ever thought possible in many of the countries. Germany, Greece, Italy, Spain, and many of the newly independent European states have TFRs of 1.3 or below.

Despite the spread of fertility decline, there is still a glaring contrast between the more-developed regions as a category and the less-developed regions. In Table 7-2, TFRs are shown for regions of the world in 1950 and 1998 and projected to 2010. Fertility among the LDRs has remained nearly double that of the MDRs even as fertility has fallen to less than half its earlier levels. Projected into the next decade, fertility in less-developed countries will continue to decline, but at a slower rate.

There is more variation among the less-developed regions than among the more-developed ones. In particular, despite fertility declines in the northern parts of the continent, fertility in sub-Saharan Africa remains high. For Africa as a whole the TFR is four times that of Europe.

Table 7-2
Estimated and Projected Total Fertility Rates for World Regions, 1950, 1998, and 2010

Region[a]	1950–55 (1)	1998 (2)	2010 (3)
World	5.0	2.7	2.5
More-Developed Regions	2.8	1.6	1.7
Less-Developed Regions	6.2	3.0	2.7
Europe	2.6	1.4	1.6
Northern America	3.5	2.0	2.1
Oceania	3.8	2.4	2.1
Asia	5.9	2.8	2.3
Latin America	5.9	3.0	2.3
Africa	6.6	5.6	4.4

[a]Regions listed in order of increasing 1998 TFR.
Source: Gelbard et al., "World Population Beyond Six Billion," 1999, figure 3; U.S. Bureau of the Census, *World Population Profile: 1998,* 1999, table A-8.

Replacement-Level Fertility

In trying to assess whether fertility is high or low, people usually are not satisfied with simply comparing populations, as we have just done. Instead they seek some more absolute benchmark against which to compare current fertility, one that shows the implications of that fertility level for the welfare of the populace. The benchmark in current use seems to be *replacement-level fertility*, which is the level at which women, on the average, have enough daughters to "replace" themselves in the population (United Nations, 1999a).

Suppose we took a hypothetical cohort of women through the age-sex-specific death rates that prevailed in the United States in 1997 and recorded how many women still survived at each age, up through the end of childbearing, say age forty-nine. Given that schedule of survivorship, and given a normal sex ratio at birth (slightly fewer daughters than sons), there is some schedule of age-specific fertility rates that would result in that particular cohort of mothers collectively producing exactly one daughter per mother.

Replacement-level total fertility rates always are above 2.0, since at least one son is born for every daughter, and some potential mothers die before age fifty, even in the healthiest hypothetical cohort. As a general estimate, replacement fertility is taken to be 2.1, and a country having a TFR below this level is said to have below-replacement fertility. According to Table 7-2, Europe and Northern America are currently below replacement-level fertility.

Nations that find themselves with fertility *below* replacement level tend to be concerned with the problems of slow population growth and population decline (see chapter 3). However, fertility is only one source of change in a country's population growth. It would be a mistake to assume that below-replacement fertility always will result in declining population size. Among the 61 countries which now have below-replacement fertility, more than half will continue to experience population growth due both to immigration and to their young age structures, with large cohorts entering ages of high fertility (United Nations, 1999a).

We also should avoid the impression that only countries of the more-developed regions have below-replacement fertility. More than a third of all countries are now below replacement fertility. Much of the developing world is even approaching replacement-level fertility (United Nations, 1999a). For example, China (still the most populous nation), over a third of all Latin American countries, and even some countries in sub-Saharan Africa now are below replacement fertility levels (United Nations, 1999a).

Malthusian and Neo-Malthusian Components

How much of these declines in fertility are caused by delay and avoidance of marriage and how much by curtailing of fertility after marriage? The Malthusian and neo-Malthusian components of the fertility transition have overlapped far more in present less-developed regions than they did in Europe. The average age of marriage in the least developed countries of the world generally remains between ages fifteen and twenty. However, average age at marriage in a large number of developing countries that have experienced greater socioeconomic and cultural development has risen to over twenty years of age (Bongaarts, 1986) and for less-developed regions as a whole has risen to just over twenty-one years of age (Population Reference Bureau, 1996).

Rising marriage age, for example, has contributed greatly to recent fertility declines in Arab countries. Increasing marriage age and an increase in the proportion of women remaining single "accounted for nearly two-thirds of the fertility decline in Tunisia and Morocco and almost all of the long-term decline in Algeria in the 1980s and 1990s" (Gelbard et al., 1999, p. 22). However, the importance of changes in marital patterns varies considerably by region, and marriage trends do not always complement fertility declines in developing countries (Bulatao, 1984).

Although changing marital patterns have played an important role, it is the neo-Malthusian fertility decline that has been the more important factor in current LDR transitions. How is it being brought about? Some of it is attributable to family-planning programs, which advocate and facilitate contraception, sterilization, and abortion. According to Bongaarts (1995), between 40 and 50% of fertility decline in the less-developed countries since the 1960s is attributable to family-planning programs alone. Some of it is due to a decrease in the number of children desired, motivating use of birth control devices provided through nonprogram, as well as program, sources. Family planning use rose from less than 10% of married women of childbearing age in the 1960s to about 50% in the 1990s (Gelbard et al., 1999).

Projections

Demographers are now informed by two sets of worldwide fertility projections. The United Nations estimates population size, population growth, and four variants of projections (depending upon assumed future fertility change) for all countries of the world every two years (United Nations, 1999a); the U.S. Bureau of the Census provides its own similar projections of world population trends (U.S. Bureau of the Census, 1999). Both projections provide, along with population size, such indicators as population growth rate, crude birth rate, crude death rate, total fertility rate, life expectancy at birth, and age-sex distribution.

Because fertility is the major determinant of world population growth, several projections are made, each assuming different fertility trends (e.g. constant, low, medium, and high). In the recent past, medium fertility estimates have tended to provide projections slightly higher than what later occurred. However, it is not possible to be certain those trends will continue and the medium projections are usually a "best guess" of future trends.

Column 3 of Table 7-2 predicts total fertility rates to the year 2010. Whatever their accuracy, demographic projections have become much less alarming every decade since the 1960s. By 2010 only Africa is projected to have fertility levels significantly higher than replacement level. Even Africa is projected to have fertility levels in 2025 below the mid-1950s levels for the more-developed regions. Asia and Latin America in 2010 would be just above replacement fertility, more similar to the current more-developed regions.

When the worldwide total fertility rate reaches about 2.1, does that mean that the world population explosion will be over? Not quite. *Crude* birth rates and *crude* growth rates could remain transitionally high for decades because of a young age structure, the heritage of previously high TFRs (see chapter 4). This point foreshadows our explanation of *population momentum* in the following section.

EXPLAINING PERIOD FERTILITY CHANGES: THE U.S. CASE

In the more-developed countries, crude birth rates dropped as part of their demographic transitions. Some of the less-developed countries seem to be starting fertility transitions as well. What are the *immediate* causes of these trends? How do changes in the age structure of the populations, in the number of children that couples have, and in the age when they have them, taken together, influence the crude birth rates? The interrelationships are complex.

Let us use the example of the United States to demonstrate how demographers explain fertility changes. It has gone through its demographic transition, and it has fertility data that are particularly complete. To set the stage, here is a thumbnail history of the U.S. crude birth rate.

History of the U.S. Crude Birth Rate

Since the birth of the nation, the U.S. population has experienced a two-century decline in crude birth rates, interrupted only in the last few decades by cyclical variations around that long-term trend. Although the data are incomplete, our best estimate is that the crude birth rate in 1800 was fifty, as high as for any current LDR subregion (Coale and Zelnick, 1963). That probably was higher than for any Western European country at that time. But by the late 1800s, the U.S. crude birth rate was below forty, like that of Western Europe (Moore and O'Connell, 1978).

Since the establishment of vital registration in the United States in the early 1900s, we have better estimates of fertility. Figure 7-4 graphs in detail the path of the crude birth rate of the United States from then until the turn of the century. The long-term decline continued, bottoming out early in the 1930s during the Depression. This was followed by the baby-boom of the 1950s and 1960s, and that was followed by the baby-bust that bottomed out in the mid-1970s. The baby-boom echo caused by childbearing of women born during the baby-boom then appears to have peaked in 1990. Since 1990, fertility has declined gradually to levels near the low of the baby-bust.

Fertility decline continues in the United States at this writing. Over almost a two-century span, the United States saw its fertility drop to less than 30% of its original high level, but it ended up with unstable fertility, subject to up-and-down cycles around the new low level. The worst of the "bulge" effects from the U.S. fertility transition are, however, likely in the past (see chapter 4) and projections into the distant future suggest there will be a gradual stabilization of fertility near current levels (Anderton et al., 1997, fig. 1.1).

Figure 7-4   U.S. Crude Birth Rates, 1910–2000

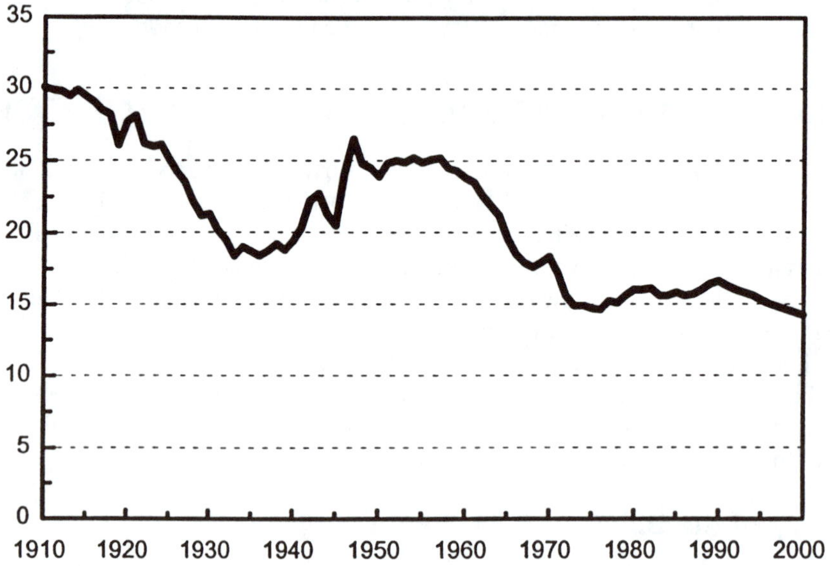

Source: Anderton et al., *Population of the United States*, 1997, fig. 1.1.

The Influence of Age Structure on Period Fertility

One factor that influences a crude birth rate is the proportion of the total population consisting of women in their childbearing years. The greater that proportion, the higher the crude birth rate, all else being equal. That proportion, in turn, can be influenced by migration and by fertility itself.

First, let us take migration. Through most of its history, the United States has had heavy positive net migration—more people moving in than out. Moreover, immigration has been dominated by young people willing and able to start lives in a new world. Thus the net effect of migration has been to add to that part of the population pyramid "at risk" of childbearing. This, in turn, tended to peg the U.S. crude birth rate at a higher level than it would have been without age-selective net immigration.

On the other hand, throughout U.S. history the proportion of the population that were new immigrants decreased. That meant the upward pressure of new immigration on fertility became less and less. Thus the decline in the U.S. net migration rate contributed to the decline in the U.S. crude birth rate.

Second, fertility change can create its own *momentum* via the age structure. A reduced crude birth rate produces a birth cohort at the bottom of the population pyramid that is smaller than it would have been with a higher birth rate. This shrunken cohort ages upward through the population pyramid until it reaches its childbearing ages. Then, because it is smaller in number than it would have been at old fertility levels, it produces fewer children, who in turn form a shrunken birth cohort at the bottom of the pyramid, and the cycle is perpetuated.

This mechanism has given *momentum* to all long-term fertility transitions. It did so in Europe and in the United States until their crude birth rates temporarily bottomed out in the 1930s. It is hoped that the same will happen in the present LDRs, once their initial fertility declines are about twenty years in duration. But this momentum also means fertility trends resist change, and thus transitions are hard to start.

Aside from such long-term trends, more-developed countries seem subject to short cycles in crude birth rates. Such cycles, by creating peaks and valleys in the population pyramid, can create echo effects in the crude birth rate a generation later. The United States is a good example, since its recent fertility cycles have been extreme.

Table 7-3 allows us to specify the timing of the positive and negative effects of past fertility cycles on crude birth rates via the age structure. Whereas age structure does influence the crude birth rate, it does not influence the total fertility rate. Thus, if we construct a ratio in which the crude birth rate is the numerator and the total fertility rate is the denominator, the size of the ratio is an index of the degree to which the age structure was enhancing the crude birth rate. We have done this in column 3 of Table 7-3.

In that column, we see that the ratio stayed stable until the late 1940s. Then it started a decline that was not to hit bottom until the early 1960s. Subtracting between twenty-five and thirty years as an average time between childbearing generations, we can figure that this decline was an echo of the smaller generations born during the declining fertility of the 1930s. The ratio then rose into the mid-1980s. Again, this is clearly an echo effect as larger numbers of women born during the baby-boom were in

Table 7-3
Comparison of U.S. Crude Birth Rates with Total Fertility Rates, 1920–1995

Years[a]	Crude Birth Rate CBR (1)	Total Fertility Rate TFR (2)	Ratio of CBR/TFR (3)
1920–24	26.8	3.248	8.25
1925–29	23.2	2.840	8.17
1930–34	19.7	2.376	8.29
1935–39	18.8	2.235	8.41
1940–44	21.2	2.523	8.40
1945–49	24.1	2.985	8.07
1950–54	24.9	3.337	7.46
1955–59	24.9	3.690	6.75
1960–64	22.4	3.459	6.48
1965–69	18.2	2.636	6.90
1970–74	16.2	2.016	8.04
1975–79	15.0	1.774	8.46
1980–84	15.9	1.817	8.75
1985–89	15.9	1.900	8.37
1990–95	16.1	2.060	7.82

[a]Five-year averages.
Source: Moore and O'Connell, *Perspectives on American Fertility,* 1978, table 1–2; NCHS, "Report of Final Natality Statistics, 1996," 1998b, tables 1 and 4.

childbearing ages. Finally, the more recent decline in the ratio has begun to reflect another echo of earlier fertility, this time of declining fertility during the baby-bust in the late 1970s.

Although there clearly are direct echo effects of past fertility cycles, fertility behavior may also respond to these cycles in such a way as to dampen, or enhance, the full effects of such cycles indirectly. In the United States, they seem more often to dampen the effects of past fertility and population structure. The 1970s baby-bust, for instance, occurred when the baby-boom cohorts were in their early childbearing years. In the 1980s there was some rise due to delayed childbearing among the baby-boomers. Baby-boomers limited and delayed their fertility, reducing the full impact their rising numbers might have had on crude birth rates. Indeed, there is some theoretical basis for saying that couples adjust how many children they have, and when they have them, on the basis of the relative size of their birth cohort in comparison with their parents' cohort (Easterlin, 1968, 1978; Ryder, 1979). That is, there may be an automatic tendency for past fertility cycles to suppress rather than reinforce future fertility cycles.

The *degree* of impact of age structure upon crude birth rates, however, is generally minor compared with the impact of cohort fertility patterns. That is, how many children couples have in their lifetimes, and when they have them, remain the major causes of trends and cycles in period fertility. For the rest of this section, let us measure fertility with total fertility rates (TFRs) rather than crude birth rates. The TFR is not affected by the age structure of the population. By using it, therefore, we are able to explore what, *beyond age structure*, can have an immediate impact on fertility trends.

The Influence of Cohort Completed Fertility

Another fertility measure that would not be affected by age structure of the population would be the eventual number of *children ever born* to a generation, or *birth cohort*, of women who had completed childbearing. This measure would not be affected by age because women belonging to the birth cohort are all nearly the same age, and because women of the birth cohort have already passed through all ages of childbearing. When we follow a cohort of women through their lives and observe, on average, how many children they have had when they are at the end of childbearing ages, we have a measure of their *cohort completed fertility rate* (Shryock and Siegel, 1976).

This rate is similar to the total fertility rate (TFR) in many ways. As you may recall, the shortcut we used to compute the TFR was to add age-specific fertility rates across all ages (and then to multiply by the number of years in each age category). That is, we added up the fertility a woman would eventually have if she went through life and experienced the current age-specific fertility rates for each year of her life as she grew older.

To compute the cohort completed fertility rate (CCFR), we actually follow women through their lives and add up the effects of their own age-specific fertility rates across time as the cohort ages. If we take, for instance, the cohort of women born between 1950–1954, they would begin significant childbearing at ages 15–19 during the years 1965–1969; ages 20–24 during 1970–1974; ages 25–29 during 1975–1979, and so on, until they reached the final years of childbearing at ages 45–49 during

1995–1999. To compute their completed fertility we would add the 1965–1969 age-specific rate for women aged 15–19 to the 1970–1974 rate for women aged 20–24, and so on, then multiply by 5 (the number of years in the birth cohort and each age group).

In sum, the computation is the same as that for the TFR; what is different is the age-specific rates we are cumulating. In the case of the cohort completed fertility rate, we are adding up the rates experienced by a cohort of women during their lives.

One frustrating limitation of cohort completed fertility rates is that they, of course, cannot measure completed fertility until the cohort has passed through childbearing ages. This problem can be dealt with in two ways.

The first way is component projection. We can assume, on whatever basis, a schedule of age-specific fertility rates that a currently childbearing cohort will experience for the remainder of its childbearing ages, add those to the rates recorded for ages already passed, and obtain a partially projected cohort completed fertility rate.

The second way is deceptively simple. It consists of asking (in survey interviews) not only how many children women have had, but also how many children the women expect to have before they complete their childbearing. Obviously, women near their forty-fifth year are better able to make such a determination than are women just starting their fecund years, and obviously younger women will have more chance to change their minds or fail to fulfill their expectations. But this is a straightforward way of using subjective plans for prediction in societies where families are largely preplanned.

Our task is to assess to what degree the ups and downs in twentieth-century U.S. total fertility rates are explained by ups and downs in cohort completed fertility. Figure 7-5 presents total fertility rates for 1925 through 1999 and cohort fertility rates for women who completed childbearing before 1994.

Some technical comments are necessary to understand this figure. In comparing period and cohort trends, one is faced with a technical difficulty: What *date* does one assign to a cohort rate? Women who were born between 1945 and 1949, for example, were of childbearing ages all the way from the early 1960s to the mid-1990s. A fairly arbitrary answer is to assign cohort fertility rates to the date of the cohort's approximate median female age of childbearing; thirty has been chosen as that age in Figure 7-5. This is why the dates in the two time scales shown at the bottom of Figure 7-5 differ consistently by thirty years.

This also explains why the CCFR graph ends in the late 1970s. The birth cohort of 1945–1949 only completed childbearing in the 1990s, but the TFR when these women were about age thirty would be that from 1975–1979. This illustrates the frustrating limitation of cohort rates, mentioned above, that they measure events which could be long past.

One can see that U.S. cohort completed fertility made significant swings, but within the limited range of about 3.2 live births to 2.2 live births per woman. The timing of the upward and downward swings certainly was such that the changing tendencies of American women to have large, then small, then large, then small families helped explain the changes in total fertility rate. Finally, if the graph included a longer historical span, one would see a long-term secular decline in the average cohort completed fertility, probably extending from the birth of the nation.

Figure 7-5 Total Fertility Rate, 1925–1999, and Cohort Completed Fertility Rates, 1895–1949

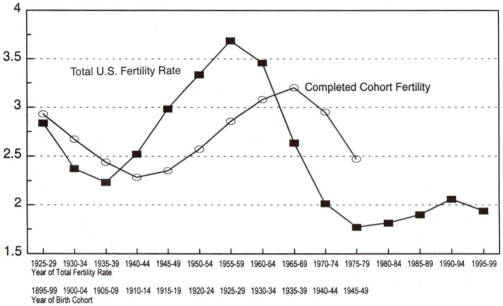

ᵃAt ages 45–49.
Source: Anderton et al., *Population of the United States*, 1997, tables 6-2 and 6-13.

A disclaimer may be appropriate. Our task has been to see whether the relation between these two trends was such that changes in CCFR could have caused observed changes in TFR, and that has been demonstrated to some extent. However, it is equally logical—given no further data—to say that changes in period total fertility rates eventually caused the swings in cohort completed fertility.

The Influence of Timing

The other aspect of cohort childbearing that can influence the total fertility rate is the timing of that childbearing. It makes a difference whether women bear their children early or late in their fecund ages. First, we will describe how this works in abstract; then we will describe how it has influenced U.S. total fertility rates in the past few decades.

Everything else being equal, a population where older women bear the children will have lower period fertility than will a population where younger women bear the children. There are two factors causing this (Coale and Tye, 1961).

Call the first the "prematernal-death" factor. Death erodes any cohort of women through its collective lifetime. That means that at every successive age between, say, fifteen and forty-nine there will be fewer women surviving. If that cohort bears its children while old, fewer of them will be alive to participate in the childbearing and they collectively will produce fewer children. (This will not be reflected in a lower cohort completed fertility rate, since that describes the performance of the women who survived.)

Call the second the "baby-spread" factor. If women bear their children at older ages and so do their daughters, and then so do their daughters, the result will be that those children will be spread over a larger number of calendar years. That means that the total fertility rate for any given year involved will be lower than it would have been under a regime of early childbearing. These two factors are *permanent* as long as the timing does not change.

In addition, there is a *transitory* effect of moving from one age schedule of childbearing to another. If a young childbearing population moves to older childbearing, there will be less overlap in the childbearing of successive cohorts than there would have been with no transition. If an old childbearing population moves to younger childbearing, there will be more of an overlap in the childbearing of successive cohorts.

In the case of the United States, the major effects of changes in age at childbearing have been due to the quick transitions in modern times. During the Depression, couples generally tended to delay childbearing; during the prosperity of the baby-boom, couples started earlier and earlier; during worldwide recession of the baby-bust, they started later again. The recent baby-boom echo happened at a time when women were bearing children at later, rather than earlier, ages. In this case the older baby-boomers finally entered into these ages and had children before they considered it too late. Most of these transitory effects have acted to *enhance* the effect of changes in U.S. cohort completed fertility. This is true even in cases such as the baby-boom echo where they may have dampened changes in period fertility.

Figure 7-5 graphs this. In this figure, the degree to which the total fertility rate line veers above or below the cohort completed fertility rate line is an index of the influence of changes in the timing of cohort fertility. Thus the TFR swooping below the CCFR line during the Depression would result from delays in childbearing. The soaring of the TFR above the CCFR during the baby-boom would be due to the late appearance of children delayed from their normal expectation during the Depression, plus the early appearance of baby-boom childbearing. The downward plunge of the TFR since 1965, even below the CCFR, registers the gap left by early-appearing baby-boom babies, plus the progressive delay of childbearing during the baby-bust. The effects of the baby-boom echo on completed fertility will not be seen until those women complete their childbearing. These echo effects can be estimated using the methods discussed above and show a continuing cyclical pattern. However, just as recent swings in TFR have been less extreme, so will be the anticipated echo effects.

Nevertheless, the potential impact of changes in timing is particularly strong in a society such as the United States. Only a portion of the U.S. women's fecund years normally are taken up with childbearing. In a typical less-developed country, in contrast, almost all of women's fecund years are taken up with childbearing. If LDR women are reproducing at all the ages they can, then there is very little room to shift the timing of their childbearing. In the United States, women have considerable choice about when to have their few children, and their decisions can have real impact on period fertility.

The Influence of Age Structure on Cohort Fertility

Here is another example of how the various immediate determinants of the crude birth rate may be subtly interrelated with each other: the relative size of birth cohorts may influence both the completed fertility of cohorts and the timing of their childbearing. How this might happen has been outlined by Richard Easterlin (1978).

Start with the observation that job opportunities for cohorts maturing into the workforce depend, everything else being equal, on the size of the cohort. Under the same business conditions, a large cohort will have to share available jobs among more people; members of a small cohort will have more choice of jobs.

Members of a cohort will see their economic situation as hopeful or hopeless not only on the basis of their actual opportunities, but also by comparing those prospects with some other standard. That standard, says Easterlin, is their family of orientation, their parents. If they see their prospects as better than those of their parents, they tend to be optimistic about improving their economic status; if they see no such chance, they respond with pessimism. Thus the relative economic opportunity of successive generations, partially determined by the relative sizes of those cohorts, influences economic optimism and pessimism.

Members express their optimism or pessimism reproductively. If they are pessimistic, they will tend to feel they can afford fewer children, voluntarily decreasing the cohort completed fertility rate for their generation. More immediately, they will tend to put off the start of childbearing until they feel more economically secure (Ryder, 1979). Both responses, of course, will reduce period fertility.

The theory is basically cyclical. Pessimistic generations (such as those becoming adults in the Depression) will produce small birth cohorts; those children, one generation hence, will see themselves as having better opportunities than their parents. They optimistically will marry early and have many children, creating a large birth cohort whose members, one generation hence, will see themselves as having poorer opportunities than their parents. They pessimistically will delay marriage and have fewer children (such as in the recent baby-bust), thus creating a small birth cohort, and so on.

One interesting, highly hypothetical implication is that this "Easterlin effect" might serve to explain dampening of the "echo effect" of peaks and valleys in the population pyramid. Everything else being equal, a relatively small birth cohort maturing into the childbearing ages is likely to produce fewer children. But here we see that a small cohort of potential parents also is likely to be economically optimistic, start childbearing early, and have more children. Of course, many other things besides cohort size can influence economic optimism and many influences other than optimism can affect childbearing decisions.

EXPLAINING COHORT FERTILITY

As we trace back through the causal chain that determines period fertility, what are the next links to study? We have established that differences in total fertility rates are caused by differences in two aspects of cohort fertility: the number of children born and the timing of the childbearing. What, then, causes these to vary?

Explanation by Background

Merely to describe fertility differences is to "explain" them in a primitive sense. Take, for instance, the fertility differences between the LDRs and the MDRs. Knowing the characteristics of people who tend to have higher fertility, for example, we can say that LDRs have higher fertility because people there are likely to be poorer and less educated, more likely of pronatalist religion, less likely to have industrial jobs, and so on. We can call this "explanation by background." It is a good first step.

The limitations of that kind of explanation become clear as soon as we undertake to *influence* fertility levels, to design fertility *policies*. Suppose, for instance, we want to reduce LDR fertility. The only guidance provided by the preceding kind of explanation in designing a policy is to suggest we change a maximum number of people from high-fertility categories to low-fertility categories. That is, make people richer, educate them better, provide them industrial jobs, and so on.

Policies that attempt to change people's fertility by changing their characteristics are indirect and gradual. When focused on particular aspects of social change, such policies can be popular among policy makers and supportive of other programs. An example is LDR policies for the improvement of female educational levels. But note that choosing a focus implies accepting some theory of how that background factor influences human behavior and thus fertility.

"Explanation by background" is simply not sufficient if we want to understand how group differences come about, or if we seek more effective ways to help people have the number of children they desire (Bulatao, 1984; Bongaarts and Potter, 1983; Burch, 1975). How many children a woman has, and when, is the result of complicated patterns of actions. She copulates or she doesn't, uses contraception or doesn't, induces an abortion or doesn't, to mention just a few of the determining acts. Those kinds of actions that have direct impact on the reproductive process we can call the *proximate determinants* of fertility levels. A more satisfactory explanation of fertility differences involves not only stating which classes of people have higher or lower fertility (describing background differentials) but also specifying how they do it (specifying differentials in the proximate determinants).

The Proximate Determinants of Fertility

Kingsley Davis and Judith Blake (1956) pioneered in outlining which categories of behavior should be taken into account in seeking to understand fertility. They saw the proximate determinants of fertility levels as *finite* and *limited*; there are just so many things that individuals can do to influence how many children they have and when. They listed these proximate determinants of fertility in order of the time sequence involved in producing babies through three stages: 1) intercourse, 2) conception, and 3) gestation and parturition. Their original list is presented in Box 7-1.

Davis and Blake called these proximate determinants "intermediate variables." This is because explanation of fertility up until the introduction of their list had been largely explanation by background. They stressed that the *only* way that a background difference (e.g. in wealth, education, or religion) could produce a fertility difference was by causing variation in one or more of the proximate determinants on their list.

Box 7-1 The "Intermediate Fertility Variables" of Davis and Blake

I. *Factors affecting exposure to intercourse ("Intercourse Variables")*
    A. Those governing the formation and dissolution of unions in the reproductive period
        1. Age of entry into sexual unions
        2. Permanent celibacy: proportion of women never entering sexual unions
        3. Amount of reproductive period spent after or between unions
            a. When unions are broken by divorce, separation, or desertion
            b. When unions are broken by death of husband
    B. Those governing the exposure to intercourse within unions
        4. Voluntary abstinence
        5. Involuntary abstinence (from impotence, illness, unavoidable but temporary separations)
        6. Coital frequency (excluding periods of abstinence)

II. *Factors affecting exposure to conception ("Conception Variables")*
        7. Fecundity or infecundity, as affected by involuntary causes
        8. Use or non-use of contraception
            a. By mechanical and chemical means
            b. By other means
        9. Fecundity or infecundity, as affected by voluntary causes (sterilization, subincision, medical treatment, etc.)

III. *Factors affecting gestation and successful parturition ("Gestation Variables")*
        10. Fetal mortality from involuntary causes
        11. Fetal mortality from voluntary causes

Source: Kingsley Davis and Judith Blake (1956), p. 212.

If we specify the proximate determinants of too-high or too-low cohort fertility for a class of people, we are in a better position for targeting a policy for influencing that fertility. If poor people have more children because they have less access to modern contraceptives, we can more easily provide such contraceptives than we can make the poor rich. Indeed, most modern fertility reduction policies in the LDRs have been family-planning programs based on this causal explanation.

Voluntary versus Involuntary Factors

Davis and Blake consistently attempted to distinguish between *voluntary* and *involuntary* intercourse variables, conception variables, and gestation variables. Let us take "voluntary" in this context to mean that the couple was adjusting its behavior with the intent of influencing how many children it would ultimately have and/or when those children would arrive. Induced abortion would be a clear case of a voluntary factor; impotence due to illness would be an extreme case of an involuntary factor.

What difference does the voluntariness of factors make? It makes a lot, not only in how you explain intercultural fertility differentials but also in what policies you might employ to change fertility levels. For instance, if you believe that the circumstances keeping LDR fertility high are mostly voluntary (people want to have large families early), then your strategy for lowering fertility requires you to change those fertility desires. If, on the other hand, you think the high fertility in the LDRs is involuntary and couples would like to have fewer children, then you undertake policies to change each one of these factors in the fertility-lowering direction. For instance, you might seek to raise the age at marriage, make contraceptives more easily available, or make induced abortion easier to obtain.

The motive for a couple's voluntarily altering its fertility isn't necessarily to reduce completed family size. They may delay the next child to give the mother more time to recover her health, to improve the next child's chances for survival, or to afford themselves temporary flexibility in responding to occupational or educational opportunities. None of these motives necessarily involves a desire to end up with a smaller family.

Let us now employ the Davis-Blake taxonomy and consider, in order, the impacts of intercourse variables, of conception variables, and of gestation variables on cohort fertility.

Intercourse Variables

The pattern of intercourse that would maximize a population's fertility is well known. It is one in which all the women in a population are sexually active throughout their fecund years and in which intercourse is optimally frequent throughout all those years. The consensus among physiologists seems to be that an average coital frequency of two to three times per week is optimal for reproduction (Trussell and Westoff, 1980); frequencies much higher than that may not give sperm a chance to develop before being ejaculated. On the average, however, deviations from the optimum in the direction of too seldom are far more likely. In the United States, for example, only around 40% of those aged eighteen to forty, and less than half of married persons, have intercourse at least two times per week (Michael et al., 1994).

Some deviations from patterns of intercourse that would maximize fertility have more impact on fertility than do others. Interruptions of sexual activity during ages of greatest fecundity, that is, among women in their twenties and early thirties, would have the most severe impact. Interruptions among women who are already pregnant, physiologically unlikely to conceive after birth (during postpartum amenorrhea and depending upon the specifics of breast-feeding, see Zohoori and Popkin, 1996), suffering from secondary sterility, or at less fecund ages, would have less impact. What follow are some of the major types of deviation from an optimal intercourse pattern that have impacted fertility in some cultures.

Being in Sexual Unions

Late entry into stable sexual unions. The term "sexual union" here refers to a heterosexual relationship in which the partners are committed to having access to each other sexually. The most normatively accepted kind of sexual union is marriage, although sizable minorities in some societies participate in nonmarital sexual unions of varying stability.

The age at which women first enter such stable sexual unions influences period fertility rates in two ways. First, it influences completed fertility of cohorts. If a cohort of women would have borne children throughout its fecund years, then forcing them to get a late start would tend to reduce their completed family size. In addition, that late start will tend to increase the average age of mothers at childbearing and, as we have seen, late childbearing has its own direct impact upon period fertility above or beyond its impact on completed family size.

Delayed entry into unions would have less impact on fertility if it occurred to women at less fecund ages or if contraceptives are widely used and couples normally have small families. Nevertheless, differences in age at first marriage are partially responsible for some of the major world fertility differentials. The low modern fertility of Western countries is attributed partially to the "European marriage pattern," that is, late female age at marriage and large proportions of women never marrying.

Interruption of stable sexual unions. Sexual unions can be broken, either by the death of the husband (widowhood) or by divorce or separation. Whatever the precipitating event, how long the women will stay nonmarried obviously depends on how rapidly and completely a new union takes place (see chapter 8). Widowhood during childbearing ages seems to be declining on a worldwide level as male mortality declines. Moreover, the negative impact of widowhood on fertility always has been limited by the fact that women are widowed mostly after their most fecund years.

The fertility impact of worldwide trends in divorce and remarriage defies easy generalization. Some LDR countries (such as those with Moslem cultures) have very low levels of divorce while others have an incidence that is quite high. Westerners are sensitive to the increasing prevalence of divorce in their countries, especially in the United States (where divorce rates have, however, stabilized and declined slightly since the 1980s). Even if continued modernization means a continued upswing in the incidence of divorce, it is unclear whether divorce will be rapidly succeeded by marriage or by other nonmarital sexual unions, stable or unstable (Yaukey, 1973).

Sexual union variables as cultural, not "intermediate." Strictly speaking, those "intercourse variables" on the Davis-Blake list (section I.A.) in Box 7-1 ("Those governing the formation and dissolution of unions . . .") do not logically belong on the list of "intermediate variables" but rather among the cultural factors that must operate through the intermediate variables. Every other variable on the Davis-Blake list has the potential for direct impact on fertility. The variables in category I.A., in contrast, can influence fertility only by influencing one of the remaining variables on the list.

Exposure within Unions

Postpartum abstinence. Sexual abstinence by females for one, two, or even three years after giving birth is normal in many societies (Heer and Grigsby, 1992). Apparently it is most prevalent in sub-Saharan Africa (Jolly and Gribble, 1993; Caldwell and Caldwell, 1977) but also has been found in Indonesia (Hull, 1975) and has been studied incompletely in other LDRs. Increasing birth intervals in this manner reduces the completed family size, delays the childbearing of these mothers, and improves infant survival. How much of an impact it has depends on how long absti-nence goes on after the mother stops breast-feeding.

Periodic abstinence. In Davis and Blake's list, periodic abstinence does not refer to either short-term interruptions of intercourse directed at contraception nor long-term interruptions that are effectively disruptions of sexual unions. We are refer-ring here to seasonal abstinence in such countries as Bangladesh (Chen et al., 1974) and Peru (Heer, 1964), where men seasonally migrate in search of employment, leav-ing their partners behind. If there were no seasonal migration fertility could increase by as much as 25% (Menken, 1979).

Infrequent intercourse. It can be difficult to get reliable representative data on the frequency of sexual intercourse. One consistent finding, however, is that the fre-quency of intercourse varies by age and by whether one is in a stable sexual union. Those in sexual unions have higher frequencies of intercourse (although those outside unions may have more sexual partners), and intercourse is more frequent at ages near the average age of marriage than it is at older ages.

In contrast to many cultural stereotypes, there is little evidence of differences in the frequency of intercourse by other major social or economic characteristics. From those data available, Nag (1968, p. 76) found no consistent difference between indus-trial and nonindustrial societies when it comes to coital frequency. In the United States, three successive fertility surveys (Trussell and Westoff, 1980) and a more recent study of sexual behavior (Michael et al., 1994) all found no association of coital frequency with socioeconomic, demographic, or even attitudinal variables.

Frequency of intercourse can clearly affect a woman's fertility. However, to sig-nificantly delay the average time to conceive among any large social group, coital fre-quency would have to be extremely low, lower than has been found on the average in *any* societal segment.

CONCEPTION VARIABLES

Under a given pattern of sexual intercourse, individuals and populations differ in the rate at which conception occurs. The factors that determine the differences in these conception rates are what Davis and Blake mean by "conception variables." These causes can be involuntary (such as sickness or malnutrition) or voluntary (such as contraception). Or, as in the case of breast-feeding, they can be a combination of the two. We will start with the clearly involuntary factors influencing conception.

Involuntary Factors

A woman is said to be fecund if she is able to conceive. The range of biological factors that somehow could influence fecundity are almost limitless. We will focus on disease and malnutrition, both of which are suspected of threatening fertility among the underprivileged.

As a starter, it helps to imagine a population with maximum fecundity. In this hypothetical population, women have early menarche (the onset of menstruation) and thus start their conception period young. Moreover, they have late menopause, allowing them to bear children late in their lives. In between these events, they have a high probability of conceiving every time they have intercourse. As part of this, they recover their capacity to conceive rapidly after each of their childbirths, having a very short period of postpartum amenorrhea (delay of the reonset of menstruation) and very few anovulatory cycles (menstrual cycles in which ovulation and thus conception do not occur). In this hypothetical population, men do their part by producing sperm adequate to their coital frequency and also of high vigor (motility), eager to seek out the female ova. Now let us describe deviations from this maximum-fecundity population.

Length of the fecund period.   Age of menopause does not vary much. For instance, the age of cessation of childbearing among noncontracepting couples seems very standard, about forty-one years on the average (Menken et al., 1981). Age of menarche, on the other hand, varies both internationally and historically. Teenage females universally become fecund over a progression of years during which they experience decreasing *adolescent sterility.* Age of menarche in part depends upon nutrition and has thus generally decreased with modernization (Heer and Grigsby, 1992; Nag, 1980). It is reportedly on the average at 12.8 years in the United States but not until 16 years in Bangladesh (Menken et al., 1981). How much of an impact age at menarche has upon fertility depends, of course, on how much intercourse, contraception, and abortion also take place in the teen years.

Subfecundity due to morbidity.   Disease and malnutrition can reduce fecundity. Infectious diseases have greater impact during reproductive ages than degenerative diseases. Both smallpox and tuberculosis, for example, produced subfecundity well into the twentieth century. Any infection accompanied by high fever can threaten spermatogenesis. Malaria is a good and pertinent illustration. In addition, many diseases can interfere with the transport of sperm or ova by inflaming or scarring the epididymis or the Fallopian tubes. Probably the most important attackers of transport are gonorrhea and genital tuberculosis (McFalls, 1979). HIV/AIDS and many other diseases also can lower fecundity through both wasting and secondary infections.

How much impact do infectious diseases actually have? Without the influence of these diseases, LDR fertility would tend to be higher, especially in parts of central Africa. Disease, with its threat to conception, also undoubtedly helps to explain conception differentials between favored and unfavored classes within societies, including the MDRs.

Very severe stoppages of nutritional intake, such as occur in famine, apparently cause cessation of ovulation, as well as loss of libido and a reduction of production of sperm (Menken et al., 1981). The effect of *malnutrition* is more controversial. Frisch (1975) suggests that women need to maintain a certain critical body weight in order to have the fat reserves necessary for regular ovulation. Coale (1974) notes there is a tendency for malnourished women to have longer periods of postpartum amenorrhea. But all investigators seem to agree that the major cause of long periods of postpartum amenorrhea is not nutrition but breast-feeding (Menken et al., 1981).

Breast-Feeding

If a woman nurses a child after giving birth, her hormonal reaction to lactation delays considerably the return of her menstrual cycles and thus her ovulation and fecundity. This tendency varies considerably among individuals and breast-feeding methods (Zohoori and Popkin, 1996; Adair et al., 1993). It does not normally work indefinitely, but on the average it can have considerable impact upon birth intervals, and can lower fertility proportionately more than other family-planning methods (Cooney, 1992). Bongaarts and Potter (1983) estimate that, with no use of contraceptives, uninterrupted breast-feeding could add eighteen months or more to average birth intervals.

Traditionally, women in less-developed countries have breast-fed in larger proportions and for longer durations than women in more-developed countries; however, there is considerable variation, even among LDRs (Sharma et al., 1991; London et al., 1985; Bongaarts and Potter, 1983). Within both LDRs and MDRs, urban and more educated women have been less likely to nurse and/or are likely to nurse for shorter periods (Hirschman and Butler, 1981; Jain and Bongaarts, 1980; Knodel and Debavalya, 1981). These differences have, however, narrowed over time (Sharma et al., 1991).

Worldwide trends in breast-feeding are mixed. Although some researchers predicted a decline in breast-feeding, especially in sub-Saharan Africa (e.g. Cochrane and Farid, 1990), others have argued that this expected decline has failed to materialize (Sharma et al., 1991). Breast-feeding trends may also become more variable as individual countries adopt the use of breast-feeding, or the Lactational Amenorrhea Method (LAM), as a heavily promoted family-planning method (Shane, 1997).

To repeat an introductory comment, whether breast-feeding is an involuntary or a voluntary variable affecting fertility is a moot question. Now we turn to a category of conception variables that is obviously voluntary.

Contraception

The geographical pattern of contraceptive use among the nations of the world probably corresponds very closely to the pattern of low fertility. Effective use of contraception is the main reason for low fertility in the nations where it is found. Box 7-2 presents a list of the prevalent contraceptive methods, ordered on the basis of when in the reproductive process they work.

How widespread is contraception? Almost all MDR couples use it; but what may surprise the reader is how widespread its use has become in the LDRs. Over the past two decades, couples in every region of the world have increasingly adopted modern contraception methods (McDevitt et al., 1996). The results of these trends as of 1998 are shown in Figure 7-6. The vast majority of these women are using modern contraceptive methods (U.S. Bureau of the Census, 1999, table A-11).

As this figure shows, there is considerable variation in the practice of contraception despite the spread of modern contraceptive methods to less-developed countries. The percentages of married reproductive-age women using contraception in eastern, middle, and western Africa remain the lowest in the world. And some parts of Asia, as well as Oceania, still have considerably lower contraceptive prevalence rates than in the more-developed regions.

Box 7-2 Prevalent Contraceptive Methods and How They Work

Prevention of Ovulation, Spermatogenesis, or Transport

Oral Contraceptives. "The pill" is a compound of synthetic hormones that suppress ovulation by keeping the estrogen level high in the female. This prevents the pituitary gland from sending a signal to the ovaries to release an egg. Although the primary effect is by suppressing ovulation, the pill also operates by keeping the cervical mucus in a state the sperm cannot penetrate and making the lining of the uterus unsuitable for implantation. Actually, there are many different types of pills, using various combinations and doses of estrogen, progestin, and other agents.

Injectable Contraceptives. Injectable contraceptives are used by over 10 million women worldwide. They are similar in composition and action to oral contraceptives and are primarily distinctive in their long-term action, which does not require daily dosages.

Surgical Sterilization. In the female, sterilization consists of cutting, tying, and removing a portion of the oviduct. In the male, sterilization (called "vasectomy") consists of cutting, tying, and removing a portion of the spermatic duct or vas deferens. In either case, transport to the potential place of union, and thus conception, is blocked.

Prevention of Contact between Sperm and Ova

Rhythm Method. Also known as *natural family planning* or *periodic abstinence*, this method capitalizes on the long-known fact that ova are available for fertilization during only a few days of the menstrual cycle. The strategy is to avoid intercourse during those few days, and the trick is to find the exact interval in which to avoid intercourse. This is attempted through estimating time of ovulation from records of past menstrual cycles, noting minor changes in the woman's temperature that signal hormonal changes following ovulation, and noting mucosal changes in the vagina throughout the entire cycle.

Withdrawal. Known more demurely as *coitus interruptus*, the method consists simply of removing the penis from the vagina before ejaculation.

Vaginal Contraceptives. The idea is to place in the vagina, not necessarily over the cervix, some substance (a spermicide) that will create a barrier to oncoming sperm and perhaps kill or immobilize them. The substances are contained in saturated sponges, suppositories, foaming tablets, and aerosol foams and creams.

The Diaphragm and Cervical Cap. These operate by covering the cervix tightly, preventing the sperm from entering the uterus. The diaphragm is a soft rubber cup with a metal spring reinforcing the rim, held in place by the spring tension, the vaginal muscle tone, and the pubic bone. Since it does not fit tightly enough to prevent the passage of all sperm, it is recommended that the diaphragm be used with a spermicidal cream or jelly. The cervical cap is a small, thimble-shaped cup, usually made of plastic, that blocks the cervix. The cap provides a more effective mechanical block than does the diaphragm; thus spermicidal mixtures are not necessary.

Condoms. The condom is a mechanical barrier that fits snugly over the penis and prevents the ejaculated sperm from entering the vagina. Condoms made from the intestines of sheep and other animals first appeared in the eighteenth century, but it was not until the vulcanization of rubber in the nineteenth century that use of condoms on a large scale became possible. Hence the popular name, the "rubber."

Douches. The postintercourse washing out of the vagina is nearly ineffective as a method of birth control, even though its use is widespread, partially for aesthetic purposes.

Prevention of Implantation of the Ovum in the Uterus

Intrauterine Devices (IUDs). The idea of placing objects in the uterus to avoid pregnancy is fairly old. Today a wide variety of intrauterine devices are available. Most are made of flexible plastic, although some also have copper wire twisted around them. It is not known exactly how IUDs prevent pregnancy, but preventing implantation is considered the most likely hypothesis.

Morning-after Pill. This pill, made of synthetic estrogen, is taken after coitus. It is a fairly new development and its introduction is being monitored carefully. Properly administered doses of oral contraceptives can provide a similar effect to morning-after pills. These medications to avert implantation are distinguished from those such as RU-486, which abort an already implanted fetus.

Menstrual Regulation. When a woman's expected menstrual flow fails to appear, menstruation may be induced. By producing a flow, this procedure prevents the development of any fertilized ovum in the uterine wall. One other technique under study involves a massive dose of a substance called prostaglandin into the vagina; this creates an endocrine imbalance that results in the appearance of menstruation.

Figure 7-6   Percentage of Married Women of Reproductive Age Using Contraception, by Region, 1998

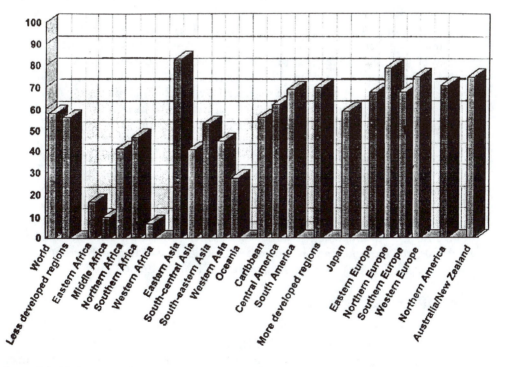

Source: United Nations, *World Contraceptive Use 1998*, 1999b. The U.N. is author of the original material.

Variation in contraceptive use among individual countries is even more dramatic. The prevalence of modern methods in China, for example, is more than two times that of India. As a result, India will have about 20% more children born in the year 2000 than those born in China, despite the greater number of married women of reproductive age in China (U.S. Bureau of the Census, 1999). According to the most recent fertility surveys, a very small percentage of women use modern or traditional contraceptive methods in some large countries such as Pakistan (9% modern and 2.8% traditional) and Nigeria (3.5% modern and 2.5% traditional).

Contraception will continue to be one of the most important proximate determinants of fertility in the coming century. The efficacy with which women can achieve lower desired family sizes is second only to those desires in determining future fertility trends. We will discuss unmet contraceptive needs and family-planning programs as a fertility "problem" later in this chapter.

GESTATION VARIABLES

Involuntary Interruption

Demographers have come to divide the nine-month gestation period into two segments, drawing the line at the end of the twenty-eighth week. Pregnancy loss before that is called *early fetal death* and corresponds to the popular notion of miscarriage. Loss after the twenty-eighth week, called *late fetal death*, corresponds to the popular notion of stillbirth (Shryock and Siegel, 1976). The demographic reason for dividing the gestation period for separate study of subperiods is that the dominant causes of death shift. In fact, after the twenty-eighth week the causes of fetal death are so similar to those for a newborn child's first week that late fetal mortality and neonatal mortality are sometimes studied together as *perinatal mortality*.

Fetal mortality is a potent force in limiting fertility. As much as 40% of conceptions may not survive through birth, even without induced abortion. Yet, since fetal deaths are relatively evenhanded across countries and are resistant to external interference, they cannot be viewed as a major explanation of differences in national fertility levels.

A variety of factors influence fetal mortality. One clearly is the age of the mother (Tafari and Zerihun, 1993); the risk curve is generally J-shaped, with minimal risk in the woman's early 20s and increasing about 9% each year to the early 40s. Another is gender; male fetuses seem to be more vulnerable than female. A variety of stressful life circumstances in developing countries increase fetal mortality, including short birth intervals, malnutrition, and limited access to health care (Tafari and Zerihun, 1993). In all regions, smoking increases fetal mortality (Hoyert, 1996).

Voluntary Interruption

Definitions are important here. As used by the medical profession, the term *abortion* denotes the termination of a pregnancy after the implantation of the blastocyst (fertilized egg) in the endometrium (uterine wall) but before the fetus has gained viability. This definition distinguishes abortion from the last category of contraception described in Box 7-2: those methods that operate by preventing implantation of the ovum in the uterus, such as the IUD or the morning-after pill. Traditionally, a fetus has been considered "viable" (able to survive outside the mother) after 28 weeks, corresponding to a fetal weight of 1,000 grams (Tietze, 1981, p. 1). An abortion is either "induced" or "spontaneous" (as in a miscarriage), depending on whether anything was done with the *intention* of ending the pregnancy. When proper medical facilities are used, intention seems unambiguous; on the other hand, there is a category of things that women can do to themselves that might result in abortions and where their intentions are not self-evident or unmixed.

Induced abortions can be either legal or illegal (criminal). Most countries, 98%, allow for abortion in cases where the mother's life is endangered. However, only 27% allow abortion on request (United Nations, 1999c). The grounds on which abortion is permitted vary widely from country to country. Less-developed countries generally have more restrictive policies than do more-developed countries. Over 80% of MDR countries, for example, permit abortion in the case of rape or incest while only 30% of those in LDRs permit abortion for the same reasons (United Nations, 1999c).

There probably are large numbers of illegal abortions in countries where the idea of birth control is well accepted by the people but where laws make induced abortion difficult, but there is no way of measuring accurately the incidence of illegally induced abortions. In fact, because abortion is stigmatized, the completeness of reporting legal abortions is also questionable (Johnston and Hill, 1996). As a result, we will focus our attention on reported legal abortions and also refer to indirect estimates that may provide more accurate measures of abortion rates.

The incidence of abortion can be measured by *abortion rates* very similar to those we use for fertility. That is, we can construct crude abortion rates, general abortion rates, age-specific abortion rates, even total abortion rates. The United States had an abortion rate of 20 abortions per 1,000 women of reproductive age in 1996 (CDC, 1998).

Abortion rates vary even more widely than do policies (United Nations, 1999c). In 1996 European abortion rates ranged from a low of just under 6 in Ireland and Spain to a high of 78 in Romania. African countries, and most other high-fertility countries, have low abortion rates. For example, South Africa had an abortion rate of only 2.7 (1997) and Tunisia of 8.6 (1996) per 1,000 women of reproductive age. However, sub-Saharan Africa may have a substantially higher incidence of abortion than is reported (Jolly and Gribble, 1993). Latin American countries, except Cuba, have generally restrictive policies and provide little information on the incidence of abortion (United Nations, 1999c). Abortion rates in Asia, by comparison, are generally high. China had an abortion rate of 26.1 (1995) while both Uzbekistan and Vietnam had rates as high as 83.3 (1996). India and Bangladesh, however, had very low abortion rates of 2.7 and 3.8 (1995/96), respectively.

Of course, the prevalence of abortion is not necessarily an indicator of how strongly it is related to overall fertility levels. Some demographers argue that no significant decline in birth rates has been achieved without some recourse to abortion, and that fertility declines often occur when abortion is made available in populations with unmet contraceptive needs (Bulatao, 1984). Using indirect abortion estimates for developing countries, Johnston and Hill (1996, p. 111) conclude:

The effect of abortion on fertility appears to be geographically clustered, suggesting that common socioeconomic situations and cultural heritages influence abortion levels. Abortion appears to have the greatest impact on fertility in Latin America, a strong influence in Southeast Asia (as measured using data from Indonesia), a varying impact in sub-Saharan Africa, and the weakest influence in the Near East (barring Turkey).

Abortion data for the United States are more reliable than that for most developing countries. In 1996 roughly 80% of all abortions were performed on unmarried women and just under half were to women with no prior live births (CDC, 1998). Availability of abortion services and restrictive policies appear to be a major influence on the variability of abortion rates from one area of the country to the next (Wetstein, 1996). Looking at trends over time, the abortion rate in the United States went from about 13 in 1972 up to 25 in 1980 and remained there until the early 1990s. Since then it has declined slowly to about 20 abortions per 1,000 women in the mid-1990s.

Another way of measuring the incidence of abortion is by means of the *abortion ratio*. The numerator of the ratio is the number of abortions. The denominator can be either the number of live births or the number of live births plus legal abortions. Using the former, the abortion ratio in the United States was around 180 abortions per 1,000 live births in 1972, rose to 359 in 1984, then fell slowly to around 314 by 1996 (CDC, 1998). Abortion ratios do not refer to the probability of any woman having an abortion but rather index the relative probability pregnancies will end with a legally induced abortion. Since we might expect abortion to vary in response to the rate of pregnancies, the abortion ratio is often preferred to the abortion rate.

Even with adequate data, is difficult to know the exact effects of abortion on overall fertility in the United States. First, efficacious contraceptive options are widely available. Second, not all abortions are of viable fetuses. As the abortion rate in the United States has declined the rate of fetal loss has risen, and as the abortion rate has increased the rate of fetal loss has fallen (Anderton et al., 1997). Finally, the dividing line between abortion and contraception is becoming increasingly blurred by a range of post-intercourse, and even post-conception, orally administered contraceptives and abortifacients. Despite the extreme emotion and political rancor surrounding induced abortion, it is only one of a range of fertility options exercised by women in the United States and certainly not the most important determinant of fertility.

FERTILITY "PROBLEMS"

Fertility, Age Structure, and Population Growth: A Review

As we discussed in chapters 3 and 4, youth dependency is caused by sustained high birth rates in many less-developed countries. In the more-developed countries, the problems of an aging population are due primarily to decreases in birth rates. And, the imbalance between the sizes of succeeding cohorts in MDR countries are due to modern short-term cycles in fertility.

We also tend to blame fertility for problems of population growth, discussed in chapter 3, but with only partial justification. Modern population explosions have been caused by changes in mortality, not in fertility, yet we tend to blame sustained high fertility for the problem. Perhaps this is because our values allow us to entertain more easily a definition of the problem that suggests a solution by decreasing childbearing, as opposed to shortening human lives.

Problems of population growth and population structure are the major purely demographic ones seen to result from fertility trends, but there are others of a more personal nature.

Maternal and Child Mortality and Morbidity

Sustained, rapid childbearing threatens the health of mothers and babies alike. The chances of the mother and the infant surviving improves if the woman is not old *and* if she has not had many previous babies. Moreover, longer intervals between births improve mothers' and babies' chances of surviving.

Shane (1997) estimates that family planning can prevent over a fourth of all maternal deaths by allowing women to space children, to avoid unwanted pregnancies and unsafe abortions, to protect themselves from sexually transmitted diseases and HIV/AIDS, and to terminate childbearing at a desired family size. She also points out that spacing births at least two years apart could, by itself, prevent an average of one in four infant deaths and improve the survival chances of next older siblings. Numerous other health advantages are possible through fertility control.

This is a case where humanitarian concern for individual health runs parallel with collective concern over population explosions and youth dependency. By having women stop their childbearing at younger ages and at earlier parities, one would not only be protecting mother and infant health but also would be reducing total fertility rates. Because the goals of reducing fertility and improving maternal and child health run parallel, policy makers frequently use health considerations as a politically acceptable justification for fertility reduction programs in the less-developed countries (Sadik, 1991).

Unmet Contraceptive Needs and Unwanted Pregnancies

If women continue to have children after they have achieved their desired number, that can place a strain on both the parents and offspring. It is this discrepancy between wish and reality that formed the ideology of the planned parenthood movement. At least originally, the movement goals were not necessarily to decrease aggregate fertility levels, but rather to minimize discrepancies between desired and actual family sizes and timings of births. That is why the movement was careful to include among its goals the helping of women who had *fewer* children than they wanted as well as those who were in danger of having *more* than they wanted.

Again, those in favor of fertility reduction programs for the LDRs have been able to appeal to this concern about couples' unmet contraceptive needs and unwanted pregnancies as a justification for reducing aggregate fertility. It is a lot easier to argue for helping couples implement their own family-size goals than it is to argue for imposing a collective low-fertility goal upon them.

A woman is considered to have unmet contraceptive needs if she would prefer to control fertility, either by spacing or limiting births, and is not currently using contraception (U.S. Bureau of the Census, 1999). Unwanted pregnancies may occur to a woman with unmet contraceptive needs or through contraceptive failure. Although surveys can obtain information on unmet contraceptive needs, it is difficult to measure the extent of unwanted pregnancies. Not all pregnancies to women with unmet contraceptive needs are unwanted. And, some women may change their preferences. A previously unwanted pregnancy may become a wanted one once it has occurred.

The unmet contraceptive needs of married women in six selected countries are shown in the columns of Table 7-4. The first column shows unmet needs among married women aged twenty to forty-nine. The percentage of women whose contraceptive needs are presently unmet range from over a third of all women in Kenya to an eighth of those in Indonesia. Unmet need is most prevalent and widespread in sub-Saharan Africa, where needs are unmet for more than a third of married women in over half of the countries with recent data (U.S. Bureau of the Census, 1999). In absolute numbers of women, unmet need is greatest in India, Pakistan, Bangladesh, Indonesia, and the Philippines. Column 2 shows unmet needs for married women in adolescent ages, fifteen through nineteen. In most countries the percentage of adolescents with unmet contraceptive needs is higher than it is for older women.

Table 7-4
Unmet Contraceptive Needs in Selected Countries, 1990–1993[a]

| | Percent of Married Women with Unmet Needs | | | |
| | Ages 20–49 | Ages 15–19 | | |
Country	(1)	Total (2)	For Spacing (3)	For Limiting (4)
Kenya	36.1	41.9	37.5	4.4
Cameroon	23.0	15.1	13.3	1.8
Philippines	26.1	31.5	27.1	4.4
Indonesia	12.5	15.6	15.0	0.6
Dominican Republic	15.6	36.3	27.5	8.8
Colombia	15.4	15.0	13.0	2.0

[a]Data are from the most recent DHS survey ranging from 1990 to 1993.
Source: U.S. Bureau of the Census, *Trends in Adolescent Fertility and Contraceptive Use in the Developing World*, 1996, tables 8 & 19.

Among adult women and adolescents, the contraceptive needs which are now unmet are most often for purposes of spacing and timing births rather than to limit eventual completed family sizes (U.S. Bureau of the Census, 1999). This is especially true for adolescents, whose thoughts of completed family size may lie in the distant future (U.S. Bureau of the Census, 1996). Columns 3 and 4 of Table 7-4 show the percentage of adolescents with unmet needs for spacing and limiting purposes. The large majority of unmet adolescent needs clearly arise from a desire to control the timing of fertility, rather than specifically to limit completed family size.

Adolescent Fertility

The extent to which adolescent fertility is considered to be a problem varies from country to country. In some regions such as Asia and Africa early marriage and early childbearing are culturally desirable. Early marriage norms are the greatest cultural cause of adolescent fertility. Yet, regardless of cultural support for early marriage and adolescent fertility, there are significant health threats associated with these births, which are high-risk for both the mother and child.

About 80% of births to adolescent women occur in the developing countries of Asia, Africa, and Latin America (U.S. Bureau of the Census, 1996). As in the United States, adolescent fertility has recently declined in most LDRs (NCHS, 1998c; U.S. Bureau of the Census, 1996). The adolescent fertility decline in less-developed regions has been even more rapid than declines in the fertility of older women.

Despite these recent declines, some groups of young women continue to suffer from higher fertility rates, unwanted pregnancies, and resulting health problems. Prominent among these are women in the highest fertility countries and in rural areas of developing countries. With generally lower education levels and with less access to family planning, these women typically have higher adolescent fertility rates, and especially in the very earliest ages which are most problematic. Because of the negative consequences for the health of mothers and children, and the especially heavy burden of adolescent fertility on disadvantaged social groups, it remains a major concern.

In sum, when we go beyond blaming sustained high fertility for its contribution to age structure and population growth problems, we tend to focus on its negative consequences for health, especially for maternal and child health. It is not surprising that the constituencies most concerned with this category of problems would be the health-medical professions and the advocates of women's rights. Indeed, within the history of the postwar family-planning movement we see a shift in emphasis from population explosion concerns to what we might call "the health and reproductive rights agenda." This shift is traced in the following section.

FAMILY-PLANNING PROGRAMS IN THE LESS-DEVELOPED REGIONS

Historically, nations have tried to raise as well as lower their fertility. During the 1930s, for instance, European policies were likely to be pronatalist, however ineffective. National policies in the post-World War II decades, however, have been largely confined to the less-developed regions, and they universally have aimed at enhancing women's reproductive control for the purposes of limiting fertility and improving maternal and child health.

Such family-planning programs have proven very successful over the past several decades. In retrospect, seldom has a social invention swept through so much of the world in such a short period with such a significant impact as has family planning. For a time, it had a marvelous combination of political acceptability, congruence with widespread social values, and technical appeal. Still, family planning has had its critics. And, the politics of family planning have changed significantly over recent years.

The Goals of Family Planning

The rationale for the existence of family planning has gone through several distinctive stages. In the 1960s through the mid-1970s these policies were dominated by concern over the need to limit population growth in developing countries.

The family-planning agenda rested upon an elegantly simple rationale: the "right" number of children per couple is generally less than the actual number of children per couple. If so, implementing individuals' and couples' wishes should simultaneously eliminate couples' future unwanted pregnancies and also reduce high growth burdens in developing countries.

Emphasizing knowledge and practices of contraception, family-planning programs were "designed to provide the information, supplies, and services of (modern) means of fertility control to those interested" (Watson, 1982, p. 205). A key feature was voluntariness, relying upon the individual's (or couple's) motivation for limiting fertility. This could be aided by noncoercive persuasion; programs include varying degrees of propaganda for small families, but they ideally only educate individuals to their own self-interest. Another feature was the involvement of modern, medically correct contraceptive methods as the proper means of achieving the desired family size. And a key aspect of these programs was government sponsorship, either directly or in combination with voluntary agencies.

Critics and Compromises

Even as family-planning programs were spreading through the LDRs, demographic critics were questioning their adequacy. One attack was directed at the underlying assumption that the collective demographic good would be served by simply implementing existing individual desires (e.g. Blake, 1969; Davis, 1967; Demerath, 1976; Hauser, 1967). Critics argued that the cultures of LDRs had evolved in the context of high mortality and short life and have had to evolve norms that support high fertility; otherwise, the societies would not have survived. There is, therefore, no escape from the necessity for basic cultural change as a prerequisite for durable and substantial fertility reduction. To these critics, the supply of contraception was not the issue. Instead, what was important was to change the social conditions generating high fertility demand (Simmons, 1986). Critics were not even necessarily convinced by the decline of fertility in many LDR countries that did have family-planning programs; they suspected that much of this decline would have occurred without the programs, due to other more fundamental cultural changes.

Another source of suspicion involved doubts about the motives of program advocates. Let us call this the "genocide threat" (Darity et al., 1971; Hartmann, 1995). To understand this perspective, it helps to recall the intellectual history of American demography during the first half of the twentieth century. Much of what were seen as population "problems" in the MDRs late in their demographic transitions were based on the belief that the "higher quality" people were having fewer children than the "lower quality" people, a *eugenics* concern. Now the critics once again saw demographers advocating smaller families—but for whom? For the citizens of the less-developed countries, who happened to be predominantly black, yellow, and brown, rather than white. Moreover, within any country, the programs were aimed mainly at those below the local (Westernized) middle class. It did not help, of course, that the programs were being advocated by former colonial or imperialist powers.

The Health and Reproductive Rights Agenda

Partly in response to criticisms, but also due to rising knowledge of the negative health impacts of high fertility for women, in the mid-1970s attention shifted to the maternal and child health aspects of family planning (Sadik, 1991; Shane, 1997). Since the mid-1980s, a series of international population and development conferences has moved the family-planning agenda to a nearly exclusive emphasis on women's reproductive rights, autonomy, status, education, and reproductive health (Harcourt, 1999; Hardee et al., 1999).

Despite these sometimes dramatic changes in emphasis, echoes of the earlier family-planning criticisms remain. Some critics maintain current programs still have the goal of imposing Western perspectives of human rights and reproduction on other cultures. Others argue that our primary concern in less-developed countries should be with developmental, rather than reproductive health and contraceptive, agendas.

Although the new emphasis on women's rights and reproductive health is laudable in its own right, it is not without controversy among the advocates of family-planning programs and more traditional agendas. Caldwell (1997a), for example, warns that these goals may be opposed to that of completing the demographic transition and that developed country governments may "never again emphasize the need for family-planning programs in developing countries."

The rhetoric of these debates has often been heated. Those advocating an emphasis on women's rights and autonomy decry the provision of contraception as an attempted cultural intrusion or genocide, while those advocating family planning argue that the new agenda is an attempt to hijack successful programs and their support by those with a different political agenda.

This controversy, however, may be overstated in the long run. Efforts to improve reproductive health, reproductive rights, and the overall status of women will most likely find few programs as helpful as family-planning programs in achieving those objectives. And, as we have seen (see Table 7-4), there is already considerable demand for family planning in most regions of the world. Based on past history, this demand and the diffusion of contraceptive technology is likely to increase rather than retreat over the coming century.

Support for Family-Planning Programs

A key element of family-planning programs is government sponsorship. In Table 7-5 government perspectives on current birth rates (column 3) and support for family planning (column 7) are given for regions of the world alongside indicators of fertility, contraception, and maternal mortality.

Government support for family planning is lowest in regions which need it most. Africa, with the highest fertility, highest maternal mortality, and lowest access to modern contraception, has a large percentage of governments that consider the

Table 7-5
Government Support for Family Planning, and Related Demographic Measures, by World Region, 1999

Region	Total Fertility Rate (1)	Maternal Deaths per 100,000 Live Births[a] (2)	Percent of Governments That Consider Birth Rate High[a] (3)	Percent of Married Women Using Contraception — All Methods (4)	Modern Methods (5)	Accessibility of Modern Contraception (6)	Government Support for Family Planning (7)
Africa	5.4	880	77	24	18	Low	Low
Asia (excl. China)	3.3	510	42	47	40	Medium	Medium-High
China	1.8	95	0	83	81	High	High
Europe	1.4	10	0	71	54	Medium-High	Medium
Latin America	2.9	180	55	68	59	Low-High	Low-High
North America	2.0	8	0	77	70	High	Medium

[a]Data for columns 2 and 3 are for 1997, and for columns 6 and 7 are undated but in the late 1980s.
Source: Population Reference Bureau, *1999 World Population Data Sheet*, 1999; *1997 World Population Data Sheet*, 1997; Simmons, "Family Planning Programs," 1986, table 1.

birth rate too high, but which lack sufficient resources and commitment to family-planning programs. Africa is followed in fertility, maternal mortality, and low contraceptive access by Asia (excluding China). However, support for family planning and access to contraceptives have been much greater in Asia. Latin America also has high fertility and moderate maternal mortality but better access to contraception. Conditions vary considerably from country to country in all regions, but this is especially true of Latin America and the Caribbean.

While family planning has been one of the most successful social inventions of the past century, and while the self-defined unmet needs in the LDRs remain evident, U.S. support for family-planning programs remains a frustratingly politicized issue.

SUMMARY

Part of the demographic transitions that accompany modernization are fertility transitions from high to low levels. These transitions theoretically start with gradual declines, followed by steeper drops, then level off around replacement levels. For European nations, initiation of the steep fertility declines bracketed the turn of the twentieth century. The transitions involved a Malthusian component, which started operating centuries ago, caused by a shift to the "European marriage pattern" of late average age at marriage and widespread nonmarriage. European fertility transitions also involved a neo-Malthusian component, the largely voluntary curtailing of marital childbearing through birth control. The social and cultural changes theorized to support the shift to family limitation are complex, including improved infant survivorship, decreasing economic valuation of children, increasing nonmaternal role options for women, spread of contraceptive technology, and so forth.

The first step in explaining differences in period fertility is to specify the *demographic causes*. In explaining crude birth rates, one such demographic factor is the proportion of the total population consisting of women in the childbearing ages. The other demographic factors are two distinct aspects of cohort fertility performance: the average number of children born to women in the birth cohort and the timing of their childbearing.

The next step is to explain these differences in cohort fertility patterns. A satisfactory explanation means specifying the actions that result in different cohort fertility. The proximate determinants of cohort fertility can be classified, following Davis and Blake, into intercourse variables, conception variables, and gestation variables. In each category, some are voluntary and some involuntary from the perspective of the couple. The importance of the various fertility variables varies widely across different settings and historical periods. Some such variables, but not all of them, are changing in such a way as to continue the worldwide fertility transition and reduce birth rates in less-developed countries.

In many less-developed countries fertility declines have now begun or are well underway. An increasing number of these countries are even approaching replacement fertility levels. Family-planning programs have been a major part of demographic policies during this fertility decline in less-developed countries. They have spread quickly and now involve much of the LDR population. Exactly how much of the current LDR fertility transition can be credited to family planning is debatable, but family planning appears to have been an effective component of the current worldwide fertility decline.

Fertility transitions underway in less-developed countries have benefited from the availability of modern, more effective contraceptive methods. However, there is still considerable unmet need for contraception and family planning throughout the world. Much of this demand is for the spacing or timing of births, which can also lower overall fertility and improve maternal and child health. Increasingly, fertility reduction policies are advocated not only on the basis of too-rapid growth rates and youth dependency but also on the basis of concerns for maternal and child health, avoidance of unwanted pregnancies, and promoting women's reproductive rights. There remains considerable need for family-planning assistance in countries with limited resources and competing demographic priorities.

EXERCISES

1. Table E7-1 presents all of the information necessary for computing a general fertility rate (GFR) and a total fertility rate (TFR) for Brazil for 1999. (The table is similar in structure to Table 7-1 in the text.)

   a. There are two missing entries each in columns 3 and 4. Fill them in, following the directions at the head of each column.

Table E7-1
Age-Specific Fertility Rates, Brazil, 1999

Age	Female Population (midyear, in thousands) (1)	Births (2)	Births per 1,000 Women per Year (col. 2 ÷ col. 1) (3)	Projected Resulting Births during Age Interval (5 x col. 3) (4)
15–19	7557	584,910	77	385
20–24	6852	937,414	137	685
25–29	6463	715,467		
30–34	5657	412,374	73	365
35–39	4866	201,450		
40–44	3974	57,223	14	70
45–49	3130	8451	3	15
Total	38,499	2,917,289		

Source: U.S. Bureau of the Census, International Data Base.

b. Compute the *general fertility rate* (GFR) by using the formula

$$GFR = \frac{B}{P_{15\text{-}49}} \times 1{,}000$$

where B is the total births in the year and $P_{15\text{-}49}$ is the total number of women aged fifteen through forty-nine in the year. Be sure to use the total of column 2 for the annual births and round to two decimal places.

GFR = _____

c. Compute the *total fertility rate* (TFR) by totaling column 4 and dividing by 1,000. Or you can add column 3, then multiply the total by 5 and divide by 1,000. Round to two decimal places.

TFR = _____

d. Compute the *gross reproduction rate* (GRR) by assuming that the proportion of total births that are female is .48. That is, multiply the (unrounded) TFR by that proportion. Round to two decimal places.

GRR = _____

2. Table E7-2 presents the data necessary for computing legal abortion rates and ratios. Compute the missing rates and ratios for the "black" and "Hispanic" categories. Follow the computations provided for whites. Enter your answers in the blank spaces in the table.

3. Compare all white women to Hispanic women using both the rate and ratio. What effect does the relative fertility of the two groups of women have on this comparison?

Table E7-2
Estimated Abortion Rates and Ratios by Ethnic Category, U.S., 1990

Ethnic Category	Number of Abortions (in 1,000s) (1)	Women Aged 15–44 (in 1,000s) (2)	Rate (per 1,000) (3)	Live Births (in 1,000s) (4)	Ratio (per 1,000 Live Births) (5)
White	926	45,844	20.2	3290	282
Black	455	7753		684	
Hispanic	140	5550		595	

Source: CDC, "Abortion Surveillance, 1996," 1998, table 1; NCHS, "Report of Final Natality Statistics, 1996," 1998b, tables 1 & 6; U.S. Bureau of the Census, *1990 Census General Population Characteristics.*

► PROPOSITIONS FOR DEBATE

1. With modernization, most of the changes in the involuntary proximate determinants of fertility are in the direction of increasing rather than decreasing fertility.
2. Malthusian transitions do not necessarily have to decrease fertility levels.
3. The more liberated women get, the fewer children couples will have.
4. LDR fertility cannot approach MDR fertility unless and until LDR societies modernize.
5. Family-planning programs are a vestige of racism and privilege on the part of the former powers of imperialism.
6. LDR fertility control policies should aim to help couples to have their desired number of offspring, not convince them to have fewer.
7. The abortion *rate* is a superior measure to the abortion *ratio*.

► REFERENCES AND SUGGESTED READINGS

Abernethy, Virginia. 1995. "The Demographic Transition Model: A Ghost Story." *Population and Environment* 17(1).

Adair, Linda S., Barry M. Popkin, and David K. Guilkey. 1993. "The Duration of Breast-Feeding: How Is It Affected by Biological, Sociodemographic, Health Sector and Food Industry Factors?" *Demography* 30(1).

Anderton, Douglas L. 1989. "Starting, Stopping and Spacing: A Commentary." *Demography* 26(3): 467–70.

Anderton, Douglas L., Richard E. Barrett, and Donald J. Bogue. 1997. *The Population of the United States.* 3rd ed. New York: Free Press.

Anderton, Douglas L., and Lee L. Bean. 1985. "Birth Spacing and Fertility Limitation: A Behavioral Analysis of a Nineteenth Century Frontier Population." *Demography* 22(2).

Becker, Gary S. 1960. "An Economic Analysis of Fertility." In *Demographic and Economic Change in Developed Countries.* Princeton, NJ: Princeton University Press.

Blake, Judith. 1969. "Population Policy for Americans: Is the Government Being Misled?" *Science* 164(19).

Bongaarts, John. 1986. "The Transition in Reproductive Behavior in the Third World." In Jane Menken, ed., *World Population & U.S. Policy.* New York: W. W. Norton & Co.

————. 1995. "The Role of Family Planning Programs in Contemporary Fertility Transitions." *Population Council Working Paper no. 71.* New York: The Population Council.

Bongaarts, John, and Robert G. Potter. 1983. *Fertility, Biology, and Behavior: An Analysis of the Proximate Determinants of Fertility.* New York: Academic Press.

Bongaarts, John, and Susan Cotts Watkins. 1996. "Social Interactions and Contemporary Fertility Transitions." *Population and Development Review* 22(4).

Bulatao, Rodolfo A. 1984. "Reducing Fertility in Developing Countries: A Review of Determinants and Policy Levers." *World Bank Staff Working Papers no. 680, Population and Development Series no. 5.* Washington, DC: World Bank.

Burch, Thomas. 1975. "Theories of Fertility as Guides to Population Policy." *Social Forces* 54(1).

Caldwell, John C. 1982. *Theory of Fertility.* London: Academic Press.

————. 1997a. "Reaching a Stationary Global Population: What We Have Learnt, and What We Must Do." *Health Transition Review* 7: Suppl. 4.

————. 1997b. "The Global Fertility Transition: The Need for a Unifying Theory." *Population and Development Review* 23(4).

Caldwell, John C., and Pat Caldwell. 1977. "The Role of Marital Sexual Abstinence in Determining Fertility: A Study of the Yoruba in Niger." *Population Studies* 31(2).

Caldwell, John C., I. O. Orubuloye, and Pat Caldwell. 1992. "Fertility Decline in Africa: A New Type of Transition?" *Population and Development Review* 18(2).

Centers for Disease Control. 1998. "Abortion Surveillance: Preliminary Analysis—United States, 1996." *Morbidity and Mortality Weekly Report* 47(December 4).

Chen, Lincoln, C. S. Ahmed, M. Gesche, and W. H. Mosley. 1974. "A Prospective Study of Birth Interval Dynamics in Rural Bangladesh." *Population Studies* 28(2).

Cleland, John, and Chris Wilson. 1987. "Demand Theories of the Fertility Transition: An Iconoclastic View." *Population Studies* 41(1).

Coale, Ansley. 1973. "The Demographic Transition." *Proceedings of the International Population Conference, Liege.* Vol. 1. Liege: IUSSP.

————. 1974. "The History of Human Population." In *The Human Population: A Scientific American Book.* San Francisco: W. H. Freeman.

Coale, Ansley J., and Roy Treadway. 1986. "A Summary of the Changing Distribution of Overall Fertility, Marital Fertility and the Proportion Married in the Provinces of Europe." In A. Coale and S. Watkins, eds., *The Decline of Fertility in Europe.* Princeton, NJ: Princeton University Press.

Coale, Ansley J., and C. Y. Tye. 1961. "The Significance of Age Patterns of Fertility in Highly Fertile Populations." *Milbank Memorial Fund Quarterly* 29.

Coale, Ansley J., and Susan Cotts Watkins, eds. 1986. *The Decline of Fertility in Europe.* Princeton, NJ: Princeton University Press.

Coale, Ansley J., and Melvin Zelnick. 1963. *Estimates of Fertility and Population in the United States.* Princeton, NJ: Princeton University Press.

Cochrane, Susan H., and S. Farid. 1990. "Socioeconomic Differentials in Fertility and their Explanation." In George T. F. Acsadi, Gwendolyn Johnson-Acsadi, and Rodolfo A. Bulatao, eds., *Population Growth and Reproduction in Sub-Saharan Africa: Technical Analyses of Fertility and its Consequences.* Washington, DC: The World Bank.

Cooney, K. A. 1992. "The Contribution of Breastfeeding and Lactational Amenorrhea Method to the Reduction of Fertility Worldwide." *Institute for Reproductive Health Occasional Paper no. 3.* Washington, DC: Institute for Reproductive Health.

Darity, William, C. Turner, and H. Thiebaux. 1971. *Race Consciousness and Fears of Black Genocide as Barriers to Family Planning*. Population Reference Bureau Selection no. 37. Washington, DC: Population Reference Bureau.

Davis, Kingsley. 1967. "Population Policy: Will Current Programs Succeed?" *Science* 158.

Davis, Kingsley, and Judith Blake. 1956. "Social Structure and Fertility: An Analytic Framework." *Economic Development and Cultural Change* 4(4).

Demerath, Nicholas J. 1976. *Birth Control and Foreign Policy: The Alternatives to Family Planning*. New York: Harper and Row.

Easterlin, Richard A. 1968. *Population, Labor Force, and Long Swings in Economic Growth*. New York: Columbia University Press.

———. 1978. "What Will 1984 Be Like? Socioeconomic Implications of Recent Twists in Age Structure." *Demography* 15(4).

Easterlin, Richard A., and Eileen M. Crimmins. 1985. *The Fertility Revolution*. Chicago: University of Chicago Press.

Eaton, Joseph W., and Albert J. Mayer. 1954. *Man's Capacity to Reproduce*. Glencoe, IL: The Free Press.

Frisch, Rose E. 1975. "Demographic Implications of the Biological Determinants of Female Fecundity." *Social Biology* 22(1).

Gelbard, Alene, Carl Haub, and Mary M. Kent. 1999. "World Population Beyond Six Billion." *Population Bulletin* 54(1).

Guinnane, Timothy W., Barbara S. Okun, and James Trussell. 1994. "What Do We Know About the Timing of Fertility Transitions in Europe?" *Demography* 31(1).

Hajnal, John. 1965. "European Marriage Patterns in Perspective." In D. V. Glass and D. E. C. Eversley, eds., *Population in History*. London: Arnold.

Harcourt, W. 1999. "Reproductive Health and Rights and the Quest for Social Justice [editorial]." *Development* 42(1).

Hardee, K., K. Agarwal, N. Luke, E. Wilson, M. Pendzich, M. Farrel, and H. Cross. 1999. "Reproductive Health Policies and Programs in Eight Countries: Progress Since Cairo." *International Family Planning Perspectives* 25, Suppl. S.

Hartmann, Betsy. 1995. *Reproductive Rights and Wrongs: The Global Politics of Population Control*. Boston, MA: South End Press.

Haupt, Arthur, and Thomas T. Kane. 1978. *The Population Reference Bureau's Population Handbook*. Washington, DC: Population Reference Bureau.

Hauser, Philip M. 1967. "Family Planning and Population Programs: A Book Review Article." *Demography* 4(1).

Heer, David M. 1964. "Fertility Differences Between Indian and Spanish-Speaking Parts of Andean Countries." *Population Studies* 18(1).

Heer, David M., and Jill S. Grigsby. 1992. *Society and Population*. 3rd ed. Englewood Cliffs, NJ: Prentice Hall.

Henry, Louis. 1961. "Some Data on Natural Fertility." *Eugenics Quarterly* 8(1).

Hirschman, Charles, and Marilyn Butler. 1981. "Trends and Differentials in Breastfeeding: An Update." *Demography* 18(1).

Hoyert, D. L. 1996. "Cigarettes and Fetal Mortality as Reported in 1990 Vital Statistics." *American Journal of Health Behavior* 20(3).

Hull, Valerie. 1975. "Fertility, Socioeconomic Status, and the Position of Women in a Javanese Village." Unpublished Ph.D. dissertation, Australian National University, Canberra.

Jain, A. K., and John Bongaarts. 1980. "Socio-biological Factors in Exposure to Childbearing, Breastfeeding and Its Fertility Effects." Paper presented at the World Fertility Survey Conference, London, July 7-11.

Johnston, Heidi Bart, and Kenneth H. Hill. 1996. "Induced Abortion in the Developing World: Indirect Estimates." *International Family Planning Perspectives* 22(3).

Jolly, Carole L., and James N. Gribble. 1993. "The Proximate Determinants of Fertility." In Karen A. Foote, Kenneth H. Hill, and Linda G. Martin, eds., *Demographic Change in Sub-Saharan Africa*. Washington, DC: National Academy Press.

Knodel, John, and Nibhon Debavalya. 1981. "Breastfeeding Trends in Thailand and Their Demographic Impact." *Intercom* 9(3).

Lesthaeghe, Ron J. 1983. "A Century of Demographic and Cultural Change in Western Europe: An Exploration of Underlying Dimensions." *Population and Development Review* 6(4).

———. 1995. "The Second Demographic Transition in Western Countries: An Interpretation." In K. O. Mason and A. M. Jensen, eds., *Gender and Family Change in Industrialized Countries*. Oxford: Clarendon Press.

London, K. A., J. Cushing, S. O. Rutstein, J. Cleland, J. E. Anderson, L. Morris, and S. H. Moore. 1985. "Fertility and Family Planning Surveys: An Update." *Population Reports Series M, Special Topics*.

Mason, Karen Oppenheim. 1997. "Explaining Fertility Transitions." Presidential Address to the Population Association of America. *Demography* 34(4).

McDevitt, Thomas M., with Arjun Adlakha, Timothy B. Fowler, and Vera Harris-Bourne. 1996. *Trends in Adolescent Fertility and Contraceptive Use in the Developing World*. U.S. Bureau of the Census Report IPC/95-1. Washington, DC: Government Printing Office.

McFalls, Joseph. 1979. "Frustrated Fertility: A Population Paradox." *Population Bulletin* 34(2). Washington, DC: Population Reference Bureau.

Menken, Jane. 1979. "Seasonal Migration and Seasonal Variation in Fecundability: Effects on Birth Rates and Birth Intervals." *Demography* 16(1).

Menken, Jane, James Trussell, and Susan Watkins. 1981. "The Nutrition and Fertility Link: An Evaluation of the Evidence." *Journal of Interdisciplinary History* 11(3).

Michael, Robert T., John H. Gagnon, Edward O. Laumann, and Gina Kolata. 1994. *Sex in America: A Definitive Survey*. Boston, MA: Little Brown.

Moore, Maurice, and Martin O'Connell. 1978. *Perspectives on American Fertility*. U.S. Bureau of the Census, Current Population Reports, Special Studies, Series P-23, no. 70. Washington, DC: Government Printing Office.

Nag, Moni. 1968. *Factors Affecting Fertility in Nonindustrial Societies: A Cross-Cultural Study*. Yale University Publications in Anthropology. New Haven, CT: Yale University Dept. of Anthropology.

———. 1980. "How Modernization Can Also Increase Fertility." *Current Anthropology* 21(5).

National Center for Health Statistics (NCHS). 1998a. "Births and Deaths: Preliminary Data for 1997." *National Vital Statistics Reports* 47(4).

———. 1998b. "Report of Final Natality Statistics, 1996." *Monthly Vital Statistics Report* 46(1).

———. 1998c. "Declines in Teenage Birth Rates, 1991–97: National and State Patterns." *Monthly Vital Statistics Report* 47(12).

Notestein, Frank. 1953. "Economic Problems of Population Change." *Proceedings of the Eighth International Conference of Agricultural Economics*. London: Oxford University Press.

Population Reference Bureau (PRB). 1996. *The World's Youth: Data Sheet*. Washington, DC: Population Reference Bureau.

———. 1997. *World Population Data Sheet*. Washington, DC: Population Reference Bureau.

———. 1999. *1999 World Population Data Sheet*. Washington, DC: Population Reference Bureau.

Reher, David, and Roger Schofield. 1993. *Old and New Methods in Historical Demography*. Oxford: Clarendon Press.

Robinson, W. C. 1997. "The Economic Theory of Fertility Over Three Decades." *Population Studies* 51(1).

Ryder, Norman B. 1959. "Fertility." In Philip M. Hauser and Otis Dudley Duncan, eds., *The Study of Population: An Inventory and Appraisal*. Chicago: University of Chicago Press.

———. 1979. "The Future of American Fertility." *Social Problems* 26(3).

Sadik, Nafis, ed. 1991. *Population Policies and Programmes: Lessons Learned from Two Decades of Experience*. United Nations Population Fund. New York: New York University Press.

Shane, Barbara. 1997. *Planning Saves Lives*. 3rd ed. Washington, DC: Population Reference Bureau.

Sharma, R. K., S. O. Rutstein, M. H. Labbok, and G. Ramos. 1991. *Trends and Differentials in Breastfeeding: Findings From the World Fertility Survey and the Demographic and Health Surveys*. Unpublished manuscript.

Shorter, Edward, John Knodel, and Etienne van de Walle. 1971. "The Decline of Non-marital Fertility in Europe, 1880–1940." *Population Studies* 25(3).

Shryock, Henry S., and Jacob S. Siegel. 1976. *The Methods and Materials of Demography*. Condensed edition by Edward G. Stockwell. New York: Academic Press.

Simmons, George B. 1986. "Family Planning Programs." In Jane Menken, ed., *World Population and U.S. Policy: The Choices Ahead*. New York: W. W. Norton.

Tafari, N., and G. Zerihun. 1993. "The Effect of Age, Parity, and Socioeconomic Factors on Perinatal Mortality and Long-Term Morbidity." In J. David Baum, ed., *Birth Risks*. New York: Raven Press.

Thompson, W. S. 1930. *Population Problems*. New York: McGraw Hill.

Thornton, Arland, and Thomas E. Fricke. 1987. "Social Change and the Family: Comparative Perspectives from the West, China, and South Asia." In J. M. Stycos, ed., *Demography as an Interdiscipline*. Oxford: Transaction Publishers.

Tietze, Christopher. 1981. *Induced Abortion: A World Review*. 4th ed. New York: The Population Council.

Trussell, James, and Charles F. Westoff. 1980. "Contraceptive Practice Trends in Coital Frequency." *Family Planning Perspectives* 12(5).

United Nations. 1999a. *Revision of the World Population Estimates and Projections, 1998 Briefing Packet*. New York: United Nations.

———. 1999b. *World Contraceptive Use 1998, Wall Chart*. New York: United Nations.

———. 1999c. *World Abortion Policies 1999, Wall Chart*. New York: United Nations.

United States Bureau of the Census. 1996. *Trends in Adolescent Fertility and Contraceptive Use in the Developing World*. Report IP/95-1. Washington, DC: Government Printing Office.

———. 1999. *World Population Profile: 1998*. Report WP/98. Washington, DC: Government Printing Office.

van de Walle, Etienne, and John Knodel. 1980. "Europe's Fertility Transition: New Evidence and Lessons for Today's Developing World." *Population Bulletin* 34(6). Washington, DC: Population Reference Bureau.

Watson, Walter B. 1982. "Family Planning Programs: Developing Countries." In John A. Ross, ed., *International Encyclopedia of Population*. New York: Free Press.

Wetstein, Matthew E. 1996. *Abortion Rates in the United States: The Influence of Opinion and Policy*. Albany, NY: SUNY Press.

Willigan, J. Dennis, and Katherine A. Lynch. 1982. *Sources and Methods of Historical Demography*. New York: Academic Press.

Yaukey, David. 1973. *Marriage Reduction and Fertility*. Lexington, MA: Lexington Books.

Zohoori, Namvar, and Barry M. Popkin. 1996. "Longitudinal Analysis of the Effects of Infant-Feeding Practices on Postpartum Amenorrhea." *Demography* 33(2).

8

Marriage and Householding

Demographers always have had a special interest in the family and household as residential units. Partially this springs from the process of census taking. It normally puts demographers in touch with intimate information about cohabitation and kinship. A U.S. census enumerator, for instance, asks one member of each household to report on him/herself and on those who live together, and to describe the kin and marital relationships among all coresidents.

But demographic interest in residential units is based on something more profound than the convenience of data. Households, and the families who reside together in them, are social units. They act together to bear children, to move, and to help each other survive. That is, they act collectively to influence the processes of fertility, migration, and mortality.

They also act collectively in other social and economic behaviors. While they may not be units of economic production as much as they once were, they still are units of consumption. Small wonder that business—for instance, marketing—is fascinated by the trends in marriage and divorce and in household size and composition.

There are so many aspects of families and households that we could describe in this chapter that it is frustrating to put some aside for lack of space. One could describe the rapidly changing patterns of household formation or the modern trend toward smaller households. One could trace the trends of illegitimacy—a subject that combines the study of fertility with that of the family.

Instead, we have chosen a set of topics centering around what demographers call *nuptiality*. This means that we will focus on the formation and breakup of marriages. It also means that we will give attention to unmarried cohabitation. After a section dealing with methodological concerns, we will deal internationally and historically with variations in the process of first marriage. Then we will focus on two features of the demographic modernization process, using the United States as an example: 1) changing patterns of widowhood and divorce and 2) the changing family life course.

233

DEFINITION AND MEASUREMENT

Definitions

The best way to introduce you to the terms used in the study of nuptiality is to take you through the imaginary marital history of a birth cohort (Cherlin, 1981). Figure 8-1 graphs this history schematically.

Everyone starts her or his life *never-married,* or *single.* The vast majority of these never-married cohort members experience, sooner or later, an event called *first marriage,* thereby entering the status of *currently married,* or *married,* for short. Demographers include the legally separated in the category of currently married.

Moving up the chart, we see that some married cohort members have their marriages dissolve: some cohort members die, leaving their spouses in the status of being *widowed.* Other married cohort members suffer divorces, putting both in the status of being *divorced.*

Figure 8-1   Schematic Marital History of a Birth Cohort

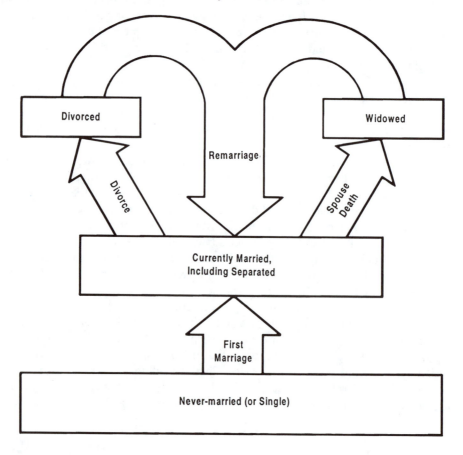

Widowed or divorced cohort members can rejoin the currently married by the process of remarriage. And once they are back in the currently married status, they may reenter a new cycle of marital dissolution by the death of their new spouse or by divorce.

Some of these statuses combine into larger categories. For instance, demographers use the term *unmarried* or *nonmarried* to combine never-married, divorced, and widowed. *Ever-married* includes the currently married, divorced, and widowed. *Formerly married* means those currently divorced or widowed.

Similarly, the processes of first marriage and remarriage combine to make up the process of *marriage.* The processes of spouse mortality and divorce combine to make up the process of *marital dissolution.*

This scheme emphasizes the legal and public statuses of individuals and changes from one status to the other; it does not pretend to capture the complexity of sexual unions and cohabitation. It does not record entering into nonsanctioned sexual unions, such as consensual unions, common-law marriages, or "living together." Being consistently legalistic, the scheme views a marriage that is annulled as a marriage that never existed. Nor does it capture the leaving of a consensual union or the separation, without divorce, from a legal marriage.

One part of the history of the birth cohort is not represented in Figure 8-1: the mortality of cohort members. The number of original members currently in any one of these marital statuses is determined not only by the processes of transition (first marriage, spouse mortality, divorce, remarriage, and so on) but also by attrition due to their own deaths. Members of any status can and do die.

Data on Marriage and Divorce

Let us distinguish between individuals' marital *events* and their marital *statuses* in Figure 8-1. The marital statuses are never-married (single), currently married (married), divorced, and widowed. The marital events mark the transitions from one status to the other: first marriage, divorce, spouse death, and remarriage. On an aggregate level, these two aspects are seen respectively as marital status *compositions* and marriage *processes.* Data about these two aspects of marriage conventionally come from different sources.

Censuses and intercensal surveys such as the Current Population Survey provide most marital *status* information. As you may remember from chapter 2, the United Nations (1998) recommends that marital status questions be asked in national censuses. Although most countries follow this advice, that does not necessarily assure internationally comparable information. "Marriage" refers to a legal recognition of a sexual union, and which unions enjoy legal standing varies somewhat from country to country. Especially bothersome is the inconsistent treatment of consensual unions in national statistical reports (Shryock and Siegel, 1976). Questions regarding marriage can even change from census to census as the cultural significance of marriage changes in a country.

Ideally, direct information about marital *events,* on the other hand, comes from the civil registration system. Just as births and deaths are certified by legal authorities, so are marriages and divorces. And in all these cases the additional step involved, for demographic purposes, is to report these events to a central office where they can be accumulated, tabulated, and reported. However, in most Western countries (including the United States) the registration of marriages and divorces is notoriously less complete than the registration of either births or deaths. Indeed, the United States even stopped collecting marriage and divorce registration information in 1996. The lack of direct registration data often forces demographers to rely upon census and survey data for estimating the marital events and processes, as well as statuses.

Censuses and surveys can give two kinds of data on marital processes. First, current marital status data taken over time (e.g. successive surveys or censuses) can be combined with age reports and used for inferring the timing of marital events in the histories of cohorts. Second, *retrospective* questions on age at marriage can provide estimates of marriage behavior among surviving women.

Most Western censuses have included such retrospective questions for decades. That information can be used not only to describe the age-timing of the first marriage process but also to allocate the marriages themselves to years of occurrence. By asking additional questions regarding household composition and relationships, censuses also provide the basis for indirect estimates of *living arrangements* that can be an alternative to marriage, such as cohabitation and same-sex unions (Casper et al., 1999).

In the less-developed countries, the main vehicles for survey questions on marriage are fertility and family-planning surveys. Interview schedules about fertility include, quite comfortably, questions about marital history. A huge advantage of such surveys is that one is able to link marital information about individuals with other extensive information about their childbearing, economic status, and the like. A disadvantage is that complete marriage histories usually are not asked for men, except as they enter into the lives of the women respondents.

In the United States, the most systematic gathering of marriage and marital status data via surveys has been the Current Population Survey, run as a separate activity by the Census Bureau. The Current Population Survey runs regular annual series on the marital and family statuses of individuals and on households and families as units. Results are described periodically in *Current Population Reports* (U.S. Bureau of the Census, 1998a) and are further analyzed in Population Division working papers (e.g. U.S. Bureau of the Census, 1998b). Most media articles monitoring changes in the U.S. marital situation undoubtedly are based on these reports.

Marital Status Composition

The main technique for describing marital status composition—or composition in general, for that matter—is by means of percentage distributions. To find the percentage of the population in any given status category, one takes the number of persons in that category, divides it by the number in the total population, and multiplies by one hundred to obtain a percentage. The upper panel of Table 8-1 gives percentage distributions by the four major marital statuses (single or never-married, married, widowed, and divorced), according to the 1950, 1970, and 1990 U.S. censuses and the 1998 Current Population Survey.

Since the mid-1950s, both men and women in the United States have experienced a nearly steady increase in the proportion of the population never-married and

Table 8-1
Marital Status of the U. S. Adult Population, by Sex, 1950–1990 and 1998[a]

	Male (%)				Female (%)			
	1950	1970	1990	1998	1950	1970	1990	1998
Marital Status	(1)	(2)	(3)	(4)	(5)	(6)	(7)	(8)
Unstandardized								
Single	26.2	28.1	30.9	31.2	19.6	22.1	23.5	24.7
Married	68.0	66.7	59.7	58.0	66.1	61.9	55.1	54.9
Widowed	4.2	2.9	2.6	2.5	12.2	12.5	12.0	10.2
Divorced	1.7	2.2	6.9	8.2	2.2	3.5	9.5	10.3
Age Standardized[b]								
Single	26.2	23.9	29.5	31.9	20.0	19.3	24.1	26.4
Married	67.4	70.8	60.8	57.4	63.9	64.9	55.7	54.3
Widowed	4.7	3.0	2.6	2.5	14.0	12.0	10.3	9.1
Divorced	1.7	2.4	7.1	8.2	2.1	3.8	9.8	10.2

[a]Adolescents excluded if less than 14 in 1950–1970 or less than 15 in 1990–1998.
[b]Standardized to 1960 age-sex distribution.
Source: U.S. Bureau of the Census, *Social Indicators*, 1976, table 2-3; *Marital Status and Living Arrangements*, 1998a.

a corresponding decline in the proportion married. The proportion widowed has generally declined since the first half of the last century, while divorce among both males and females has increased steadily throughout the past century (Anderton et al., 1997). The crude divorce rate, however, began to level off, or even slightly decline, in about 1980 (Goldstein, 1999).

However, one cause of a changing marital status composition could be a changing age structure during the period covered. The age structure of the U.S. population did change considerably between 1950 and 1998. Demographers have developed techniques for discounting the influence of such age structure differences in making marital status composition comparisons. These also are illustrated in Table 8-1.

A first step is to confine oneself only to the segment of the age distribution at risk. For instance, in Table 8-1 (and in most tabulations of marital status), adolescent women are excluded, on the assumption that they are rarely at risk of being anything besides single (never-married).

A more complete method of controlling for the effects of age composition is age *standardization*. It attempts to answer the following hypothetical question: If the age structures of all populations being compared were the same (some specified percentage distribution by age), then what percentage would fall into each of the marital status categories?

The bottom panel of Table 8-1 presents such standardized percentages. The age structure used as a standard was that for 1960; therefore, the bottom panel of the table shows the percentages that would fall into each of the marital status categories if the populations of 1950, 1970, 1990, and 1998 all had the age structure (for each sex) of the population of 1960.

The standardized percentages in Table 8-1 show that changes in the age composition, largely caused by the baby-boom, affected marital status composition in the 1970s. Although the unstandardized percentage of those married decreased in 1970 for males and females, the standardized percentages married actually increased. The opposite is true for the proportion single; the unstandardized proportion single increased while the standardized proportion actually decreased. This difference is due to the largely young and still single baby-boom cohort in the 1970s. The increase in single status and decrease in married status in 1970 thus were due to changing age structures.

The choice of the standard population is somewhat arbitrary. When comparing more than one population, one choice is to select a standard population close to the average of the populations being compared. However, the use of multiple standards confuses statistical comparisons so there is an advantage in choosing some convention. Government agencies, for example, frequently choose a single standard which is then used to allow comparisons across different publications or studies. At the time of this writing, the year 2000 population is being widely adopted as a "new" standard.

Standardization is a very flexible and useful technique in demography, not confined to the study of marital status or to standardization of age. We most frequently see standardization of age because age influences so many other demographic characteristics and processes. The same basic process also can be used in standardizing for race, education, and so on. Exercise 1 at the end of the chapter demonstrates one technique of age standardization.

Annual Rates

One can measure the processes of marriage and marital dissolution with rates (just as one does the vital processes of mortality and fertility), using crude rates, refined rates, specific rates, or total rates. *Refined* rates are favored, however. In refined rates, the numerator contains *all* of the specified marital events that occurred in the year, while the denominator includes not the total population but rather a segment of it considered to be at risk of experiencing that event.

Clearly not everybody in the population is equally at risk of being first married, divorced, widowed, or remarried. Some *age* categories can be eliminated as being "not at risk." For example, in most societies those under fifteen can be considered "not at risk" for all marital events. Moreover, what can happen to an individual, marriage-wise, depends upon that person's present status. Looking back at Figure 8-1, we see confirmation of some obvious points: A first marriage can happen only to those who never have married; only those currently married can get divorced or widowed; only those divorced or widowed can be remarried. Therefore, refined rates for these processes confine their denominators to the population in the proper marital status category, as well as the proper age categories.

The set of refined rates for nuptiality has not been conventionalized. Instead demographers tend to be pragmatic and flexible, using the limited data at hand in a given situation. This makes for a certain lack of exact comparability between reported rates. The "divorce rate" does not mean the same thing in all reports. It is necessary for the reader to always check for definitions of the rates being employed.

WORLD VARIATIONS IN FIRST MARRIAGE

Since we all are born single, the first nuptial event we can encounter is first marriage. How many of us take that step, and when, varies considerably from culture to culture and cohort to cohort. We start this section describing something that is shared, the first-marriage curve. Then we demonstrate the current wide international variation in other aspects of the first-marriage process. Turning to history, we then trace the changes that seem to have accompanied the modernization of the West, ending with specific attention to the United States.

The First-Marriage Curve

Let us once again use the example of a hypothetical birth cohort and follow it through a marital process, this time the process of first marriage alone. For simplicity, let us suppose that we are dealing with a cohort of females only. Obviously, all women in the cohort were born never-married (single). Somewhere around age fifteen, cohort women start to marry, gradually at first, changing their status from never-married to ever-married. During the next few years, first marriage spreads like an epidemic through the surviving singles in the cohort, changing the status of most to ever-married before their thirtieth birthday. The first-marriage epidemic spends itself as it runs out of singles and as it finds the few remaining singles harder to marry. Demographers have found that women who are never-married at the age of fifty are very unlikely ever to marry.

Figure 8-2 graphs this process for five different countries and five historical times. Coale (1971) chose these countries and these times to present a wide variety of marital patterns for which data were available.

Figure 8-2   Proportions of Women Ever-Married, by Age, Selected Populations

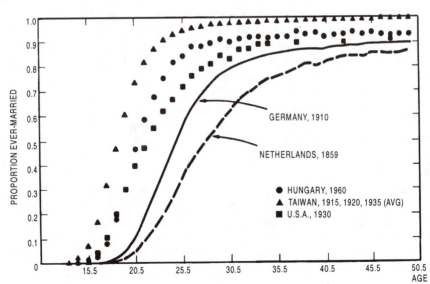

Source: Coale, "Age Patterns of Marriage," 1971, figure 3.

What is striking is the similarity in the *form* of the curve, given the variety of cultures involved. In all countries graphed, the proportions ever-married increase in an S-shaped curve, but not a symmetrical one. The left side is compressed; the right side is spread out.

Coale and his team started investigating the prevalence of this form after noticing it in all of the European demographic transitions they happened to be studying. Intrigued by the regularity, Coale attempted, unsuccessfully, to find exceptions to the pattern outside of the region and time he had been studying. He observed:

> The most puzzling feature of the common pattern . . . is its very prevalence. We have seen evidence of the same basic curve . . . in cohorts that marry early and cohorts that marry late, in cohorts in which marriage is virtually universal and in cohorts in which one-quarter remain single. Moreover, the uniform age structure of nuptiality occurs in societies in which most marriages are arranged by families with little regard for the preference of bride and groom and in societies in which marriages result from self-selection of mutually preferred partners. (Coale, 1971, p. 203)

Figure 8-2 dramatizes the formal similarity among countries in the first-marriage process, but it also alerts us to the ways in which countries *vary* in this process. First, the countries vary in the proportions of women who ever do marry, represented by the heights of the curves at their termination at the right of the figure. The proportion ever-married at about age fifty ranges from virtually 100% in Taiwan to between 80 and 90% in the Netherlands. Second, the countries vary in the age at which nuptiality begins and peaks. The steepest part of the curve is earliest for Taiwan and latest for the Netherlands. Finally, countries differ in the speed with which marriage spreads though the nubile population. That is, the *steepness* of the curve varies, again from a very rapid pace in Taiwan and Hungary on the one hand, to a slower pace in the Netherlands.

Current Variations among Less-Developed Countries

Table 8-2 presents data about the timing of first marriage in selected less-developed countries. Not all countries of the world have enough information even for estimates. From among those countries that do, only a couple have been chosen to represent each of the world's subregions. Generally, we have included the country with the second youngest marriage pattern and the country with the second oldest for females in the subregion; therefore, the countries in the table demonstrate not only the variety *among* less-developed regions when it comes to age at marriage, but also the variety *within* subregions.

The table uses two measures. In column 3 is the proportion of women aged fifteen through nineteen in a marital union. This figure reflects the timing of first marriage among females but is especially sensitive to the prevalence of *very* early marriage among females.

The other measure is the *singulate mean age at first marriage,* computed separately for men and women. The first step in computing one of these means is to array the five-year age categories from fifteen through forty-nine sequentially, and for each category to tabulate the percentage single. The data usually come from a census, sometimes from a survey. We interpret the array of percentages as though it were the history of a hypothetical cohort. Then we estimate what the mean age at first marriage must be for a cohort that left such a trail.

Table 8-2
Estimated Current Age at First Marriage, Selected Countries from Less-Developed Regions

| Region and Country | Singulate Mean Age at Marriage | | Percent Currently Married Age 15–19 |
	Female (1)	Male (2)	(3)
Africa			
North			
Morocco	22.3	27.2	12.1
Sudan	24.1	..	26.0
West			
Burkina Faso	17.4	27.0	33.0
Mauritania	23.1	29.8	14.3
East			
Madagascar	20.3	23.5	34.3
Mauritius	22.8	27.8	11.3
Middle			
Central African Republic	18.9	24.1	40.8
Congo	21.9	27.0	15.7
South			
Botswana	25.0	..	5.1
South Africa	25.7	27.8	4.3
Asia			
West			
Syria	21.5	25.7	24.6
Jordan	24.7	27.8	9.3
South Central			
Nepal	17.9	21.5	45.7
Pakistan	21.7	26.5	29.1
Southeast			
Myanmar	22.4	24.6	16.0
Philippines	23.8	26.3	9.3
East			
Korea (South)	24.7	27.8	0.5
Hong Kong (China)	26.6	29.2	1.6
Latin America			
Central			
Mexico	20.6	24.1	15.1
Panama	21.9	25.4	21.3
Caribbean			
Dominican Republic	20.5	24.3	17.4
Jamaica	29.7	30.8	0.5
South			
Venezuela	21.2	24.8	18.4
Argentina	22.9	25.3	12.3

Note: Only countries with available data were included. Notably, data was not available for former Soviet republics and some least-developed countries. Where singlulate mean age of marriage for males was not available it is indicated by ".." as the cell entry.
Source: United Nations, *The World's Women 1995*, 1997, table 1-4.

The technology of computation is beyond the scope of an introductory text (Shryock and Siegel, 1976, p. 166), but readers may remember this general line of thinking from both our treatment of life expectancy in chapter 5 and the total fertility rate in chapter 6.

One can make several preliminary generalizations from Table 8-2. In all the countries, males normally marry later than females. In most countries this age difference is roughly between two and five years of age. There usually is less variation among the countries with respect to male average age at first marriage than with respect to female average age at first marriage; therefore, the age gap between the husband and the wife at first marriage tends to be greatest where female marriage is earliest. But there seems to be considerable variety, both among and within less-developed regions.

However, no single table can capture the LDR variety in marital patterns. What follows, therefore, is a region-by-region summary of the timing of first marriage and trends in that timing. These summaries are based largely on a comparison of detailed marriage data from the Demographic and Health Surveys of less-developed countries between 1986 and 1992 and are limited to countries with available DHS data (Westoff et al., 1994).

Africa. In Africa as a whole marriage is nearly universal. There are, however, important exceptions to this rule. *Cohabitation* without marriage occurs to some degree in most African countries. Liberia and Rwanda have the highest reported rates of cohabitation. In Liberia cohabitation is even more common than marriage, with nearly 40% of women between fifteen and forty-nine years of age cohabiting, while only 30% are married. Other relationships less familiar than marriage or cohabitation are common in some African countries. In Botswana and Namibia, for example, many women are in *stable childbearing relationships* that appear to endure but do not involve either marriage or regular cohabitation. These alternatives to marriage confound the measurement of marriage patterns by simple indicators such as the percentage ever marrying or singulate mean ages of marriage. They also have led to very different estimates of the proportion of women in a union, depending upon whether survey questions ask whether women are "married," "living with a man" or have a "partner" (Westoff et al., 1994).

Even for women who are married, there are considerable variations in the types of marriage across Africa. In some regions marriage is frequently polygamous. For example, over half of all married women age thirty or greater in Mali, Niger, Nigeria, Senegal and Togo are in polygamous unions.

The timing of first marriage is generally early in Africa but varies widely. In sub-Saharan Africa marriage generally occurs at younger ages than in Northern Africa. Sub-Saharan countries with high proportions of polygyny also tend to have much higher percentages of women married before age twenty. For example, over 70% of women between fifteen and nineteen years of age in Mali are married, as are more than half of such young women in Niger. In contrast, few women under twenty years of age are married in Northern Africa and the Near East. Moreover, 85% of women under twenty in Egypt, Morocco, and Tunisia, for example, have never married.

Differences in the timing of marriage across regions of Africa, however, have grown larger over the past three decades as increasing marriage ages in Arab countries have contributed to the differences between Northern and sub-Saharan Africa. Age at first marriage has risen in every Arab country since the 1970s, ranging from an increase in median age at first marriage of almost eight years in Bahrain to less than one year in Yemen (Gelbard et al., 1999).

Asia. Regions of Asia also vary dramatically in the timing of first marriage for women. At one extreme, women in most countries of South Central Asia (e.g. the Indian subcontinent) marry very early. At the other extreme, marriage patterns in most countries of East Asia (e.g. Japan, Korea, Taiwan, and China) are more similar to Europe in terms of late average age at marriage and a small proportion of women marrying early. Between these extremes are the countries of Southeast Asia and West Asia.

The rising age of marriage in Arab countries also has increased differences among countries within West Asia. The percentage of women aged fifteen to nineteen who are unmarried has risen to over 85% in Jordan as it has in many Arab countries of Northern Africa. However, nearly a fourth of women in this age group are married in nearby Syria.

Although Asian women vary regionally in terms of the timing of their first marriages, most of them eventually do marry. For instance, among the countries covered by the Demographic and Health Surveys, the proportions still single at age forty-five through forty-nine are universally low. The highest reported was 3.9% for Thailand; the lowest, 1.4% for Indonesia. The proportion of women married at these older ages is correspondingly very high, for example, nearly 91% in Pakistan.

Latin America. There are two conventional types of sexual unions coexisting side by side in many Latin American countries. Marriage, meaning unions that have legal or religious sanction, are supplemented by consensual unions, which differ in their cultural meaning from region to region. Unlike the stable unions without cohabitation in Botswana and Namibia (already discussed), consensual unions in Latin America most often involve cohabitation.

If we ignore consensual cohabitation, Latin America is relatively late marrying among the less-developed regions, though not quite as late as most countries of East Asia. Almost 90% of Peruvian women aged fifteen to nineteen, for example, were unmarried. Even in Guatemala, with the youngest marriage pattern in Latin America, about three-fourths of Guatemalan women ages fifteen through nineteen were still never married.

Obviously, this is only part of the picture. In many Latin American countries the proportion of women cohabiting is greater than those marrying, especially at younger ages. And fertility rates for women aged fifteen through nineteen are high enough to suggest marriage data alone undercount stable sexual unions. In the Dominican Republic, for example, only 2.4% of women aged fifteen to nineteen are married; 15.3% are cohabiting. Cohabitation ranges from about 9% of all women aged fifteen to forty-nine in Brazil to 33% of those in the Dominican Republic.

International contrasts illustrated. The previous summaries make the point that marital patterns vary immensely, not only among less-developed regions but also within regions. To dramatize these cultural contrasts, Figure 8-3 gives extreme examples of three different marriage patterns, selected from countries of Africa, Asia, and Latin America.

Figure 8-3 Illustrative Age-Specific Marriage Patterns in Selected Less-Developed Countries

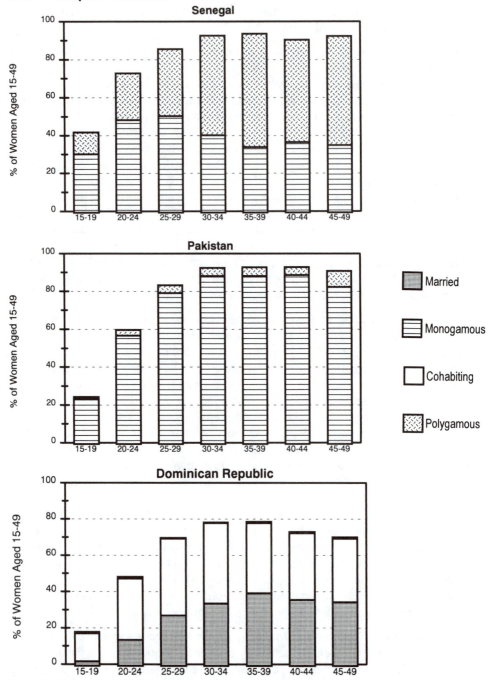

Source: Westoff et al., Marriage and Entry into Parenthood, 1994, tables 3.1 and 3.5.

The first graph illustrates the pattern of polygyny in one African country, Senegal. Each bar of the graph shows the percentages of Senegalese women at a given age who are in marriages (monogamous and polygamous). Polygyny is substantial, involving more than half of all marriages over age thirty; and the older the wife is, the more likely she is to be in a polygamous marriage, possibly because additional younger wives are taken as a woman grows older. Or it could imply a declining practice of polygamy in more recent marriages. Characteristic of most sub-Saharan countries, timing of marriage is early, with over 40% of women aged fifteen to nineteen being married.

The second graph tells us that marriage is almost universal in Pakistan. Comparing the first two graphs, we see that age at marriage is clearly later in Pakistan than it is in Senegal. Less than a fourth of Pakistani women aged fifteen to nineteen are married compared to over 40% in Senegal. In fact, the age of marriage has been increasing in Pakistan in recent decades. However, age at marriage is still early when compared to more-developed regions or most countries of East Asia. The marriage pattern of Pakistan also reflects the nearly universal marriage in most Asian and African countries; by age thirty nearly all women in both Pakistan and Senegal are married.

In Pakistan, polygyny is practiced by a relatively small fraction of the Islamic population and is not nearly as widespread as in Senegal. There is, however, another cultural variation in marriages that is not reflected in Figure 8-3: between 60 and 80% of marriages in Pakistan are *consanguineous,* or between blood relations, with the most common being marriage among cousins (Hussain and Bittles, 1998). Consanguineous marriage in Pakistan further illustrates the variability of cultural marriage patterns throughout the world and is of interest to demographers because of possible biological impacts on mortality and fertility.

Unions among women of the Dominican Republic are shown in the third graph of Figure 8-3. Notice that fewer than 40% of women in any age group are legally married. In this case, it makes more sense to consider both married and cohabiting women in studying the formation of sexual unions. Even this broader definition does not insure all women in unions are included in the percentages reported. Confusion over the meaning of survey questions and social reluctance may result in underreporting of cohabitation even where it is widely practiced. Nonetheless, combining marriage and cohabitation, the third graph is more nearly similar to those of marriage in Senegal and Pakistan. Timing of union formation is relatively late and not nearly so universal as marriage in other less-developed regions, even including reported cohabitation.

These three extremes serve to remind us of the tremendous variation in marriage practices and patterns throughout the world. The nature of sexual unions, the timing of women's entry into different types of unions, and the ultimate percentage of women in a stable union vary widely across less-developed countries.

At the same time, we should not lose sight of the common features of marriage across countries and cultures. Three seem worth remembering: 1) most women in all countries join with men to form stable marital/sexual unions, 2) there are worldwide similarities in the general form of the cumulative marriage distribution, and 3) where marriage behaviors are undergoing change, recent trends are generally in the direction of rising age of marriage and declining universality of marriage.

Europe, Past and Present

As we have done with fertility and mortality, we might reasonably ask how the marriage patterns and trends of current less-developed countries compare with the historical marriage patterns of Europe. Were rising marriage ages and declining universality of marriage features of historical modernization and demographic transitions in the present more-developed countries? If so, are there changes in marriage we might expect to accompany demographic transitions that are now underway throughout much of the less-developed world? What did mid-transition European censuses of, say, 1870 though 1900 find with respect to the timing and universality of first marriage?

In Europe, too, there were regional variations. There was a split between Western and Eastern Europe, the dividing line running roughly from Leningrad to Trieste (Hajnal, 1965, p. 101). In Western Europe, more females remained unmarried throughout their lives, and those who did marry were doing so later. In Eastern Europe, more women married, and they did so earlier. In the Western European pattern, at the turn of the century, the average age of women at first marriage must have been about twenty-four years or older. In most of these countries, 10 to 20% of women aged forty-five through forty-nine were never-married (Hajnal, 1965, p. 102). In both of these respects, Eastern Europe fell somewhere in between the pattern for Western Europe and that for the non-European countries.

Where did this Western European marriage pattern come from? From his historical review, Hajnal concludes:

> . . .(1) that the distinctively [Western] European pattern can be traced back with fair confidence as far as the seventeenth century in the general population; (2) that its origins lie somewhere about the sixteenth century in several of the upper class groups available for study, and in none of those groups was the pattern "European" before the sixteenth century; (3) the little fragmentary evidence which exists for the middle ages suggests a non-"European" pattern, as do scraps of information from the ancient world. (1965, p. 134)

As Hajnal implies, statements about times prior to the mid-1800s have to rely upon considerably more scanty and heterogeneous information plumbed by the various techniques of historical demography. Nevertheless, what emerges from this analysis is the birth and spread of a unique marriage pattern in Western Europe over several centuries prior to the 1800s.

The divergence between Eastern and Western Europe peaked around the end of the nineteenth century. From then until the 1970s there was a tendency toward convergence. This was due largely to the retreat by Western European countries from their unique pattern of late marriage, especially during the "marriage boom" that followed World War II (Hajnal, 1953; Watkins, 1981). Between 1950 and 1970 the average age at first marriage for both women and men continued downward in almost all the countries of Europe; however, this trend seems to have been more extreme in Northern and Western Europe than in Eastern Europe. The result was less variation in Europe in 1970 than there had been in 1950. That is not to say, however, that the overall Western/Eastern distinction disappeared.

In the last part of the twentieth century, the Western European marriage boom became a bust. Since the 1970s female age at marriage has risen in Northern and Western Europe and the proportion of women never marrying has increased. This decline of marriage has caused a slight resurgence in differences among European marriage patterns.

Table 8-3 presents some typical cases from the current European scene. Comparing regions of Europe, the singulate mean age at marriage for women is two or more years younger in the East than in other parts of Europe. In addition, the percentage married at young ages is considerably higher in some countries of the East. The percentage of older women never married in the East is much lower than in other regions. Together these differences show the persistence, and even resurgence, of later and less universal marriage in Western Europe with earlier and more universal marriage in Eastern Europe. That is not to say, of course, that the young in Western Europe have been avoiding sexual unions. Cohabitation has increased within many of these countries as marriage has declined (Festy, 1980).

The United States, Past and Present

Regarding timing of first marriage in the United States, we have census figures starting in 1890 but have to make an educated guess about prior times. As of then, the

Table 8-3
Estimated Current Age at First Marriage, Selected Countries of European Settlement

| Region and Country | Singulate Mean Age at Marriage | | Percent Currently Married | Percent Never Married |
	Female (1)	Male (2)	Age 15–19 (3)	Age 45 and Over (4)
Europe				
North				
Norway	24.0	26.3	0.5	7.6
Sweden	24.7	27.4	0.5	8.8
West				
Luxembourg	23.1	26.2	2.4	8.4
France	24.5	26.4	0.8	7.7
East				
Bulgaria	21.1	24.9	16.1	1.9
Hungary	21.0	24.8	4.0	4.0
South				
Italy	23.2	27.1	4.6	11.3
Spain	23.1	26.0	2.3	10.4
Oceania				
Australia	23.5	27.0	2.7	9.0
North America				
United States	23.3	25.2	3.9	5.0

Source: United Nations, *The World's Women 1995*, 1997, table 1-4.

median age at first marriage was 26.1 years for males and 22.0 years for females. That would imply that U.S. females were marrying about two years earlier than their Western European contemporaries. Since U.S. age at marriage declined for decades after 1890, it is tempting to suppose that it also declined before 1890, but fragmentary data do not confirm such a prior trend (Davis, 1972). The safest guess is that there had not been much variation from the 1890 level in prior decades (Monahan, 1951).

Figure 8-4 shows the male and female median ages at first marriage, estimated from the censuses of 1890 through 1990 and the Current Population Survey of 1998. Before we discuss the rising and falling age of marriage over the past century, note one consistent trend: the age difference between husbands and wives has shrunk steadily over the century. In 1890 husbands were on average more than 4 years older than their wives; by 1998 they were only 1.7 years older. Other trends in age at first marriage have been anything but consistent over the century. In general, one can see that the long time span of Figure 8-4 is best broken in the middle, after World War II, and that trends vary considerably before and after that war.

From 1890 to 1950, the overall trend in the United States was towards earlier marriage. That trend was strongest up to 1920. In the 1920s and 1930s, through the Depression years, marital age leveled off for males and even rose slightly for females. By 1940, the stage was set for even more dramatic changes.

Figure 8-4 Estimated Median Age at First Marriage for U.S. Males and Females, 1890–1998

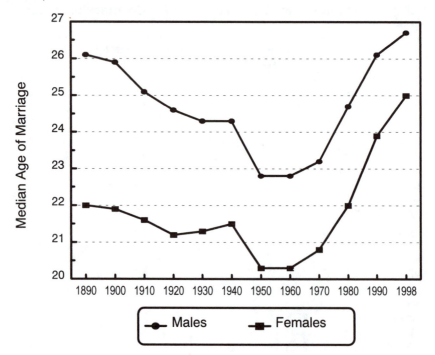

Source: U.S. Censuses 1890–1990; U.S. Bureau of the Census, *1998 Current Population Reports,* Internet Release, 1999, table MS-2.

Just as Europe experienced a marriage boom early in the optimistic postwar years, so too did the United States. The female median age at first marriage dropped from 21.5 in 1940 to an estimate of 20.1 in 1956; the male drop was even more extreme, from 24.3 in 1940 to 22.5 years in 1956. Not only did the average age at first marriage plummet, but also most marriages tended to cluster around those averages; variation diminished. Early marriage appeared to be in fashion.

Then, just as dramatic as the prewar decline in age at marriage, came its reversal after 1956. Figure 8-4 shows resurgent median age at first marriage for males and females since the 1950s. Since 1956, the median age at first marriage has gone up by more than four years for males and nearly five years for females to the highest levels ever recorded for the U.S. population.

The rising postwar age at marriage has been cited as evidence for the demise of marriage, supposedly brought on by a decline in childbearing, increasing economic independence of women, acceptability of sexual relations outside marriage, and so on. As described by the National Marriage Project's *1999 State of Our Unions* report:

> Americans have become less likely to marry. When they do marry their marriages are less happy. And married couples face a high likelihood of divorce. Over the past four decades, marriage has declined as the first living together experience for couples and as a status of parenthood. Unmarried cohabitation and unwed births have grown enormously. . . (Popenoe and Whitehead, 1999, p. 2)

At this point perhaps we should, without lament or judgment, take a lesson from the variety of sexual unions we have documented worldwide. The recent trend toward later marriage should be interpreted in the context of increasing cohabitation and stable sexual unions *without* marriage; otherwise, one gets an exaggerated picture of the degree to which young adults are delaying setting up sexual unions. Women who cohabit are also more likely to marry or to begin childbearing than those who do not (Brien et al., 1999).

Tracking such nontraditional unions poses methodological problems. For instance, how would the Census Bureau get information about the extent of unmarried sexual unions? It would seem unsuitable for such a government agency to ask questions about sex life. However, in its Current Population Surveys, the Census Bureau does ask information about membership in households, kin relationships among members, and age. With these data, it defines *unmarried couples* as households occupied by two unrelated adults of the opposite sex. The vast majority of these unmarried couples consisted of partners who were either in the same or adjacent ten-year age categories and probably were sexually involved.

The changing nature of couple householding can be seen in Figure 8-5. In this graph the percentage of households which included a married couple declined from nearly 75% of all households in 1960 to just over half of all households in 1998. Figure 8-5 graphs the rise in households with unmarried couples during this same period. Since these households are more rare, we graph the rate of unmarried couples per thousand households (per mil) rather than per hundred (percent). Unmarried couple households rose steadily after 1970, from under 10 per thousand to over 40 per thousand (or under 1% to over 4%). While there has been a clear rise in unmarried couple

Figure 8-5 Married and Unmarried Opposite-Sex Couple Households, United States, 1960–1998

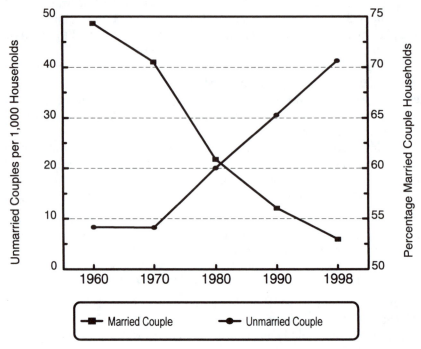

Source: U.S. Bureau of the Census, *1998 Current Population Reports*, Internet Release, 1999, tables HH-1 and AD-2.

households, only a fraction (just over 15%) of the decline in married couple households has been replaced by households with unmarried opposite-sex couples.

Figure 8-5 does not show trends in same-sex unmarried couple householding. Recent estimates suggest there are nearly half as many same-sex couple households as opposite-sex couple households in the United States (Anderton et al., 1997, table 11-15). Assumptions as to the nature of these households are, however, difficult to make. While at least some are formed for sexual union and child rearing, it is impossible to establish the extent of such behavior without further data.

Clearly not all segments of the population are equally likely to live together unmarried. Divorced people—and especially young divorced people—seem particularly prone in this matter (Anderton et al., 1997). Another likely segment of the population is couples in which both partners have started but not yet finished college.

What about the eventual universality of marriage? Conventionally, demographers measure this by the percentage of males or females in the age category forty-five through fifty-four who ever have married. From the earliest detailed census records, that proportion has been consistently high for the United States compared with Northern and Western European countries. It has hovered around 90% for males and slightly less for females since the late 1800s. If anything, it has risen gradually from 1910 to a high in recent decades of about 95% for men and more than 95% for women.

What will happen in the future to universality of marriage is anybody's guess. Recent projections, assuming no sudden rush to marry by young adults now delaying marriage, predict a decline to about 85% ever marrying (Popenoe and Whitehead, 1999). Other studies suggest the current rise in cohabitation may serve the purpose of trial marriages which could eventually end in marital unions (Willis and Michael, 1994). Will those young men and women now putting off marriage end up opting out of it entirely? Has the "need" to marry fallen as fertility has declined and the economic independence of women has risen? Or will those delaying marriage and later cohorts revert to the traditional U.S. pattern of almost universal marriage?

As marriage and married couple households have declined in the United States, a tremendous variety of householding arrangements appear to be replacing these traditional households and the child-rearing role they have fulfilled in the past. *Cohabitation* is only one adaptation. As young adults wait longer to marry, for example, they are *living with their parents* longer and returning more frequently to their parents' home after attending college. The percentage of young males aged eighteen to twenty-four living at home has increased by about 13.5%, and of females by about 37.1% since 1960 (U.S. Bureau of the Census, 1999, table AD-1). Men and women aged twenty-five to thirty-four and still living with their parents has increased by about a third over the same time. The percentage of men and women *living alone* also has increased dramatically: since 1970, men under thirty-five years of age and living alone have increased by over 150% each decade; women living alone increased by the same rate up to 1980, but at a much slower rate since then (Anderton et al., 1997). The percentage living as *single parents* also has risen dramatically, as childbearing outside marriage and divorce has increased. The percentage of children residing in such households has more than doubled since 1970 (Anderton et al., 1997). Over the same period *grandparent maintained households* have increased by over 76% (Casper and Bryson, 1998). The idea of a single "normal" type of household is being challenged by reality.

Nevertheless, despite the rising variety of living arrangements, marriage rates in the United States are not dramatically low by either historical or international standards. Current marriage rates are no lower than their historical low in the late 1950s, and the percentage of current cohorts projected to ever marry remains higher than that of many industrialized countries (De Vita, 1996). Recent declines in marriage may signal changing views of when and whether to marry, but marriage remains the primary stable form of sexual union within the United States.

MARITAL DISSOLUTION TRENDS IN THE UNITED STATES

Let us look back at Figure 8-1 to remind ourselves of the processes involved in marital dissolution. The population at risk of suffering marital dissolution is the currently married population only. Current marriages can dissolve through either of two events, death of a spouse (thrusting any surviving spouse into the widowed status) or divorce (thrusting both survivors into the divorced status). In either case, survivors can

Box 8-1   The Marriage Market in the United States

Demographers sometimes refer to the composition of the marriageable population as a *marriage market.* Try to imagine such a market. For heterosexual marriages, it contains all the women and men who, at a given time and place, are eligible as mates for each other. Each sex in the market has its own population composition with respect to traits that make them more or less eligible and desirable as marriage partners for others. For one thing, both female and male components have age structures. Moreover, each society has its own rules of endogamy with respect to characteristics beyond age, probably including such traits as kinship, race and ethnic identity, and to some degree, socioeconomic status.

We can say that a marriage market is *efficient* to the degree that individual women and men have an easy time finding mates with acceptable combinations of marriage-significant traits. Efficient markets, on the aggregate level, tend to be ones where there is minimal delay in finding mates and thus—everything else being equal—potentially earlier marriage.

Efficiency can be enhanced in several ways. The market can increase in size through a breakdown of localism, greater mobility of population, and easier communication or transportation. All of these broaden one's options, effectively increasing the size of one's pool of eligibles. The size of the pool of eligibles also can be increased by high divorce rates, thus inserting young divorced persons back into the market. Beyond that, the pool can be increased by relaxing exogamy limitations: for instance, increasing intermarriage across racial, ethnic, or socioeconomic lines. Something also can happen to equalize in a category the number of males and females who are eligible to each other.

All but the last of these processes almost surely have been operating in the United States over the past decades (De Vita, 1996). Potential partners no longer are confined to their home neighborhoods, but have become more and more free to roam the country—or surf the Internet—to find partners. Greater and greater proportions of our young people are clustering in those magnificent local marriage markets we call colleges and universities. Divorces and the number of individuals not currently married have increased. Racism and ethnic exclusiveness have declined allowing greater intermarriage across those lines.

There is one respect, however, in which the efficiency of the marriage market in the United States has been limited, at least theoretically. Demographers have come to call this the *marriage squeeze* (Goldman, et al., 1993; Schoen, 1983). It refers to shortages in the correct *age* categories of the pool of eligibles. Most societies have cultural norms regarding the relative ages of husbands and wives with husbands being generally a few years older than wives. Another feature of societies experiencing transition or change, however, is a population pyramid with age-specific bulges and busts (see chapter 4). The combined result of these two features can be a chronic marriage squeeze. For every bulge moving up the population pyramid, the female component will hit its prime marriage ages before the males do; when that male bulge hits its prime ages, females a few years younger may be in a bust. To the degree this continues, men and women looking for mates can be faced with either a feast or famine of eligible partners; and, of course, one sex's feast is the other sex's famine—but either sex's famine would reduce the efficiency of the market.

reenter the marriage market and change those statuses by remarriage, thus reentering the currently married population and again being at risk of marital dissolution.

By implication, there are demographic limits on the number of marital dissolutions. How many divorces or widowings occur depends on how many people get married in the first place. The number of divorced or widowed people depends not only on the rates of spouse death and of divorce, but also on the mortality rates for widowed and divorced former spouses. More forcefully, the number of former spouses left divorced and widowed at a given moment depends on the rates of marriage, including remarriage.

Although there are some obvious similarities between widowhood and divorce, there also are some important differences. Both create unmarried spouses, but divorce creates two, whereas spouse mortality creates one. Widowhood happens later in life on the average than does divorce. At any age, the chances of remarriage apparently are different for the widowed compared with the divorced. The cause of widowhood is involuntary, whereas the cause of divorce is voluntary, although that distinction may not be as clear-cut as it sounds. Partially because of the differing age patterns of incidence, the number and ages of the children left with only one parent at a time varies from widowhood to divorce.

The modernization of the present more-developed countries has changed considerably the relative roles of widowhood and divorce in the marital dissolution process. We have chosen the United States as a dramatic example. There are several reasons for this choice. One is that the United States presents an extreme case of high divorce along with relatively low spouse mortality, both of these features having manifested themselves in many more-developed countries over the past century. Looking at one country alone also avoids the difficulties of noncomparable definitions of divorce, separation, annulment, and so on, which bedevil international comparisons. Furthermore, partially because of U.S. concern over its rising divorce rate, this country has kept relatively good statistics over a long period of time.

Widowhood in the United States

Let us start with a description of the present situation in the United States. Table 8-4 shows the percentage of persons widowed in 1998, by sex, for all adult age classes. It presents the same information for the divorced, both for contrast and for future reference.

The difference between the patterns for widowhood and divorce is dramatic. Widowhood is overwhelmingly a female phenomenon, much more so than is divorce. In the fifteen-and-over population, there are more than four times as many widows as widowers, and sizable differentials in that direction hold true in every age category. For fifteen-and-over females the prevalence of widowhood is about equal to that of divorce; widowhood is far less common than divorce for males.

If widowhood and divorce are equally common for adult women, why do we carry around the idea that divorce is the major cause of marital dissolution? One explanation probably has to do with the age patterns of widowhood and divorce. After retirement ages, widowhood—and especially female widowhood—rises to considerable proportions; being divorced, on the other hand, is more evenly spread over the age distribution, peaking somewhat in the middle ages. Why would this age differen-

Table 8-4
Percentage Widowed and Divorced by Sex and Age, United States, March 1998

Age	Widowed		Divorced	
	Male (1)	Female (2)	Male (3)	Female (4)
In 5-Year Intervals				
20–24	0.0	0.2	1.5	2.5
25–29	0.1	0.4	4.2	5.5
30–34	0.2	0.5	7.7	9.4
35–39	0.4	1.2	10.7	13.0
40–44	0.5	1.5	13.0	15.8
In 10-Year Intervals				
45–54	0.9	4.0	13.9	18.1
55–64	2.6	13.2	11.9	14.4
65–74	8.8	31.9	7.8	8.9
75–84	19.6	55.6	3.7	5.4
85 and Over	42.0	77.4	3.6	3.7
15 and Over	2.5	10.2	8.2	10.3

Source: U.S. Bureau of the Census, *Marital Status and Living Arrangements: March 1998*, 1998a, table 1.

tial affect our consciousness of divorce relative to widowhood? One reason might be that marriages broken by divorce are much more likely to involve parents of still-dependent children than are marriages broken by widowhood, in modern times.

Which historical demographic changes have produced this age and sex pattern of widowhood? As the life expectancy of everyone in the United States went up, so did the average age of the dying spouse and probably that of the surviving mate at the time of that death. This in itself probably was the major factor in bringing about the progressive centering of widowhood in the senior years.

Another aspect of the mortality decline would be, of course, the remaining life expectancy due the surviving spouse. The direction of change in this factor, however, is not quite so clear. Although remaining life expectancy at every age was going up, the death of the spouse also was occurring later in the surviving spouse's life.

Another historical demographic trend to take into account is the sex difference in mortality declines. For most of the mortality transition, male longevity did not improve as rapidly as did female and thus female widowhood did not decrease as rapidly as did male. The present extreme imbalance between male and female widowhood is a generally modern phenomenon. These differences have, however, declined over the past two decades as the gap between male and female longevity has narrowed (see chapter 5).

The net results of demographic changes in developed countries like the United States have been an overall decline in the prevalence of widowhood and a focusing of widowhood in the elderly population, especially the female elderly. For elderly women, the decline in the proportion widowed has been minor at best, and one should be reminded that the segment of our total population that is growing most rapidly are the elderly. Issues raised by widowhood, therefore, are not about to go away.

Divorce in the United States

The divorce process normally is measured by a *refined* rate, called the *general divorce rate,* rather than a crude one. In the general divorce rate, the total events (divorces) compose the numerator, but only that part of the population at risk of participating in the event is in the denominator. Actually, the "population" at risk is of marriages, not people. Since there is one married woman in each such couple, the number of married women of adult age is used as a denominator, that number being more easily accessible.

Figure 8-6 traces the U.S. annual general divorce rates from 1920 to 1998. Divorce experienced a relatively steady, but slow, increase for more than a half century leading up to 1920 (Cherlin, 1981). The general divorce rate was just over one per 1,000 married women in 1860 and increased to over seven by 1919. The overall trend since 1920 also is clearly upward, dramatically so. But within that upward trend there are sharp fluctuations, lasting from a year or so to decades. Remember, these are annual rates and are extremely sensitive to external events that might encourage couples to break up (or postpone a breakup) in particular years. After major wars, for instance, there normally have been some temporary rises in the divorce rate, the peak after World War II being the most dramatic example in Figure 8-6. On the other hand,

Figure 8-6   Annual General Divorce Rates, United States, 1920–1998

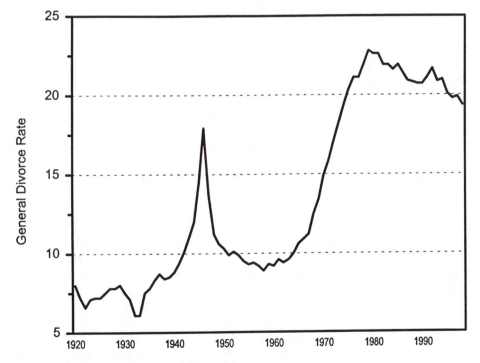

Note: The GDR is the rate of divorces per 1,000 married women.
Source: Anderton et al., *Population of the United States,* 1997, figure 5-3; NCHS, *National Vital Statistics Reports,* 47(12), 1999; *Monthly Vital Statistics Reports,* 45(12), 1997; 42(13), 1994; 41(13), 1993.

there was a temporary retreat from divorce during the depths of the Depression. After the post-World War II temporary peak there was a rather unprecedented holiday from upward divorce trends between 1950 and 1962. Since that time, however, and especially through the 1970s, the upward trend in divorce rates resumed with a vengeance. Although the divorce rate remains higher than at any time prior to 1975, it has declined slightly since its peak in 1979.

Demographers sometimes use a *cohort* perspective rather than a *period* perspective in studying or measuring divorce. The purpose is to estimate the lifetime chances of divorce implicit in period rates. Since current cohorts in a population have not completed their marital history, an estimate of their lifetime chances of divorce requires projecting the future marriage behavior of the cohort. This is done in the same way that life tables are used to project the future mortality of a cohort (see chapter 5). A group of married women are aged forward in time assuming they experience the same age-specific divorce rates that the current population does. Using such a method allows demographers to spell out the implications of sequences of rates for the marital life chances of individuals belonging to particular cohorts (see Bogue et al., 1993, vol. 4).

Again using the United States as an example, Figure 8-7 presents cohort measures of divorce for women who were ever married by 1990 from the birth cohorts of women born between 1935 and 1970. For each birth cohort across the bottom of the graph, the gray area shows the percent of those marriages that ended in divorce prior to mid-year 1990. The white area above the gray shows the additional percentage of the birth cohort that may eventually experience a divorce if, over the remainder of their lives, they have the same age-specific divorce rates as women had during 1985–1990. Thus the line at the top of the white area tells for each birth cohort the percentage of first marriages which have ended, or are projected to end, in divorce. The top panel of the graph is for women's first marriages. With caution for the assumptions of such a projection, the graph suggests that the percentage of first marriages ending in divorce may peak with the birth cohort of 1950–1955, who are now about forty-five to fifty years old, and may fall for younger cohorts. Remarriages are, however, an increasing percentage of all marriages and are also subject to marital disruption. The bottom panel of the graph gives the percentage of all remarriages ending in divorce. Except for the cohorts from 1945 to 1955 the percentage of remarriages ending in divorce is projected to be higher than for first marriages. According to these projections, the percentage of remarriages ending in divorce will also continue to rise up through more recent birth cohorts.

Cohort projections of divorce are not, however, generally reliable. Projecting the chances of divorce into the future for a cohort makes the unlikely assumption of stable divorce rates over time. The dramatic variability in divorce rates which is apparent in Figure 8-6, in contrast, suggests divorce is highly responsive to contemporary, or period, events. As predictions, these projections are very tentative.

With levels of divorce near historically high levels, how does the United States compare with other countries? International comparisons relying on legal divorce statistics are difficult to make. In those countries where many of the sexual unions are consensual rather than legal, unions can be dissolved voluntarily without that ever being recorded. Indeed, census reports from Latin American countries imply that

Figure 8-7 Percent of Women Whose Marriages May End in Divorce, U.S., Birth Cohorts 1935–1970

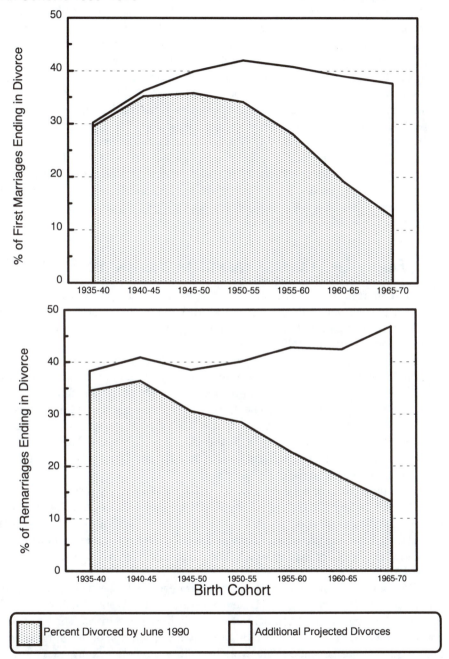

Note: Projected divorce percentages assume the birth cohort will experience the same age-specific divorce rates as older cohorts did over the period of 1985–1990.
Source: Anderton et al., *The Population of the United States*, 1997, table 5-22.

many people who have gone through this process (without remarriage) describe themselves as "single" rather than "divorced." Beyond that there is the process in Catholic countries of erasing the record of a legal marriage by annulment. Finally, there is the vague category of "separation," which may involve large proportions of the population but is poorly and inconsistently reported. So, it is more precise to say that the United States has peaked at the highest divorce rate in the world, rather than to say that it has the highest rate of voluntary marital breakup.

The total rate of marital dissolution, from divorce and widowhood combined, remained remarkably stable over the past century until rising during the divorce boom of the 1970s (Cherlin, 1981). In terms of rates, widowhood declined and divorce rose over this same period. It is tempting—probably too tempting—to interpret these rates as suggesting that divorce has simply replaced widowhood as a form of marital dissolution as spouses live longer. It was, perhaps, a lot easier to keep the vow of marital commitment "till death do us part" when that terminal date was due in a couple of decades, rather than in a couple of generations. Consequently, there may now be less readiness to confine oneself to only one marriage in life.

FAMILY LIFE COURSE TRENDS IN THE UNITED STATES

The cohort measures of divorce shown in Figure 8-7 are only one example of the cohort perspective (versus the period perspective) in describing marital trends. Generally, cohort measures seem to have more meaning for individuals assessing their marital-life prospects (Aldous, 1990).

One notion that demographers and sociologists employ in the cohort study of the family is that of a family life course, sometimes referred to as the family life cycle. A family life course specifies a *sequence of events* that might occur in the life of a nuclear family, such as first marriage, then bearing children, then death of both spouses. In a given society and time period, obviously a whole array of sequences will have been experienced by families, with varying frequencies. It is the relative frequency of these sequences that is of primary interest. A second important aspect of a life course is the *timing* of those events that make up the sequence.

A chronic problem with employing the cohort perspective is that recent cohort histories are yet incomplete. That means family life course descriptions of *real* cohorts will be limited to those cohorts who might have experienced all the specified family events. To describe the life course implications of current marital event rates we have to employ the strategy of hypothetical cohorts, just as we did in constructing life tables (chapter 5).

We provide examples of each of these strategies below, necessarily describing somewhat different time periods. Uhlenberg's pioneering work (1978) deals with a sequence of *real* cohorts and compares their family life course arrays. The latest cohort represented, however, was born in 1930, roughly the generation of the grandparents of most of our college-age readers. The work by Schoen and Weinick provides more contemporary information, but necessarily about *hypothetical* cohorts. From their work, we have chosen three recent years whose rates they interpret, 1970 (before the peak in the divorce rate), 1980 (about the peak in that rate), and 1988 (after the divorce peak). The emphasis in Uhlenberg's study is on the array of event sequences involved; the emphasis in our data from Schoen and Weinick is on the *timing* of events.

Changes in Completed Family Life Courses

Using a combination of census and vital statistics data, Uhlenberg (1978) described the changing array of marital life courses in the United States for birth cohorts that had reached, or neared, average life expectancy by the end of the twentieth century. Table 8-5 presents the data for females. Each row is a birth cohort selected at twenty-year intervals from 1870 to 1930. One can read down a given column in order to see the direction of any trend in marital experiences across the cohorts. The numbers in the column for each life course type tell how many (per thousand women in the birth cohort who reached age twenty) experienced a specified life course sequence.

A major conclusion is that the proportion who experienced the "normatively expected course" (column 5) consistently *increased* over that half century. This life course involves marrying, bearing children, and surviving to age fifty with marriage still intact. The major reason for the ascendance of the normatively expected pattern was the decline of early death (column 1). As a result, more, not fewer, women lived out the cultural ideal.

The three remaining life course types offer a variety of trends. "Spinster" (column 2), surviving never-married to age fifty, declined dramatically in prevalence. "Unstable marriage with children" (column 4), defined as having a marriage with children end by divorce or death of husband before the woman reaches age fifty, increased dramatically. "Childless" (column 3), marrying and surviving without having any children, first went up during these decades and then decreased dramatically.

Several well-known demographic trends during this period are behind the changing patterns of life course experience. Foremost was the decline in *mortality* associated with the demographic transition. Fewer women died between ages fifteen and fifty, reducing the proportion of women who failed to survive and shrinking the "early death" column. Aside from mortality, *marriage* became more universal in the

Table 8-5
Distribution of 1,000 White Females in the United States, by Type of Life Course Experiences, Birth Cohorts from 1870–1930

Birth Cohort	Early Death (1)	Spinster (2)	Childless (3)	Unstable Marriage with Children (4)	Normatively Expected (5)
1870	235	80	70	175	440
1890	170	85	115	170	460
1910	90	60	145	185	520
1930	50	45	40	265	600

Note: Confined to those who survived to age 20.
Source: Uhlenberg, "Changing Configurations in the Life Course," 1978, table 2.5.

later cohorts, reducing the number of spinsters. Rising marriage also raised the percentage of the population at risk for each of the last three columns of the table. The increase in the "unstable marriage with children" column reflects increased divorces, separations, and widowings among rising numbers of marriages. In the table women are considered childless only if married, so the rise and fall of percentages in the "childless" column also reflect an initial rise in marriages (column 5) and a later rise in marriage dissolution (column 4).

Table 8-6 presents comparable information from Uhlenberg (1978) about males. The life course types are not exactly the same as those for females, for two reasons. The typical family life course experiences of males are empirically different from those of females. Moreover, censuses normally do not record as much information about the relationship between men and their offspring as they do for women. Nevertheless, some similarities appear. The decline in mortality also led to a decline in early death among males (column 1) and an even greater decline in widowhood (column 3). And, as with females, the proportion never marrying (column 2) declined as the culturally preferred intact marriage (column 5) increased.

Both men and women *improved* their likelihood of living out the culturally preferred life course in their middle years across these cohorts. Much of that change in both male and female life course experiences was due to declining mortality coupled with a rise in the universality of marriage.

Recent Changes in Timing of Marital Events

To examine marital timing during recent times, we will use marital life tables computed from period rates of marriage, divorce and widowhood. We have seen (in Figure 8-6) the dramatic rise in general divorce rates that occurred between 1970 and 1980 and the subsequent drop in those rates from 1980 to 1988. To examine the effects of these changes on marital timing, Table 8-7 presents selected marital life table estimates from 1970, 1980, and 1988 tables computed by Schoen and Weinick (1993). (We trust the reader will remember that these life table estimates are only what would *hypothetically* occur if a cohort were to experience the period rates of 1970, 1980 or 1988 respectively over the cohort's life course.) The first three columns of the table

Table 8-6
Distribution of 1,000 White Males in the United States, by Type of Life Course Experiences, Birth Cohorts from 1870–1930

Birth Cohort	Die Between 20 and 50 (1)	Bachelor (2)	Wife Died (3)	Other Broken Marriage (4)	Spouse Present (5)
1870	245	95	110	60	490
1890	190	90	90	85	545
1910	115	60	50	145	630
1930	75	55	25	210	635

Note: Confined to those who survived to age 20.
Source: Uhlenberg, "Changing Configurations in the Life Course," 1978, table 2.5.

give estimates for females in each of the three periods while the next three columns provide similar figures for males.

The first three rows of the table give *marriage* and marriage timing estimates. For both sexes, the percentage ever marrying (first row) declined and the average age at first marriage (second row) rose substantially throughout. The average duration of marriages (third row) declined as divorce rose, but then rose slightly as divorce rates fell. Marriages became less universal, occurred at an older age, and lasted a shorter number of years across the three life tables.

Table 8-7
Marital Life Table Estimates Before, During, and After Peak Divorce Years, United States

	Female			Male		
Life Table Estimates	Pre-Peak 1970 (1)	Divorce Peak 1980 (2)	Post-Peak 1988 (3)	Pre-Peak 1970 (1)	Divorce Peak 1980 (2)	Post-Peak 1988 (3)
Marriage						
Percent Ever Marrying	96.5	90.8	87.9	96.0	89.2	83.5
Average Age at First Marriage	21.8	24.1	25.1	23.4	26.3	27.5
Average Duration of a Marriage	26.8	24.4	24.8	26.5	23.8	24.5
Divorce						
Percent Ending in Divorce	35.7	42.9	43.2	37.3	44.4	42.7
Average Age at Divorce	33.9	33.1	34.4	36.4	37.1	37.7
Average Duration of a Divorce	9.4	10.8	13.4	4.3	6.0	7.9
Widowhood						
Percent Ending in Widowhood	45.3	40.0	39.3	18.7	17.1	18.3
Average Age at Widowhood	65.2	67.9	68.9	67.8	71.1	72.3
Average Duration of Widowhood	14.8	15.0	15.3	7.4	7.7	8.4
Remarriage						
Percent of Divorced Remarrying	80.2	78.3	72.3	86.0	82.7	78.3
Average Age of Remarriage for Divorced	35.5	34.7	36.1	37.3	38.5	40.1
Percent of Widowed Remarrying	10.3	7.6	6.3	27.0	20.8	17.3
Average Age of Remarriage for Widowed	53.9	56.0	56.5	58.8	61.9	62.9
Expectation of Life at Birth	74.8	77.6	78.5	67.2	69.7	70.7

Source: Schoen and Weinick, "The Slowing Metabolism of Marriage," 1993, table 1.

The next three rows provide *divorce* estimates. Not surprisingly, the percentage of marriages ending in divorce rose as divorce rates rose and increased very little (for females) or declined (for males) as divorce rates fell. The average age at divorce, however, dropped for women during peak divorce years and then rose again while it rose steadily for males across all three periods. These trends echo the balance between changes in the age and duration of marriages. Most importantly, the average duration of a divorce, before it is ended by remarriage or death, rose considerably across all three periods and for both sexes. The time spent living as divorced steadily increased regardless of whether divorce rates increased or fell.

As divorce rose, the percentage of marriages ending in *widowhood* declined. Yet the age at widowhood and the average duration of widowhood increased steadily. Both estimates are largely explained by rising life expectancy. The percentage *remarrying* after either divorce or widowhood declined for both sexes just as first marriages declined. The age at remarriage after divorce fell for women who both divorced and remarried at younger ages during the divorce peak, and then rose. The age at which divorced males remarry rose steadily as did the average age at remarriage for widows of both sexes.

Table 8-7 demonstrates that the timing of the marital life course was clearly affected by the rising divorce rates from 1970 to 1980. However, these estimates also reveal that during these dramatic changes in divorce, the marital life course was also profoundly shaped by two more consistent trends, a decline in marriage (both universal and early marriage) and an increasing life expectancy. It is important, however, to remember these images are drawn from period rates and that younger women during these years have not yet completed their marital life course. Some of the trends seen, especially the declining universality of marriage, may well change in the future if women who remained single turn out to be only delaying, rather than avoiding, marriage.

WHICH MARITAL TRENDS ARE PROBLEMS?

Apparently, it is universal to feel nostalgic when judging any current marriage trends (Goode, 1963). This is not new. The family always has seemed to be on the decline and in disarray at any given moment, as compared with the past. Because family institutions and the roles associated with them are central to all cultures, any change can seem threatening because it requires compensating changes in many interconnected cultural norms, including some of our most deeply held values. On the other hand, in periods of general social change, some members of society might find the family changes to be in keeping with the other changes in their lives. To them, the old family pattern often may seem an anachronism and a bad fit.

Thus, in a changing culture, there is not likely to be much agreement on the definition of "problems" associated with changes in marriage and marital dissolution, not nearly as much as there is concerning trends in mortality, fertility, and age structure. We do not even find well-articulated problem definitions held by sizable segments of the public. Instead, we seem to have widespread ambivalence or a mix of opposing views about almost any given trend.

Summarizing recent changes in American families, DaVanzo and Rahman (1993) identify four important trends: 1) increased proportions of children living in single-parent families due to increasing divorce and childbearing outside marriage, 2) increased proportions of nontraditional living arrangements, 3) increased female labor force participation across the life course, and 4) an increasingly older composition of families due to declining mortality and fertility. We will briefly discuss the impacts of these trends and why some are labeled "problems."

1. *More children are living in single-parent families.* Children in single-parent families have fewer economic resources and represent one of the most rapidly growing groups living in poverty over the past half century. Two parents may also be capable of providing more of other types of social support than can one parent. At the same time, it can be argued that poverty among single-parent families is a problem of inadequate social support rather than a problem of single parenthood itself. Although one parent provides only one income, problems of poverty among children of single-parent families are not due solely to having only a single income. Rather, such poverty is due to both the burdens of child rearing and limited opportunity or income of the average single parent. These problems may arise from the abdication by society at large for responsibility to children and include the lack of affordable child care, absence of educational assistance for young single parents, and so on. Indeed, a single-parent family may provide far better social support to a child than a traditional married-couple family where a spouse is not committed to the family or may even be abusive.

2. *More couples are living together in nontraditional ways.* It is disturbing to some segments of the population that strong couple commitments associated with sex and childbearing, referred to as "family values" by proponents, are being undermined by permitting cohabitation and nontraditional family arrangements. On the other hand, nonmarital cohabitation among the young may reinforce the stability of marriage when it does occur, by providing a trial marriage and delaying marriage until people generally less committed to marriage are somewhat more mature. Many nontraditional living arrangements may also provide social and economic stability for individuals who are simply unable to form a suitable traditional union, for whatever reason. Proponents of greater flexibility in living arrangements can point to eroding governmental and extended family support, greater geographic dispersion of families, rising social and economic independence of women, greater acceptability of same-sex couples, and similar social trends as requiring more flexible householding arrangements.

3. *More women are working before marriage and outside the home after marriage.* Some segments of the population view women working outside the home as being at the root of the marriage decline. There is evidence to support that view. Working before marriage may increase the likelihood marriage will be delayed and working in marriage takes a woman away from traditional domestic roles and child rearing. Implicit in this critique of women entering

the wage labor force is the assumption that the marital decline, and the first two trends mentioned above, are themselves obvious problems. Others genuinely lament the loss of respect for the domestic labor women traditionally have provided and the economic and social benefits it afforded the family. Married-couple single-wage-earner families will clearly remain an optimal solution for at least some segment of the population. At the same time, others point to the economic benefits of a dual-income family, the overall (and marital) satisfaction a career may bring to a woman, the role model working mothers provide to their daughters, and so forth. They also can point to the oppressive patriarchal aspects of trying to keep a wife "barefoot and pregnant" under her husband's control. It is not surprising that some women would prefer the satisfactions and productivity of a more traditional domestic lifestyle to many stressful or unsatisfying wage labor jobs. Understandably, others may prefer the excitement, independence, and earnings of a career outside the home. It also is not surprising that some men would prefer to have the comforts, status, and security they find in a traditional one-earner family division of labor, while others would prefer to share in public working lives, a sense of independence, and dual incomes as a couple.

4. *Families are growing older with delay of marriage and childbearing.* Parenting is occurring later, for better or worse. Older families may have greater financial security, greater stability, and fewer distractions (such as career building) competing with children for attention. At the same time, the social distance of parents from children, the physical stress of childbearing and rearing, and the uncertainty of surviving children's formative years are all potentially greater in older families. The aging of U.S. families, however, has not generated the same level of public concern as the first three trends we have discussed—not yet, at least.

SUMMARY

As a birth cohort matures, its members experience demographic events (marriage, divorce, death of spouse) that place them for periods of time in different marital statuses or sexual unions (single, married, divorced, separated, widowed, remarried, cohabiting, noncohabiting stable sexual unions, multiple unions, etc.). Societies track changes in population composition with respect to stable sexual unions by means of censuses and interim sample surveys. They sometimes track the transitional events by civil registration and by retrospective survey or census questions. As registration systems have been criticized and even curtailed in the United States, sample surveys have added greatly to the fund of information for the demographic study of nuptiality and sexual unions.

Marriage remains the dominant form of stable sexual union in nearly all countries. The general pattern of spread of first marriage through a birth cohort appears nearly universal. Yet societies do differ in terms of when the process starts, how fast it spreads once started, and how many are never married. Although the less-developed regions generally have earlier marriage of females than the more-developed regions, there is considerable variety among the LDRs and a marked recent trend toward delay of marriage in increasing numbers of less-developed countries.

Over the past several centuries, Europe—and in particular Western Europe—developed a distinctive pattern of late marriage of women combined with high proportions never marrying. This seems to have peaked at the turn of the century. More recently, both Europe and the United States have experienced a pattern of marriage booms and busts, perhaps facilitated by the increasingly voluntary nature of marriage and responding to demographic compositional swings.

In the United States, marriage has increasingly been delayed and the universality of marriage has declined. Widowhood has been delayed, yet has increased in duration, due to the increase in longevity during the mortality transition and the fact that this increase has favored women. Divorce has taken over as the cause of marital dissolution during the young and middle ages, and the trend rose sharply in the 1970s before leveling and even slightly declining in more recent times. Divorce rates remain at a high plateau.

These changes have had their impact on the family life courses followed by successive cohorts in the United States. Perhaps surprisingly, the proportion of women and men who lived out the culturally preferred sequence of events—getting married, having at least one child, and having the marriage survive until their fiftieth birthday—actually increased over past cohorts. Timing of marriage events has, however, changed over more recent decades, and marriage in cohorts still living out their marital histories has become later, less universal, and shorter in duration. The time spent living as divorced has continued to increase although divorce rates peaked at the end of the 1970s.

Some nostalgia for the supposedly better family life of the past seems universal. Yet the pros and cons of any given marriage trend in a changing society is debatable, and debated. For example, we summarize the debate surrounding four salient trends in the United States. Individuals who value traditional arrangements view these trends as problematic, while those who value new alternatives welcome them.

EXERCISES

1. Age Standardization

   Suppose you are making a historical contrast between the 1890 and the present (1999) U.S. male marital status compositions. You are aware that one reason for a change in marital status composition might be an aging male population during that century (see chapter 4). You might want to know how much of the marital status change is attributable to changes in age structure, that is, what the 1890 marital status composition would have been if it had that older 1999 age structure. To do this you could *standardize* 1890 to the 1999 age distribution using the *direct method,* as follows:

   First, record different information about the two dates in a standardization table, such as Table E8-1. The number of males in each age category (excluding those under age fourteen) for the standard population of 1999 would be recorded in column 1 of the top panel in Table E8-1. For the 1890 population, record the proportion in each age category falling into each marital status (see columns 2, 3, 4, and 5 of the top panel of Table E8-1).

Using these source data, make the following computations, filling in the blanks in the exercise table.

a. Multiply each of the proportions for 1890 in columns 2 through 5 against the 1999 population for the appropriate age category found in column 1. Record the resulting "expected number in marital status" in the lower panel of Table E8-1.

b. For each marital status, accumulate the expected numbers, at all ages, at the foot of columns 2 through 5. Together, these totals form the expected frequency distribution by marital status.

Table E8-1
Calculation of Percent Distribution by Marital Status for U.S. Males in 1890, Standardized by Age to the 1999 U.S. Male Population Distribution

Age	Male Population June 1, 1999 (thousands) (1)	Proportional Distribution by Marital Status, 1890			
		Single (2)	Married (3)	Widowed (4)	Divorced (5)
14–19	12,147	0.9957	0.0042	0.0001	0.0001
20–24	9,178	0.8081	0.1889	0.0025	0.0005
25–29	9,081	0.4607	0.5278	0.0099	0.0016
30–34	9,797	0.2655	0.7140	0.0181	0.0024
35–44	22,254	0.1537	0.8102	0.0327	0.0035
45–54	17,453	0.0915	0.8400	0.0602	0.0043
55–64	11,134	0.0683	0.8245	0.1024	0.0048
65 and over	14,305	0.0561	0.7063	0.2335	0.0040
		Expected Number in Marital Status			
14–19		12,095	51	1	1
20–24		7,417	1,734	23	5
25–29			4,793	90	15
30–34				177	24
35–44		3,420			78
45–54		1,597	14,661		
55–64		760	9,180	1,140	
65 and over		803	10,104	3,340	57
Total	105,283	32,877		6,550	308
Percent in Status					
1999 Standardized		31.2			0.3
1890 Unstandardized		43.8	52.3	3.8	0.2

Source: Shryock and Siegel, *The Methods and Materials of Demography,* 1976, table 10-2; U.S. Bureau of the Census Population Estimates Program, Population Division, Internet Release, 1999.

c. Convert this frequency distribution into a percentage distribution. Divide the expected number in each status category by the expected number in all categories combined (105,283).

The bottom row of Table E8-1 presents, for comparison, the actual (non-standardized) percentage distribution by marital status of the 1890 male population aged fourteen and over. The main difference is that standardization, or the hypothetical assumption of a 1999 age structure, would reduce the proportion of those who would be single and increase the proportions married and widowed. That is consistent, since older men are less likely to be single and more likely to be married or widowed.

2. Calculating Annual Rates

Table E8-2 contains data to compute the United States crude marriage and divorce rates (per 1,000 population) and the general divorce rate (per 1,000 married adult women) for the years 1998 and 1997. Complete the table by filling in the blank cells for each rate in 1998. Also apply the crude divorce rate in 1997 to the population to fill in the blank cell for the number of divorces in that year.

Table E8-2
Calculation of Marriage and Divorce Rates, United States, 1997–1998

	Year	
	1998	**1997**
Total Population (1,000s)	270,299	267,744
Married Females 15 Years Old and Over	58,633	57,923
Marriages	2,244,000	2,384,000
Divorces	1,135,000	
Crude Marriage Rate		8.9
Crude Divorce Rate		4.3
General Divorce Rate		19.9

Source: NCHS, *National Vital Statistics Reports,* 47(12), 1999.

▶ PROPOSITIONS FOR DEBATE

1. Rising proportions of people living as single in the United States demonstrates a fundamental decline in the desire to live as a couple.

2. We should expect marriage to decline and divorce to rise as fertility decreases.

3. We should expect both the age at first marriage and the divorce rate to rise as life expectancy increases.

4. The divorce rate will fall again as the population grows older.

5. We should expect the divorce rate to continue to rise as even more women enter into the labor force and gain greater economic independence.

6. Cohabitation, same-sex couples, and alternatives to marriage will continue to rise in the MDRs.

7. Over the coming years it appears that the MDRs will become more like the LDRs as far as the prevalence of civil marriage is concerned.

▶ REFERENCES AND SUGGESTED READINGS

Aldous, J. 1990. "Family Development and the Life Course: Two Perspectives on Family Change." *Journal of Marriage and the Family* 52(3).

Anderton, Douglas L., Richard E. Barrett, and Donald J. Bogue. 1997. *The Population of the United States*. 3rd ed. New York: Free Press.

Becker, Gary S. 1981. *A Treatise on the Family*. Cambridge: Harvard University Press.

Bianchi, Suzanne. 1995. "Changing Economic Roles of Women and Men." In Reynolds Farley, ed., *State of the Union: America in the 1990s*. Vol. I: *Economic Trends*. New York: Russell Sage Press.

Blau, Peter M. 1977. *Inequality and Heterogeneity: A Primitive Theory of Social Structure*. London: Free Press.

Bogue, Donald J., Eduardo Arriaga, and Douglas L. Anderton, eds. 1993. *Readings in Population Research Methodology*. United Nations Fund for Population Activities. Chicago: Social Development Center.

Brien, Michael J., Lee A. Lillard, and Linda J. Waite. 1999. "Interrelated Family-Building Behaviors: Cohabitation, Marriage and Nonmarital Conception." *Demography* 36(4).

Burch, Thomas K. 1982. "Household and Family Demography." In John A. Ross, ed., *International Encyclopedia of Population*. Vol. 1. New York: Free Press.

Casper, Lynne M., and Kenneth R. Bryson. 1998. *Co-resident Grandparents and Their Grandchildren: Grandparent Maintained Families*. United States Bureau of the Census Population Division Working Paper no. 26. Washington, DC: Government Printing Office.

Casper, Lynne M., Philip N. Cohen, and Tavia Simmons. 1999. "How Does POSSLQ Measure Up? Historical Estimates of Cohabitation." United States Bureau of the Census Population Division Working Paper no. 26. Washington, DC: Government Printing Office.

Cherlin, Andrew J. 1981. *Marriage, Divorce, and Remarriage*. Cambridge, MA: Harvard University Press.

Coale, Ansley J. 1971. "Age Patterns of Marriage." *Population Studies* 25(2).

Coale, Ansley J., and D. R. McNeil. 1972. "The Distribution by Age of the Frequency of First Marriage in a Female Cohort." *Journal of the American Statistical Association* 67(340).

DaVanzo, J., and F. K. Goldscheider. 1990. "Coming Home Again: Returns to the Parental Home of Young Adults." *Population Studies* 44(2).

DaVanzo, J., and M. O. Rahman. 1993. "American Families: Trends and Correlates." *Population Index* 59(3).

Davis, Kingsley. 1972. "The American Family in Relation to Demographic Change." In Charles F. Westoff and Robert Parke, Jr., eds., *Demographic and Social Aspects of Population Growth*. Vol. 1. Washington, DC: Government Printing Office.

DeVita, Carol J. 1996. "The United States at Mid-Decade." *Population Bulletin* 50(4).

Festy, Patrick. 1980. "On the New Context of Marriage in Western Europe." *Population and Development Review* 6(2).

Fu, H., and N. Goldman. 1996. "Incorporating Health into Models of Marriage Choice: Demographic and Sociological Perspectives." *Journal of Marriage and the Family* 58(3).

Gelbard, Alene, Carl Haub, and Mary M. Kent. 1999. "World Population Beyond Six Billion." *Population Bulletin* 54(1).

Glick, Paul C. 1977. "Updating the Life Cycle of the Family." *Journal of Marriage and the Family* 39(1).

Goldman, Noreen. 1993. "Marriage Selection and Mortality Patterns: Inferences and Fallacies." *Demography* 30(1).

Goldman, Noreen, Charles F. Westoff, and Charles Hammerslough. 1993. "Demography of the Marriage Market in the United States." In Bogue, Arriaga, and Anderton, eds., *Readings in Population Research Methodology*. United Nations Fund for Population Activities, Chicago: Social Development Center.

Goldstein, Joshua R. 1999. "The Leveling of Divorce in the United States." *Demography* 36(3).

Goode, William. 1963. *World Revolution and Family Patterns*. New York: Free Press.

Grossbard-Schechtman, A. 1985. "Marriage Squeezes and the Marriage Market." In Kingsley Davis, ed., *Contemporary Marriage: Comparative Perspectives on a Changing Institution*. New York: Russell Sage Foundation.

Hajnal, John. 1953. "The Marriage Boom." *Population Index* 19(2).

———. 1965. "European Marriage Patterns in Perspective." In D. V. Glass and D. E. C. Eversley, eds., *Population in History*. London: Arnold.

Hernes, Gudmund. 1972. "The Process of Entry into First Marriage." *American Sociological Review* 37(2).

Hiedemann, B., O. Suhomlinova, and A. M. Rand. 1998. "Economic Independence, Economic Status, and Empty Nest in Midlife Marital Disruption." *Journal of Marriage and the Family* 66(1).

Hussain, R., and A. H. Bittles. 1998. "The Prevalence and Demographic Characteristics of Consanguineous Marriages in Pakistan." *Journal of Biosocial Science* 30(2).

McLanahan, Sara S., and Lynne Casper. 1995. "Growing Diversity and Inequality in the American Family." In R. Farley, ed., *State of the Union: America in the 1990s*. Vol. II. New York: Russell Sage Press.

Monahan, Thomas P. 1951. *The Age at Marriage in the United States*. Philadelphia: Stephenson.

National Center for Health Statistics. 1993. "Annual Summary of Births, Marriages, Divorces, and Deaths: United States, 1992." *Monthly Vital Statistics Report* 41(13).

———. 1994. "Annual Summary of Births, Marriages, Divorces, and Deaths: United States, 1993." *Monthly Vital Statistics Report* 42(13).

———. 1997a. "Births, Marriages, Divorces, and Deaths for 1996." *Monthly Vital Statistics Report* 45(12).

———. 1997b. "Fertility, Family Planning, and Women's Health: New Data from the 1995 National Survey of Family Growth." *Vital and Health Statistics* 23(19).

———. 1999. "Births, Marriages, Divorces, and Deaths: Provisional Data for 1998." *National Vital Statistics Reports* 47(21).

Oppenheimer, Valerie K. 1994. "Women's Rising Employment and the Future of the Family in Industrial Societies." *Population and Development Review* 20(2).

Oppenheimer, V. K., and V. Lew. 1995. "American Marriage Formation in the 1980s: How Important was Women's Economic Independence." In Karen O. Mason and An-Magritt Jensen, eds., *Gender and Family Change in Industrialized Countries*. Oxford: Clarendon Press.

Popenoe, David, and Barbara Dafoe Whitehead. 1999. *The State of Our Unions: The Social Health of Marriage in America*. National Marriage Project Report. New Brunswick, NJ: Rutgers University.

Regan, Milton C. 1993. *Family Law and the Pursuit of Intimacy.* New York: New York University Press.

Ross, C. E. 1995. "Reconceptualizing Marital Status as a Continuum of Social Attachment." *Journal of Marriage and the Family* 57(1).

Ruggles, Steven. 1993. "Historical Demography from the Census: Applications of the American Census Microdata Files." In David S. Reher and Roger Schofield, eds., *Old and New Methods in Historical Demography.* Oxford: Clarendon Press.

———. 1997. "The Rise of Divorce and Separation in the United States." *Demography* 34(4).

Schoen, Robert. 1983. "Measuring the Tightness of a Marriage Squeeze." *Demography* 20(1).

Schoen, Robert, and J. Baj. 1985. "The Impact of the Marriage Squeeze in Five Western Countries." *Sociology and Social Research* 70(1).

Schoen, Robert, and Robin M. Weinick. 1993. "The Slowing Metabolism of Marriage: Figures from 1988 U.S. Marital Status Life Tables." *Demography* 30(4).

Shryock, Henry S., and Jacob S. Siegel. 1976. *The Methods and Materials of Demography.* Condensed ed. by Edward G. Stockwell. New York: Academic Press.

Uhlenberg, Peter. 1978. "Changing Configurations in the Life Course." In Tamara K. Hareven, ed., *Transitions: The Family and Life Course in Historical Perspective.* New York: The Academic Press.

United Nations. 1983. *Marital Status and Fertility: A Comparative Analysis of World Fertility Survey Data for Twenty-One Countries.* ST/ESA/SER.R/52. New York: United Nations Population Division.

———. 1997. *The World's Women 1995: Trends and Statistics.* ST/ESA/SER.K/WWW/12/Rev.1. New York: United Nations Population Division.

———. 1998. *Principles and Recommendations for Population and Housing Censuses.* ST/ESA/STAT/SER.M/Rev.1. New York: United Nations.

United States Bureau of the Census. 1976. *Social Indicators, 1976.* Washington, DC: Government Printing Office.

———. 1998a. *Marital Status and Living Arrangements: March 1998 (Update).* Current Population Reports, Series P-20, no. 514. Washington, DC: Government Printing Office.

———. 1998b. *Trends in the Marital Status of U.S. Women at First Birth: 1930 to 1994.* Population Division Working Paper no. 20. Washington, DC: Government Printing Office.

———. 1999. *Current Population Reports.* Internet Release. Washington, DC: Government Printing Office.

Waite, Linda J. 1995. "Does Marriage Matter?" *Demography* 32(4).

Watkins, Susan C. 1981. "Regional Patterns of Nuptiality in Europe, 1870–1960." *Population Studies* 35(2).

Westoff, Charles F., Ann K. Blanc, and Laura Nyblade. 1994. *Marriage and Entry into Parenthood.* Demographic and Health Surveys Comparative Studies no. 10. Maryland: Macro International Inc.

Westoff, Charles F., and Robert Parke, Jr., eds. 1972. *Demographic and Social Aspects of Population Growth.* Vol. 1. Washington, DC: Government Printing Office.

Willis, Robert J., and Robert T. Michael. 1994. "Innovation in Family Formation: Evidence on Cohabitation in the United States." In John Ermisch and Naohiro Ogawa, eds., *The Family, the Market and the State in Ageing Societies.* Oxford: Clarendon Press.

9

Migration

In this chapter we introduce the remaining component of population growth, migration. Thereafter, in chapters 10 and 11, we discuss two major consequences of migration, i.e. urbanization and population diversity.

This chapter starts with the knotty problem of defining migration. It then proceeds to describe the major patterns of international and internal migration and theories about the causes or determinants of migration. Finally, we address the consequences and policy concerns of international migration, especially the flow of population from the less-developed regions to the more-developed regions of the world.

WHAT IS MIGRATION?

Migration is more difficult to define than are mortality or fertility. Whereas all births contribute to fertility and all deaths contribute to mortality, not all moves contribute to migration. A vacation trip, a move to a neighboring apartment, an errand to the shopping mall, a daily commute to work: these moves are *not* migrations.

Which Moves Are Migrations?

So, which moves do demographers consider to be migrations? One answer to this question can be seen in the population growth equation of chapter 1. Migrations are those population movements that add or subtract from the *members* of a population or society. For demographers, membership in a population is closely linked to the idea of *residence*. Residence, in this context, means more than just being physically present at a geographic location at a moment in time; it implies being socially *affiliated* with a population.

By this limitation, we focus on those moves which are demographically and socially important. The society in the area of origin (the *donor* society) wants to know

271

how many people, of what kind, it is losing. The society in the area of destination (the *host* society) wants to know how many people, of what kind, it is gaining. And, from the perspective of *individuals*, changes in residence that involve the tearing up of old roots and the setting down of new ones are psychologically, socially, and economically more important than casual moves.

Migration, or change in population membership, is then demographically identified as a change in residence. Being more precise, demographers require a move to satisfy three conditions to qualify as a migration: 1) It must involve a permanent or semi-permanent change in one's residence; 2) it must cross some administrative boundary; 3) it must occur during a given time or period (Pressat, 1985). This is the simplest definition of migration, a change in residence across some geopolitical boundary in a given period of time.

Note that this definition of migration uses neither a *distance* criterion nor a *duration* criterion, at least not directly. A change in residence by moving across the street might be a migration if it crosses administrative boundaries, while a vacation trip around the world might not. A citizen of one country might live for years in another without changing his citizenship, while a refugee might immediately adopt her new home as a country of residence. Demographers sometimes do use distance of move and duration of stay—or even intended duration—as a proxy or indicator for the change of residence (Shryock and Siegel, 1976), but reaffiliation remains the underlying criterion.

Which kinds of moves are left out of this demographic definition of migration? One exclusion would be moves of people who have no geographically durable residence, either before or after the moves, such as nomadic or homeless populations. Another exclusion would be short-term movements of a periodic sort, for instance, commuting to and from work or annual vacation trips. Another categorical exclusion would be a change of residence within a geopolitical unit, such as moving from one's present house to another in the same administrative area.

This last exclusion raises a complication in our definition. Determining which moves are going to be called migrations depends on the scale of geopolitical units one is considering, the *migration defining area* (Pressat, 1985). If one is dealing with international migration, one does not count the moves that might take place between provinces or states within nations. If one is dealing with interprovince or interstate migration, then one does not count moves between communities within states or provinces.

Because of this ambiguity, demographers are careful to specify which scale of migration they are talking about. For instance, they universally distinguish between international and internal migration, and within internal migration, they are careful to specify further. Within the United States, for example, they distinguish between interregional, interstate, and intercounty migration.

Which Dimensions of Migration Are Important?

The vocabulary of migration is more easily introduced if we have before us the simplified migration schematic diagram shown in Figure 9-1. We have two areas, A and B, each with a specified residential population at the beginning of a year. During

Figure 9-1 Schematic Diagram of Migration Between Two Areas

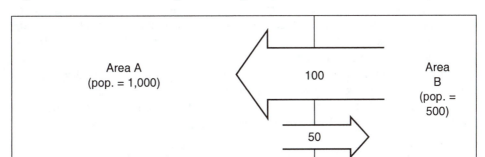

that year, one set of people crosses from area A to area B and another set crosses from area B to area A. Let us assume that these border crossings mean changes of residence—that they are migrations.

This migration situation can be viewed either from a wide perspective or from a narrow one. Broadly, we can think of areas A and B as parts of some larger whole, such as when studying migration among regions of a country. More narrowly, we can identify with only one of the areas and view the migration only in terms of its impact on that one area, such as most nations view their international migration.

Let us start with the wider perspective and introduce its terms. The focus of interest is likely to be on migration *streams*. A migration stream consists of the people who migrate from one specified area to another in a given period of time. The arrows in Figure 9-1 show two streams. The numbers within the arrows tell how many people are in the stream and the size of the arrow represents the size of the stream. Each stream has an area of *origin* and an area of *destination*. Demographers sometimes are concerned about the collective force of the two streams, and sometimes about the balance between the two streams; that is, they might focus upon *gross* migration (or the *volume* of migration), the sum of the two streams (150 in our figure), or the *net* migration, the differences between the two streams (50 in our figure).

From a narrow, local perspective, priorities are different. Let us take, for a moment, the position of area A, and let us say that area A is a nation (albeit a tiny one). From that position, the 100 who move from area B to area A represent *immigration*; the 50 who move from area A to area B represent *emigration*. If the areas were not nations but subunits (that is, if the migration were internal), then the processes might be labeled *out-migration* rather than emigration, and *in-migration* rather than immigration. The net migration for area A would be the in-migration (100) minus the out-migration (50), for a gain of 50 people. Net migration for area B would be *minus* 50. Exercise 1 at the end of this chapter provides practice in applying these concepts.

Migration *rates* can be computed for each of these aspects of migration. But their meaning tends to be less clear than either death rates or birth rates. Emigration (or out-migration) rates make some sense. The total resident population in an area bears some resemblance to the number of people who could move out. So crude, or even age-specific, rates can be used to measure emigration (or out-migration) relevant to a resident population at risk of leaving. But the rate of immigration (or in-migration) among current residents makes less sense. The resident population is not at risk of immigration and its absolute size has little to do with the number of people who could move into the area. When immigration (in-migration) rates are constructed, it is usually to indicate the rate at which immigration *impacts* the resident population in the area of destination. Similarly, the rate of net migration frequently is used to indicate the net impact of immigration and emigration on the population in the area of destination. Generally, however, you will see demographers using migration rates sparingly and reporting instead the absolute size of migration movements (Shryock and Siegel, 1976).

One more important dimension of the migration process is *selectivity*. Demographers, you will remember, are interested not only in changes of population size but also in population *composition*. To the degree that the composition of the net migration stream differs from the composition of the resident population of the destination area, migration will have an impact on the composition of the resident population; the same will be true at the origin area. Exercise 2 at the end of this chapter gives readers a closer look at this process of selective migration.

DATA SOURCES

Of the three population processes in the growth equation (i.e. fertility, mortality, and migration), our data on migration are the least complete. Among migration data, those on international migration, and especially illegal international migration, are the worst.

One reason for this negative distinction is that we do not have a true world government. Such an authority could insist upon all nations cooperating in tracking moves from one country to another, just as nations (ideally) track moves among their regions, provinces, and states. Instead, what we have is a mishmash of differing national definitions, priorities, and procedures, mostly based on national rather than international concerns.

It is helpful to remind ourselves what would constitute ideal data, as applied to international migration. One should have the same kind of information on migrations that one is supposed to have about births and deaths. All moves that might later be classed as migrations should be recorded, as well as the time of each move. Enough information about the ultimate reaffiliation (change of residence, membership) of the mover should be gathered so that later decisions can be made as to which moves were migrations. Enough information also should be gathered about the characteristics of the migrants so that, minimally, the composition of migrant populations could be compared with the composition of resident populations. Simply to describe the ideal is to warn the reader that we fall woefully short, especially on the international plane. The description also reminds us how unlikely it is to achieve such an ideal anytime soon, so let us return to the real world.

Estimates of both international and internal migration come from four main sources: 1) administrative records, 2) registrations of border crossings, 3) inferences made from past and present residences as reported in censuses or surveys, and 4) estimations of migration made from knowledge of growth and the other components of growth (United Nations, 1998a). The weight placed on these data sources differs between the study of international and internal migration.

Administrative Records

Administrative sources of migration data include population registers, registers of foreigners, applications (for visas, residence, and work permits), exit clearances, and any other source of information generated by the bureaucratic processing of movers. Administrative data generally are available for *international* migrations. However, they are not designed primarily to collect migration information and are of limited use for that purpose (United Nations, 1998a). Most often, for example, they apply only to the movements of foreigners and not to the international movement and relocation of citizens; thus emigration is less well attended than immigration. Another drawback is that in many records, such as visas or tourist permits, there can be considerable difference between the time at which data are collected and when migration occurs.

Administrative records are rarely kept for events related to *internal* migration. An exception is population registers, which require continuous recording of demographic events including migrations by resident household members. This tradition, however, is confined to only a few countries (Shryock and Siegel, 1976).

Registering Border Crossings

One way to track a demographic process—be it mortality, fertility, or migration—is to register the events making up the process as they occur. Data collected at border crossings occur at the time of movements and have the advantage of being frequently collected for both foreigners and citizens. Unfortunately, "only in a few countries do border statistics provide reliable data on international migration" (United Nations, 1998a, p. 5). Even then, there are some special problems with the data.

One problem springs from the fact that officials at the border do not know, at the time of crossing, what the mover ultimately will do. The United Nations (1998a, table 1) recommends asking how long the migrants lived at their prior residences and how long they *intend* to live at their new residences, to distinguish immigrants and emigrants (with long previous and expected durations of residence) from other types of travelers. Even following such guidelines, border officials would know only the mover's stated intentions, and even honest intentions change.

A related problem is that the two nations involved—that of origin and that of destination—might differ in their priorities and in their records. Nations tend to be more concerned with detailed information about people who are joining them (immigrants) than about people who are leaving them (emigrants). Moreover, decisions about how to determine residence (or affiliation) and which characteristics of movers are important to record vary from nation to nation. The upshot is that the two countries involved in any given migration stream are likely to record it differently. This makes combining their data to estimate net migration difficult.

Another category of problems is logistical. Simply recording all the border crossings that later might prove to be migrations can be a difficult job (United Nations, 1998a). It is easier for nations whose ports of entry and exit are limited, such as islands. At the other extreme, some countries have long land borders that normally are not fully patrolled, such as the northern and southern borders of the United States. And, finally, the borders of political units *within* the nation are usually relatively unimportant, so nations seldom monitor the crossings of internal borders as they do external ones.

Asking Retrospective Census or Survey Questions

Most governments rely on household inquiries, in the form of censuses and surveys, to estimate migration. Every census asks, minimally, the residence of each respondent at the time of the census. Most ask the respondent's place of birth as well. Some, like recent U.S. censuses, even ask about residence at some specified prior time, say five years ago or one year ago. Where the present residence is not the same as the place of birth or of prior residence, some move must have occurred, probably a migration. This indirect measurement of migration from census data is relied upon more generally than border-crossing data, especially among the less-developed countries (United Nations, 1998a). Because these methods identify migrants, but not the exact timing of migration, they are more useful in measuring the size of a population's stock of international migrants than they are for measuring the migration flow.

The method is not airtight. People can and do conceal their foreign origins, especially if they feel they can pass as a native and have some reason for doing so (see chapter 11). More importantly, some kinds of moves are not recorded, such as moves by those who emigrate and are abroad at the time of the census, by those who emigrate but return to the same location before the census, and by those who immigrate but leave or die before the census. It is particularly limited in measuring emigration, requiring a complex procedure of comparing censuses over time to identify those who have left and then comparing these people with death records to identify those who were lost via emigration rather than death.

If national censuses ask similar questions about place of birth or prior residence for more detailed geographic areas within the nation, then internal migration can be estimated. United States censuses since 1850 have asked state or country of birth. Since 1940 the U.S. census and the Current Population Survey have asked detailed place-of-residence questions either one or five years prior to the census. Asking such questions in censuses is highly recommended by the United Nations and is becoming more widespread.

There are advantages to asking place-of-prior-residence (over place-of-birth) questions: the shorter period between the prior-residence data and the census date means fewer intervening moves will go unrecorded. Moreover, the timing of those that are recorded is bracketed more narrowly and recent migrations are often of greatest interest. The disadvantage is that the data refer to a very limited calendar period.

Because sample surveys are less costly than censuses, they can be used to probe more deeply into the migrations of their fewer respondents. On the other hand, surveys have the weakness of not supplying information about every local area, only those that are included in the sample. The ideal balance seems to be to include as many questions as can be afforded in decennial censuses or large national samples, and then to supplement those with periodic and more intensive surveys. This is the practice in the United States, where the Current Population Survey has contained detailed questions about prior residence and decennial censuses have asked general questions about prior residence one or five years earlier.

Intensive *retrospective* migration surveys attempt to record the entire sequence of lifetime moves for respondents, the areas of origin and destination, the timing of migration and related life-course events which may reveal the determinants or conse- quences of migrations. Alternately, *repetitive* surveys which follow a cohort through time (e.g. the National Longitudinal Surveys) can trace the history of individuals' migrations as it unfolds.

Estimating from Intercensal Growth

If a country has repetitive censuses and either ongoing counts or estimates of mortality and fertility, it can use these to deduce *net* migration. Because this strategy does not involve the actual counting of moves as they happen, or even inferring partic- ular moves from changes in reported residence, these techniques have been called *indi- rect* or *residual* (Bogue, 1993).

One technique is the *vital statistics method*. Remember the growth equation from chapter 1? It was stated as

$$P_2 - P_1 = (B - D) + M$$

For estimating net migration, the equation can be converted to

$$M = (P_2 - P_1) - (B - D)$$

That is to say: the net migration between censuses (M) is equal to the total growth between the censuses $(P_2 - P_1)$ minus the natural increase between the censuses (B – D). Since most countries are relatively confident of their census totals and have devel- oped methods for making at least rough estimates of their total deaths and births, this method is usually considered the most reliable for gauging *net* migration (Bogue, 1993). Exercise 3 at the end of the chapter illustrates the use of this vital statistics method.

Aside from being limited to net migration, the vital statistics method also can be inaccurate. Censuses do err, and (especially in LDCs) the estimates of fertility and mortality can be approximate. Moreover, since the migration component in the equa- tion is usually small compared with those of growth and natural increase, even a small absolute error in those other components can result in a large proportional misestima- tion of net migration (Bogue, 1993).

A refinement of the same strategy makes estimates for one age-sex class at a time. If one knows the size of a given living cohort at the end of the interval and at the beginning of the interval, and if one can estimate the deaths that occurred to that age class in between, then one can infer the net migration of that cohort. The logic is pre- cisely the same as for the vital statistics method, but applied to one category at a time.

These methods are also applicable for geographic units smaller than nations, where separate data are available for such units. Additional options for estimation are afforded when one has demographic information on a whole set of contiguous geographic areas, such as regions within a nation. For instance, Rees and Wilson (1977) use model multiregional life tables for inferring not only net migration but migration flows among regions. A method requiring less data is the *national growth rate method*, which compares the growth in any subnational area with that in the nation as a whole and attributes deviations to net migration (Shryock and Siegel, 1976).

Accuracy aside, indirect methods are limited in the completeness of information they provide. They estimate net migration but do not describe migration streams unless supplemented with other data. They do not automatically identify the *composition* of the residual net migrant population unless they are applied to birth, death, and population data available separately for each such group. Yet, in the imperfect world of migration statistics, they play a major role.

Table 9-1 illustrates the application of the vital statistics method to estimate net migration for world regions during the year preceding 1996. Column 1 of the table shows the population at the end of the period. Columns 2 and 3 record estimates of the births and deaths in the preceding year (using the annual averages from the five years 1990–95). Column 4 is the natural increase resulting from the excess of births over deaths, obtained by subtracting column 3 from column 2. The population growth in column 5 is the difference between the 1996 population and the preceding year's population (estimated by subtracting the average annual growth over the preceding five years). Subtracting natural increase, column 4, from the total growth, column 5, then leaves a residual change that must be due to net migration—column 6.

Table 9-1
Net Migration Into World Regions, 1995–1996, Estimated by the Vital Statistics Method

Region	P_2 1996 Population (1)	1990–95 Annual Averages				
		B Births (2)	D Deaths (3)	$B - D$ Natural Increase (4)	$P_2 - P_1$ Total Growth (5)	M Net Migration (6)
World	5,767,774	132,091	51,129	80,961	80,961	
More-Developed Regions	1,175,039	14,341	11,760	2580	4653	2073
Less-Developed Regions	4,592,734	117,750	39,369	78,381	76,309	-2073
Africa	738,730	27,769	9616	18,153	18,022	-131
Asia	3,488,027	79,640	27,583	52,057	50,689	-1368
Europe	728,777	8333	8174	159	1186	1027
Latin America and the Caribbean	484,301	11,373	3044	8330	7763	-566
Northern America	299,252	4454	2499	1955	2925	970
Oceania	28,686	524	213	310	376	66

Note: In thousands.
Source: United Nations, *World Population Monitoring 1997*, 1998, table A.1.

We will elaborate on the substantive global net migration pattern revealed in Table 9-1, but we can use the table as a global preview now. We can see that less-developed regions lost migrants (i.e. had a negative net migration) to the more-developed regions. Asia had the largest negative net migration, in absolute numbers; Africa had the smallest. Europe and Northern America were the regions with the greatest net gain of migrants, with fewer going to Oceania.

Estimating Illegal Immigration

The data sources discussed so far are not completely satisfactory in measuring even *legal* migration, so one can imagine how difficult it is to estimate *illegal*, or *undocumented*, migration, where the migrant usually has the intention of remaining uncounted. The United Nations (1998a) cites recent efforts in the United States as illustrating the best attempt to document illegal immigration. The Immigration and Naturalization Service (INS) has greatly improved its estimates since the early 1990s (INS, 1998).

The procedures developed by the INS incorporate all of the methods for estimating migration discussed previously. Administrative records provide data for illegal immigrants who entered legally but overstayed their permitted visit, mortality among illegal immigrants, and so on. Border-crossing data are used to identify visits not completed by subsequent departures. Censuses and Current Population Surveys are used to adjust foreign-born populations for undercounting, subtract legally resident populations, and derive estimates of illegally resident populations. More complex procedures are used to estimate the departures, or emigration, of illegally arriving populations. The vital statistics method then incorporates these various resources to derive estimates of net illegal immigration. Although the integration of these data sources and estimation methods allows for considerable error, the size of the error has been reduced to "a few hundred thousand rather than a few million, which was the error range during the late 1970s and into the 1980s" (INS, 1998, p.3). The resulting estimate for 1996 was about five million illegal immigrants (see Table 9-4).

Few countries have invested as much effort in estimating illegal and undocumented migration as has the United States. However, all countries use the same basic types of data to estimate migration trends and make some efforts to monitor otherwise undocumented migrations.

INTERNATIONAL MIGRATION

Much of the history of human migration, of course, occurred before demographers ever began collecting data on migration. And, to place our discussion in a historical context, it is useful to briefly review these prehistoric and historic migration patterns. In this section we trace the different forms, or types, of human migration from prehistoric to modern times. We end our discussion with a more detailed treatment of modern migration streams and their impacts on receiving nations.

Prehistoric and Historic Variety

The earliest human populations migrated. We believe that the first humans were wanderers, hunters of game and gatherers of food. Many of these movements were long enough to cross continental and regional boundaries; some would have been international if there had been nations then. Yet the nature and meaning of human migration has changed over time—with respect to the migratory forces that cause people to move, the typical size of the social unit doing the moving (e.g. groups, families, individuals, or masses), and the degree of choice enjoyed by the movers (Petersen, 1975).

Primitive migration refers to moves forced by an ecological push, such as a deterioration in the resources necessary to support a people. Many prehistoric migrations were likely of this sort. A more technically advanced people might have responded with innovations that would have enabled them to adapt to the changing environment; peoples with primitive technologies historically have responded by collectively moving. Early primitive migrations probably could be called *wandering*, moving away from one place but without a definite destination. For instance, those people who most likely moved from Siberia to Alaska over the land bridge between 26,000 and 8000 B.C. probably were not aiming to settle in North America; they knew nothing of it. More contemporary forms of primitive migration would be groups of people (clans, tribes) *ranging* over perhaps fixed traditional routes, gathering food in season or, more prevalently now, raising cattle as *nomads*. Another contemporary form of primitive migration would be illustrated by rural peoples in less-developed countries, where the agricultural land has been overused or overpopulated, who flee to the cities (see chapter 10).

Impelled or *forced migration* in various forms results, indirectly or directly, from state expansions and conflicts. Expanding nations often set up trading outposts, such as did the Phoenicians and the Greeks around the Mediterranean. A step up in scale would be the establishment of colonies, such as during Europe's mercantile period. American readers, of course, are familiar with this kind of immigration, which occurred during their colonial history. On a larger, and more dramatic, scale would be the invasions that historically took the form of a culturally more advanced people subduing a less advanced one. An early example would be the Roman conquest of Gaul and Britain. There are many modern examples as well. In these, the invading state's intention is not necessarily to move large numbers of its people into the new territory, but rather to control. Increasingly important refugee movements of modern times bear witness to the persistence of forced migrations.

Slavery and *indentured servitude* are further examples of forced migrations. *Slavery* in the Western Hemisphere was dominated in premodern times by the trade of Africans to the New World, extending from the sixteenth century to the abolition of slavery at various dates in the nineteenth century (McEvedy and Jones, 1978). It is estimated that about 9.5 million slaves were imported into the Americas between 1550 and 1850, the vast majority to the Caribbean and Brazil (7.5 million). The relatively smaller number of African slaves imported to the United States, however, has had a disproportionately greater impact on its current population diversity (see chapter 11). As for *indentured servitude*, Davis gives a dramatic account:

When slavery was abolished in the British Empire in 1833, the British, who controlled a large share of the world's tropical lands, substituted indentured labor, and the Dutch did the same. Instead of coming from Africa, however, indentured plantation labor came overwhelmingly from densely settled areas such as southern China, Java, and India, which not only were closer to new zones of plantation agriculture in Malaya, Sumatra, Burma, Ceylon, and Fiji but also were societies in which thousands of illiterate and landless workers could be induced to risk their fate in unknown places. . . .16.8 million Indians left India, of whom 4.4 million stayed away permanently. It seems probable that several million Chinese left China and hundreds of thousands left Java. . . . total volume probably exceeded that of slave migration. (1974, p. 97)

Free migration is the kind of migration with which American readers are most familiar. The outstanding example was the migration of some 60 million Europeans between the sixteenth and twentieth centuries. The principal destinations were the United States, Argentina, Canada, Brazil, Australia, New Zealand, South Africa, and the British West Indies. The surge in European emigration corresponded with two important changes. One was the demographic transition in Europe, the reduction in the death rate prior to a lowered birth rate, resulting in national population explosions first in Northern and Western Europe and then in the rest of Europe. The other was the improvement in transportation, such as the invention of the steamship. The important thing for readers to realize, however, is that this immense wave of free migration was something of an isolated phenomenon in the long prehistory and history of human migration.

Premodern Migration Streams, 1500–1965

Figure 9-2 maps the major intercontinental net migration streams from 1500 until the beginning of the modern migration period in 1965 (adapted from Woytinsky and Woytinsky, 1953). The seven major, largely intercontinental, migration streams of the premodern period are numbered on the map.

The first three streams identified were primarily made up of free migration: 1) the mass migration from all parts of Europe to North America, 2) the north to south migration from Latin countries of Europe to Central and South America, and 3) the migrations of colonial expansion from Great Britain to Africa and Australia. Colonial expansions did include indentured servants, forced migration of slaves and convicts, and so on. The great majority of the migrants in these streams, however, were freely migrating to less-developed regions of the world in the hopes of building a better life or to escape political and religious bounds.

Two of the migration streams identified were exclusively or largely forced migrations: 4) the importation of slaves from the western parts of Africa to the Caribbean and South and North America, and 5) the (partly intercontinental, partly intracontinental) migrations from China and India abroad. While migrations from China and India included free migrations, we identify them with forced migration because of the substantial role of indentured labor in these migration streams.

Also shown on the map are two important streams of interregional but internal migration: 6) the westward and then southward movement of the population within the United States, and 7) the eastward and northward movements in Russia to settle hostile northern environs (later to be government sponsored). Especially in North America, these internal migrations were frequently simple extensions of the great transatlantic voyages. It is not so much that the eastern U.S. population moved westward as that the destinations for transatlantic immigrants moved westward.

The list of migration streams in Figure 9-2 is not exhaustive; population movements are widespread, continual, and fluctuating over this premodern period. Even the listed streams were far from constant over time. The mass migration from Europe to North America (numbered 1 in Figure 9-2) is an example.

Figure 9-2   Major World Migration Streams, 1500–1965

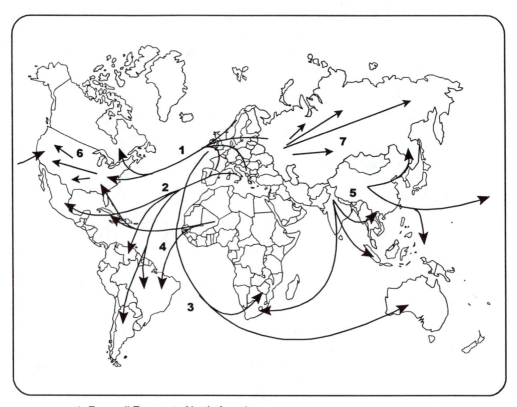

1. From all Europe to North America
2. Latin European countries to Central and South America
3. Great Britain to Africa and Australia
4. African slavery to Caribbean, Latin America, and North America
5. China and India abroad (Inter- and Intracontinental)
6. American westward and southward expansion
7. Russian eastward and northern expansion

Note: Political boundaries circa 1965.
Source: Adapted from Woytinsky and Woytinsky, *World Population and Production*, 1953; McEvedy and Jones, *Atlas of World Population History*, 1978.

This immigration stream, familiar to U.S. readers, actually consisted of a series of *migration waves* (Martin and Midgley, 1994). The first wave occurred from 1790 to 1820 and consisted primarily of English, as well as Scotch, Scotch-Irish, German, Dutch, French, and Spanish immigrants seeking religious and political freedoms or economic betterment. The second wave, from 1820 to 1860, consisted of German, British, and Irish immigrants, many displaced by the industrial revolution in Europe and local hardships such as the Irish famines. The third wave, from 1880 to 1914, came largely from countries of southern and eastern Europe and flowed into the eastern and midwestern United States (at more or less the same time as the migration from Asian countries numbered 5 in Figure 9-2 flowed into the western United States). More than with earlier waves, the promise of a better life in the rapidly industrializing United States constituted a pull, rather than a push, underlying this third migration wave. After these three great waves, immigration from Europe ceased or remained low from World War I until the 1960s. Postwar immigration restrictions (after a slight resurgence of migration in the 1920s) had much to do with this lull in migration. When immigration restrictions were eased in the mid-1960s, a fourth wave of modern immigration began which has lasted until the present.

Modern Migration Streams

With continuous and changing streams, choosing a starting point to introduce *modern* migration is difficult. We have chosen 1965 to separate Figures 9-2 and 9-3, although the shift from premodern to modern migration patterns actually spanned the period from the end of World War II until then. During this couple of decades, migration patterns underwent a fundamental change from migrations largely influenced by European population expansion and political history, to migrations increasingly influenced by global economic development, the demographics of post-transition countries, and conflicts within the developing world. Figure 9-3 maps the major migration streams of the modern period.

Free migration. In the United States, as we have observed, when immigration restrictions were eased in the mid-1960s, the twentieth-century lull in immigration gave way to a fourth wave. The countries from which the fourth wave of immigrants have come, however, are vastly different than before or during the World Wars (Martin and Midgley, 1994). Immigration to the U.S. from Europe continued, but at diminished levels (labeled number 1 in Figure 9-3). Immigrations came increasingly from less-developed countries of Latin America (labeled number 2). Thus, regarding the Americas, the dominant stream of migration changed from Europeans into South and North America to Latin Americans into North America.

In *Europe*, the postwar political realignments, rebuilding, and prosperity of the West drew immigrants from the East, lasting until the dissolution of the Soviet Union. Contemporary prosperity in Europe and the aging of the European work force have attracted recent immigrants from northern Africa and the Mideast (labeled number 3). These changes have resulted in a shift, as in the Americas, from north→south to south→north migration streams.

Although the causes are quite different, a similar reversal of premodern free migration patterns has occurred in the *Russian Federation* and Commonwealth of Independent States. Following the breakup of the Soviet Union, the former migration streams to settle the less-developed regions to the north and south have been reversed by migrations back to central Russia and by ethnic minorities returning to ancestral homelands (labeled number 4 in Figure 9-3). In 1991 some 25 million Russians were living in non-Russia successor states. Return migrations to Russia from

Figure 9-3 Major World Migration Streams, 1965–2000

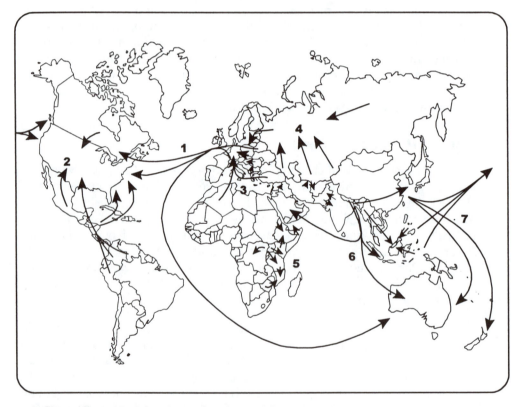

1. Slowed European migration to America and Oceania
2. Latin America and Canada to the United States*
3. North Africa, developing countries and Eastern Europe to Western Europe*
4. Returns to Central Russia after breakup of the USSR
5. Refugees (e.g. African, Afghan, Balkan, Pakistani, Iranian, Palestinian, and Southeast Asian)
6. Bangladesh, Pakistan and Sri Lanka abroad*
7. Philippine and Asian abroad*
* (including temporary labor migrations)

Note: Political boundaries circa 1965.
Source: Zlotnick, *International Migration 1965–96*, 1998; National Geographic, "Migration," 1998; United Nations, *World Population Monitoring 1997*, 1998.

the Transcaucasian Republics (Armenia, Azerbaijan, and Georgia) alone has exceeded 300,000 per year since 1992 and peaked at nearly 600,000 in 1993 (United Nations, 1998a). Despite differences, this change has some similarities to the European and American cases.

In all three areas described above, prewar migration streams that flowed from the more-developed regions into the less-developed ones shifted direction. In modern times migration streams flow into the MDRs. This change in direction is one mark of modern migration patterns.

But postwar migrations differ from the prewar migration streams in other ways. Not all these migrations are permanent relocations in the sense that an arduous transatlantic crossing once implied. Temporary migrations and refugee moves outnumber permanent migrations by more than ten to one in modern times. Another difference in modern free migration patterns is hidden somewhat in Figure 9-3: since 1965 there has been a substantial increase in the variety of countries from which immigrants enter the more-developed countries (Zlotnick, 1998). This increase in variety of migrant origins is in part due to the shift in direction of migration from the numerous LDRs into the fewer MDRs.

Forced migration. A second major change in the modern migration period is a shift in the levels and patterns of forced migration. Since the end of World War II the size of forced migration has increased. The global refugee population, for example, increased from under 2 million in 1965 to more than 13 million persons in 1997 (United Nations, 1998a). The sources of refugee movements have also changed: in the 1940s and 1950s forced migrations were mostly consequences of the European wars and declining European empires. Growing out of these postwar and postcolonial conflicts, forced migrations have increasingly been the result of conflicts among less-developed countries. The changing origins of refugees admitted to the United States reflect this change: in the 1950s, refugees to the U.S. were largely from European countries; by the 1970s, they were mostly from Asia and Central America (Martin and Midgley, 1994).

Forced migrations during and after World War II (e.g. millions of Jews streaming from Germany as political refugees during Hitler's rise to power in the 1930s) foreshadowed the rising importance of refugee movements in the modern period. The close of World War II and the ensuing Cold War resulted in immense forced migrations. About 20 million people in Eastern and Central Europe were involved in various kinds of flights, exchanges, expulsions, and transfers. Most of these people relocated within Europe; some ended up in North America or other frontier countries. In Asia, 3 million Japanese who had moved to far-flung parts of the empire were returned by decree to the homeland.

Postwar emergence from the colonial system also resulted in forced migrations. The partition of India and Pakistan in 1947, for example, resulted in about 7 million Hindus fleeing to India and an equal number of Moslems fleeing to Pakistan. In 1948, following the establishment of the state of Israel, about 700,000 Palestinian Arabs fled. The Communist victory in China in 1949 caused the migration of uncounted millions to elsewhere in Asia, such as Taiwan. The Cuban revolution sent a wave of migrants across the South Atlantic to the shores of Florida and beyond. The Indo-Pakistani war in 1971 gave birth to the state of Bangladesh and triggered the exchange of millions more among that country, India, and Pakistan.

The establishment of postcolonial African states, with boundaries arbitrarily designated by former colonial powers, resulted in massive migrations and set the stage for current conflicts in the region. Such streams are labeled number 5 in Figure 9-3 and actually were more widespread than represented here. Conflicts among, and civil wars within, African states have resulted in significant refugee migrations to Somalia and Sudan in the 1980s and to Malawi, Ethiopia, Sudan, Kenya, the Democratic Republic of the Congo, Rwanda, and Tanzania, among others, in the 1990s. Refugees from the Iran-Iraq conflicts and the Gulf War illustrate refugee movements beyond sub-Saharan Africa. Ethnic conflicts in the Balkans also have resulted in refugee movements in Bosnia, Croatia, Kosovo, and surrounding countries.

In sum, the characteristic changes of forced migration in the modern migration period are both 1) the substantial rise in the number of international refugees and 2) the primary relation of these movements to conflicts in the less-developed regions of the world (United Nations, 1998a).

Temporary labor migration. The third major change creating modern migration patterns has been the rise of large-scale temporary labor force relocations from the less-developed to the more-developed economies. Perhaps it stretches our definition of "migration" to include moves not crowned with potential full reaffiliation in the destination country. However, international streams of this sort have become too sizable to ignore, and the compromise status of temporary immigrant (or guest worker) has acquired recognition in many host countries.

Temporary labor migrations are part of both free and forced migrations in the modern period. The same conditions which have attracted free immigration into Europe and North America (i.e. an aging labor force and relative prosperity), when coupled with immigration restrictions, encourage the importation of foreign migrants with a nonpermanent, guest worker, or illegal alien status to fulfill labor force needs. The free migration streams into these countries from less-developed regions (labeled 2 and 3 in Figure 9-3) also include substantial temporary labor migrations. Conflicts also can result in temporary labor migrations. Dislocations following the Gulf War, for example, resulted in a dramatic increase in temporary labor migrations from Asian countries such as Pakistan to the Gulf States, as the importation of laborers from other Arab countries declined (United Nations, 1998a).

Two migration streams from Asia consist substantially of temporary labor migrations. The first of these streams has been from South-Central Asia (e.g. Bangladesh, India, Pakistan, and Sri Lanka) to other Asian countries and, much less so, abroad to the Middle East and Oceania (labeled number 6 in Figure 9-3). Another major migration stream is that from Southeast Asia (e.g. Indonesia, the Philippines, and Thailand) and eastern Asia (e.g. China and Korea) to western Asia and abroad (labeled number 7). While almost all of these migration streams have remained within Asia, since 1990 a majority of migrants from China, in particular, have gone to non-Asian countries including the United States.

Not all labor force migration streams are temporary migrations, of course, and even those which begin as temporary in intent may not remain so. These migration streams are, however, a salient part of modern migration patterns. As we shall see in the next section, they pose particular problems to host countries due to the ambiguous status of temporary immigrants.

Impact on Resident Populations

Let us turn from the study of international migration as a population process to the study of the impact of that process on population size and composition. It is these net results, rather than the movements themselves, that cause the most concern, especially in countries of destination.

We have used Table 9-1 to introduce a method of estimating net migration. Let us use it now to summarize net migration for world regions in the mid-1990s. We can see that the less-developed regions lost migrants and that the more-developed regions, of course, gained the same migrants. Asia had the largest negative net migration, with most other net migration loss coming from Latin America and the Caribbean. Europe and Northern America (U.S. and Canada) were the regions with the greatest net gain of migrants. Africa and Oceania were less heavily involved numerically in either plus or minus net migration.

Table 9-2 allows us to assess roughly the impact of net migration on destination region populations during the modern period. Specifically, it tells the percentages of regional populations that were foreign born in 1965 and in 1990, and the increase (or decrease) between those two years.

As expected, the more-developed regions have a greater proportion of foreign born than do the less-developed, and the gap widened over the modern period. Note

Table 9-2
Migrants As a Percent of World Regional Populations, 1965–1990

Region	Foreign-Born Population As Percent of Region's Population		
	1965 (1)	1990 (2)	Increase (3)
World	2.3	2.3	0.0
More-Developed Regions	3.1	4.5	1.4
Less-Developed Regions	1.9	1.6	-0.3
Africa	2.5	2.5	0.0
Asia	1.7	1.4	-0.3
Latin America and Caribbean	2.4	1.7	-0.7
Northern America	6.0	8.6	2.6
Europe*	3.6	6.1	2.5
Former Soviet and Transition Economies	2.3	1.6	-0.7
Oceania	14.4	17.8	3.4

*Excluding former Soviet states and transitional Eastern European economies.
Source: United Nations, World Population Monitoring 1997, 1998, table 6.

that the impact of net migration on a country or region is influenced not only by the number of net migrants it receives, but also by the size of the resident receiving population. Oceania (dominated by Australia-New Zealand) dramatizes this point. Although it was singled out in Table 9-1 as a low importer of net migrants numerically, it stands out in Table 9-2 in terms of the impact of those immigrants on its small resident population.

The high proportion of MDR populations that are foreign born, then, is a result of both a numerically large net migration and a numerically small resident population. These high national net migration rates in the MDRs clearly are altering the ethnic compositions and diversity of more-developed countries, as we will detail in chapter 11.

INTERNAL MIGRATION: THE U.S. CASE

Which internal moves (that is, intranational moves) are migrations? Internal migration can be interregional, interstate, interprovince, intercounty, intercommunity, even interneighborhood. Again, whom you call a migrant depends on which kind of boundaries you are using and how fine a net you are casting over the movers.

Of all the patterns of internal migration that nations could study, three seem to have been of particular interest. One is interregional migration, as typified by the shifting regional population of the United States, which we address here. Another is rural-to-urban (and sometimes urban-to-rural) migration. We are saving separate treatment of that for chapter 10. The third is the migration and spatial distribution of ethnic populations within countries, a subject we will address in more detail in chapter 11.

We focus here on the example of regional migration salient to most readers—that within the borders of the United States. By choosing interregional migration, we are viewing the "big picture" of internal migration. Remember, however, that a demographer advising local community planning officials, for example, might zoom in on a different level of internal migration, such as state, community, or even neighborhood.

A Brief History of U.S. Interregional Migration

Using census and iPUMS data (see chapter 2), Farley (1996) summarizes internal migration trends in the United States from 1790 to the mid-1990s. Initial settlement of the thirteen colonies concentrated on what is now the East Coast of the United States. At the time Thomas Jefferson supervised the first census in 1790, the population was equally divided among the northern and southern states. Although northeastern states attracted immigrants from abroad, they lost population, partially through out-migration, to other regions. The percentage of the national population in the Northeast steadily declined over the past two centuries and is now less than one-fourth of the population.

The opening of rich croplands in the Ohio River valley initially drew migrants from New England. Later, migration to the Midwest boomed as industry in the region expanded after the Civil War. At its peak in 1890, the Midwest held more than one-third of the country's population, and in the 1940s midwestern cities drew substantial numbers of blacks migrating northward from the southern states, as they now attract immigrants from Latin America and the Caribbean. Yet throughout the twentieth century the Midwest grew more slowly than did the rest of the country.

For almost two centuries after the revolution, the population of the South continued to grow, but more slowly than the rest of the nation. Until 1970, the percentage of the national population residing in the South declined to a low of less than one-third. Since 1970, internal and international migration have attracted a resurgence of southern growth. The emergence of major southern commercial cities attracted a migration stream from the Northeast and Midwest to the sunbelt states which continues to the present. Meanwhile, immigration from Latin America and the Caribbean also contributes to rapid growth in the South. The South has, at this time, the greatest share of the nation's population.

Western states were admitted to the union between 1848 (California) and 1959 (Hawaii). The West has continued to attract in-migration since the admission of California, the ensuing gold rush, dustbowl migrations westward in the Depression years, and the postwar economic boom. It owes recent growth to a share in more recent internal sunbelt migrations and to immigration from Latin America and Asia. At the time of the Civil War, only one in fifty residents lived west of the Rocky Mountains; in 1990 one in four residents lived in the West. Today the West has a larger population than either the Northeast or Midwest.

Although international migration and natural increase (births minus deaths) can affect the distribution of the nation's population across regions, internal migration accounts for many of these U.S. regional changes. The western flow of the population out of the Northeast, and later out of the Midwest (and to a small degree from the South), has been sustained. The other major net migration stream flowed from the South to the North until after World War II. During its prime it had a heavy component of blacks and poor whites seeking opportunity in the industrializing Northeast and Midwest. By the 1960s, the net flow had reversed and by 1970 migration from the Northeast and Midwest to the sunbelt states of the South was well-established. By the 1990s, even the southern exodus of the black population to the North was reversed (Frey, 1998; see also chapter 11).

Current Interregional Net Migration

Table 9-3 lists Census Bureau estimates of interregional net migration in the United States from 1990 to 1998. Looking at the number of migrants in the top half of the table, we see that the Northeast and Midwest continued to have net out-migration while the South and West continued to gain from internal migration. The biggest losses were in the Northeast and the biggest gains in the South. Looking at the *rates* in the bottom half, we see that the net loss from the Northeast is even more impressive when the small population from which it flowed is taken into account.

However, interregional migration is only one factor influencing the regional distribution of population. Especially in a country with heavy international migration, such as the U.S., this also can be a major determinant. International migration (column 2) has profoundly altered the impacts of U.S. internal migration over the past decade. Over 60% of the Northeast's losses from internal migration were

Table 9-3
Interregional Net Migration, United States, 1990–1998

Region	Internal (1)	International (2)	Total (3)
	Number (1,000's)		
Northeast	-2800	1718	-1082
Midwest	-573	665	92
South	3331	1773	5104
West	42	2540	2582
	Rate (per 1,000 Residents)		
Northeast	-54.1	33.2	-20.9
Midwest	-9.1	10.6	1.5
South	34.9	18.6	53.5
West	0.7	42.2	42.8

Source: U.S. Bureau of the Census, Datafile ST-98-7 (Press Release CB98-242), 1998.

negated by international immigration. Losses in the Midwest were canceled out by immigration gains. Meanwhile, the internal migration gains in the South were boosted by more than half as many immigrants, and almost the entire gains of the West were due to immigration.

Several demographers have established a close connection between international migration and subsequent internal migration during the past two decades. As immigrants enter population centers they increase the supply of labor in an area, especially of lower-skilled labor. An oversupply of labor may encourage domestic internal migration out of the region by those in the same labor market (White and Liang, 1998; Frey and Liaw, 1998; Frey, 1996). However, we might anticipate this connection between immigration and internal migration to be less important with the rising employment rates of recent years.

Effect of Population Age Composition

The changing age composition of the United States (see chapter 4) also has affected internal migration in recent years. The chances that a person will migrate are highest for those entering the labor market and migrating to employment opportunities, normally young adults. Since these young adults often have families, the next most likely group to migrate is children. In the United States, there also is a tendency for individuals to migrate at retirement ages.

As an example of age selectivity, Figure 9-4 analyzes the recent internal migration in the sunbelt states. In-migration rates at each age are shown as upward arrows from the zero line; out-migration rates are shown as downward arrows from the zero line. The total length of the vertical arrows, then, measures the *gross* migration for each of the age categories. The *net* migration rate is indicated by the location of the box within each bar relative to the zero horizontal line.

The variety in the lengths of the vertical arrows shows the considerable age selectivity in *gross* migration, 1996–1997. As expected, the individuals most likely to

Figure 9-4   Age Selectivity of Sunbelt Internal Migration, 1996–1997

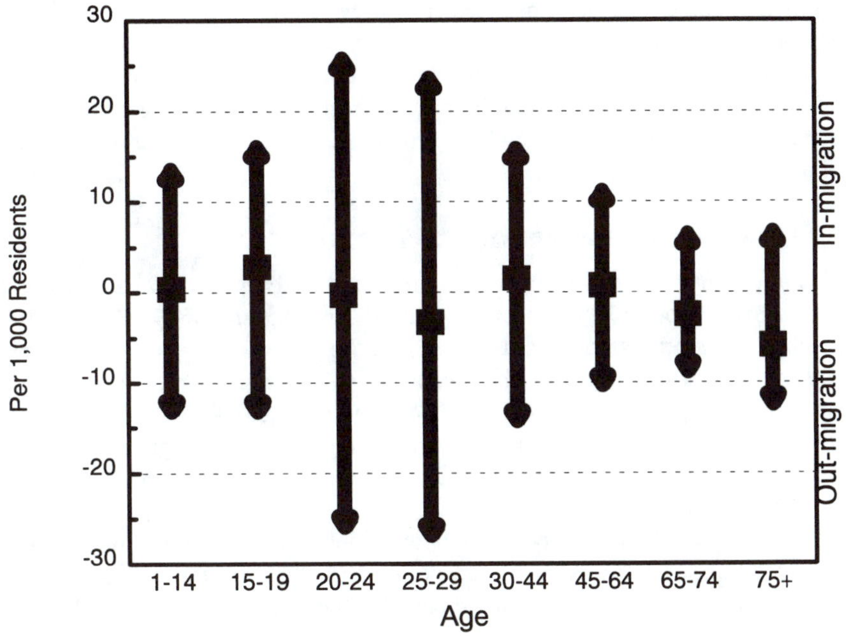

Source: U.S. Bureau of the Census, *Current Population Reports P2--510*, 1998, table 43.

migrate in or out of the sunbelt were those newly entering the labor force at ages twenty to twenty-nine. However, the *net* migration was almost balanced for these ages. As for the elderly, even though many migrated to the sunbelt to retire in the recent past (Longino, 1994), in this particular year the gross migration rates were not large and the net migration was outward.

What is the relevance of such age selectivity to internal migration in the United States? Over the past several decades the impact of the baby-boom generation on the age structure and thus on internal migration has been significant. During the 1970s the baby-boom reached employment ages and the migration streams out of the Northeast and Midwest to the South and West generated levels of net migration nearly three times the previous two decades (Plane, 1992). Yet many of the baby-boomers delayed moving (as they delayed marriage and fertility) and then moved during the 1980s, keeping internal migration high during that decade (Plane and Rogerson, 1991). In the 1990s, internal migration declined in all regions as the baby-boomers settled in (the exception being a recent increase in out-migration from the Midwest (U.S. Bureau of the Census, 1998b).

Migration is selective not only with age, but potentially with sex and other migrant characteristics. Empirical generalizations about selectivity in migration are presented in the next section.

DETERMINANTS OF MIGRATION

Why do people migrate? The *theoretical* study of migration began with observations that 1) not everybody is equally likely to move and 2) knowing which people are most likely to move might help us understand the forces underlying migration (Lee, 1966; Ravenstein, 1889). Identifying the groups most likely to migrate provides *empirical generalizations* about migration which might then contribute to *theoretical explanations* of migration (Pressat, 1985).

From Empirical Generalizations to Theories

The first empirical generalizations of this sort were those of E. G. Ravenstein, who wrote his editions of "Laws of Migration" in 1885 and 1889 (Pressat, 1985). Ravenstein's observations attempted to describe the general characteristics of migration and migrants. He also provided the basis for the *size-distance* rule, a concept later developed into the *gravity model* of George Zipf and S. A. Stouffer (see Pressat, 1985). The gravity model simply states that the number of migrants over a given distance will be proportional to the opportunities at the destination but inversely related to opportunities at a nearer distance.

Ravenstein's observations and the gravity model's notion of intervening influences were expanded upon by several more recent demographers including E. S. Lee (1966, pp. 52–56), whose reformulation is quoted here. On the volume of migration, Lee states:

1. The volume of migration within a given territory varies with the degree of diversity of areas included in that territory.
2. The volume of migration varies with the diversity of people.
3. The volume of migration is related to the difficulty of surmounting the intervening obstacles.
4. The volume of migration varies with fluctuations in the economy.
5. Unless severe checks are imposed, both volume and rate of migration tend to increase with time.
6. The volume and rate of migration vary with the state of progress in a country or area.

On migration streams and *counterstreams*, he asserts:

1. Migration tends to take place largely within well-defined streams.
2. For every major migration stream, a counterstream develops.
3. The efficiency of the stream (the ratio of the stream to the counterstream) is high if the major factors in the development of a migration stream were minus factors at origin.
4. The efficiency of stream and counterstream tends to be low if origin and destination are similar.
5. The efficiency of streams will be high if the intervening obstacles are great.
6. The efficiency of a migration stream varies with economic conditions, being high in prosperous times and low in times of depression.

Lee went on to observe that migration is not only *selective*, but the *degree* of selectivity varies (1966, pp. 56–57). Where migration is influenced mostly by the attractions to the area of destination, then migrants are likely to be *positively selected*. That is, those who are most likely to win in the competition for those attractive qualities (e.g. jobs) are most likely to migrate. On the other hand, where migration is impelled mostly by negative forces at the area of origin (such as political upheaval or natural calamity), then the emigration is likely to be less selective. Obstacles between the area of origin and destination—distance, legal barriers, threats to survival—tend to make the migration more selective. And, over time, there is a tendency for selectivity in a migration stream to erode as in pioneer migrations, in which adventurous young males start the stream and later on send for their families and friends.

Lee also observed that migration is especially likely at transitions between life's stages: getting married, entering the work force, having the children leave home, getting divorced, retiring, being widowed, and so on. As we have seen, one expression of this is the nearly universal age selectivity of migration as young adults enter the labor force. In the United States, for example, the highest rates of moving are found among those twenty to twenty-nine years of age (U.S. Bureau of the Census, 1998a). Migration also selects by sex, but the nature of that selection varies, depending upon such things as the definition of sex roles. Traditionally, migration selected for young males seeking work or fortunes abroad. But sex selectivity in more-developed, and some less-developed, regions is becoming more varied as more women enter the labor market and barriers to their migration are breached (Chant and Radcliffe, 1992). Nearly as many women as men now cross international borders (United Nations, 1998a). Finally, culturally and politically defined identities (e.g. race and ethnicity) may affect mobility directly, or indirectly through differences in occupation or educational opportunity, cultural preferences, and the momentum created by existing migration streams (see chapters 10 and 11).

Lee incorporates these observations into a broad conceptual model of migration selectivity in *individual, voluntary* migration. The model is presented as Figure 9-5. Lee explains his *push-pull* migration model as follows:

Figure 9-5 E. S. Lee's Model of Voluntary Migration

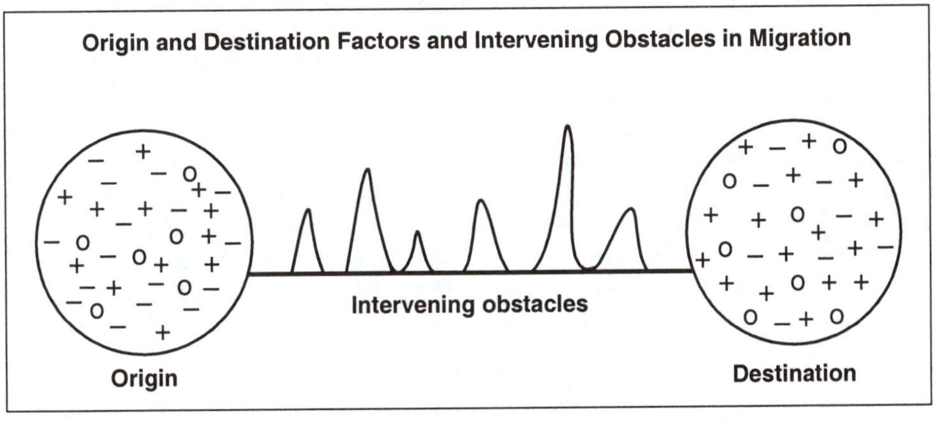

Source: Based on Lee, "A Theory of Migration," 1966, chart 1.

In every area there are countless factors which act to hold people within that area or attract people to it, and there are others which tend to repel them. These are shown in the diagram as + and − signs. There are others, shown as 0s, to which people are essentially indifferent. Some of these factors affect most people in much the same way, while others affect different people in different ways. (1966, p. 50)

Between the two locations is a set of "intervening obstacles," which can be viewed as "costs" involved in moving from the origin to the destination. An abundance of pluses at the destination would attract, or "pull," migrants, while an abundance of minuses at the origin would "push" migrants to move. Intervening obstacles decrease the potency of these effects.

Migration Theories

Migration theory has been one of the most fruitful and rapidly developing areas of demography in recent decades. Several authors have recently reviewed and assessed the prevailing theories of migration (e.g. United Nations, 1998a, 1998b; Stahl, 1995; Massey et al., 1994, 1993). A review of the major current migration theories is presented below.

Neoclassical economics (macro theory). One of the earliest migration theories, the neoclassical economic theory attempts to explain the relationship between labor migration and economic development by theorizing that mass migration will tend to flow from countries with an oversupply of labor to those with unmet demands for labor. In theory, capital, including highly skilled human capital, also will tend to migrate from areas of abundance to those of scarcity where it can earn higher returns (i.e. usually moving in the opposite direction of mass labor migrations). Left unrestricted, migration of labor and capital will continue until an international equilibrium of labor supply and demand is reached. This is a macro theory in the sense that it does not pay much attention to the characteristics or motivations of migrants except for their skill, or human capital, and the wages available to them in different areas.

Neoclassical economics (micro theory). Related to the macro theory, this view is formulated at the level of the individual migrant. According to this theory, individuals make rational choices to migrate or not based upon cost-benefit calculations. These calculations are not limited to immediate gains and losses but also include future expectations (see chapter 10 for a discussion of how this impacts rural-urban migration). In theory, and barring migration restrictions, a migrant will move to where the *expected value* of future returns is greatest. As Massey et al. (1993) note, this micro-level theory leads to somewhat different conclusions than does macro-level neoclassical theory. Two important differences are that the micro-level model affords some explanation of differential migration within countries (not simply between countries) and that individuals may migrate based upon future expectations (not just current wage differences).

New economics of migration theory. This viewpoint challenges the conclusions of neoclassical economic theory and assumes it is not only individuals but social units such as families and households that make migration decisions. Units such as families are able to make more complex migration plans because of the possible diversification of family labor. Some family members can remain at home, for example, while others migrate to distant labor opportunities and may send earnings, or *remittances*, back to their families. Especially in developing countries, these strategies can be used to minimize risks faced by a family. Sending a family member abroad, for example, can provide a source of income to insure against local hard times from unemployment, crop failures, falling crop prices, lack of capital, and so on. This suggests the source, not just the amount, of income matters. Household members may migrate for the insurance remittances provide even when wage differences would not result in migration according to neoclassical theories. Similarly, a family's sense of *relative deprivation* influences migration decisions in ways not explained by wages alone. If, for example, economic development raises lifestyle expectations in a community, individuals may have greater motivation to seek gains from migration even if their wage has also improved during the development.

Dual labor market theory. This theory explains migration as a result of labor force needs and migration policies of modern industrial societies. Developed countries evolve dual labor markets, with a high-skill, high-wage, and capital-intensive sector affording attractive job opportunities and a low-skill, low-wage, and labor-intensive sector affording the least attractive employment. More-developed countries find it increasingly difficult to fill low-status jobs from their high-aspiration native labor pool. Demographic trends in developed countries compound the shortage of less skilled labor. Fertility declines have lowered the proportion of young unskilled laborers willing to temporarily take low-status jobs. Later marriage, rising divorce rates, and access to higher education have encouraged women to enter the primary high-skill labor force, also making them less willing to take low-status jobs. Acceptable raises in wage will not sufficiently improve the relative status of low-skill jobs and may simply push the entire wage scale and aspirations even higher. So, to fulfill needs for low-skill labor, developed economies recruit migrant labor from abroad, which does not require raising wages. In fact, wages are most often held in check through institutional mechanisms and migration policies. As a result, wages are not likely to rise with greater demand but may fall with increased supply, increasing the gap between sectors.

World systems theory. This is a broad sweeping view of global development which argues that migration simply follows from the political and economic organization of an ever-expanding capitalist world market or world division of labor. Capitalist penetration into the developing economies creates disruptive development and an uprooted mobile population at the periphery of the world economy. The use of force by capitalist countries seeking to protect investments abroad and to expand the world economy can also create dislocated refugee populations. At the same time, strong material and cultural ties are formed with the core countries during capitalist penetration (and earlier colonial rule). International migration of disrupted populations then flows in the opposite direction of capital penetration, toward the newly familiar culture, aspirations, and opportunities in the core economies. Economic considerations may influence migrants' decisions, but they are not the primary cause of migration.

The impetus for migration in developing countries is the dislocation of population arising from capitalist penetration.

Migration systems theory.   This theory is somewhat different from the other theories in that it focuses on the self-perpetuation of migration streams. Once a migration stream has begun, systematic effects can arise which support continuing migration. Whatever the original cause of migration, it may become less important as these migration systems become stronger. *Network theory,* for example, emphasizes that social networks are a form of social capital. When enough migrants with a common social identity arrive in an area they may constitute a network that can then offer aid to new arrivals—from material comfort to simply lowering the psychic costs of migrating to a strange place. Members of the network also retain ties to their community of origin and can reach out to offer information or assistance to prospective migrants. In both ways networks contribute to a self-sustaining immigration stream. *Institutional theory* emphasizes the similar role of social organizations ranging from voluntary humanitarian organizations to private black-market immigration services. Like networks, these institutions can perpetuate, and sometimes profit from, migration regardless of the initial reasons for the migration stream. Both of these theories reflect *cumulative causation* where each migration decision changes the context in which subsequent decisions are made, usually perpetuating migration (Massey, 1990). Our discussion of relative deprivation illustrates cumulative causation: as some families in an area of origin receive remittances from a family member working abroad, others will see a fall in their income relative to these neighbors and will, in turn, be more likely to then send a family member abroad, and so on (Stark and Taylor, 1991). Migration systems and cumulative causation can explain significant migration effects that are not explained well by the other major theories. Some of these explanations are now well-developed theories such as network theory. Others, however, are more nearly empirical generalizations. This remains a rapidly developing area of demographic theory.

With several major migration theories to choose from we might naturally ask which theory is correct? However, migration theories are not so much contradictory as they are potentially complementary. As Massey et al. conclude:

> Our review produced little substantial evidence that would lead to the rejection of any of the theoretical models we have surveyed. On the contrary, each model received at least some empirical support, suggesting that each theory captures an element of the truth. . . . What is unclear is how well the various models perform against each other, and how much of an independent contribution to explanatory power each model might retain in a simultaneous examination. (1994, p. 739)

Each of the major migration theories has been used to explain internal as well as international migration. The study of *internal* migration does, however, have unique concerns that have also given rise to a number of specific *middle-range* theories (e.g. United Nations, 1994; Frey, 1998; Fokkema et al., 1993; Todaro, 1997). Some of these specifically internal migration theories are taken up in later chapters on urbanization (chapter 10) and population diversity (chapter 11).

MIGRATION PROBLEMS AND POLICIES

Consequences of migration are felt both by individual migrants and by the social collectivities (e.g. nations) they leave and join. On the individual level, most migration theories suggest we would ultimately expect a positive effect for immigrants. That, supposedly, was the expectation of the individual migrants, at least in free migration. However, population problems and policies usually are defined on a collective level.

What are the collective effects of migration on origin and destination populations? Obviously, moving numbers of people about can directly affect the size and growth rates of both origin and destination populations. Migration also can change the size and composition of the labor force in both countries. An exchange of residents between populations also alters the social and cultural composition of each.

Are these collective consequences population problems? Using the questions we identified in chapter 1 as our guides, we will ask *who* views these consequences as a source of problems, *what* the perceived problems are, and *why* they are considered to be problems.

Spread of National Policies

Let us start with the first of these questions; that is, who views the consequences of migration as problematic? This question is the easiest one to answer. An increasing number of countries view at least some consequences of immigration and emigration as significant problems. This is seen in a growing tendency of countries to intervene politically in immigration and emigration streams; that is, a declining willingness to leave migration unchecked.

Figure 9-6 shows the percentage of countries *not* intervening with immigration in 1976 and in 1995. The percentage of countries leaving immigration unrestrained was cut in half over this period. This change was even more extreme in the more-developed countries. Parallel changes were worldwide in all regions (except North America, which already had immigration restrictions before 1976).

The situation is different for *emigration*, shown in Figure 9-7. Again, the percentage of countries leaving well enough alone fell by almost half between 1976 and 1995. But increasing policy intervention in emigration was concentrated in the more-developed countries. Intervention was even reduced in the less-developed regions of Africa and Latin America.

In sum, increasing numbers of governments view migration as a source of problems which require intervention. Almost all regions appear to have become more concerned with immigration. Emigration, however, seems of less concern to less-developed countries than it is to more-developed ones.

Why? What specific migration consequences are viewed as problems and why are they so considered? Why is emigration of less concern to less-developed countries? To answer these questions we will need to discuss the general consequences of migration in a bit more detail.

Figure 9-6 Percentage of Countries with Immigration Non-Intervention Policies, 1976 and 1995

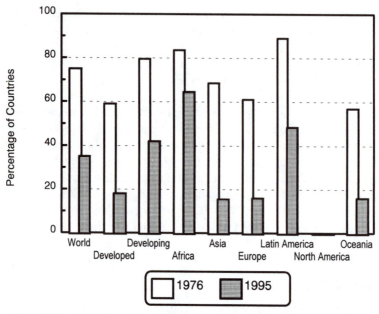

Source: United Nations, *World Population Monitoring 1997*, 1998, figure 8.

Figure 9-7 Percentage of Countries with Emigration Non-Intervention Policies, 1976 and 1995

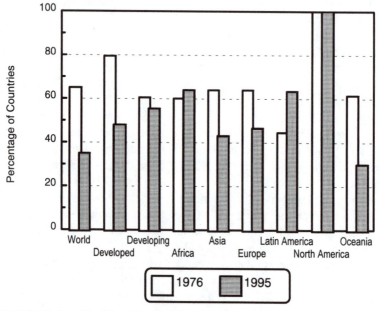

Source: United Nations, *World Population Monitoring 1997*, 1998, figure 8.

Impact on Size and Growth Rates

International migration increases the size and growth rate of the population in the country of destination and decreases them in the country of origin. It is obvious that net migration from one population to another would decrease the origin population by the same absolute number that it would increase the destination population. Less obviously, the degree of impact on the *growth rate* of the two populations would *not* be the same. That impact depends upon the size of the net migrant population *relative to* the size of the resident population. Net migration from a small to a large population, for example, would cause a greater decrease in the growth rate of the small origin population than increase in the growth rate of the larger destination population. Conversely, net migration from a large to a small population would have a greater impact on the growth rate of the destination country.

The point is not trivial. It implies that the degree to which social units experience growth or shrinkage depends somewhat on how narrowly focused the migrant streams are, either at their origin or destination. A small village, for example, might have its population devastated by sending most of its former inhabitants to a large, more-developed city, whereas that city's inhabitants might hardly feel the addition. Conversely, a particular destination city might feel overwhelmed by its growth if it became the exclusive destination of a migrant stream (which, as we will see in chapters 10 and 11, is frequently the case).

Indirect effects of migration also can alter growth rates. Separations, costs of migration, and especially age selectivity can change fertility, nuptiality, and mortality rates in both origin and destination populations. Higher levels of migrant fertility (see chapter 11) can also operate indirectly to increase growth rates in destination countries. In international migration streams most effects operate in the same direction— to *increase* the population size and growth rates of the receiving more-developed countries while decreasing those in the less-developed countries.

Migration effects on population growth might at first seem to offer one reason why emigration may not be as great a concern in the less-developed countries as it appears to be in more-developed ones. LDRs may gain some relief from the strains of their rapid growth from emigration. In contrast, for MDRs emigration may aggravate problems arising from their already aging populations and slow growth rates.

This logic appears to have affected government migration policies. That is not to say, however, that demographers have proven emigration to serve as an effective release valve for high-growth LDRs. Indeed, indirect evidence questions such a generalization (United Nations, 1998a; Yang, 1995). Empirically, immigration also has had little overall impact on the size or growth rates of total populations of large nations in the short term.

Impact on the Labor Force

Of more immediate concern has been the impact on the *composition* of the populations, especially in the receiving countries (United Nations, 1998a). One focus of this concern has been the effect of composition changes on the labor force. It turns out that the labor force effects of international migration are anything but simple. Let us start with the least complicated effect, that of *age selectivity*, then proceed to the complications.

Theoretically, immigration to more-developed countries from less-developed ones explicitly selects young adults. Since MDRs have older resident populations, they gain the benefit of a needed increase in their young labor force. In contrast, LDRs have very young populations and removal of working-age adults would make already high age-dependency ratios even worse. In general, destination MDRs would benefit from the age selectivity of migration while LDRs would suffer.

International immigration also generally favors *employable* adults, needed in the destination countries. Depending upon the migration stream, it might favor highly educated and high-skill labor (as in the case of migration from other developed countries to the United States, Canada, and Australia) or less educated low-skill labor (as with migrant farm workers in the United States, guest workers in Europe, and Asian laborers in the Gulf states). Supposedly, then, international migration of workers would benefit economies of destination countries, but due to indirect effects destination economies may not always benefit from such immigration. Importation of foreign labor, for example, can forestall other economic readjustments needed in developed countries and may bring with it problems of social inequality arising from the marginalization of foreign workers (United Nations, 1998a).

The impact of skill selectivity on the labor force of origin countries is equally complex. Theoretically, origin economies would gain from emigration; it could, for example, boost the demand for workers remaining in LDR labor forces, and thus their employment rates and wage levels. However, those most likely to emigrate are the most skilled.

The loss of the most highly educated individuals to migration, called a *brain-drain*, is of concern to many countries. However, the impact of such a drain has been greatest in those regions already facing shortages of highly skilled workers and stagnating economies. In sub-Saharan Africa, for example, nearly 30% of the skilled personnel in the region left between 1960 and 1987 (United Nations, 1998a).

Although emigration is likely to drain the most employable from a country of origin, these "positively selected" migrants may still suffer by comparison with the resident work force in the destination country. In fact, one theory, that of dual economies, suggests that immigrants will tend to be among the least skilled, least educated, and lowest-paid laborers in the destination country. Wages of migrant workers, for example, are only about three-fourths those of the native population in Germany, and less than half those of the native population working in many of the same industries in the Republic of Korea (United Nations, 1998a). The low-skilled native laborers in destination countries may also suffer from decreased competitiveness and inability to bargain for higher wages, ultimately increasing the wage-status gap in the dual economy.

Because of household migration strategies, many workers abroad send *remittances* to their families, improving national income and providing an important source of foreign exchange. The flow of capital involved should not be underestimated. In 1990 remittances amounted to $71 billion, far greater than the $47 billion in official development aid in the prior year from countries belonging to the Organization for Economic Cooperation and Development (United Nations, 1998a). But countries depending heavily on such remittances leave themselves vulnerable to changes in employment conditions and/or immigration policies at the country of destination. In addition, relative deprivation and social inequality in the home community can be widened by unequal access to remittances as, for example, in poor rural districts of Pakistan (United Nations, 1998a).

In short, the labor force effects of migration are mixed. In general, the economies of destination MDRs likely benefit from net immigration even though some segments of their populations, especially new immigrants, may suffer; and in general the economies of origin LDRs likely suffer from net emigration, but gain through remittances from abroad. Such a complex picture does not easily lead to migration policy formulation.

Finally, a nation's policy regarding legal migration is necessarily affected by the facts of its illegal migration and refugee admittances. Policy changes in the United States have increased control of illegal immigration and thereby allowed reduced constraints on legal immigration. In contrast, Europe's tightened legal immigration requirements have encouraged growth in illegal avenues of migration (United Nations, 1998a). Problems of labor force migration are likely to be dominated in the near future by issues of illegal and undocumented migrant workers (United Nations, 1998a).

Impact on Social Composition

It is hard to review past and present MDR immigration policies without suspecting that they are motivated strongly by *xenophobia*. This fear and contempt of ethnically distinct foreigners has resulted in many groups of migrants being viewed as "problems" by the populations in countries of destination. This attitude has been rationalized with negative ethnic stereotyping in the policy debates. Indeed, nearly all immigrant groups with any identifiable difference from the host population have been discriminated against in migration policies, differing mainly in degree (see, for example, Cummings and Lambert, 1998; Layton-Henry, 1994; Cohen, 1995). Immigration policies have, in turn, perpetuated and solidified discriminatory attitudes toward immigrants (Fassin et al., 1997). Unfortunately, this has not been rectified by the recent reform attempts of more-developed countries; policies continue to reflect discriminatory objectives and to promote discriminatory stereotypes (Jones, 1995; Lowell et al., 1995).

Such discrimination is easier to justify publicly if it is supported by rationalizations. Migrants have been characterized at various times, for example, as a danger to public health, a threat to job security, a drain on social welfare systems, and a threat to the dominant groups or cultures of the host country. Such sentiments toward migrants are more likely to affect migration policy if they are plausible, whether or not they are true.

At various times in history some discriminatory concerns with the composition of migrant streams were clearly plausible. An historical example is the quarantine of migrants. Quarantines from specific countries with widespread endemic diseases, for example, have been justifiable, even if discriminatory, in some past cases. Yet, in other cases, the same reason has been used to detain migrants without plausible evidence of a public health threat.

It is also important to recognize that at any given time the view of migrants as a "social problem" may be genuine for some and an excuse for discrimination by others. For example, fears that importation of foreign labor might result in falling wages for low-skill occupations in the host country is a currently held *belief* among many—a genuine concern for some and an excuse to discriminate for others.

Demographers seem strangely silent on the subject of xenophobia in immigration policies (United Nations, 1998a), but it would be naive of us to limit our discussion by ignoring the evidence that migration policies throughout history—and in the present—have been profoundly shaped by these sentiments among host populations. The United States is no exception.

IMMIGRATION POLICY: THE U.S. CASE

We will use the case of the migration policies in the United States to illustrate immigration concerns and policies in the more-developed regions. Although the United States case does not represent all more-developed countries, it is a reasonable representative of the frontier receiving nations, such as Australia and Canada. Focusing upon one case will allow us to provide specific examples of past migration issues and policies.

A Brief History

Immigration policies in the United States have gone through several distinct stages (Martin and Midgley, 1994; Keely, 1982a), described serially as follows:

Laissez faire: 1790 to 1875. A welcoming viewpoint held sway for the first century of the nation's life. Until 1875, there were no federal laws abridging or forbidding immigration. Exceptions were very specific and minor. In 1808, the importation of slaves was prohibited. In 1798, the Alien and Sedition Act empowered the president to deport any alien he deemed dangerous, but this power was not renewed two years later. The influx of Roman Catholics in the 1840s set off the first organized antiforeign movement in the country, the "Know Nothing" movement, but did not result in congressional action on immigration.

Qualitative restrictions: 1875 to 1920. The Supreme Court in 1876 held that Congress was empowered by the interstate commerce clause to regulate immigration. During the next forty-five years, Congress passed three kinds of laws restricting certain types, or quality, of immigrants. The first excluded people with various physical and mental diseases or who had criminal, moral, or political beliefs or behaviors that made them unfit. Second were the contract-labor laws, prohibiting persons contracted abroad to work in the United States, the intent being to reduce competition with American labor.

Third, foreshadowing the future, was the categorical exclusion of groups because of race or nationality, specifically, Oriental race and nationality. In 1882 Congress passed the Chinese Exclusion Act. In 1907 came the "Gentleman's Agreement," which required Japan to refuse passports to the United States for Japanese laborers. In 1917, Congress set up an Asiatic Barred Zone that declared any native of India, Burma, Siam, the Malay States, the East Indies, or the Polynesian Islands to be inadmissible to the United States (Bouvier et al., 1977). As the decades passed, exclusionist sentiment held sway but the target changed.

Quantitative restrictions: 1921 to the present. Immigration quota acts passed in 1921 and 1924 changed the basis for limiting immigration from the countries outside the Western Hemisphere and reserved fixed proportions of the total visa allotment for natives of specific countries. Asian immigrants continued to be barred. The first quota act, passed in 1921, limited migrants from Europe to a small annual percentage of their non-U.S.-born countrymen enumerated in the U.S. census as of 1910. The Immigration Act of 1924 went even further, lowering the percentage and basing it not on the most current census but that of 1890, when the population composition of the country had been less influenced by recent immigration from southern and eastern Europe. The 1952 McCarran-Walter Act continued the restrictionist emphasis; however, the fact that it had to be passed over President Truman's veto implies that antirestrictionist sentiment was rising. Immigration restrictions have continued in some quantitative form to the present; the basis of these restrictions, however, has changed.

Family reunion and labor needs: 1965 to 1980. In 1965 ethnic quotas were relaxed and replaced with those which gave preference to close relatives of U.S. citizens and those with special skills. Public Law 89-236 went into full effect in 1968. There remained in place a form of earlier quantitative restrictions. No more than 20,000 immigrants were to come from any single country. Initially the Eastern Hemisphere as a whole could send no more than 170,000 immigrants (with no limit on those from the Western Hemisphere). In 1978 these hemispheric limits were abolished and a worldwide ceiling was established (initially 290,000 and later changed to

Figure 9-8   Give Me *Some* of Your Tired, Your Poor . . .

Source: © 1981 John Trever, *Albuquerque Journal.* Used with permission of John Trever.

270,000). A complicated, and fluid, system of preferences was used to determine qualification and priority for migration.

Recent Immigration Reforms

In a more recent effort to reform the complex and continually changing migration system, Congress enacted three major reforms: the Refugee Act of 1980, the Immigration Reform and Control Act of 1986 (IRCA), and the Immigration Act of 1990 (IMMACT). Not surprisingly, the first two of these acts were to address rising modern migration streams, refugees, and illegal immigration.

The Refugee Act (1980) gave special status to that kind of potential immigrant. It empowered the attorney general to admit for up to two years any persons whose entry was deemed in the national interest. Further, it enlarged the definition of *refugee* to conform to the United Nations definition—basically, any person who faces persecution or who has a well-founded fear of persecution on account of race, religion, nationality, political beliefs, or membership in a social group (Keely, 1982b).

The Immigration Reform and Control Act (1986) was intended to reduce the number of illegal aliens resident in the country. The act legalized most undocumented workers then employed in the country and followed this with harsh sanctions on employers for hiring new unauthorized workers. The dramatic impact of IRCA on United States immigration can be seen in Figure 9-9. The tremendous 1990–1992 peak in admissions, exceeding any other time in the twentieth century, reflects the admission of undocumented workers through IRCA.

IRCA, however, had modest success in its objectives. Fraud was considerable: more than two-thirds of those admitted as agricultural workers did not satisfy the program's requirements (Martin and Midgley, 1994). This fraud and lax enforcement of sanctions have encouraged continued illegal immigration. The Immigration and Naturalization Service estimates show a fairly constant level, but declining rate, of growth in the undocumented resident population from 1988 to the present (INS, 1998). Continued illegal immigration has, in turn, prevented newly legalized workers from improving their wages and benefits.

Figure 9-9   Legal Immigration to the United States, 1901–1997

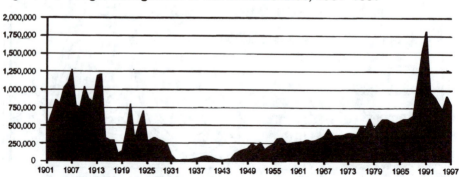

Source: Immigration and Naturalization Service, *Annual Report*, 1999, chart 1.

Table 9-4 presents the INS estimates of illegal immigration populations in the United States as of 1996. The panel on the left presents the top ten countries from which illegal immigrants originated, and the number from each country. The panel on the right presents the top ten states in which illegal immigrants resided as of 1996. According to this table, the origins of illegal immigration to the United States were largely in the Western Hemisphere and geographically close (the only exceptions in the top ten countries being the Philippines and Poland). Over half of all illegal immigrants to the United States came from Mexico. Not surprisingly, more than half of illegal immigrants reside in California and Texas, both border states with Mexico. Other states in which illegal immigrants reside have large metropolitan areas with substantial foreign-born populations.

Not shown in Table 9-4 is a fact that some readers may find surprising. According to the INS estimates, almost four of every ten illegal immigrants residing in the U.S. are those who entered legally but overstayed their permitted time. These cases receive considerably less attention in the media than do surreptitious border crossings.

The Immigration Act of 1990 has received less attention than IRCA. It has been heralded for increasing the number of skilled immigrants who may enter the United States. But Martin and Midgley (1994) suggest it may be remembered only for making already complex policies even more so. The effects of IMMACT remain to be seen in future migration trends.

To these three reform acts, one might add NAFTA. The North Atlantic Free Trade Agreement is not a migration policy per se, but is expected by some demographers to have a profound impact on migration. It exemplifies the increasing intertwining of migration with more general global economic considerations. NAFTA was an agreement for "free trade" to encourage laissez-faire movement of capital resources among North American countries at the same time immigration policies restrict the flow of human resources.

Proponents of NAFTA argued that the free flow of capital would have equalizing economic impacts which would eventually lessen migration pressures and result in a

Table 9-4
Estimated Illegal Immigrant Population for the Top 10 Countries of Origin and States of Residence, United States, 1996

Country of Origin (1)	Population (2)	State of Residence (3)	Population (4)
All Countries	5,000,000	All States	5,000,000
Mexico	2,700,000	California	2,000,000
El Salvador	335,000	Texas	700,000
Guatemala	165,000	New York	540,000
Canada	120,000	Florida	350,000
Haiti	105,000	Illinois	290,000
Philippines	95,000	New Jersey	135,000
Honduras	90,000	Arizona	115,000
Poland	70,000	Massachusetts	85,000
Nicaragua	70,000	Virginia	55,000
Bahamas	70,000	Washington	52,000

Source: INS, *Illegal Alien Resident Population*, 1998, table 1.

reduction of south-to-north migration into the United States. However, it is likely any decrease in migration would come only later, after an increase, or "bump," in migration from the displacement of agricultural labor likely to result from the flow of capital into Latin American countries (Martin, 1993). Projections suggest that by the mid-2000s, Mexico-to-U.S. migration, for example, will decline and stabilize (Martin and Midgley, 1994). However, despite much anticipation ranging from optimism to doom-and-gloom scenarios, there is thus far little evidence for any impact of NAFTA on migration (Amuedo-Dorantes and Huang, 1997; Smith, 1997; Schiff, 1996; Andreas, 1994).

It may take time for the immigration reforms of the past two decades to have any substantial impacts, especially those which require long-term changes in the economic conditions underlying migration. In the meantime, the lesson of recent immigration reforms appears to be that migration streams such as the current south-to-north flow from Latin America are much easier to start than they are to alter or stop.

SUMMARY

Migration is harder to define than the other demographic growth processes, mortality and fertility. Not all moves across geographic boundaries are migrations, since not all of them involve changing residence (that is, reaffiliation with a new population). Nor are there consistent attempts to register all moves across geographic borders as they occur. Thus, demographers rely upon indirect information to infer migration. One such method is to note changes in residences reported at succeeding times. Another is to measure the degree of population growth, deduct the amount of natural increase, and infer the net migration that must have occurred.

International migration has taken widely various forms throughout history. The voluntary migration, both individual and mass, that has been so prominent in modern Western history is unusual in the overall picture. Patterns of migration have shifted rapidly in the modern period and probably will continue to do so. Temporary labor migrations have grown to significantly outnumber permanent migrations. Former migration streams from more-developed countries to less-developed have reversed. Conflicts, increasingly within less-developed regions, have increased the numbers of people forced to migrate as refugees.

People migrate for a variety of reasons, of course, but there are regularities. Differential rates relate to stage in the life cycle (age), employment status, ethnic identity, gender, and so on. Young adults entering the labor force and their offspring are the most likely to move. The most general model for interpreting migratory motivation is one that features a place of origin and a place of destination, each with attractive *pull* and unattractive *push* qualities, separated by a series of intervening *obstacles*. These empirical generalizations about migration have given rise to several modern migration theories which increasingly reflect the complexity of migration.

Migration theoretically favors population growth at the place of destination at the expense of growth at the place of origin, both directly through the simple exchange of population and indirectly through age selectivity and differential fertility. In the long term, migration is also likely to favor the workforce at the place of destination, to the detriment of the place of origin. Selectivity will bring younger laborers and skills in demand to the destination's workforce while removing these from the population of origin. However, remittances to less-developed countries are substantial and may provide families with some insurance against economic risks while providing much needed capital to less-developed economies.

Large-scale migration into more-developed countries can involve difficult adjustments, at least in the short term, for both migrants and destination communities. Resistance to immigration in MDRs can reflect concerns over the socioeconomic burdens of new immigrants on social services, loss of jobs and lowered competitiveness among less skilled workers, greater social inequality, and so forth. But much of the resistance to immigration seems the result of xenophobia and fears over the loss of dominance by majority cultural and political groups in the population of destination. These concerns have found expression in the immigration policies of many countries.

The United States is an example of a developed destination country with a history of shifting immigration policies. Despite recent reforms, the greatest challenge to contemporary U.S. immigration policies is that of controlling largely self-perpetuating migration streams from less-developed countries, which can result in substantial illegal or undocumented migration streams when legal migrations are restricted. It is too early to see the ultimate effect of recent policy reforms and global economic agreements on international migration streams.

EXERCISES

1. Table E9-1 is a matrix showing U.S. regions of residence for those who migrated between March 1996 and March 1997, according to the Bureau of the Census Current Population Survey. Define as an *interregional migrant* anyone who had a different U.S. region of residence in 1997 than she or he reported for 1996. Answer the following questions:

   a. The migration *stream* from the Northeast to the South had 392,000 people. How many were in the migration stream from South to Northeast?

Table E9-1
Region of Residence for Those Who Migrated Between Regions, March 1996 to March 1997, United States

	Residence March 1997			
Residence March 1996	**Northeast** (1)	**Midwest** (2)	**South** (3)	**West** (4)
Northeast	—	107	392	101
Midwest	94	—	492	228
South	256	333	—	358
West	131	221	454	—

Note: In thousands
Source: U.S. Bureau of the Census, *Current Population Reports*, P20-510, 1998, table 20.

b. The *volume* of (gross) migration between the South and the Northeast was 648,000 people. What was the volume of migration between the Midwest and the South?

c. The *net* migration from the Northeast to the South was plus 136,000. What was the net migration from the South to the Northeast?

d. What was the *net* migration from the Midwest to the South?

2. Suppose you had the hypothetical interregional migration situation in Table E9-2.

Table E9-2
Resident and Interregional Migration Populations Between Areas A and B, by Sex, 2000–2005

Sex	Resident, Area A, Jan. 2000 (1)	Resident, Area B, Jan. 2000 (2)	Migrant, 2000–2005, Area A to B (3)	Migrant, 2000–2005, Area B to A (4)
Male	1000	2000	300	100
Female	1000	2000	100	300
Ratio	100	100	300	33

Note: In thousands, hypothetical illustration.

a. What would be the resulting net migration stream (in raw numbers) to Area B from Area A? (Specify plus or minus.)

of males _____

of females _____

b. What would be the influence of this sex-selective net migration on the sex ratio of the new resident population of Area A? (Check one.)

_____ raise it

_____ lower it

_____ no influence

c. The influence would be in the opposite direction in Area B, but would the *degree* of effect be more, or less, in Area B, given Area B's larger initial resident population? (Check one.)

_____ more

_____ less

_____ the same

3. Lacking direct counts of migration, nations often infer net migration between censuses by the vital statistics method. The appropriate formula is

$$M = (P_2 - P_1) - (B - D)$$

You may recognize this as a transformation of the growth equation presented in chapter 1.

Table E9-3 shows the required calculations of net migration for the United States from 1995 to 2000. Following that model, estimate the net migration for Mexico from 1995 to 2000. Enter your answers in the blank spaces in the table.

Table E9-3
Estimating Net Migration by the Vital Statistics Method

| | Population 1995 (1) | Population 2000 (2) | Components of Population Change, 1995–2000 | | | | |
			Net Change (3) = (2) – (1)	Births (4)	Deaths (5)	Natural Increase (6) = (4) – (5)	Estimated Net Migration (7) = (3) – (6)
United States	263,119	275,636	12,517	19,600	10,520	9080	3437
Mexico	90,464	98,787		11,170	2215		

Note: Projections, in thousands.
Source: Bos et al., *World Population Projections 1994–95 Edition*, 1994.

If these estimates are to be believed, which country had the higher crude *rate* of net migration, on the average, for the years 1995 to 2000? (Check one.)

_____ Mexico

_____ U.S.

► PROPOSITIONS FOR DEBATE

1. "Seasonal migration" of agricultural workers from Mexico to the U.S. should not be defined as true migration.
2. The country of destination loses and the country of origin wins through international migration.
3. More-developed countries have no right to restrict immigration from less-developed countries.
4. Economic motivations completely explain illegal or undocumented immigration.
5. As the U.S. baby-boomers enter their senior years, age selectivity of interregional migration will decrease.
6. International migration promotes [or reduces] economic inequalities among countries.
7. International migration streams probably will continue to increase even if population growth in the less-developed countries continues to decline.
8. Migration policies are inherently xenophobic and racist.
9. In the next few decades, population "problems" will be defined increasingly around migration and decreasingly around fertility.

▶ **REFERENCES AND SUGGESTED READINGS**

Amuedo-Dorantes, C., and W. C. Huang. 1997. "Unemployment, Immigration, and NAFTA: A Panel Study of Ten Major U.S. Industries." *Journal of Labor Research* 18(4).

Andreas, P. 1994. "The Making of Amerexico: (Mis)Handling Illegal Immigration." *World Policy Journal* 11(2).

Bean, Frank D., Allan G. King, and Jeffrey S. Passel. 1983. "The Number of Illegal Migrants of Mexican Origin in the United States: Sex Ratio-based Estimates for 1980." *Demography* 20(1).

Bogue, Donald J., ed. 1993. "Spatial Mobility and Migration Research." In Bogue, Arriaga, and Anderton, eds., *Readings in Population Research Methodology.* United Nations Fund for Population Activities, Chicago: Social Development Center.

Bos, Eduard, Mu T. Vu, Ernest Massiah, and Rodolfo A. Bulatao. 1994. *World Population Projections 1994-95 Edition: Estimates and Projections with Related Demographic Statistics.* World Bank, Baltimore: Johns Hopkins University Press.

Boserup, Ester. 1981. *Population and Technological Change.* Chicago: University of Chicago Press.

Bouvier, Leon F., with Henry S. Shryock and Harry W. Henderson. 1977. "International Migration: Yesterday, Today, Tomorrow." *Population Bulletin* 32(4). Washington, DC: Population Reference Bureau.

Chant, S., and S. A. Radcliffe. 1992. "Migration and Development: The Importance of Gender." In Sylvia Chant, ed., *Gender and Migration in Developing Countries.* London: Belhaven Press.

Cohen, R. 1995. *The Cambridge Survey of World Migration.* New York: Cambridge University Press.

Cohen, S. 1995. "The Mighty State of Immigration Controls." *Social Policy Review* 7.

Committee on Urbanization and Population Redistribution. 1979. *The Territorial Mobility of Population: Rethinking its Forms and Functions.* IUSSP Papers, no. 13. Liege: IUSSP.

Crewdson, John. 1983. *The Tarnished Door: The New Immigrants and the Transformation of America.* New York: New York Times Books.

Cummings, S., and T. Lambert. 1998. "Immigration Restrictions and the American Worker: An Examination of Competing Interpretations." *Population Research and Policy Review* 17(6).

Da Vanzo, Julie. 1982. "Techniques for Analysis of Migration-History Data." Rand Note, no. N-1824 AID/NICHD. Santa Monica, CA: Rand Corporation.

Davis, Kingsley. 1974. "The Migration of Human Populations." *Scientific American* 231(3).

———. 1981. "Emerging Issues in International Migration." In *International Population Conference: Solicited Papers.* Vol. 2. Liege, Belgium: IUSSP.

De Jong, Gordon F., and Sarah Harbison. 1981. "Policy Intervention Consideration: The Relationship of Theoretical Models to Planning." In Gordon F. De Jong and Robert W. Gardner, eds., *Migration Decision Making: Multidisciplinary Approaches to Microlevel Studies in Developed and Developing Countries.* New York: Pergamon Press.

Farley, Reynolds. 1996. *The New American Reality: Who We Are, How We Got Here, Where We Are Going.* New York: Russell Sage.

Fassin, D., A. Morice, and C. Quiminal. 1997. *The Laws of Inhospitality: Immigration Policies and the Test Posed by Undocumented Immigrants.* Paris, France: Editions La Decouverte.

Flanders, Stephen A. 1998. *Atlas of American Migration.* New York: Facts on File.

Fokkema, T., G. J. De Jong, and P. Nijkamp. 1993. *Internal Elderly Migration: An Exploration of the Literature.* NIDI Report no. 32. The Hague, Netherlands: Netherlands Interdisciplinary Demographic Institute.

Frey, William H. 1996. "Immigrant and Native Migrant Magnets." *American Demographics* 18(11).

———. 1998. "Black Migration to the South Reaches Record Highs in 1990s." *Population Today* 26(2).

Frey, W. H., and K. L. Liaw. 1998. "The Impact of Recent Immigration on Population Redistribution within the United States." In J. P. Smith and B. Edmonston, eds., *The Immigration Debate: Studies on the Economic, Demographic, and Fiscal Effects of Immigration*. Washington, DC: National Academy Press.

Goldscheider, Calvin, ed. 1983. *Urban Migrants in Developing Nations: Patterns and Problems of Adjustment*. Boulder, CO: Westview Press.

Goldstein, Sidney, and Alice Goldstein. 1981. "The Use of Multiplicity Surveys to Identify Migrants." *Demography* 18(1).

Immigration and Naturalization Service. 1998. *Illegal Alien Resident Population*. Internet Release (June).

———. 1999. "Legal Immigration, Fiscal Year 1997." *Office of Policy and Planning Statistics Branch Annual Report 1*.

Jones, H. 1995. "The Continuing Ethnic-Origins Dimension of Australian Immigration Policy." *Applied Geography* 15(3).

Keely, Charles B. 1982a. "Illegal Migration." *Scientific American* 246(3).

———. 1982b. "Illegal Immigration." *Scientific American* 246(3).

Land, Kenneth C., and Andrei Rogers, eds. 1982. *Multidimensional Mathematical Demography*. New York: Academic Press.

Layton-Henry, Z. 1994. "Britain: The Would-Be Zero-Immigration Country." In Wayne A. Cornelious, Philip L. Martin, and James F. Hollifield, eds., *Controlling Immigration: A Global Perspective*. Stanford: Stanford University Press.

Lee, Everett S. 1966. "A Theory of Migration." *Demography* 3(1).

Longino, C. F. 1994. "From Sunbelt to Sunspots." *American Demographics* 16(11).

Lowell, B. L., J. Teachman, and Z. Jing. 1995. "Unintended Consequences of Immigration Reform: Discrimination and Hispanic Employment." *Demography* 32(4).

Lucas, R. E. 1997. "Internal Migration in Developing Countries." In Mark R. Rosenzweig and Oded Stark, eds., *Handbook of Population and Family Economics*. Amsterdam: Elsevier.

Martin, Philip L. 1993. "Trade and Migration: The Case of NAFTA." *Asian and Pacific Migration Journal* 12(3).

Martin, Philip, and Elizabeth Midgley. 1994. "Immigration to the United States: Journey to an Uncertain Destination." *Population Bulletin* 49(4). Washington, DC: Population Reference Bureau.

Massey, Douglas S. 1990. "Social Structure, Household Strategies, and the Cumulative Causation of Migration." *Population Index* 56(1).

Massey, Douglas S., Joaquin Arango, Graeme Hugo, Ali Kouaouci, Adela Pellegrino, and J. Edward Taylor. 1993. "Theories of International Migration: A Review and Appraisal." *Population and Development Review* 19(3).

———. 1994. "An Evaluation of International Migration Theory: The North American Case." *Population and Development Review* 20(4).

McEvedy, Colin, and Richard Jones. 1978. *Atlas of World Population History*. New York: Penguin.

National Geographic. 1998. "Migration." *National Geographic* no. 4 (October).

Petersen, William. 1975. *Population*. 3rd ed. New York: Macmillan.

Plane, D. A. 1992. "Age-Composition Change and the Geographical Dynamics of Interregional Migration in the U.S." *Annals of the Association of American Geographers* 82(1).

Plane, D. A., and P. A. Rogerson. 1991. "Tracking the Baby Boom, the Baby Bust, and Echo Generations: How Age Composition Regulates U.S. Migration." *Professional Geographer* 43(4).

Potts, L. 1990. *The World Labour Market: A History of Migration*. London: Zed Books.

Pressat, Roland. 1985. *The Dictionary of Demography*, edited by Christopher Wilson. New York: Basil Blackwell Ltd.

Ravenstein, E. 1889. "The Laws of Migration." *Journal of the Royal Statistical Society* 52.

Rees, P. H., and A. G. Wilson. 1977. *Spatial Population Analysis.* London: Edward Arnold.

Schiff, M. 1996. *South-North Migration and Trade: A Survey.* World Bank Policy Research Working Paper no. 1696. Washington, DC: World Bank.

Shryock, Henry S., and Jacob S. Siegel. 1976. *The Methods and Materials of Demography.* Condensed edition by Edward G. Stockwell. New York: Academic Press.

Smith, P. H. 1997. "NAFTA and Mexican Migration." In Frank D. Bean et al., eds., *At the Crossroads: Mexican Migration and U.S. Policy.* Lanham, MD: Rowman and Littlefield.

Stahl, C. W. 1995. "Theories of International Labor Migration: An Overview." *Asian and Pacific Migration Journal* 4(2–3).

Stark, O., and J. E. Taylor. 1991. *Relative Deprivation and Migration: Theory, Evidence, and Policy Implications.* World Bank Policy, Research and External Affairs Working Paper no. WPS 656. Washington, DC: World Bank.

Stouffer, Samuel A. 1940. "Intervening Opportunities: A Theory Relating Mobility and Distance." *American Sociological Review* 5.

Teitelbaum, Michael S. 1980. "Right versus Right: Immigration and Refugee Policy in the United States." *Foreign Affairs* 59(1).

Thomlinson, Ralph. 1962. "The Determination of a Base Population for Computing Migration Rates." *Milbank Memorial Fund Quarterly* 40(3).

Todaro, Michael P. 1997. *Urbanization, Unemployment, and Migration in Africa: Theory and Policy.* Population Council Policy Research Division Working Paper no. 104. New York: Population Council.

Treyz, G. K., D. S. Rickman, G. L. Hunt, and M. J. Greenwood. 1993. "The Dynamics of U.S. Internal Migration." *Review of Economics and Statistics* 73(2).

United Nations. 1994. *The Migration of Women: Methodological Issues in the Measurement and Analysis of Internal and International Migration.* Santo Domingo: International Research and Training Institute for the Advancement of Women.

———. 1998a. *World Population Monitoring 1997: International Migration and Development.* Population Studies, no. 169. ST/ESA/SER.A/169. New York: United Nations.

———. 1998b. *Population Distribution and Migration.* ST/ESA/SER.R/133. New York: United Nations.

———. 1999. *Migration Potential in Central and Eastern Europe.* New York: United Nations, 1999.

United States Bureau of the Census. 1998a. "Geographic Mobility: March 1996 to March 1997 (Update)." *Current Population Reports,* Series P-20, no. 510. Washington, DC: Government Printing Office.

———. 1998b. *State Population Estimates and Demographic Components of Population Change: Annual Time Series, July 1, 1990 to July 1, 1998.* Press Release CB98-242 and Data File ST-98-7.

White, M. J., and Liang Z. 1998. "The Effect of Immigration on the Internal Migration of the Native-Born Population, 1981–1990." *Population Research and Policy Review* 17(2).

Working Group on the Methodology for the Study of International Migration. 1981. *Indirect Procedures for Estimating Emigration.* IUSSP Paper no. 18. Liege: IUSSP.

Woytinsky, Wladimir S., and E. S. Woytinsky. 1953. *World Population and Production.* New York: The Twentieth Century Fund.

Yang, Philip Q. 1995. *Post-1965 Immigration to the United States: Structural Determinants.* Westport, Connecticut: Praeger.

Zipf, George K. 1949. *Human Behavior and the Principle of Least Effort.* Reading, MA: Addison-Wesley.

Zlotnick, Hania. 1998. "International Migration 1965–96: An Overview." *Population and Development Review* 24(3).

10 Urbanization

The history of civilization has also been a history of urbanization, the concentration of populations in cities. And, in modern times, the industrial revolution has triggered a veritable urban explosion, first in the world's more-developed regions and then in the less-developed ones. The UN now projects that by the year 2030, 84% of the population in the more-developed regions and 57% of the population in the less-developed regions will reside in urban areas (United Nations, 1998a).

So important is this ongoing evolution in human settlement patterns that we devote a separate chapter to it. We start the chapter with a descriptive history of world urban growth and urbanization. We soon discover that the process of urbanization is different in the less-developed regions of the world than in the more-developed ones, and so we devote separate sections to urbanization trends in each of the two regional categories.

WORLD URBANIZATION: PAST, PRESENT, AND FUTURE

Definition and Measurement

Before one can measure urbanization or urban growth, one has to define *urban*. What characteristics of a population settlement allow us to call it a "city" or a "town"? Good answers could easily refer to 1) the size and concentration of a population settlement, 2) politically designated areas such as towns or cities, 3) the location of central features in an urban lifestyle, 4) a concentration of economic activities or occupations, or 5) the presence of specific local institutions (Pressat, 1985). In demographic terms, the fundamental criteria are the size and concentration of the population settlement: an urban community is one that has a relatively large population density settled in an area surrounded by a less dense settlement (Golden, 1981, p. 28). The other sociological traits mentioned are correlates of these demographic ones.

313

But population size and density are matters of degree, and so is being urban. How do we determine the cut-off point between the smallest urban community and rural? Supposedly, there is some minimum community size below which the style of life, the occupational structure, and the political institutions clearly are rural. But that cut-off point varies somewhat from culture to culture.

Therefore, we rely upon the national census bureaus to establish their cut-off points. Most countries use some combination of the criteria mentioned above. This reliance on national censuses introduces a bothersome lack of standardization into international comparisons. For this reason, we tend to have more confidence in comparative statements about cities of larger population sizes, such as 100,000 and above, or one million and above—everyone could agree that these are cities.

If we have decided what "urban" means, then what is *urbanization?* Actually, it has two meanings. One is a present condition, the *degree* of urbanization. This conventionally is measured as the percentage of the total population residing in places that are called urban. The other meaning is urbanization as a process, the *pace* of urbanization. This pace often is measured by the rate of change over time in the percentage of the population residing in urban places (Arriaga, 1982).

Urbanization should be distinguished from *urban growth.* Just as the total population of a country has its growth rate, so do the rural population and the urban population. It is the *relative* speed of urban versus rural population growth that determines the pace of urbanization. But a country can have rapid urban growth without necessarily having rapid urbanization; the rural population may be growing at about the same speed as the urban. Moreover, rapid urban growth, the multiplication of cities and increase in their size, can have its own consequences, above and beyond the consequences of urbanization. So it is important that we keep these conceptually separate.

A final aspect of the process worth attending to is which *size of city* seems to be growing most rapidly. Being urban, remember, is a matter of degree. A particularly important aspect of the modern urban explosion has been the disproportionate growth of metropolitan mega-cities, first in the more-developed and now in the less-developed regions.

A History of Urbanization

Towns, and even some great cities, have been with us since antiquity. In the first century A.D., for example, Rome had a population estimated at over one million, nearly as large as London in 1800 or Philadelphia in 1900 (Hopkins, 1978). Pre-industrial population centers were, of course, very different from what we think of as a modern city. Ancient cities generally were concentrations of political power that lived off the surplus of agricultural activities in rural areas and colonies. In contrast, industry brought the center of economic activity into the heart of the city, and as nonagricultural enterprises gained in importance, so did the cities.

As economic activity moved into towns and cities, people followed, with hopes of securing livelihood there. The *pull* of cities was often compounded by a *push* from agricultural areas, as prime farming lands and agricultural work for growing rural populations were in increasingly short supply. Industrialization, providing livelihoods not tied to the ownership of land, opened the new urban frontier for settlement.

Yet the first industrial cities were not necessarily technologically modern. The early industrial revolution even hindered modernization through difficult labor conditions and harsh social inequalities within emergent cities (Wrigley, 1981). Rapid urban growth, especially in the new industrial cities, brought with it problems of disease and severe population crowding (Hautaniemi et al., 1999). After the industrial revolution, most of the world's population, even in what were becoming the more-developed countries, still lived in rural areas and worked in agricultural occupations.

The tremendous growth of urban areas that shaped the modern city came in the form of a "second industrial revolution" that would expand the horizons of urban growth and tilt the balance to bring a majority of the world's population into the cities. This happened first in the regions of the world that industrialized first—the present-day MDRs. In the United States this urban explosion began soon after the Civil War. In 1860 less than 20% of U.S. residents lived in urban areas; by 1920 a majority of the U.S. population were urban dwellers.

Technology was once again the key to rapid urban growth. In the thirty years after the Civil War, more than twelve times as many inventions were patented as in the entire history of the country to that time (Flanders, 1998). Two crucial developments were the shift from steam to electrical power and the concurrent rise of the steel industry. Electricity and steel, in turn, shaped the skyline of the emerging modern city. The first steel-framed skyscraper, a "towering" twenty-two stories, was completed in New York City in 1904 as elevators opened a new vertical habitat. Less than ten years later, the fifty-five-story Woolworth building dominated the skyline.

Urban growth was as explosive as the urban skyline. By the turn of the century three U.S. cities had over a million residents each: New York with 3.4 million; Chicago with 1.7 million; and Philadelphia with 1.3 million. By 1950 New York had more than doubled in size and these three cities had as many residents as they have now (Flanders, 1998). The influence of these industrial and technological revolutions worldwide is graphed in Figure 10-1.

Figure 10-1 charts the estimated, observed, and projected increase in urbanization from 1650 to 2015. The top line refers to the percentage of the world's population living in all urban areas. The line below that refers to the percentage of the population living in cities of one million or more and the lowest line gives the percentage living in cities of over ten million. Historical time goes from left to right in the graph in equal fifty-year intervals, the ones before 1800 being largely estimates based upon historical observation, those from 1950 to 1995 being direct observations, and those from 1995 to 2015 being projections. The height of each line tells us the *degree* of urbanization in different-sized cities.

The slope of each line shows the *pace* of urbanization. The vertical scale is logarithmic (i.e. the graph is semi-logarithmic). That means that a straight line ascending on the graph would imply a constant pace of urbanization. A line curving upward implies an increasing pace of urbanization, while one curving downward would show a decreasing pace of urbanization.

We see that the pace of urbanization in general increased slowly but steadily up to 1800. Then, with the coming of the first industrial revolution, the pace of urbanization increased dramatically and remained nearly constant into recent decades, where it has

Figure 10-1 World Urbanization, by City Size, 1650–2015

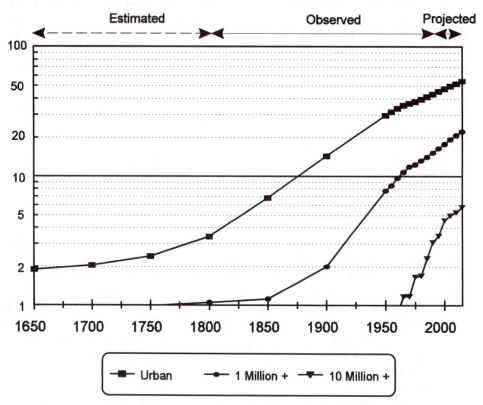

Source: Golden, *Urbanization and Cities*, 1981, figure 6.2; United Nations, *World Urbanization Prospects*, 1998, tables A2 and A17.

slowed slightly. The percentage of the population living in large cities of over one million did not increase substantially until 1850, with the second industrial revolution, when the pace of growth in large cities increased rapidly. As it did for urbanization overall, the pace of large city urbanization slowed slightly in the 1970s. Yet the pace of increase in large cities remains very rapid, more so than the rate of growth in urbanization overall. The most rapid increase shown in Figure 10-1 is the recent growth in the percentage of the population living in mega-cities of over ten million residents. Note that the pace of increase in these mega-cities is projected to slow down, but has not yet done so.

Rapid urbanization and the modern city skyline emerged first in the more-developed countries. By the 1950s a majority of the population in MDRs lived in urban areas. Only later did the urban explosions start in the less-developed regions. The current percentage of LDR urban populations is still considerably less than for the MDRs in 1950. Figure 10-2 illustrates the growth in the percentage of urban population for the world, for more-developed regions, and for less-developed regions from 1950 to 1995 and makes projections extending to 2015.

Figure 10-2 Percentage of Urban Population in More-Developed and Less-Developed Regions, 1950–2015

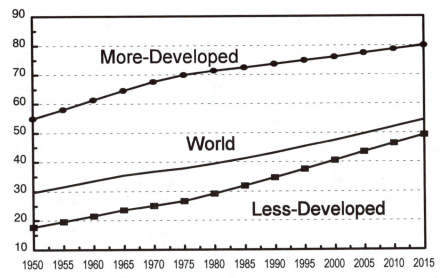

Source: United Nations, *World Urbanization Prospects*, 1998, table A2.

Although urbanization in the less-developed regions has historically lagged behind that in the more-developed regions, the recent *pace* of LDR urbanization has been higher than that of the MDRs, and is projected to continue. In Figure 10-2 there is only a slightly higher absolute yearly increase in the percentage urban of the less-developed regions compared with the more-developed regions—but that increase represents a greater proportional change: for the LDRs, the 2015 figure is about 1.7 times the 1980 figure; for the MDRs, that ratio is only about 1.1. (If we were to graph Figure 10-2 in a semi-logarithmic scale like Figure 10-1 is graphed, the LDR pace of increase in urbanization—the slope of that line—would be greater than for MDRs.)

The Components of Urban Growth

What has produced the rapid growth in the percentage of populations living in urban areas throughout the world? To answer this question we must first ask how urban populations grow.

Urban growth must come from either *natural increase of the urban population* or the net movement of people who were not previously urban residents into urban areas. The movement of population into urban areas occurs in two ways. First, individuals can become urban residents by *migration* to existing urban areas (from rural areas or from abroad). Second, they may live in rural areas which grow to the point where an entire area and its population are *reclassified* from rural to urban. Urban natural increase, net migration, and reclassification are the three components of urban population growth. So, being more specific, we might ask whether the rapid growth of urban populations is a result of natural increase in existing urban centers or of net migration and reclassification into urban areas.

To begin to answer this question it is important to consider stages in the history of urban areas. In the early history of urban settlements the population is relatively small and migration may have a dramatic impact on growth. New York City at the turn of the eighteenth century provides an example. The small city population, only 33,131 in 1790, nearly doubled over the next ten years almost entirely from migration. During this early stage of city growth, it does not take a large number of migrants to contribute substantially to the growth of the urban population. However, as an urban population grows this situation changes. It takes a much larger migration stream to have such large effects on the size of the urban population. Two hundred years later, in 1990, the population of New York City was over 8.5 million. This larger city population would not have doubled even if all the immigrants to the United States over the next decade came only to New York City. As cities grow large, migration tends to make proportionately less of a contribution to urban growth and, if demographic behavior does not change, the natural increase of the very large urban population becomes proportionately more important. But other demographic behaviors have changed as cities have grown larger and these changes also have had significant effects on the components of urban growth.

In the MDRs urban growth and the demographic transition have worked in tandem. During early stages of urban growth both the small size of urban populations and their high mortality made migration a very significant component of urban growth. Then, as many MDR cities grew to have large populations mortality also declined, both of which made urban natural increase more significant in urban growth. With high fertility and controlled immigration, the contribution of migration to urban growth in the MDRs eventually fell below that of natural increase. Indeed, by the early 1980s almost two-thirds of urban growth in the MDRs was due to urban natural increase (United Nations, 1998b). However, in recent years the contraceptive revolution, which led to declining fertility and the aging of MDR populations, also has led to a dramatic decline in urban natural increase. Migration's importance in urban growth is again rising in the MDR cities.

Figure 10-3 shows the changing percentage of urban growth in the LDRs and MDRs attributable to net migration and reclassification since 1980. The contributions of migration and reclassification to MDR urban growth increased significantly by the early 1990s. The United Nations (1998a, 1998b) projects that in the early 2000s most urban growth in the MDRs will again be due to net in-migration and reclassification.

Regional Urbanization Trends

Degree of urbanization. Table 10-1 presents the percentage of the total population of various world regions that was urban in 1950 and 1975 and is projected to be urban in 2000 and 2025. For the world as a whole, nearly half of the population already lives in urban places. The more-developed regions are the more urban, with nearly three of every four persons in the MDRs living in urban areas, compared with less than half of those in LDRs. The degree of urbanization is increasing in both more- and less-developed regions, and is projected to continue to do so. Some of these results already have been presented graphically in Figure 10-2.

Figure 10-3   Percentage of Urban Growth Due to Migration and Reclassification, World Region, 1980–1985, 1990–1995, and Projections for 2000–2005

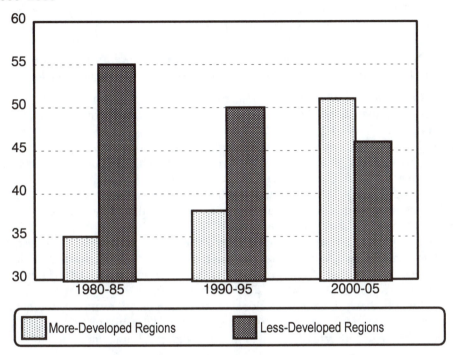

Source: United Nations, *Population Distribution and Migration,* 1998b, table 2.

Table 10-1
Percentage Urban Population, World Regions, 1950, 1975, 2000, and 2025

Region[a]	Percentage Urban			
	1950 (1)	1975 (2)	2000[b] (3)	2025[b] (4)
World	29.7	37.8	47.4	58.9
More-Developed Regions	54.9	69.9	76.1	82.6
Less-Developed Regions	17.8	26.7	40.5	54.7
North America	63.9	73.8	77.2	83.3
Latin America and Caribbean	41.4	61.2	75.4	82.1
Europe	52.4	67.2	74.9	81.7
Oceania	61.6	71.8	70.0	73.5
Africa	14.6	25.2	37.8	51.7
Asia	17.4	24.6	37.6	52.4

[a] Sorted in order of percentage urban in 2000.
[b] Projections.
Source: United Nations, *World Urbanization Prospects,* 1998a, table A2.

What is new in Table 10-1 is the comparison among specific world regions. We have ranked the regions from most urban to least urban as of 2000. The three more-developed regions (North America, Latin America and the Caribbean, and Europe) are the most urbanized. Oceania was one of the most urbanized regions in 1950 but has not experienced the same increase in urbanization over the last half of the twentieth century as other MDRs or Latin America. The Asian regions and Africa have been and will be relatively rural. Nevertheless, the percentage urban has more than doubled for Asia and Africa in the past half century and a majority of their population is projected to be urban by 2025.

Urban growth and the pace of urbanization. *Urban growth* has its own consequences, and the balance between urban and rural growth determines the pace of urbanization. Table 10-2 presents the average annual growth rates for urban and for rural populations for world regions during the periods 1950 to 1975 and 1975 to 2000. Throughout this entire span the world's population in both urban and rural areas continued to grow, but more so in the urban areas, increasing world urbanization.

However, the *pace* of world urbanization varied within the span. From 1950 to 1975 the urban populations grew at an annual rate twice that of the rural population. Then, from 1975 to 2000, as lower levels of fertility spread throughout much of the world (see chapter 5), growth slowed in both urban and rural areas. However, the decline in rural growth was more severe than the decline in urban growth, resulting in an increase in the pace of urbanization even as urban growth slowed. The ratio of urban to rural growth from 1975 to 2000 increased to about 2.5.

Table 10-2 reveals complex regional differences in the postwar pace of urbanization. For the *more-developed* regions as a class, the pace of urbanization slowed, 1975 to 2000, as urban growth rates declined more rapidly than did rural ones. The slowing of

Table 10-2
Average Annual Rate of Growth, Urban and Rural Populations, World Regions, 1950–1975 and 1975–2000

| | Average Annual Rate of Growth | | | |
| | 1950–1975 | | 1975–2000 | |
Region	Urban (1)	Rural (2)	Urban (3)	Rural (4)
World	2.88	1.44	2.51	0.93
More-Developed Regions	1.99	-0.60	0.83	-0.42
Less-Developed Regions	3.92	1.83	3.59	1.09
Europe	1.84	-0.64	0.73	-0.77
North America	1.98	0.11	1.13	0.40
Oceania	2.73	0.88	1.28	1.62
Latin America and Caribbean	4.19	0.97	2.73	0.09
Asia	3.55	1.79	3.40	0.96
Africa	4.63	1.93	4.36	2.00

Note: Sorted in order of annual urban growth 1975–2000.
Source: United Nations, *World Urbanization Prospects*, 1998a, tables A6 & A7.

urbanization is most pronounced in Oceania and North America, both of which experienced an increase in rural growth rates.

For the *less-developed* regions, both urban and rural growth rates were considerably higher than in the MDRs over the last half century, and the very high urban growth rates resulted in relatively rapid urbanization. Moreover, because growth in rural areas fell considerably more than in urban areas during 1975–2000, the pace of LDR urbanization has increased over this period. However, Table 10-2 also reveals considerable difference among LDR regions. Asia experienced the greatest increase in the pace of urbanization as rural growth fell to almost half what it was in 1950–1975 and urban growth remained high. Growth in rural and urban Africa did not change considerably over the past half century. In Latin America and the Caribbean urban growth actually slowed more than the decline in rural growth, slowing urbanization.

City Size, Mega-Cities, and Urban Corridors

So far in this section, we have dealt with the simple dichotomy between urban and rural. But cities come in many sizes, from small towns to mega-cities. Has urban growth been spread evenly over the range of city sizes or has it favored mega-cities?

The postwar picture is complex. In what one might call the middle range, cities between half a million and ten million residents, the proportion of the urban population living in each size class of city has remained fairly constant since 1950 and is projected to remain so through 2015 (United Nations, 1998a, p. 28). But the biggest change, especially over the past decade, has occurred at the low and high ranges of the city-size distribution: the rising percentage of urban dwellers who live in mega-cities of over 10 million and the declining percentage living in cities of less than half a million. The percentage of urban dwellers living in mega-cities increased from 1.7 to 7.1% from 1950 to 1995, and by 2015 it is projected that one of every ten urban dwellers will live in such a mega-city (United Nations, 1998a, p. 29).

This tendency to disproportionate growth of mega-cities is not equally strong worldwide. Table 10-3 shows the number of mega-cities for regions of the world in 1975, 1995, and projected to 2015. Mega-cities are predominantly located in less-developed regions, especially in Asia. This disparity will increase markedly in the coming years. The number of mega-cities in less-developed regions is projected to more than double, and those in Asia to more than triple, by 2015, while the number in more-developed regions remains constant.

As the number of mega-cities in Asia and elsewhere grows, they are more likely to merge and integrate into even larger global *urban corridors* (Lo and Yeung, 1998). Regional urbanization is so common in Asian countries, for example, that some demographers have argued that the European notion of separate cities is not appropriate in less-developed countries (Lin, 1994). Instead, they argue, we should consider broad regional urbanization trends in the LDRs. The Beijing-Seoul-Tokyo urban corridor (see Figure 10-4; Choe, 1996) and the Singapore-Johor-Riau growth triangle (Choe, 1998) are two examples of linked mega-cities or region-wide patterns of urbanization in Asia. The Central European and the Boston-New York-Washington, D.C. axis are two examples of urban corridors in more-developed countries.

Table 10-3
Number of Mega-Cities in World Regions, 1975, 1995, and 2015

Region	Number of Mega-Cities		
	1975 (1)	1995 (2)	2015 (3)
World	5	14	26
More-Developed Regions	2	4	4
Less-Developed Regions	3	10	22
Asia (excluding Japan)	1	5	16
Latin America and the Caribbean	2	4	4
Japan	1	2	2
Northern America	1	2	2
Africa	0	1	2

Note: Japan is included in the more-developed regions of this tabulation.
Regions sorted in order of the number of mega-cities in 1995.
Source: United Nations, *World Urbanization Prospects*, 1998a, table 4.

Figure 10-4 Beijing-Seoul-Tokyo Urban Corridor

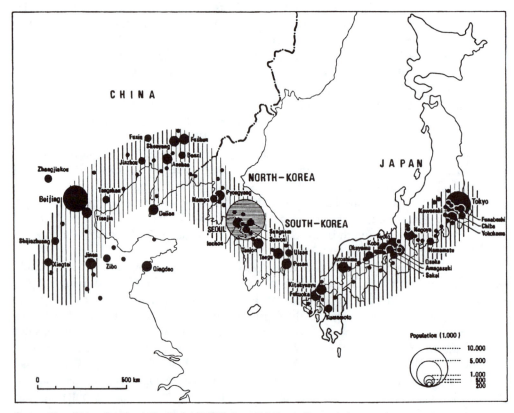

Source: Choe, "Urban Corridors in Pacific Asia," 1998, figure 7.2. Used with permission.

Table 10-4
World's Largest Urban Agglomerations, Ranked by Size, 1950 and 2015

1950		2015	
City (1)	**Population in Millions** (2)	**City** (3)	**Population in Millions** (4)
New York	12.3	Tokyo	28.9
London	8.7	Bombay	26.2
Tokyo	6.9	Lagos	24.6
Paris	5.4	São Paulo	20.3
Moscow	5.4	Dhaka	19.5
Shanghai	5.3	Karachi	19.4
Essen	5.3	Mexico City	19.2
Buenos Aires	5.0	Shanghai	18.0
Chicago	4.9	New York	17.6
Calcutta	4.4	Calcutta	17.3
Osaka	4.1	Delhi	16.9
Los Angeles	4.0	Beijing	15.6
Beijing	3.9	Metro Manila	14.7
Milan	3.6	Cairo	14.4
Berlin	3.3	Los Angeles	14.2

Source: United Nations, World Urbanization Prospects, 1998a, table 3.

One result of this clustering in less-developed regions will be a change in the hierarchy of the world's largest cities. This is dramatized in Table 10-4, showing the largest fifteen cities in 1950 and as projected in the year 2015. In 1950 the top five cities, and most of the top fifteen, were in the more-developed countries. By 2015, only one of the top five cities (Tokyo), and few of the top fifteen, will be in the more-developed regions. In 2015 all of the top fifteen cities will be mega-cities and larger than the largest urban agglomeration (New York City) was in 1950. The new mega-cities will be headed by Tokyo, which is projected to have 28.9 million people (nearly the size of the entire U.S. population at the onset of World War I). Los Angeles, at the bottom of the list, is projected to have a mere 14.2 million! Only six of the largest cities in 1950 will still be among the world's largest cities by 2015. The second through sixth largest cities in the world will all be from less-developed countries and were not even on the list in 1950.

URBANIZATION "PROBLEMS" AND POLICIES IN THE LESS-DEVELOPED REGIONS

Governmental Concerns

Most governments of less-developed countries do not consider urban growth itself to be a problem. In fact, in less-developed countries urban settlements "generate 60% of gross national product and, if properly managed, can develop the capacity to sustain their productivity, improve the living conditions of their residents, and manage natural resources in a sustainable way" (United Nations, 2000). Many international agreements about urban growth, such as the United Nations' *Agenda 21* and *Habitat II* (United Nations, 1996), actually encourage urban growth, albeit especially of mid-sized cities.

At the same time, most governments have grave concerns over the many city problems, such as urban poverty, homelessness, unemployment, crime, inadequate sanitation, and so on, which can result from poorly managed and/or rapid urban growth. In 1992, more than 178 countries adopted a strategy for urban and rural development at the United Nations "Conference on Environment and Development" in Rio de Janeiro, Brazil. In this *Agenda 21* agreement governments recognized that rapid urban growth has strained their ability to 1) provide adequate shelter, 2) manage human settlements, 3) plan for sustainable land use, 4) provide adequate integrated public health infrastructures (e.g. water, sanitation, sewage), 5) promote sustainable energy and transportation systems, 6) plan for disasters, 7) promote sustainable construction industry, and 8) develop human resources.

Of course, one way to limit the extent of such urban problems would simply be to control urban growth. So, why do governments increasingly prefer policies that try to manage urban problems rather than limit urban growth? One reason is economic. Urban areas are the primary source of most countries' economic productivity and growth. Another reason is more practical. Policies to control urban growth and internal migration to urban areas have been implemented, including 1) policies to control out-migration from rural areas through transforming the rural economy, 2) policies to limit the growth of large cities through migration control, and 3) policies that try to slow the growth of large cities by redirecting migration flows to mid-sized cities and smaller urban centers (United Nations, 1998b, p. 334). Unfortunately, these policies have had limited success.

> [P]opulation distribution policies implemented during the postwar period by developing countries did not succeed in improving the territorial distribution of production, employment and population. On the contrary, in almost all countries, internal migration to the major cities grew and the trends towards population concentration and urban primacy were strengthened. (United Nations, 1998b, p. 183)

What demographic concerns have led governments to pursue these specific policies and why have they largely failed?

Out-Migration from Rural Areas

In discussing the pros and cons of international migration in chapter 9, we noted the country of origin suffers from the selective loss of its young adults, especially since the emigrants tend to be the best educated and perhaps the most ambitious. This also is the case in most rural-to-urban migrations. Because of the agrarian nature of most rural areas, the loss of productive agricultural workers is of special concern to the communities of origin and to the nation.

On the positive side, migrants to urban areas may remain in contact and send remittances back to their families or villages, and migrants from many rural areas often move to urban areas only on a temporary basis, returning for seasonal agricultural labor (Gugler, 1997; United Nations, 1998b). However, when agricultural productivity suffers from out-migration the negative impacts on those remaining in rural areas is only partly compensated by remittances sent back by migrants (United Nations, 1998b). Moreover, many who do migrate and who maintain contact with home tend to become a successful elite from the village perspective and giving financial support to their kin can exacerbate income disparities on the village level.

In-Migration to the Cities

The people who make out best as a result of rural-to-urban migration in LDRs are the *individual migrants* themselves. Usually they are motivated either by a desire to have a better job or to get a better education. Apparently, some succeed in these goals; otherwise the migration streams would eventually dry up. But even if migration turns out well for the migrants as individuals, it could be less so for the collectives of which they are parts: the receiving communities and the nations involved.

Positive selection of the most educated and ambitious from the villages contributes to a more productive urban workforce. Thus, in the *long* term, receiving cities should benefit. If that is so, then why is rural-to-urban migration and rapid city growth considered problematic?

Part of the problem is simply coping with the speed of population growth in the *short* term. Rapidly growing cities in the LDRs seem never to catch up with the need for rapidly developing social services, housing, infrastructure, and especially employment opportunities; and they characteristically develop huge budget deficits in their attempts. City economies may grow more slowly than urban populations and are thus incapable of providing immediate employment opportunities for all migrants. These concerns are especially severe in slowly developing economies such as the Central and Eastern European economies in transition from communist rule (United Nations, 1998b). Although many migrants may benefit from moving to urban areas, others enter the informal city economy and do not earn a sufficient wage to avoid poverty, or remain unemployed.

The problem of supplying urban jobs relates to a concern over "premature" urbanization. Urbanization on a massive scale occurred fairly late in the industrialization and technological development of the present MDRs. In LDR cities, the massive influx from villages came before cities had industrial economy jobs for migrants to fill. A symptom of this is the large proportion of the workforce in LDR cities in service jobs, as opposed to manufacturing. Optimistically, these cities—with their surpluses of labor—will be motivated to evolve a style of development that is labor-intensive rather than capital-intensive, as has been the Western model.

Maldistribution of Cities

Another concern is that LDR cities are of the wrong size and in the wrong locations. There is a tendency for a country's largest city and/or its capital to grow disproportionately large. This polarizing of the urban population in a few huge agglomerations means that whatever benefits come from urbanization are not spread throughout the country.

Urban problems also are generally easier to manage in mid-sized cities. Perhaps what these countries need are more Cincinnatis and Omahas and fewer New York Cities. The dominant cities in most LDRs, after all, were located primarily in response to the needs of a colonial arrangement that is long since past. What may be needed are decentralized cities located more favorably to the development of the domestic economy.

Reasons for Limited Migration Policy Success

Why have policies to limit LDR rural-urban migration and urban growth had such limited success? Three major reasons probably explain much of the difficulty: 1) the strength of the attraction that urban areas have for migrants, 2) the weak and conflicting commitments governments have made to controlling population redistributions, and 3) the continuing high rates of natural increase in less-developed countries.

Expected eventual benefits of urban migration. In chapter 9 we discussed migration theories that emphasized the role of expected eventual benefits in migration decisions. Such calculations appear to play a large part in migration from rural to urban areas in the LDRs. Migrants often enter the unfamiliar landscape of the large city only to find themselves at a social and economic disadvantage. Many end up joining the ranks of the urban poor. Why would they migrate to such dismal prospects?

The answer involves both the push from rural areas and the pull of urban areas. It is not only the *current* push and pull factors but also the prospects for the future that matter. Many rural areas appear to provide very limited possibilities for the future while growing urban centers seem to offer boundless opportunity. Migrants continue to face the costs of migration and move to the urban areas because the *expected* benefits from such a move seem high.

Figure 10-5 schematically illustrates such migration decisions. The figure shows two patterns of expected income in the years after deciding whether or not to migrate. If potential migrants choose simply to remain in the rural area, they might expect little change in income over the coming years. If they choose to migrate they may expect to encounter costs of moving, interruption of employment, retraining, etc.; so for the first few years they may expect to actually experience a loss of income. However, if they have high expectations for the future, their expected income may eventually rise to much higher levels than if they had not moved to the city. If these expectations are sufficiently high, then they will likely decide to make the move and suffer the temporary costs of migration. Because the decision to migrate is a personal judgment, migration to urban areas may continue even when the immediate prospects for migrants are dismal and their future uncertain. So long as they believe the promise of urban futures are brighter than the more well-known and predictable drudgeries of remaining at home, they will continue to move to the growing urban centers.

Direct limits on migration to urban areas have had only limited success where migrants continue to perceive future benefits of migration (United Nations, 1998b), and it is difficult for a government to change the conditions of rural and urban life to the extent required for people to have a different vision of their possible future in these areas. It is equally difficult to resist a spreading dominance of capitalism's *urban cul-*

Figure 10-5   Expected Value of Rural-Urban Migration Decisions

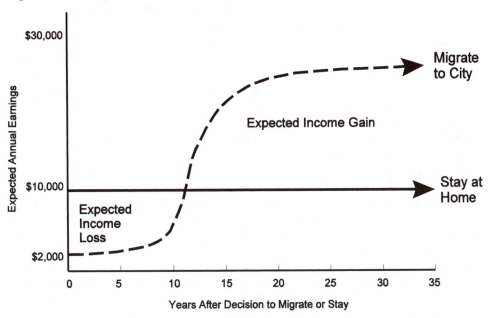

Source: Adapted from Martin and Midgley, "Immigration to the United States," 1994, figure 4.

ture, which increases the value placed on the fast-paced, gleaming, technological urban lifestyle and neglects or denigrates the slow, pastoral, agricultural rural life.

If the poor are more likely to migrate and their prospects in the city are uncertain, is the migration of the rural poor into the cities the cause of urban poverty? It may be tempting to think so, but there is little evidence to support this conclusion. As Hjerppe and Berghäll (1996) observe, urban poverty does not increase in proportion to urbanization in the less-developed countries. The proportion of poor actually tends to decline as city size increases; and a much larger proportion of the world's rural population is poor than is the city population. New immigrants to the city also are no more likely to be excluded from the formal economy than are others. In the absence of urbanization, poverty might, in fact, be much worse. Urban poverty is the result of disadvantages in education, health, nutrition, family planning, and so on, and, although some migrants may bring such disadvantages with them, decisions to move to urban areas generally do benefit migrants. So long as that remains the case it is difficult for migration policies to reverse the rural-to-urban migration stream.

Conflicting aims and weak commitments.   What might a comprehensive LDR policy to discourage and/or accommodate rural-to-urban migration require? To reduce the push from rural areas, investments in rural economies are needed. Support for the informal economies of cities is required to expand the employment opportunities of newly arriving migrants. Decentralization would require the creation of new mid-sized urban centers—but such investments have difficulty competing with the other national development priorities, and resulting weak commitments and limited funding for such programs have led to the dismal record of rural-urban migration policies in LDRs.

Policies to decentralize urbanization from very large cities to medium-sized ones offer an example (United Nations, 1998b). Relocation of industrial activities to outlying areas has, instead of decreasing urbanization, tended simply to increase the boundaries of urban areas. Simply relocating administrative or industrial activities to entirely new or small cities has failed to attract populations away from the large urban areas where migrants perceive greater opportunities and social services. The success of such programs generally would require much more ambitious, and costly, development programs.

Indeed, policies to reduce rural-urban migration may even contradict aspects of accepted economic development policy. As less-developed countries struggle to expand their international economies they are led further in the direction of developing export-oriented industries within major urban centers (United Nations, 1996; 1998b). At the same time, attempts to modernize agriculture have promoted a green revolution that has decreased, rather than increased, the demand for rural labor (United Nations, 1998b). These efforts to enhance national development have amplified rather than limited urbanization, rural-to-urban migration, and the growth of large cities.

In the face of competing demands and priorities, migration policies have been weakly funded and conflicted. Governments have not made (and perhaps cannot make) the large investments that would be required to reverse the push-pull forces underlying rural-urban migration streams (Becker and Morrison, 1997). Even given the means to address urban growth, many governments may not wish to limit patterns of urbanization that contribute to national development and rising standards of living overall.

Continued population growth. Another reason for the failure of many migration policies in the less-developed countries has been their high rate of natural increase. As populations increase, the expanding opportunities of urban areas provide an outlet for such growth while rural areas and agricultural enterprises have more limited abilities to absorb growing populations. In many countries that have attempted to improve rural retention through land reform, for example, these programs have simply been overwhelmed by continuing population growth, and land reforms have not improved the problem of land scarcity (United Nations, 1998b). As increasing proportions of the population live in urban areas their own natural increase also contributes to the growth and reclassification of urban communities. Consequently, attempts to decentralize have resulted in cities which have been absorbed into new, even larger, urban corridors and metropolises.

URBANIZATION "PROBLEMS" IN THE MORE-DEVELOPED REGIONS

It is ironic that the most salient and troublesome urbanization trends for the more-developed regions are almost the opposite of those typical for less-developed regions. The LDRs generally are plagued by rapid urbanization, especially metropolitanization. In contrast, many MDR countries have been surprised in recent decades by an "urban deconcentration" or "counter-urbanization" with population flowing out of their largest cities.

Urbanization and Counter-Urbanization in More-Developed Regions

During the 1950s and 1960s most MDR populations continued increasing in concentration in major cities, but in the 1970s there was a net out-migration from the largest cities (Illeris, 1990). Then, just as suddenly, in the 1980s this counter-urbanization appeared to stop in many countries. Some demographers considered the counter-urbanization of the 1970s a temporary event which had finally ended (United Nations, 1998b). But, once again fortunes turned and counter-urbanization reappeared in the 1990s (Johnson, 1999).

The more recent rise in U.S. counter-urbanization is widespread (Johnson, 1999). It is not, however, as uniformly widespread throughout the world as counter-urbanization in the 1970s. Some more-developed countries have resumed earlier growth in urbanization, while in other countries the growth of urban centers remains at or below the national average (Illeris, 1990). The broad counter-urbanization of the 1970s was, in most cases, due to rapid changes in industrial activities and changing job opportunities across geographic regions of the MDRs (Illeris, 1990; Frey, 1995; Kasarda, 1995; United Nations, 1998b). More recent and varied patterns of population deconcentration in the 1990s appear to reflect complex underlying causes. In Europe, counter-urbanization reflects a continuing process of industrial restructuring with local economic conditions and activities determining regional patterns of counter-urbanization (Illeris, 1990; United Nations, 1998b). In the United States, industrial restructuring has also continued and perhaps has even been reinforced by recent economic "good times." However, a large part of the recent growth in rural areas of the United States is not due to migration but to a rise in rural "retention," or declining migration from rural to urban areas (Johnson and Beale, 1994).

Counter-urbanization is clearly concentrated in the more-developed countries, but is not confined to the MDRs. Several of the mega-cities in less-developed countries, such as Cairo, Lagos, Abidjan, and Johannesburg, have begun to experience similar trends (El-Shakhs, 1997).

Detailed comparative study of urbanization and counter-urbanization, even in the more-developed countries, is a methodologically daunting task. Not only do the countries not have a standard definition of "urban" but they also do not have standard classifications of various sizes of cities. Even within given countries, definitions may change over time. To further explore the trends of counter-urbanization in the more-developed countries requires careful consideration of the way in which urban centers are defined and counter-urbanization measured. To simplify the matter, we will narrow our focus for the moment to the United States and the most recent trends in urban deconcentration.

Metropolitan Growth: The U.S. Case

Definition and measurement. A metropolitan area consists of a large population nucleus and adjacent counties that are socially or economically integrated with the population center. Despite changing terminology over the years, that core meaning has remained in U.S. census designations since 1910. Census data in 1990 distinguished three types of metropolis: large *consolidated metropolitan statistical areas* (CMSAs) of over a million people, smaller independent *metropolitan statistical areas* (MSAs), and the *primary metropolitan statistical areas* (PMSAs) making up the huge urban belts of the United States.

Within metropolitan areas data are available for a variety of geographic subdivisions including the *central cities* of the MSA, other *urban fringe* areas, and adjacent *rural areas* in the counties (see Anderton et al., 1997, figure 2-3 for more detail). Cities and places within the metropolitan areas also are distinguished by size. These complex geographic designations provide considerable detail on the movement of population between not only rural and urban areas, but between different types of more and less urbanized areas.

One can see from the way in which metropolitan areas are defined that it is important to distinguish the *concentration* of population, or clustering in areas of high density surrounded by areas of lesser density, from *centralization,* or the functional connection of many areas with a central economy. We will use *counter-urbanization* and *deconcentration* interchangeably to refer to the decline of a population's concentration. It could be evident in a smaller proportion of the population living in metropolises, or movement from center cities to the rings around them or to less densely settled metropolitan areas.

Metropolitan growth. First, let us deal with metropolitanization, the relative growth of metropolitan compared with nonmetropolitan populations. Metropolitanization was an established pattern in the United States during the post-World War II decades, but it was a declining one (Long, 1983). Figure 10-6 contrasts metropolitan and nonmetropolitan growth from the 1960s through the 1990s. Growth in metropolitan areas is divided into the growth in MSAs with over one million population and those with less than one million population.

In the 1960s metropolitan areas grew rapidly and nonmetropolitan areas grew very little, but during the urban deconcentration of the 1970s smaller metropolitan areas and nonmetropolitan areas grew much faster than did the largest MSAs. With the reversal of deconcentration in the 1980s metropolitan areas again grew faster than nonmetropolitan ones, but less dramatically so than in the 1960s. Finally, in the 1990s it appears that smaller metropolitan areas and nonmetropolitan areas are again experiencing a resurgence of growth with a resulting deconcentration from major metropolitan areas.

Components of metropolitan growth. What were the components of this metropolitan growth? Metropolitan populations can grow through natural increase, through net migration to metropolitan areas, by increasing their territory, or by creating new metropolitan areas. Forstall and Fitzsimmons (1993) studied the historical components of change in the population of metropolitan areas from 1940 to 1990. This is a difficult task because of the changing boundaries and definitions of metropolitan areas. Table 10-5 gives a summary of their results for major metropolitan areas.

In the 1940s most metropolitan growth was due to natural increase and net migration to metropolitan areas. By the 1950s the creation of new metropolitan areas

Figure 10-6 Metropolitan and Nonmetropolitan Growth, United States, Observed Through 1960–1997 and Projected to 1999

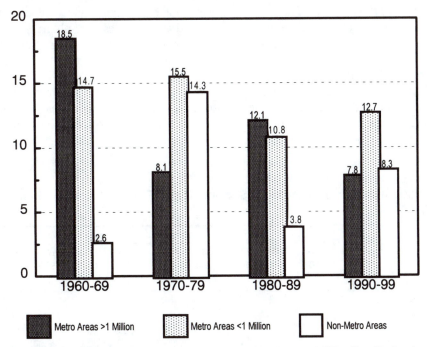

Note: Census estimates for 1990–97 projected through 1999 by authors for comparability with earlier decades.
Source: Frey, "The New Geography of Population Shifts," 1995, figure 6.1; U.S. Bureau of the Census Internet Release, 1998, table A-3.

Table 10-5
Components of Population Growth in Major Metropolitan Area Populations, United States, 1940–1990

Source of MMA Increase	1940–1950 (1)	1950–1960 (2)	1960–1970 (3)	1970–1980 (4)	1980–1990 (5)
Population Increase	34.7	49.6	39.6	13.2	23.3
Natural Increase	12.1	18.9	13.7	6.6	8.8
Net Migration	9.8	11.9	7.6	1.5	4.4
Territorial Increase	4.3	4.4	3.4	2.2	4.8
New MMAs	8.6	14.5	15.0	3.0	5.2

Source: Forstall and Fitzsimmons, "Metropolitan Growth and Expansion in the 1980s," 1993, table 4 (updated 1999).

contributed more to the growth in the metropolitan population than did net migration, and by the 1960s newly emerging metropolitan areas were the greatest source of metropolitan growth. All four components of metropolitan growth fell during the urban deconcentration of the 1970s, but the most dramatic changes were the declines in net migration and in the emergence of new metropolitan areas. During the reversal of the 1980s, all four components of metropolitan growth rose again. However, in the years since this historical study, components of metropolitan growth have again declined (Fuguitt and Beale, 1996; Fulton et al., 1997; Johnson and Beale, 1994).

Regional contrasts. These changes were not happening equally all over the country. A major contrast is between the so-called *frostbelt* cities of the Northeast and north central regions and the *sunbelt* cities of the South and western regions. Table 10-6 shows the population growth in selected metropolitan statistical areas of both categories from 1900 to 1996.

Since the postwar period, metropolitan growth and new metropolitan areas have been concentrated in the sunbelt states. Most sunbelt MSAs continued to grow rapidly throughout the 1970s. In contrast, metropolitan areas in the frostbelt experienced a net population loss during the counter-urbanization of the 1970s. The frostbelt MSAs

Table 10-6
Population Growth in Selected U.S. Sunbelt and Frostbelt Metropolitan Areas, 1900–1996

	Percent Growth in Decade									
	1900–1910	1910–1920	1920–1930	1930–1940	1940–1950	1950–1960	1960–1970	1970–1980	1980–1990	1990–1996
Area	(1)	(2)	(3)	(4)	(5)	(6)	(7)	(8)	(9)	(10)
United States	21.0	14.9	16.1	7.2	14.5	19.0	13.3	11.4	9.5	6.4
Sunbelt MSAs										
Atlanta	—	—	—	17.5	29.7	39.9	36.7	27.4	32.5	19.7
Dallas/Ft. Worth	—	—	—	19.3	56.4	69.7	39.9	28.3	32.5	13.3
Denver	—	—	—	—	38.3	51.8	32.1	30.7	13.6	15.0
Houston	—	—	—	47.2	52.5	54.1	40.0	45.3	20.7	14.1
Los Angeles	183.5	85.3	133.2	25.3	49.8	54.4	16.4	6.2	18.5	3.0
Miami	—	—	—	—	—	88.9	35.6	28.3	19.2	7.2
Phoenix	—	—	—	—	—	100.0	45.8	55.3	39.9	22.7
San Diego	—	—	—	—	92.4	85.5	31.4	37.1	34.2	6.3
Frostbelt MSAs										
Chicago	31.5	27.9	32.8	3.2	13.9	20.1	12.2	1.8	2.3	4.4
Cleveland	43.3	47.2	27.9	1.9	15.6	22.6	8.1	-8.0	-3.3	1.4
Detroit	43.8	112.7	66.7	9.2	26.9	24.7	11.6	-1.9	-4.4	1.3
New York	39.6	20.5	27.9	7.4	10.7	11.9	8.2	-8.6	3.3	1.1
Philadelphia	19.9	19.7	15.6	2.0	14.7	18.3	10.9	-2.2	2.9	0.6
St. Louis	25.3	13.5	19.3	5.3	17.4	19.8	12.3	-2.3	3.2	2.2

Note: Data begin with the decade when the metropolitan area first attained a population of 500,000. Prior to 1950 data represent metropolitan area boundaries recognized in 1950. After 1950 data refer to boundaries in effect at the end of each decade.
Source: Long, *Population Redistribution in the U.S.,* 1983, table 1; U.S. Bureau of the Census, *Statistical Abstract of the United States,* 1998, table 43.

have only slowly recovered to have small population gains in recent years. Without international immigration many of these frostbelt cities would have lower, or even negative, rates of growth at the present.

Of course, the frostbelt cities are not only colder, they also tend to be older, with economies based more on heavy industry. Many of these cities are in the *rustbelt* of declining heavy-industry economies. The difference between declining growth of the rustbelt cities and sustained growth in the sunbelt cities is largely explained by a shift in employment opportunities out of the primary industries of the rustbelt and into manufacturing, service, and technology sectors in the sunbelt (Kasarda, 1995).

Suburbanization. Another face of counter-urbanization and deconcentration has been the relatively slow growth of central cities compared with surrounding areas. Ever since the 1940s the rings immediately around the center cities of metropolises have been growing relatively rapidly; this is known as suburbanization. Table 10-7 shows the percentage growth in central cities and suburbs between 1960 and 1990 for the same MSAs as in the previous table.

In the United States, suburbs grew more rapidly than central cities throughout all three decades. Although nearly all of the frostbelt MSAs, and some sunbelt MSAs,

Table 10-7
Population Growth in Selected U.S. Sunbelt and Frostbelt Central Cities and Suburbs, 1960–1990

	Percent Growth in Decade					
	Central City			Suburbs		
Area	1960–1970 (1)	1970–1980 (2)	1980–1990 (3)	1960–1970 (4)	1970–1980 (5)	1980–1990 (6)
United States	17	11	12	23	20	15
Sunbelt MSAs						
Atlanta	2	-13	-4	58	45	42
Dallas/Ft. Worth	31	8	16	56	56	48
Denver	4	-4	-5	62	58	23
Houston	34	27	3	53	83	48
Los Angeles	12	5	18	22	8	19
Miami	24	12	9	45	40	25
Phoenix	67	44	36	-5	104	56
San Diego	28	28	30	36	48	39
Frostbelt MSAs						
Chicago	-5	-11	-7	40	13	7
Cleveland	-14	-24	-12	27	1	0
Detroit	-8	-19	-13	31	10	2
New York	1	-10	4	22	2	2
Philadelphia	-3	-14	-6	25	6	8
St. Louis	-11	-22	-9	31	9	7

Source: Frey, "The New Geography of Population Shifts," 1995, table 6.6.

even had a net population decline in their central cities, all experienced growth in their suburbs. Regional differences in suburbanization are, however, pronounced. The decline in metropolitan growth of the frostbelt metropolitan areas after 1970 also ended the rapid growth of their suburban areas. Nonetheless, in the 1960s the majority of metropolitan residents lived and worked in the central city and by the 1980s they were suburbanites (Frey, 1995).

Metropolitan "Problems": The U.S. Case

When Americans think of urban problems, what come first to mind probably are the everyday struggles of urban life—traffic, smog, crime, noise, etc. But do these collectively constitute the major urban problem? Rusk, for example, thinks not:

> Jobs, housing, streets and highways, water and sewer systems, pollution, and revenues are common issues for urban areas everywhere, but collectively they do not seem to add up to America's urban problem. In fact, compared with most urban populations throughout the world, America does not really have an urban problem as such. Most urban Americans are better employed, better housed, better served by transportation systems and public facilities, and live in better environmental conditions than the rest of the world. America's *real* urban problem [italics ours] is the racial and economic segregation that has created an underclass in many of America's major urban areas. (Rusk, 1993, p. 1)

There is an admirable degree of consensus among social scientists that the *concentration of poverty* in high-poverty neighborhoods within central cities is the single greatest urban problem in the United States.

Migration into urban areas has played a central role in shaping the nature of poverty in the city. The composition and geographic distribution of socioeconomic groups in U.S. cities reflect the effects of migrations long past as well as current migration streams. Immigrants, minorities, and the socially disadvantaged have historically migrated to the metropolis in search of a better life. Most have struggled, yet found it; many others have not. Instead, they have found themselves in a city segregated across social groups and with barriers blocking the social mobility of the disadvantaged, the different, and the disabled (see chapter 11).

Sometimes segregation is voluntary and sometimes it is not. Many in-migrants to the cities already face social disadvantages such as language barriers, lower skill or education levels, less access to financial capital, and so forth. Facing such disadvantages, voluntary segregation has historically been a choice of some social groups who have benefited from the support that a cultural and residential enclave of like individuals can offer. Unfortunately, especially for such groups already at a social disadvantage, involuntary segregation has had more lasting and negative historical effects on the city landscape. Many of the disadvantaged in the city, recent arrivals or long-term residents, have become trapped in a cycle of discrimination, disadvantage, and poverty. In addition, this urban underclass has been concentrated and further isolated from opportunity in high-poverty neighborhoods suffering from inadequate social services, urban decay, few employment opportunities, high crime rates, and unhealthy environments (Jargowsky, 1997; Wilson, 1997; Massey, 1996).

Out-migration and urban deconcentration have contributed to these problems. Counter-urbanization and suburbanization have been unevenly spread across social groups. Migration streams to suburbs and rural areas (along with rural retention) have favored the relocation of more "well-to-do" and middle-class residents out of central metropolitan cities (Fuguitt and Beale, 1996; Fulton et al., 1997). The migration patterns of both the poor and the non-poor have reinforced the concentration of poverty, chronic unemployment, and social disadvantage in segregated areas in the central cities of the United States (Massey, 1996; Nord et al., 1995; Rusk, 1993). Even within relatively affluent cities, migration patterns contribute to concentrated pockets of poverty and urban decay (Rusk, 1993; Jargowsky, 1997; Wilson, 1997).

Geographic restructuring of industry and regional migration shifts in the United States also have contributed to urban poverty problems.

> Between 1980 and 1990, the Frostbelt (Northeast and Midwest census regions) lost 1.5 million manufacturing jobs and $40 billion (in constant 1989 dollars) in aggregate manufacturing worker earnings, whereas the Sunbelt (South and West) added 450,000 manufacturing jobs and gained $21 billion in manufacturing worker earnings. . . . Metropolitan areas captured nearly 90 percent of the nation's employment growth; much of this growth occurred in the 'edge cities' at the metropolitan periphery . . . with information-processing jobs that typically require higher education replacing low-education jobs, while the city residential bases became increasingly dominated by less-educated minorities and immigrants. (Kasarda, 1995, p. 215)

This mismatch of skills and opportunities has further limited the chances for social and geographic mobility of those in areas of concentrated poverty at the same time that it has diminished the attraction of such areas to new enterprises seeking skilled laborers.

These same trends also have had a fiscal impact on city governments and their ability to provide for the social needs of their citizens. As these migration trends have led to a movement of the middle class out of many cities and a concentration of poverty within central cities, they have impacted the tax base and fiscal health of many metropolitan areas. And as Rusk (1993) notes, older cities, primarily in the Northeast, that are densely populated and surrounded by competing cities are *inelastic* and cannot readily expand to include the new rapidly growing suburbs. In contrast, many other cities, especially those in the South and West, are *elastic* and continue to expand through the annexation and incorporation of the growing suburbs. As economic growth expands in the suburbs, and dwindles or stagnates in central cities, the inelastic cities cannot expand to encompass this activity and garner the tax revenues needed to address the needs of the central city. Rusk argues that metropolitan growth is inhibited in inelastic cities and that when their growth through expansion stops, counter-urbanization begins and the concentration of poverty worsens. Older, more mature cities are more likely to find themselves confronting such difficulties.

SUMMARY

Although the world had been moving toward urbanization throughout history, industrialization has triggered an urban explosion. The present more-developed regions industrialized and started their urban explosions first, and at the moment they are the most urbanized. The less-developed regions, however, now have the more rapid growth of their urban populations; they also have the more rapid pace of urbanization, as urban population growth far outstrips that of rural population. This rapid pace of urbanization is projected to continue in the LDRs. Moreover, we can expect the largest mega-cities and urban corridors of the near future to be found in the less-developed regions. Net migration always has been the major demographic cause of urbanization and it continues to be so, although now urban natural increase also contributes to urban growth, just as it does to rural growth, in the LDRs.

There is widespread concern in less-developed countries about the consequences of massive rural-to-urban migration. Although migrations may improve the circumstances of the individual, and although in the long run the receiving community may gain desirable kinds of migrants, the constant immediate strain of rapid city growth masks any such benefits. Migration policies to control this rural-to-urban migration stream have, however, had little effect. One reason for the inefficacy of migration policies is the strong expectation many migrants have that the city offers a more promising eventual future, regardless of the immediate costs of migration. Another reason migration policies have had little impact is that they often conflict with economic development policies that encourage continuing economic growth in urban areas and lower the demand for agricultural labor in rural areas.

Ironically, while the less-developed regions are concerned with metropolitan growth, the more-developed regions are experiencing the opposite. Since the 1970s deconcentration has occurred in many European and American cities. In the 1970s, some of the largest U.S. cities actually began to shrink. This was largely in response to regional shifts in industrial activities and employment opportunities from the frostbelt states to those in the sunbelt. Since the 1970s, concentration-deconcentration trends have responded to cycles in economic activity and have accordingly been erratic. Although deconcentration has seen a revival in the 1990s with the return of prosperity, it is difficult to predict how lasting this trend will be.

Counter-urbanization in the United States has also involved migration by more affluent residents out of the central cities and into metropolitan-edge cities and suburbs, where economic opportunities are increasingly concentrated, or even into rural areas, remote from the problems of urban life. Meanwhile, segregation, discrimination, and persistent social disadvantage have all contributed to a concentration of high-poverty neighborhoods and urban decay in the inner cities. Cities that cannot expand to incorporate the economic growth at their fringes see their social needs grow as their tax revenues dwindle.

▶ EXERCISES

1. Compute measures of the degree of urbanization, using the data and examples in Table E10-1.

Table E10-1
Degree of Estimated and Projected Urbanization in South America, 1980–2030

	1980 (1)	1990 (2)	2000 (3)	2010 (4)	2020 (5)	2030 (6)
Population (in 1,000s)						
Urban	163,450	218,324	272,495	323,913	369,853	410,103
Rural	76,930	74,436	68,939	65,001	62,940	60,242
Total	240,380	292,760	341,434	388,914	432,793	470,345
Percentage Urban	68.0		79.8	83.3		87.2
Ratio Urban/ Rural x 100	212.5	293.3		498.3	587.6	

Source: United Nations, *World Urbanization Prospects,* 1998a, tables A3 and A4.

> a. Compute the percentage of the total population living in urban places for 1990 and 2020, rounding to one decimal place, and record them in the blank spaces of the table.
>
> b. Compute the ratio of the urban population to the rural population for 2000 and 2030, rounding to one decimal place, and record them in the blank spaces in the table.

2. Compute measures of the pace of urban growth and of urbanization, using the data in Table E10-1 and examples in Table E10-2.

Table E10-2
Pace of Urban and Rural Growth and of Urbanization in South America, 1980–2030

	1980–1990 (1)	1990–2000 (2)	2000–2010 (3)	2010–2020 (4)	2020–2030 (5)
Decade Growth Ratio (x 100)					
Urban	133.6		118.9		110.9
Rural	96.8		94.3		95.7
Ratio of Urban Growth Ratio to Rural Growth Ratio (x 100)					
		135		118	116

Source: Derived from table E10-1.

> a. Compute ratios of urban growth for 1990–2000 and 2010–2020. Do this by dividing the later urban population by the earlier urban population and multiplying the quotient by one hundred. Round to one decimal place and record in the blank spaces in Table E10-2.
>
> b. Compute the ratios of rural growth for 1990–2000 and 2010–2020, using the same procedure. Round to one decimal place and record in the blank spaces in Table E10-2.

c. Compute the ratio of the urban-growth ratio to the rural-growth ratio for 1980–1990 and for 2000–2010. Multiply by one hundred, round to the nearest whole number and record in the blank spaces of Table E10-2. This is one measure of the pace of urbanization.

d. If the figure in the bottom row for a given decade were less than one hundred, that would mean that (check one)

_____ the urban growth ratio was less than the rural growth ratio.

_____ the urban population did not grow.

_____ less than half the population lived in urban places during the decade.

_____ all of the above.

3. Compute net internal migration and net total migration for the United States between 1996 and 1997 using the data in Table E10-3.

Table E10-3
In-Migration, Out-Migration, and Net Migration for Metropolitan Areas, United States, 1996–1997

	In-Migrants (1)	Out-Migrants (2)	Net Internal Migration (3)	Net Movers from Abroad (4)	Net Total Migration (5)
Metropolitan Areas	1787	2002		1201	986
Central Cities	3297	6295		622	
Suburbs	6611	3829	2782	578	3360
Nonmetropolitan Areas	2002	1787		103	

Source: U.S. Bureau of the Census, Internet Release, 1998, table A-3.

a. Compute the net internal migration for metropolitan areas, central cities, and nonmetropolitan areas in column 3. Enter your answers in the blank spaces of the table.

b. Compute the net total migration (including movers from abroad) for central cities and nonmetropolitan areas in column 5. Enter your answers in the blank spaces of the table.

▶ PROPOSITIONS FOR DEBATE

1. In countries where population growth is rapid, urbanization also tends to be rapid, everything else being equal.

2. On balance, less-developed countries actually are better off if their urbanization is rapid.

3. One of the reasons for the deconcentration of the U.S. population in recent decades may have been the change in marriage and family norms.

4. Any problems resulting from urban deconcentration in the U.S. have been min-imized by the steady arrival of international migrants into metropolitan areas.

5. Deconcentration is a stage of a city's life cycle; all old cities eventually will stop growing and will experience deconcentration.

6. Since problems of racial and ethnic relations seem most severe in metropoli-tan central cities, the U.S. should welcome any deconcentration of its metro-politan populations.

▶ REFERENCES AND SELECTED READINGS

Anderton, Douglas L., Richard E. Barrett, and Donald J. Bogue. 1997. *The Population of the United States*. 3rd ed. New York: Free Press.

Arriaga, Eduardo. 1982. "Urbanization: Measurement." In J. A. Ross, ed., *International Encyclo-pedia of Population*. Vol. 2. New York: Free Press.

Becker, C. M., and A. R. Morrison. 1997. "Public Policy and Rural-Urban Migration." In J. Gugler, ed., *Cities in the Developing World: Issues, Theory, and Policy*. Oxford: Oxford Uni-versity Press.

Chandler, Tertius, and Gerald Fox. 1974. *3000 Years of Urban Growth*. New York: Academic Press.

Choe, Sang-Chuel. 1996. "The Evolving Urban System in North-East Asia." In Fu-chen Lo and Yue-man Yeung, eds., *Emerging World Cities in Pacific Asia*. Tokyo: United Nations University Press.

———. 1998. "Urban Corridors in Pacific Asia." In Fu-chen Lo and Yue-man Yeung, eds., *Globalization and the World of Large Cities*. Tokyo: United Nations University Press.

El-Shakhs, Sala. 1997. "Towards Appropriate Urban Development Policy in Emerging Mega-Cities in Africa." In Carole Rakodi, ed., *The Urban Challenge in Africa: Growth and Manage-ment of Its Large Cities*. Tokyo: United Nations University Press.

Flanders, Carol M. 1998. *Atlas of American Migration*. New York: Facts On File Inc.

Forstall, Richard L., and James D. Fitzsimmons. 1993. "Metropolitan Growth and Expansion in the 1980s." Population Division Working Paper no. 6. Washington, DC: U.S. Census Bureau.

Frey, William H. 1995. "The New Geography of Population Shifts: Trends Toward Balkaniza-tion." In Reynolds Farley, ed., *State of the Union: America in the 1990s*. Vol. II, *Social Trends*. New York: Russell Sage Press.

Frey, William H., and Kao-Lee Liaw. 1998. "The Impact of Recent Immigration on Population Redistribution Within the United States." In James P. Smith and Barry Edmonston, eds., *The Immigration Debate: Studies on the Economic, Demographic, and Fiscal Effects of Immigra-tion*. Washington, DC: National Academy Press.

Fuguitt, Glenn V., and Calvin L. Beale. 1996. "Recent Trends in Nonmetropolitan Migration: Toward a New Turnaround?" *Growth and Change* 27(Spring).

Fuguitt, Glenn V., and Timothy B. Heaton. 1995. "The Impact of Migration on the Nonmetro-politan Population Age Structure, 1960–1990." *Population Research and Policy Review* 14(2).

Fulton, J. A., G. V. Fuguitt, and R. M. Gibson. 1997. "Recent Changes in Metropolitan-Non-metropolitan Migration Streams." *Rural Sociology* 62(3).

Golden, Hilda H. 1981. *Urbanization and Cities*. Lexington, MA: D.C. Heath.

Goldscheider, Calvin. 1983. "Modernization, Migration, and Urbanization." In Peter A. Mor-rison, ed., *Population Movements: Their Forms and Functions in Urbanization and Develop-ment*. Liege, Belgium: Ordina Editions.

Gugler, J. 1997. "Life in a Dual System Revisited: Urban-Rural Ties in Enugu, Nigeria, 1961–1987." In J. Gugler, ed., *Cities in the Developing World: Issues, Theory, and Policy.* Oxford: Oxford University Press.

Hauser, Philip M., Robert W. Gardner, Aprodicio A. Laquian, and Sala El-Shakhs. 1982. *Population and the Urban Future.* Albany: State University of New York Press.

Hautaniemi, Susan I., Alan C. Swedlund, and Douglas L. Anderton. 1999. "Mill Town Mortality: Consequences of Industrial Growth in Two Nineteenth-Century New England Towns." *Social Science History* 23(1).

Hopkins, Keith. 1978. "Economic Growth and Towns in Classical Antiquity." In Philip Abrams and E. A. Wrigley, eds., *Towns in Societies.* Cambridge: Cambridge University Press.

Illeris, S. 1990. "Counter-Urbanization Revisited: The New Map of Population Distribution in Central and North-Western Europe." *Norwegian Journal of Geography* 44(1).

Jargowsky, Paul A. 1997. *Poverty and Place: Ghettos, Barrios, and the American City.* New York: Russell Sage Foundation.

Johnson, Kenneth M. 1999. *The Rural Rebound. Population Reference Bureau Reports on America* 3(1).

Johnson, Kenneth M., and Calvin L. Beale. 1994. "The Recent Revival of Widespread Population Growth in Nonmetropolitan Areas of the United States." *Rural Sociology* 59(4).

Kasarda, John D. 1995. "Industrial Restructuring and the Changing Location of Jobs." In Reynolds Farley, ed., *State of the Union: America in the 1990s.* Vol. I, *Economic Trends.* New York: Russell Sage Press.

Lin, G. C. 1994. "Changing Theoretical Perspectives on Urbanisation in Asian Developing Countries." *Third World Planning Review* 16(1).

Lo, Fu-chen, and Yue-man Yeung, eds. 1998. *Globalization and the World of Large Cities.* Tokyo: United Nations University Press.

Logan, John R., and Harvey L. Molotch. 1987. *Urban Fortunes: The Political Economy of Place.* Berkeley: University of California Press.

Long, Larry H. 1983. "Population Redistribution in the U.S.: Issues for the 1980s." *Population Trends and Public Policy,* no. 3. Washington, DC: Population Reference Bureau.

Martin, Philip, and Elizabeth Midgley. 1994. "Immigration to the United States: Journey to an Uncertain Destination." *Population Bulletin* 49(4). Washington, DC: Population Reference Bureau.

Massey, Douglas S. 1996. "The Age of Extremes: Concentrated Affluence and Poverty in the Twenty-First Century." *Demography* 33(4).

Nord, M., A. E. Luloff, and L. Jensen. 1995. "Migration and the Spatial Concentration of Poverty." *Rural Sociology* 60(3).

Pressat, Roland. 1985. *The Dictionary of Demography,* Christopher Wilson, ed. New York: Basil Blackwell Ltd.

Rusk, David. 1993. *Cities Without Suburbs.* Washington, DC: Woodrow Wilson Center Press.

United Nations. 1980. *Patterns of Urban and Rural Growth.* Population Studies, no. 68. ST/ESA/SER.A/68. New York: United Nations.

———. 1996. *United Nations Conference on Human Settlements (Habitat II).* A/CONF. 165/14 (part). New York: United Nations.

———. 1998a. *World Urbanization Prospects: The 1996 Revision.* ST/ESA/SER.A/170. New York: United Nations.

———. 1998b. *Population Distribution and Migration.* ST/ESA/SER.R/133. New York: United Nations.

———. 2000. *Earth Summit: Agenda 21—The Rio Declaration on Environment and Development.* A/CONF. 151/26 (Vol. I–III). New York: United Nations.

United Nations, Commission on the Status of Women. 1994. "Development: Women in Urban Areas—Population, Nutrition and Health Factors for Women in Development, Including Migration, Drug Consumption and Acquired Immunodeficiency Syndrome." E/CN.6/1994/3. New York: United Nations.

United States Bureau of the Census. 1998a. *Population of the 100 Largest Cities and Other Urban Places in the United States: 1790–1990.* Population Division Working Paper no. 27. Washington, DC: Government Printing Office.

———. 1998b. *Statistical Abstract of the United States, 1998.* Washington, DC: Government Printing Office.

Wilson, William J. 1997. *When Work Disappears: The World of the New Urban Poor.* New York: Vintage Press.

Wrigley, E. A. 1981. "The Process of Modernization and the Industrial Revolution in England." In Theodore K. Rabb and Robert I. Rotberg, eds., *Industrialization and Urbanization.* Princeton: Princeton University Press.

11

Population Diversity

Throughout history one effect of migration has been to bring people from diverse origins and cultures increasingly into contact with one another. Through migration from different areas of origin, and subsequent growth of immigrant groups, most countries of the world now have a population with a considerable diversity of cultures and origins. Cultural diversity, therefore, is a fundamental dimension of population composition of interest to demographers.

DEMOGRAPHIC TERMINOLOGY

Even for demographers, the identification and labeling of culturally diverse groups can be, with good reason, a sensitive undertaking. In the past, such categorizing of cultural groups has too often been used to stereotype minority populations and to facilitate discrimination against those marked as different. Thus, even the most innocent attempts at classification are understandably met with suspicion. In such an atmosphere, it is important to recognize what is, and what is not, implied by demographers in the labels they use to identify culturally diverse groups.

Race, Ethnicity, and Ancestry

The concept of *race* offers perhaps the clearest illustration of an abused demographic concept. During the early twentieth century race was regarded as an objective trait reflecting biological heredity and inherent social differences between identified racial groups (Soloway, 1990). The use of race often reflected an underlying ideology of *racism* (i.e. that humans are divided into genetic physical types with traits intrinsically related to their cultures and to their physical or cultural superiority). As the world recoiled from the horrors of World War II and Hitler's quest for a super race, growing scientific evidence of genetic commonality across—and of cultural variability

343

within—identified race groups cast increasing doubt on the biological validity of race categories. Identified races differ from culture to culture and across history, lending recognition to race as an essentially cultural, rather than biological, definition of social groups. "Whether the idea of race is meaningful in a biological sense remains a controversial and seemingly unresolvable issue . . . the importance of race for the study of intergroup relations clearly lies in its social meaning" (Marger, 2000, p. 23). Yet, even as a reference to social groups, race is not without problems. The use of the term "race" is so arbitrary and so emotionally charged that it is difficult to employ in any useful analytical fashion. Adding to the confusion, race categories, such as black or white, are sweeping combinations of very different cultural populations.

> As a result of its confusing usage and questionable scientific validity, many sociologists and anthropologists have dispensed entirely with the term race and instead use *ethnic group* to describe those groups commonly defined as racial. . . . [or,] for those groups that are particularly divergent from the dominant group . . . the term *racial-ethnic group.* (Marger, 2000, pp. 25–26)

Although the terms *ethnic group* and *ethnicity* are now familiar, these terms did not appear in standard English dictionaries until the 1960s. What constitutes an ethnic group is still not entirely clear. Martin Marger (2000), for example, identifies ethnic groups as subcultures that have unique cultural traits (e.g. language, religion), a sense of community, varying degrees of ethnocentrism, most often ascribed membership, and frequently some distinct territoriality or regional concentration.

Ethnic group identity is sometimes, but not always, related to *ancestry,* in the simplest case defined as the birthplace of one's parents. In a broader sense, however, ancestry can refer to more remote heritages than one's own parents. People often claim ancestry, such as Irish-American, Italian-American, or African-American, many generations removed from any contact with ancestral homelands and after such heritage is blurred by repeated intermarriage with those of different ancestries. Self-identified ancestries are often so strong that the individuals involved have a strong sense of community and constitute an ethnic group. In contrast, many first-generation foreign-born residents with a clearly identified ancestry may become thoroughly involved and assimilated in the dominant culture with little cultural identity as an ethnic group.

Population diversity among race, ethnic, or ancestry groups clearly depends upon exactly how these subgroups are defined and measured. It also is likely that the population diversity of importance in one culture will not be the same as that in another. Race and ethnic groups or issues in India, for example, are considerably different from those in the United States.

For that reason we will focus more narrowly on the United States in this chapter than we have in earlier chapters. We will begin with issues of defining and measuring population diversity in the United States. We then provide a brief demographic comparison of major ethnic groups in the United States with respect to the topics of earlier chapters: growth, age and sex structure, mortality, morbidity, health, fertility, marriage, migration, and urbanization. The chapter ends with a treatment of the problems and policies that seem to spring from those demographic realities.

Definition and Measurement in the United States

Since ethnic groups are culturally defined, they tend to change even within a single culture over time. The measurement of race, ethnicity, and ancestry has changed repeatedly over the centuries of U.S. censuses. Questions asked about these social distinctions in the 1870, 1970, and 1990 censuses are shown in Table 11-1. In the earliest of these three censuses, only four racial categories were used. By 1970, nine categories of race, six Hispanic-origin groups, and three ancestry questions were included. By

Table 11-1
Race, Ethnicity, and Ancestry Questions on the U.S. Census Questionnaire, 1870, 1970, and 1990

1870 (1)	1970 (2)	1990 (3)
White	White	White
Black, mulatto	Negro or Black	Black or Negro
Indian	Indian (Amer.): print tribe	Indian (Amer.): print tribe
Chinese	Japanese	Eskimo
	Chinese	Aleut
	Filipino	Asian or Pacific Islander:
	Hawaiian	Chinese
	Korean	Filipino
	Other: print race	Hawaiian
		Korean
		Vietnamese
		Japanese
		Asian Indian
		Samoan
		Guamanian
		Other Asian or Pacific Islander: print race
		Other race: print race
		IS THIS PERSON OF SPANISH/HISPANIC ORIGIN OR DESCENT?
		No (not Spanish/Hispanic)
		Yes, Mexican, Mexican-Am., Chicano
		Yes, Puerto Rican
		Yes, Cuban
		Yes, Other Spanish/Hispanic: print one group
SAMPLE (LONG FORM) ITEMS		
[None]	Where was this person born? What country was his father born in? What country was his mother born in? Is this person's origin or descent Mexican; Puerto Rican; Cuban, Central or South American, Other Spanish; None of these? Is this person naturalized?	In what U.S. state or foreign country was this person born? Is this person a citizen of the United States? What is this person's ancestry or ethnic origin?

Source: Edmonston and Schultze, *Modernizing the U.S. Census,* 1995, tables 7.1 and 7.2.

1990, Asian race categories were expanded and Hispanic origin was collected from all respondents (not just on the sample long form—see chapter 2). These most recent changes reflect attention to the growing percentage of Asian and Hispanic residents in the United States.

Growing cultural diversity of the population has led to concerns about whether these race, ethnicity, and ancestry questions are sufficient to reflect the population's heterogeneity. Partially this is a result of modern complex patterns of international migration (see chapter 9). In addition, however, the increasing number of children of multiracial parents, from less than half a million in 1970 to more than two million in 1990, could indicate a growing group who do not wish to identify with any single race in census questions.

Self-identities also change over time for race and ethnic groups, and there are continuing questions about the best terminology to identify any one group. For example, should the census refer to African-American, black, or Negro? Ask about Guamanians or Chamorro? Distinguish Hawaiian or Native Hawaiian? These are not equivalent identities and some demographers fear that such changes in question wording will result in incomparability across successive censuses (U.S. Bureau of the Census, 1999). Yet such labels are socially defined and do change over time; in the long run the census has little choice in the matter.

To determine the race, ethnicity, and ancestry questions for use in the year 2000 census the Census Bureau conducted an intensive study of the effects that multiracial categories, alternative racial and ethnic terminology, and the order in which such questions were asked would have on the enumeration of population subgroups. Given the results of this study, the continuing increase in population diversity, and evolving self-identity among social groups, it is likely that census questions about race, ethnicity, and ancestry will necessarily continue to change over time (U.S. Bureau of the Census, 1999; Bureau of Labor Statistics, 1996).

Throughout the rest of this chapter we will focus upon the five major *ethnic groups* identified in Census Bureau publications: white, black, Hispanic, Asian, and American Indian. Since ethnic groups identified by the Census Bureau have changed over time, and vary in different reports, there is some variability in the data available. Most notably, some tabulations will further identify non-Hispanic white and non-Hispanic black populations. It is important to remember throughout this discussion that there are a considerable variety of ethnic identities within any one of these major ethnic groups.

THE DEMOGRAPHY OF U.S. ETHNIC GROUPS

Relative Growth

A population's diversity rises as the variety of ethnic subgroups increases or as people are spread more evenly across ethnic groups. Many of the more-developed regions have experienced substantial increases in diversity through immigration, lower birth rates of resident populations, and a relatively young age structure among ethnic minorities conducive to higher rates of growth. The United States is a case in point.

There have always been diverse groups in the U.S. population. However, the variety of ethnic groups and the percentage of the population expressing ethnic identities that differ from that of the majority are both increasing. Over the last half-century the proportion of the U.S. population accounted for by "majority" non-Hispanic whites has declined as, between 1950 and 1998, other groups have more than tripled in size. By 1998 the "minority" nonwhite or Hispanic population of the United States was greater than the population of Great Britain, France, Italy, or Spain (Pollard and O'Hare, 1999).

Figure 11-1 shows the percentage composition of the United States population among five major ethnic groups identified by the census. In 1980 nearly four of every five people in the United States were white and non-Hispanic. The largest minority ethnic group was the black and non-Hispanic population. Hispanic and Asian populations, however, have been increasing at a faster rate than other groups in Figure 11-1. As a result, projections over the next half-century show rising percentages of these ethnic populations. By 2050 it is predicted that just over half of the people in the United States will be traditional "majority" white non-Hispanics. The percentage of black non-Hispanic will not significantly decrease or increase. The percentage Hispanic will increase significantly, as they replace blacks as the largest ethnic minority, and Asians will rise to be a substantial percentage of the population. More complex diversity

Figure 11-1 Projected Ethnic Composition of the U.S. Population, 1980–2050

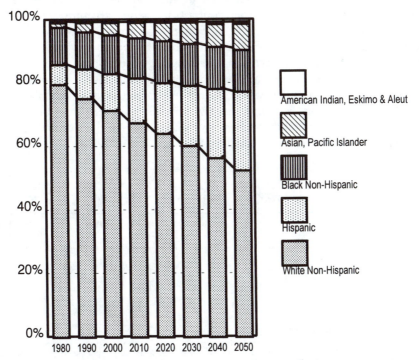

Source: U.S. Bureau of the Census, *Population Projections of the United States, by Age, Sex, Race, and Hispanic Origin: 1993 to 2050*, 1993, table 2; census data from 1980 and 1990.

within these major ethnic groups has in some cases increased, such as among Asians, and in other cases decreased, such as among Hispanics, due to changes in migration over the recent past (O'Hare, 1992).

Age and Sex Structures

In chapter 4 we saw that the age-sex structure of a population reflects its past mortality, fertility, and selective net migration. This is true of ethnic group populations as well as national populations. Moreover, ethnic groups within a nation can vary considerably in their structures, as the U.S. case attests. In turn, the varying age and sex structures of ethnic groups will influence their demographic futures.

Figure 11-2 presents population pyramids (discussed in chapter 4) for each of several large U.S. ethnic groups. The non-Hispanic white population composition is similar to that of the total population, having a higher percentage of its population in the oldest age categories and a lower percentage in the youngest age categories compared to other ethnic groups. This composition reflects the recent low fertility and mortality of this group. The Hispanic population, in contrast, has the greatest percentages of population in the very young ages, reflecting the higher fertility of this population in the recent past. Asians and Pacific Islanders have a population bulge at the working ages, in part due to age selectivity among immigrants and recent fertility declines.

Measures introduced in chapter 4, the age-dependency ratio and the sex ratio, can be used to summarize ethnic group contrasts in age-sex structure. Table 11-2 presents these ratios. The bulge of working-age population among the Asian and Pacific Islander group is reflected in their remarkably low age-dependency ratio, just as the high fertility of Hispanics is reflected in a very high age-dependency ratio.

Non-Hispanic blacks have the lowest sex ratio in Table 11-2. This relative shortage of male population is due in part to higher risks of mortality among black males. The high sex ratio among Hispanics has two sources: a higher percentage at young ages where biological sex ratios at birth favor a temporary surplus of males, and sex selectivity among migrants reinforcing this difference into older ages.

Table 11-2
Age-Dependency and Sex Ratios of Selected U.S. Ethnic Groups, 2000

Ethnic Group[a]	Age-Dependency Ratio (1)	Sex Ratio (2)
Total Resident Population	51.6	95.6
White (Non-Hispanic)	51.2	95.9
Black (Non-Hispanic)	51.4	90.0
Hispanic	56.4	101.1
Asian & Pacific Islander	45.5	91.7
Amer. Indian, Eskimo & Aleut	52.9	96.9

[a]All groups other than Hispanic exclude those of self-identified Hispanic origin. Ethnic groups are presented in order of total population size January 1, 2000.
Source: U. S. Bureau of the Census, Population Estimates Program, Population Division, Internet Release.

Figure 11-2
Estimated Population Pyramids of Selected U.S. Ethnic Groups, 2000

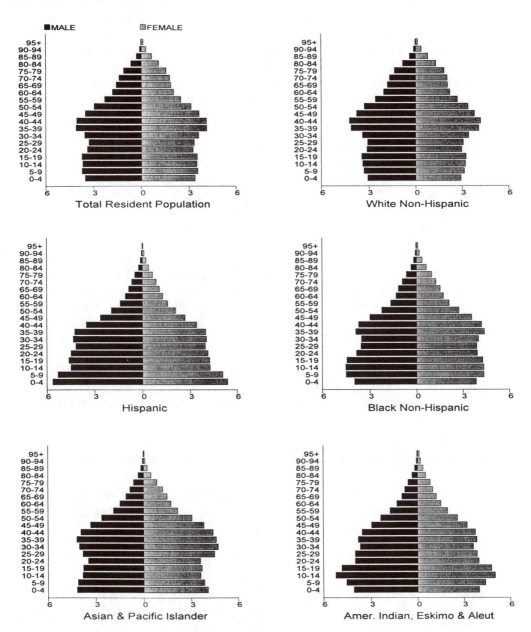

Source: Population Estimates Program, Population Division, U.S. Census Bureau Internet Release.

Mortality

There also are substantial differences in the mortality experience of the United States' ethnic groups. Table 11-3 presents age-standardized mortality rates separately for males and females of selected ethnic groups. The reader may recall that age standardization is a method for controlling the effects of age composition when making comparisons across populations (see chapter 8, Exercise E8–1). The first column of Table 11-3 shows age-standardized mortality rates for males and the second column for females. Overall, age-standardized mortality is higher for males, but this is dramatically more so for black males. For both sexes, black mortality is relatively high, especially when compared with Asians and Hispanics.

Percentage declines in the age-adjusted mortality rates since 1980 are presented in columns 3 and 4. These data show that white males have had a larger mortality decline over recent decades than any other sex-ethnicity group. Despite a higher initial mortality rate, black males have not experienced the same proportionate decline in mortality that white males have since 1980. Asian males and females have had the least mortality declines in recent decades because of their already low mortality rates.

What is responsible for the higher mortality of some ethnic groups? In chapter 5 we suggested that one way to identify vulnerable groups was to look at cause-specific mortality rates to see if certain segments of the population suffer disproportionately from mortality that is premature and largely preventable. The National Center for Health Statistics (1999a) identified the two causes of death in 1997 that were most significantly higher among the black population as HIV/AIDS and homicide. Figure 11-3 shows the crude death rates for these two causes among the white, black, and Hispanic populations of the United States in 1997. The crude death rate for both causes was more than six times higher for blacks than for whites (7.5 times and 6.0 times higher using age-standardized rates). The crude cause-specific death rates for HIV/AIDS and homicide among Hispanics were also considerably higher than for

Table 11-3

Age-Standardized Mortality Rates by Ethnic Group and Sex, United States, 1997

	Age-Standardized Rate		1980 to 1997 % Change	
	Male (1)	Female (2)	Male (3)	Female (4)
Total	602.8	375.7	-22.4	-13.2
White	573.8	358.0	-23.0	-12.9
Black	911.9	545.5	-18.1	-13.6
American Indian, Aleut and Eskimo	584.1	359.9	-20.3	-13.1
Asian or Pacific Islander	350.3	214.7	-15.9	-4.4
Hispanic	447.7	263.4	—	—

Note: In NCHS calculations Hispanics are not distinguished among other ethnic groups and Hispanic age-standardized rates are not provided for 1980. Rates are standardized to the age distribution of the 1940 U.S. population. *Source:* NCHS, *Deaths: Final Data for 1997*, vol. 47, no. 19, 1999, tables 2 and 3.

Figure 11-3   Crude Death Rates for Homicide and HIV in Selected Ethnic Groups, United States, 1997

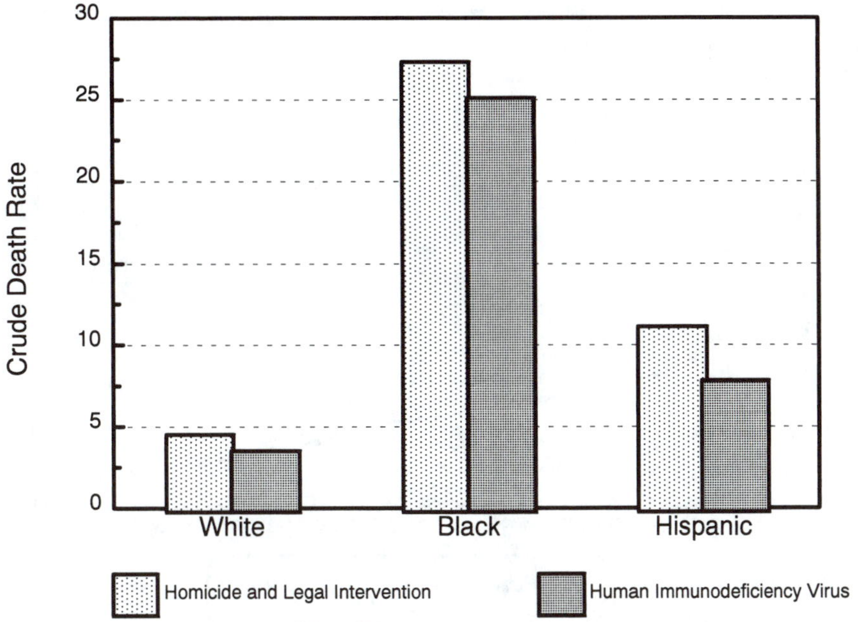

Note: Rates per 100,000 population. Age-standardized rates are not provided by NCHS for these causes of death among Hispanics.
Source: NCHS, Deaths: *Final Data for 1997*, vol. 47, no. 19, 1999, tables 9 and 13.

whites but significantly lower than for blacks. These two cause-specific mortality differences are important because they are the two largest ethnic differences in leading causes of death and because they both identify preventable causes of mortality among vulnerable groups.

Although HIV/AIDS and homicide are clearly special health problems, it is important to remember that for most of the ten leading causes of death mortality rates are higher in the black population than among whites (NCHS, 1999a). Only a few leading causes, such as suicide or Alzheimer's disease, have higher rates in the white population.

A general indicator of differences in health conditions among population groups (introduced in chapter 5) is the infant mortality rate. The reader may recall that deaths in the first year are particularly preventable through medical care, and that infant mortality is often used as an index of general medical and public health conditions. Infant mortality rates in the United States are higher among socioeconomically disadvantaged populations and among many ethnic groups. Figure 11-4 shows the infant mortality rates for white and black populations of the United States from 1980 through 1997. The infant mortality rates of both ethnic groups have declined steadily over this period. While the absolute decline was slightly greater for blacks, the proportional decline was less. The ratio of black to white mortality rates actually increased,

Figure 11-4 Infant Mortality Rate for Selected Ethnic Groups, United States, 1980–1997

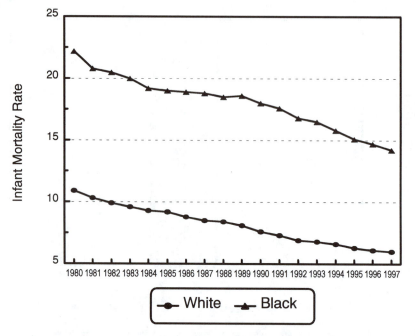

Note: Rate per 1,000 live births. Comparable data for other ethnic groups are not provided in NCHS reports. *Source:* NCHS, *Deaths: Final Data for 1997*, vol. 47, no. 19, 1999, table 27.

from a black infant mortality that was 2.0 times higher than whites in 1980 to one that was 2.4 times higher than whites in 1997.

In sum, these data combine to suggest that mortality differences among ethnic groups in the United States are largely due to an excess of preventable deaths in some ethnic populations.

Morbidity and Health

Not surprisingly, health and morbidity also vary among ethnic groups. Poorer health in some ethnic groups is largely due to differential access to health care and health insurance (e.g. Kass et al., 1999; Rogers, 1992). But differences in health-related behaviors and lifestyle risk factors also contribute to ethnic health differences (e.g. Santelli et al., 1998; Kallan, 1998). Less important, it also appears there are some genetic predispositions toward specific types of morbidity (e.g. Garner et al., 2000; Austin, 1993).

General patterns of ethnic morbidity are similar to those of mortality. In Table 11-4 self-assessed health status in the United States is given by sex for selected ethnic groups. These data are drawn from the National Health Interview Survey (see chapter 6). The percentages of those who consider themselves to be in poor-to-fair health (rather than good health) are given for males (column 1) and for females (column 2).

Fewer whites and Asians consider themselves to be in less than good health while more American Indians, blacks, and Hispanics rate themselves as having only poor to fair health.

One major morbidity measure introduced in chapter 6 is the *years lived with disability,* or YLD. Using life table methods (see chapter 5) and age-specific rates of both mortality and disability, Hayward and Heron (1999) estimated the adult working-age YLD for ethnic groups of the United States. Figure 11-5 shows these estimates for the

Table 11-4
Self-Assessed Health Status by Sex and Ethnic Group, United States, 1996

Ethnic Group	Percentage in Poor or Fair Health, 1996	
	Male (1)	Female (2)
White, Non-Hispanic	7.6	8.1
Black, Non-Hispanic	13.7	15.9
Hispanic	11.8	14.1
Asian or Pacific Islander	6.5	10.0
American Indian or Alaska Native	19.2	17.8

Source: CDC, *Health, United States, 1999,* 1998, table 60, original data drawn from the National Health Interview Survey.

Figure 11-5   Years Lived with Disability Between Ages 20 and 65 for Selected Ethnic Groups by Sex, United States, 1990

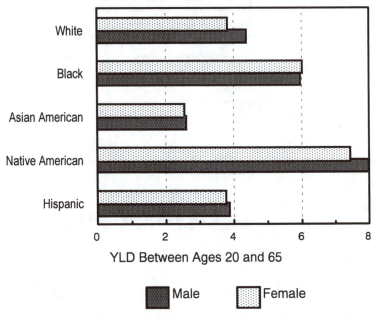

Source: Hayward and Heron, "Racial Inequality in Active Life Among Adult Americans," 1999, table 6.

years lived with disability between ages twenty and sixty-five for various ethnic groups. There are not great differences by sex, but males generally have a slightly higher YLD during working ages. Native Americans have, by far, the greatest estimated YLD in working ages. Blacks have the second-highest and Asian Americans have the lowest estimated working-age years lived with disability. Whites and Hispanics are between these extremes and nearly equivalent at about four years, or roughly 10% of the adult working-age years lived with disability.

Differences in health and morbidity among ethnic groups are clearly related to differences in socioeconomic status. African Americans, for example, are more likely than other Americans to suffer from chronic health problems, and lower socioeconomic status has historically accounted for their higher incidence of long-term disability (O'Hare et al., 1991; Ries, 1990).

Many health behavior risk factors also are associated with ethnic identity. Cigarette smoking provides an important example. Figure 11-6 shows the percentage of male and female adults who smoke in selected ethnic groups. For both men and women, rates of cigarette smoking are highest among American Indians and Alaskan Natives. For men, cigarette smoking varies less than for women but is lowest among Hispanics. For women, cigarette smoking is least common among Asians or Pacific Islanders.

Figure 11-6 Percentage of Adults Who Are Cigarette Smokers, by Sex and Ethnic Group, United States, 1993–1995

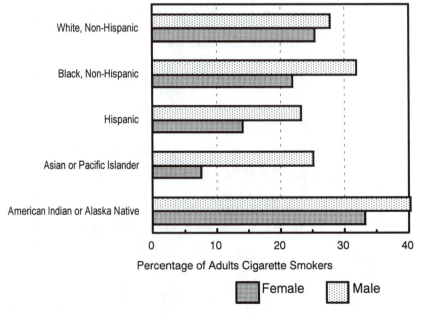

Source: CDC, *Health, United States, 1999*, 1998, table 63, original data drawn from the National Health Interview Survey.

Fertility

Table 11-5 summarizes differences in fertility for selected ethnic groups, using three different fertility measures introduced in chapter 7: the crude birth rate (CBR), the general fertility rate (GFR), and the total fertility rate (TFR). The Hispanic crude birth rate and general fertility rates are by far the highest. Focusing on the general fertility rate, a GFR of over 100 births to every 1,000 women of childbearing age suggests that approximately one of every ten Hispanic women in these ages gives birth each year. There are at least 30 more births to every 1,000 Hispanic women of childbearing ages in a year than there are to the same number of women in any other ethnic group. These high Hispanic crude birth and general fertility rates help explain two ethnic differentials noted earlier: the very rapid projected increase in the percentage of the future United States population that will be Hispanic (Figure 11-1), and the much more broadly based population pyramid, showing a younger age composition (Figure 11-2).

Table 11-5
Crude Birth, General Fertility, and Total Fertility Rates for Selected Ethnic Groups, United States, 1997

Ethnic Group	Crude Birth Rate (1)	General Fertility Rate (2)	Total Fertility Rate (3)
Total	14.5	65.0	2.0
White	13.9	63.9	2.0
Black	17.7	70.4	2.2
American Indian, Aleut and Eskimo	16.6	69.7	2.1
Asian or Pacific Islander	16.9	66.3	1.9
Hispanic	24.2	102.8	3.0

Source: NCHS, *National Vital Statistics Reports* 47:18, 1999, tables 1, 6, 9, and 13.

The TFR in the third column of Table 11-5 gives the average number of children that would be born alive to a woman during her lifetime if she were to pass through all her childbearing years conforming to the current age-specific fertility rates of her ethnic group (see Table 7-1 for an example of the TFR computation). According to the TFR, Hispanic women might be expected to have an average of three children over their life course while most other ethnic groups could be expected to have below, or near, replacement fertility of roughly 2.1 children per woman (see chapter 7).

A glance back at the population pyramids in Figure 11-2 provides indirect evidence of historic fertility changes in the ethnic groups. All ethnic groups other than Hispanics have population booms, or bulges, at post-childhood ages. These births occurred before recent declines in fertility to replacement levels or below. The age of individuals in these bulges indicates how recently fertility has declined to lower levels for these groups. Whites and Asians have had lower fertility for a longer period of time and thus have population bulges at much older ages. Relatively young population bulges in black and American Indian populations suggest a more recent decline to lower fertility levels.

Within general fertility, there are specific ethnic differences in fertility behaviors that are potentially problematic. Over recent history, for example, demographers have been concerned with high fertility among women of very young ages. Each year roughly a million pregnancies occur to American teenagers between fifteen and nineteen years of age. These babies are often unintended, are of low birthweight, have disproportionately high infant mortality rates, and are also far more likely to be poor (NCHS, 1999b). Although the number of teenage pregnancies has declined since a peak in 1990, the prevention of teenage pregnancies remains a major concern and national health initiative.

Ethnic group teenage fertility rates are given in Figure 11-7. The variations are wide. The fertility rate for Hispanic or black teens is nearly twice that of whites. American Indians have a teenage fertility rate that is one-and-a-half times that of white teens, while Asians have a rate only half that of whites and one-quarter that of Hispanics.

Differences in fertility rates reflect only the difference in pregnancies that result in a live birth. There also are significant ethnic differences in how "wanted" these pregnancies are and how many are ended through abortion. Pregnancies among non-Hispanic black women, for example, are about twice as likely to end in abortion as are pregnancies among non-Hispanic white and Hispanic women (NCHS, 1999b).

As we learned in chapter 7, fertility research suggests that large differences in ethnic fertility levels will probably continue to decrease over time as all groups of women move to lower fertility levels. Many ethnic, religious, and social groups have followed such a course in the recent past in the more-developed regions. However,

Figure 11-7   Fertility Rates Among Mothers Aged 15–19 for Selected Ethnic Groups, United States, 1998

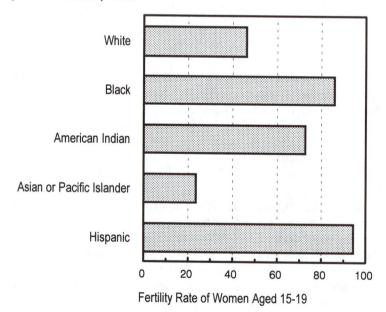

Fertility Rate of Women Aged 15-19

Source: NCHS, *National Vital Statistics Reports* 47:29, 1999, table 1.

higher fertility among some ethnic groups and lower fertility among others is likely to continue into the near future.

These past and present fertility differences are the source of some of the major demographic contrasts among ethnic groups noted previously. They help explain differences in growth rates among these groups, and thus the ethnic composition of the population. They also help explain the differences in age composition of ethnic groups, differences that have their own social and cultural consequences as well as demographic ones.

Marriage

Marital status. There are, as we have seen in chapter 8, tremendous cultural differences in the prevalence and acceptability of different types of stable sexual unions among different countries. Not surprisingly, there are also significant differences in the marital and cohabitation patterns of ethnic groups within most countries, including the United States. The percentages of U.S. adults in each major marital status are given in the top panel of Figure 11-8 for white, black, and Hispanic populations. Among adults, Hispanics and whites are most likely to be living in marital unions. Hispanics are also likely to marry at younger ages than whites or blacks (Anderton et al., 1997). Black adults are the least likely of these three groups to be living as married couples and indeed are more likely to be living as never married than married.

Presumably, some adults in all ethnic groups are also living in what the Census Bureau has designated as unmarried couples and partnerships, including cohabitation and same-sex partnerships. However, it has been difficult to accurately estimate these alternative living arrangements (Anderton et al., 1997). Using a broad definition of cohabitation with data from the 1990 Survey of Income and Program Participation, Bauman (1999) estimated that the highest percentage of population cohabiting was among blacks, followed by Hispanics, Asians, and then whites. It is unlikely that cohabitation alone accounts for the differences in marital status of adults in Figure 11-8.

Differences in the marital status of adults influence the living arrangements of children. The bottom panel of Figure 11-8 shows the percentage of children in various living arrangements among white, black, and Hispanic populations of the United States. Given ethnic differences in the marital status of adults, it is not surprising that white and Hispanic children are more likely to live with both parents than are black children. Black children are much more likely than white and Hispanic children to live with their mother only or with their grandparents.

Ethnic intermarriage. Intermarriage is a significant demographic mechanism through which ethnic identities are combined and changed over time. The first column of Table 11-6 shows the percentage of all U.S. couples, with at least one member of the ethnic group identified by the row heading, that are interethnic. Of all couples with at least one white member, for example, only 3% are interethnic couples. The highest percentage of interethnic couples is among the American Indian, Eskimo, and

Figure 11-8   Marital Status of Adults over 18 years of Age, and Living Arrangements of Children under 18 years of Age, for Selected Ethnic Groups, United States, 1998

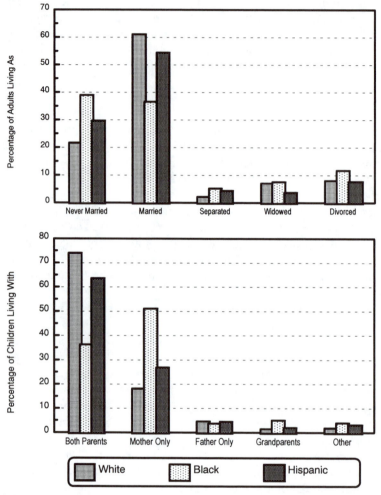

Source: U.S. Bureau of the Census, *Marital Status and Living Arrangements March 1998* (update), P20-514, 1998, tables 1 and 4.

Aleut population. Nearly three of every four such couples are interethnic. Within Hispanic ethnicity groups the highest percentages of ethnic intermarriage are between Puerto Ricans and other smaller Hispanic groups.

Because of their sheer numbers, majority groups tend to be a larger percentage of all interethnic couples than minority groups, so a somewhat different picture is shown by the percentage of interethnic couples which have at least one member of each ethnic group. The second column of Table 11-6, for example, shows that 92% of all interethnic couples are with a white person while only 17.3% of such couples are

Table 11-6
Interethnic Couples, United States, 1990

Couples, at Least One of Whom is:	Percent Interethnic (1)	Percent of All Interethnic (2)
Race/Ethnicity:		
White	3.0	92.0
Black	7.2	17.3
American Indian, Eskimo and Aleut	73.6	23.3
Asian and Pacific Islander	30.0	32.5
Other Race	25.3	26.9
Hispanic Ethnicity:		
Not Hispanic	2.7	87.4
Mexican	30.6	48.6
Puerto Rican	45.1	12.8
Cuban	36.8	6.6
Other Hispanic	50.3	32.0

Source: 1990 PUMS, Census Internet Release, 6/10/98.

with a black person. Whites also are the most common partners in Hispanic interethnic couples (87.4%), while couples with a Cuban partner are least common.

Ethnic intermarriage, like ethnic groups, is not equally common in all parts of the country. One of every five interracial couples in the United States resides in California, which has the largest concentrations of nearly every ethnic group. As a result, interethnic babies were the third-largest category of births in California after Hispanics and whites (Pollard and O'Hare, 1999).

Through ethnic intermarriage there are increasing numbers of individuals with multiethnic heritage. This rising interethnic population has led to questions over the classification of ethnic groups in demographic data (see chapter 2; Edmonston and Shultze, 1995). Many children of ethnic intermarriage have cross-cutting cultural identities. Across several generations the multiplicity of ethnic influences may become very complex or even fade in importance. Ethnic divisions, for example, among European immigrants (e.g. Irish, Polish, German, English, Italian, etc.) to the United States were once far more stark than they now appear. It is not uncommon to find traditional ethnic identities are of greater importance to older generations than to younger ones. Ultimately, significant intermarriage helps to blur the boundaries of ethnic diversity and complicates any simple view of the origins and intergenerational transmission of ethnicity.

Migration

Ethnicity affects both international and internal migration streams. Just as there are age and sex selectivities to migration (noted in chapter 9), not all ethnic groups are equally likely to emigrate from, or immigrate to, an area. In this section, we will focus on the impact of this ethnically selective immigration on the diversity of the U.S. population.

Figure 11-9   Multiethnic Census Classification

Non Sequitur © 2000 Wiley Miller. Distributed by Universal Press Syndicate. Used with permission.

Ethnic selectivity in international migration, of course, potentially affects the population composition of both the country of origin and of destination. Historically, however, the ethnic impacts of international migration have been greater for receiving countries. The purely demographic effects of forced migration and slavery on population composition have been, for example, far greater on the North American population than they were on African nations (McEvedy and Jones, 1978). Contemporary impacts of immigration on more-developed country population compositions are pronounced. This is because, as in the United States, the ethnic composition of the recent immigrant populations to the MDRs is often very different from that of the resident population.

Let us first attend the ethnic composition of the legal immigrant population. Country of birth is often used as a proxy for ethnic origins of immigrants, although it is a crude measure since many different ethnic groups may have been born in any given country of origin. Table 11-7 classifies the legal immigrants admitted to the United States in 1998 by place of birth. The largest groups of immigrants are those from Asia and North America, followed by Europe. Of those immigrants born in North America most were born in Mexico. Indeed, Mexican-born immigrants account for nearly one of every five legal immigrants admitted to the United States. About one of every three immigrants comes from an Asian country. This selective immigration obviously contributes to the high rate of increase in the Hispanic and Asian populations described earlier.

As we suggested in chapter 9, the impact of immigration on population diversity is also determined by where immigrants locate once they come to the

Table 11-7
Immigrants Admitted to the United States by Region and Selected Countries of Birth, 1998

Region/Country	Percentage of All Immigration	
Africa	6.2	
Asia	33.3	
China		5.6
India		5.5
Philippines		5.2
Vietnam		2.7
Europe	13.7	
Russia		1.7
United Kingdom		1.4
Poland		1.3
North America	38.3	
Mexico		19.9
Dominican Republic		3.1
Cuba		2.6
Haiti		2.0
Oceania	0.6	
South America	6.9	
Unknown	1.1	

Source: INS, *Legal Immigration Fiscal Year 1998*, 2000, table 2.

United States. As Figure 11-10 shows, over 25% of immigrants intend to reside in the state of California. About half of the immigrants admitted in 1998 intended to live in either California, New York, or Florida. This concentration of ethnic immigrants in specific states or regions is in large part a result of migration into border states and areas, or enclaves, which already have a large population of immigrants with a similar background (O'Hare, 1992). In turn, the tendency to migrate into areas that already have large ethnic populations has created greater regional differences in ethnic diversity, with large concentrations of various ethnic groups in some places and few in others.

The present regional distribution of ethnic groups in the U.S. is largely the product of contemporary and historical ethnically-selective migrations. Table 11-8 describes that distribution. Non-Hispanic whites are the most widely diffused population. In contrast, as column 2 shows, over half of the black population resides in the southern United States. In large part this is a historical vestige of slavery. Similarly, over half of the Asian and Pacific Islander population lives in the western states, which are traditional destinations of Pacific transoceanic migration. Nearly half of the American Indian, Eskimo, and Aleut population lives in the western states, both as a result of native populations in that region and the forced progressive displacement of Native Americans to western reservations. The higher percentage of Hispanics in the South and West is similarly a result of their migration history and proximity to the southern borders of entry to the United States.

Figure 11-10 Immigrants Admitted to the United States by Intended State of Residence, Top Ten States of Destination, 1998

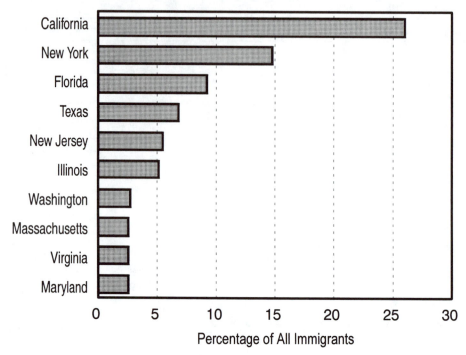

Percentage of All Immigrants

Source: INS, Legal Immigration, Fiscal Year 1998, 2000, table 3.

Table 11-8
Estimated Regional Distribution of U.S. Ethnic Groups, 1995, and Projected Percentage Growth by 2025

Region	White Non-Hispanic (1)	Black (2)	Hispanic (3)	American Indian, Eskimo and Aleut (4)	Asian and Pacific Islander (5)
Percentage Distribution:					
Northeast	20.6	18.9	16.4	6.3	18.4
Midwest	27.0	18.7	7.7	16.5	10.5
South	33.3	52.8	30.5	27.6	16.5
West	19.0	9.6	45.4	49.5	54.6
Projected Percentage Growth 1995–2025:					
Northeast	-5.2	37.1	94.4	42.6	139.0
Midwest	3.5	32.3	110.2	57.3	119.9
South	16.1	48.3	115.8	46.0	129.2
West	14.8	51.6	131.2	47.4	138.4
Total	8.1	43.5	118.9	48.3	135.0

Source: U.S. Bureau of the Census, Projected State Populations, by Sex, Race, and Hispanic Origin: 1995–2025, Internet Release, resident population, Series A projections.

Although the regional distribution of ethnic populations is revealing, it also can be somewhat misleading. Most immigrants initially locate in metropolitan areas of the United States. Many ethnic enclaves exist in the major metropolitan areas of states which have, overall, few ethnic residents. Figure 11-11 illustrates this fact. The top metropolitan areas of destination for immigrants admitted to the United States generally reflect the states with large ethnic populations and those in which immigrants intend to reside. More than one in five immigrants, for example, planned to locate in either the New York or the Los Angeles-Long Beach MSAs. However, many immigrants also intended to locate, for example, in the metropolitan areas of Chicago, Washington, DC, and Boston even though these cities are not in the top five states of immigrant destination (see Figure 11-10) or in regions with the largest ethnic populations (see Table 11-8). As ethnic populations grow in the major cities, metropolitan areas have often become increasingly more diverse than regional or state populations.

PROBLEMS AND POLICIES

Our procedure in earlier chapters has been to discuss the demographic *problems* arising from trends discussed, and to approach these problems by first questioning *who*

Figure 11-11   Immigrants Admitted to the United States by Intended Metropolitan Area of Residence, Top Ten MSAs of Destination, 1998

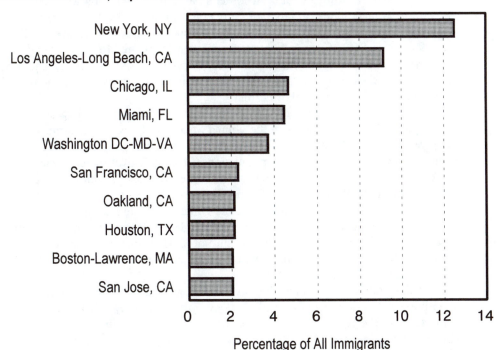

Percentage of All Immigrants

Source: INS, *Legal Immigration, Fiscal Year 1998,* 2000, table 3.

considers them to be problematic. Relatively few people consider population diversity itself to be a demographic problem. At the same time, there are a variety of specific demographic problems and policy concerns that have been associated with different ethnic subpopulations. We will limit ourselves here to discussing a few general demographic concerns which apply broadly across many ethnic minorities and which have received considerable demographic attention over recent decades. These central concerns are about the grievous persistence of segregation, the poor health and higher fertility among ethnic groups, and accommodating changing patterns of ethnic immigration.

Urban Segregation

Since international migrants tend to locate in major urban areas, we might expect that over time ethnic minorities would also be more likely to concentrate in urban areas. Unfortunately, given the continuing worldwide discrimination against minority populations, we might also expect these populations are likely to live in segregated urban enclaves. Many different national studies confirm these expectations. Minority populations in European countries are more likely to be urban residents and to live in segregated urban areas (Friedrichs, 1998; van Kempen and van Weesep, 1998; Kesteloot et al., 1997; Bonvalet et al., 1995). Minorities are also more likely to live in urban areas of the former Soviet republics (Harris, 1993) and areas of Southeast Asia (Banister, 1992). However, in some cases, most notably China, minorities are more likely to live in rural, outlying, or even border areas (Pannel and Torguson, 1991).

In the United States, all large minority ethnic groups, except American Indians and Alaska natives, are more likely to live in metropolitan areas (Waldinger, 1989). In the 1990 census, 86% of ethnic "minority" members, compared to 75% of "majority" non-Hispanic whites, lived in metropolitan statistical areas (O'Hare, 1992), and in six of the eight U.S. cities with over a million residents, ethnic "majority" non-Hispanic whites were actually numerical minorities.

Table 11-9 shows the ten metropolitan statistical areas with the largest numbers of black and Hispanic residents in the United States as of 1997. In column 1 of this table we can see that New York, Washington, DC, and Chicago were the three metropolitan areas with the largest black populations. Column 3 gives the percentage of all black residents of the United States who lived in each MSA. Summing the percentages for New York, Washington, DC, and Chicago it is clear that over 20%, or more than one of every five, black residents of the United States live in one of these three metropolitan areas; over 40% live in one of the ten MSAs listed. The concentration of Hispanics is even more dramatic. Over a third of all Hispanics are located in the Los Angeles, New York, or Miami metropolitan areas, and well over half live in one of the ten MSAs listed in Table 11-9.

Within the cities in which they live, ethnic groups often are segregated from other populations (Massey and Denton, 1993; Farley and Frey, 1994). Much of this segregation is the result of historical discrimination in housing and employment opportunities (Massey et al., 1994). However, recent migration has also played a role. Black segregation is, for example, a historical legacy of slavery, the postwar migrations to the northern cities, and housing discrimination. Recent black immigration,

Table 11-9
Metropolitan Statistical Areas with the Largest Numbers of Black and Hispanic Residents, 1997

MSAs with Largest Black Populations (1)	Black Population in 1,000s (2)	Percent of Total Black Population (3)	MSAs with Largest Hispanic Populations (4)	Hispanic Population in 1,000s (5)	Percent of Total Hispanic Population (6)
Total U.S.	33,973		Total U.S.	29,160	
New York	3856	11.4	Los Angeles	6002	20.6
Washington, DC	1858	5.5	New York	3392	11.6
Chicago	1662	4.9	Miami	1308	4.5
Los Angeles	1301	3.8	San Francisco	1283	4.4
Philadelphia	1162	3.4	Chicago	1169	4.0
Detroit	1133	3.3	Houston	1050	3.6
Atlanta	937	2.8	San Antonio	804	2.8
Houston	790	2.3	Dallas	727	2.5
Miami	691	2.0	San Diego	697	2.4
Dallas	664	2.0	Phoenix	575	2.0
Top 10 MSAs	14,054	41.4	Top 10 MSAs	17,007	58.3

Source: U.S. Bureau of the Census, Statistical Abstract of the U.S., 1998, table 45; Population Estimates Program, Internet Release, 12/23/99.

nonetheless, reinforces these historical patterns. The influx of immigrants into cities that are major ports of entry in particular can significantly increase residential segregation in these cities (Pollard and O'Hare, 1999). Segregation can also reflect migrants' choices of destination (South and Crowder, 1998). Hispanic segregation is more heavily influenced by recent immigration. The specific influences underlying segregation have changed considerably more over time than the basic realities of discrimination and the persistence of segregation.

Demographers have several different indices to measure how segregated populations are. Measuring segregation involves a comparison of how a specified minority is distributed across the neighborhoods (usually census tracts or block areas) of a city compared to the majority population. A commonly used measure of segregation is the *dissimilarity index*. As an equation, the index is simply

$$D = \frac{1}{2} \sum_{i=1}^{n} \left| m_i - o_i \right|$$

where m_i is the percentage of the city's total minority population that live in neighborhood i and o_i is the percentage of the total of all other city residents that live in the neighborhood. If every neighborhood has the same proportion of the city's minority residents as it has of the city's other residents, then the two populations are equally distributed and the dissimilarity index will be zero. At the other extreme, if minority and majority populations live in entirely different neighborhoods, the index will be 100. Although few would propose forced migrations to resolve segregation, the value of the dissimilarity index is easily interpreted as the percentage of minority residents who would have to move to other neighborhoods for them to have the same distribution as the rest of the population. (See Exercise 11-2 for an example of computing the dissimilarity index.)

Table 11-10 lists dissimilarity indices for both non-Hispanic blacks and Hispanics in the largest metropolitan statistical areas of the United States. In column 1 the MSAs are ordered from those in which non-Hispanic blacks are most segregated, such as Detroit, Chicago, and Cleveland, to those in which they are least segregated, such as Phoenix, San Bernadino, and Anaheim. It is apparent that the most segregated cities for blacks are generally those in the old industrial North while the least segregated are those in the West and South. Blacks migrating to the North in search of employment, and to escape from southern segregation, instead found discriminatory housing and employ-

Table 11-10
Segregation of Non-Hispanic Blacks and Hispanics in the 25 Largest MSAs[a], United States, 1990

Non-Hispanic Blacks		Hispanics	
Metropolitan Statistical Area (1)	Dissimilarity Index (2)	Metropolitan Statistical Area (3)	Dissimilarity Index (4)
Detroit	88.0	Newark	67.0
Chicago	85.9	New York	66.0
Cleveland	85.3	Philadelphia	63.9
Newark	82.9	Chicago	63.8
New York	82.4	Los Angeles	61.2
Philadelphia	77.8	Boston	57.5
Nassau/Suffolk	77.4	Cleveland	56.4
St. Louis	77.3	Miami	50.4
Los Angeles	73.4	Anaheim	50.2
Miami	71.9	Dallas	49.8
Pittsburgh	71.7	Houston	49.5
Baltimore	71.6	Phoenix	48.4
Boston	70.8	Denver	46.8
Tampa	70.2	Tampa	46.2
Oakland	68.2	San Diego	46.1
Atlanta	67.9	Detroit	45.2
Houston	67.0	Pittsburgh	44.7
Denver	65.1	Nassau/Suffolk	43.0
Dallas	63.2	Minneapolis	40.5
Minneapolis	63.1	Oakland	38.8
San Diego	59.1	Atlanta	36.9
Seattle	57.9	Baltimore	36.3
Phoenix	50.8	San Bernadino/Riverside	36.0
San Bernadino/Riverside	43.5	St. Louis	31.6
Anaheim	40.7	Seattle	24.5

[a]Excluding Washington, DC.
Source: Author's calculations from 1990 Census STF3a data.

ment practices (Sugrue, 1996). The resulting segregation persists to the present. Looking at column 2, for example, the dissimilarity index for Detroit suggests that almost nine of ten non-Hispanic blacks in the city would have to move to achieve an equal integration of neighborhoods in the city. Even in the least segregated of these MSAs, Anaheim, four of ten non-Hispanic blacks would have to relocate to achieve an equal integration.

Columns 3 and 4 give similar data for Hispanics. The regional nature of segregation is less consistent for Hispanics, yet the four most segregated of these MSAs are cities of the old industrial North, and the three least segregated are more recent western or southern cities. Also apparent from column 4 is the fact that Hispanics are in general less segregated than non-Hispanic blacks.

Why is segregation a problem and who considers it a problem? The answer may seem self-evident to many of our readers. There is a long history of demographic research showing that segregation limits opportunities and results in a spatial concentration of poverty and economic inequality (e.g. Jargowsky, 1997; Wilson, 1997; Massey and Denton, 1993; Massey, 1996). The concentration of poverty in segregated ethnic neighborhoods is both a cause and a consequence of limited social and economic opportunities for individuals in these areas worldwide (Massey, 1996).

The limits segregation places upon population groups are universally acknowledged as social problems. At the same time, as we've seen in Figures 11-10 and 11-11, many ethnic immigrants choose to live in the same regions and cities as other members of the same ethnic group. In fact, many immigrants wish to live in the specific neighborhoods, or enclaves—such as "Little Havana" in Miami, Florida—where others share the same culture. These voluntary assortative residential decisions must be distinguished from segregation, which is the imposed or forced separation of population groups. However, decisions to live in an ethnic enclave may limit some long-term opportunities and reinforce segregation even as it fulfills short-term desires.

There is considerable interest among demographers in the trends of ethnic segregation and their possible causes. There have been some recent, but slight, declines in U.S. segregation (Farley and Frey, 1994). Yet segregation has increased in many of the very largest metropolitan areas (Massey and Denton, 1993). Immigration has reinforced segregation patterns. Internal migration patterns of net black migration out of white neighborhoods and net white migration out of black neighborhoods reinforce and recreate segregation (South and Crowder, 1998). At the same time, it does not appear to be the case that socioeconomic differences in migration—for example, wealthy blacks leaving ethnic neighborhoods—are responsible for the concentration of poverty in ethnic neighborhoods (South and Crowder, 1998; Massey et al., 1994). Instead, both segregation and the concentration of ethnic poverty are substantially increased by persistent job discrimination and segregated housing markets (Fishman, 1999; Massey et al., 1994).

Inequities in Health

Although the health of the U.S. population has improved over the past century, as we have seen in chapters 5 and 6, the largest of the ethnic minority groups, i.e. blacks and Hispanics, still have poorer health and higher mortality. For example, over the past two decades life expectancy has increased more rapidly for whites than for blacks, causing the gap in average life expectancy actually to increase.

Ethnic health inequities are a social problem for all who see these differences in health as a reflection of more basic social injustices. Indeed, much of the difference in ethnic group health arises from the lower socioeconomic status and more limited access to health care among ethnic minorities. Only about 12% of non-Hispanic whites had no health care coverage in 1997; in comparison, 21% of both blacks and Asian Americans, 25% of American Indians, and 34% of Hispanics reported no health care coverage (Pollard and O'Hare, 1999). These inequities are also a special epidemiological concern to public health officials who see the greatest potential for overall improvement in public health in lowering the high morbidity and mortality of these more vulnerable groups. With an infant mortality rate twice that of whites, reducing infant mortality among blacks is, for example, critical to continued overall declines in infant mortality.

Social inequities are reflected in many specific health problems that disproportionately burden ethnic minorities. Many ethnic groups face higher mortality from HIV/AIDS at all ages, much higher rates of mortality from homicide among males, low-birthweight babies with more frequent developmental problems, and higher diabetes mortality among women, among other inequities in health (Pollard and O'Hare, 1999). These health problems reflect the less adequate residential environs, socioeconomic resources, and nutrition than the more privileged non-Hispanic white population enjoys. Alas, these inequities in health are unlikely to be eliminated without a reduction in basic social inequality.

Higher Ethnic Group Fertility

Many ethnic groups also have much higher fertility than do non-Hispanic whites. Overall, in 1997 ethnic minority births comprised 40% of all births, although these ethnic groups accounted for only 28% of the population (Pollard and O'Hare, 1999). The generally younger age composition of ethnic minorities (see Figure 11-2) is partly responsible for this difference. In a younger population more women are likely to be of childbearing ages. However, age-specific fertility rates of women in the largest ethnic groups are also higher than those of white women at the same age (see chapter 7).

Who considers this higher fertility a problem? Is higher minority fertility a problem only to radical racists who fear the loss of numerical dominance by current majority groups? Certainly, ethnic and racial defensiveness does play a role in concern with higher minority fertility. Many aging white communities, for example, have expressed political aversion to taxes needed to support the education and schooling of predominately ethnic minority children.

Yet there are other reasons for concern with high fertility among ethnic groups. A primary one is higher rates of teenage motherhood and childbearing out of wedlock. In 1997 teenagers accounted for 22% of black births, 21% of American Indian births, 17% of Hispanic births, 10% of non-Hispanic white births, and 5% of Asian and Pacific Islander births. Higher levels of teen childbearing are, in turn, associated with negative health, social, and economic consequences for mothers and children (Pollard and O'Hare, 1999; Ventura et al., 1998).

Accommodating Ethnic Immigrants

Immigration is a major component of growth in the ethnic populations of the United States, accounting for about two-fifths of the growth in Hispanics and two-thirds of the growth in Asian Americans in the last decade (Pollard and O'Hare, 1999). This means that many people in these ethnic groups came to this country recently. In fact, most Asian Americans were not born in the United States.

Who considers this immigration a problem? Of course, there are again some people and politicians who simply have a xenophobic fear of immigrants and view all immigration as a problem. However, many others have more specific concerns over the changing nature of ethnic immigration.

One concern, as we have suggested, is with the growth of segregated immigrant communities. While immigrant communities and ethnic enclaves do provide support for newcomers, they can also isolate immigrant groups, slowing the acquisition of English and the assimilation of newcomers into mainstream society (Pollard and O'Hare, 1999).

Another concern is the very young age structure of some ethnic groups, resulting from age-selectivity in migration and high fertility after arrival. On the one hand, this young ethnic population can serve as an antidote for the aging of the non-Hispanic workforce. However, Pollard and O'Hare note there are special concerns with preparing this new generation to fulfill their role as the future workforce of the United States:

> Minorities' growing share of U.S. children—the future workforce—has implications for American businesses and public policy. Minorities have lower educational attainment and higher poverty rates than whites, on average. Because such a large percentage are immigrants or the children of immigrants, many Asian and Hispanic children have limited English skills and require special language classes. Policymakers will need to ensure that minority children from disadvantaged homes receive adequate education, nutrition, and health care in order to provide the nation with a trained and competitive work force in the years ahead. (1999, p. 7)

In sum, there is a glaring lack of national consensus about the value of heavy immigration into the United States, especially from less-developed regions (Pollard and O'Hare, 1999). Some groups fear the loss of less-skilled jobs to recent ethnic immigrants while others feel immigrants are needed to fill demands for such labor. Political movements in some high-immigration states have been formed by taxpayers opposing provision of basic social services to recent or illegal immigrants.

Accordingly, there is little consensus on immigration policy issues:

> Should we try to slow or increase the flow of immigrants? Should we give a greater preference to foreign relatives of U.S. residents or immigrants with valuable skills and financial resources to invest in our economy? How much should we spend to apprehend and deport illegal immigrants? Events outside Americans' control—population pressures, racial and ethnic strife, and poor economic opportunities—will determine the origins and numbers of people who want to come to this country. But, U.S. policies will determine how many and whom we will accept and, in part, reflect Americans' assessment of the effect of minorities on society. (Pollard and O'Hare, 1999, p. 3)

SUMMARY

Diversity refers to the variety of cultural groups in a population and the even distribution of the population across these groups. Ethnicity, race, and ancestry are common demographic terms which refer to diverse cultural groups. Some countries, such as Ethiopia (with over thirty official ethnic groups), have been diverse since their national inception, but most nations have experienced rapidly increasing population diversity over the past century. Growth in international migration has been the greatest source of this increasing population diversity.

Because ethnicity, race, and ancestry are culturally defined, groups identified vary from one national population to another. Definitions also change dramatically over time within nations. These unstandardized definitions complicate the measurement of diversity over time and across populations.

Nonetheless, it is clear that in the United States diversity is increasing. In the last half-century the "minority" ethnic population (i.e. nonwhites and Hispanic groups) has more than tripled in size. By 2050 it is projected that nearly half of the country's population will be nonwhite and/or Hispanic. Hispanics and Asian Americans are the fastest growing ethnic groups in the country—and in the first decade of this century Hispanics will overtake blacks as the largest ethnic minority in the country.

Most ethnic minorities in the United States have a young age composition and high growth rates. Because of young ethnic populations, diversity in the working-age population is even greater than in the total population, and will increase rapidly in the near future. Diversity of young adults is also producing a sharp increase in ethnic intermarriage, further confounding ethnic identity in the coming century. Today's ethnic youth, disproportionately disadvantaged, will need the training and education to be the nation's future workforce.

Youthfulness of ethnic populations is a result of higher fertility and age-selective immigration. One concern with higher ethnic fertility rates is the negative effects of adolescent fertility on mothers and children. More generally, most ethnic minorities experience poorer health and have higher mortality. The poorer health of these populations is largely due to their lower average socioeconomic status, inadequate access to health care, and greater lack of health insurance. There is widespread concern over the generally poorer health and higher mortality of ethnic minorities in the United States.

Most ethnic immigrants migrate to a relatively few states and major metropolitan areas, increasing differences between regions of the United States and concentrating ethnic populations within major urban areas. Concentration in urban areas and in ethnic enclaves in the cities has contributed to the persistence of urban segregation in recent decades. Ethnic segregation, in turn, has historically resulted in concentrated pockets of poverty and social disadvantage that are difficult to escape. Ethnic enclaves, which may provide support and comfort to arriving immigrants, may ultimately sustain segregation or slow immigrants' entry into mainstream society and the opportunities it affords.

Rising diversity is a major demographic trend, not only in the United States but also in more-developed regions generally, as resident populations age and younger ethnic immigrants arrive. Because these arriving cultural groups often have different demographic behaviors, diversity will impact the demography of many countries throughout the coming century. Changes in population diversity will present both new challenges and new opportunities to these nations.

▶ **EXERCISES**

1. The projected age composition of several ethnic groups in 2025 is summarized in Table E11-1. Using this information, and formulas from chapter 4, compute and fill in the missing age dependency ratios for Hispanics and non-Hispanic whites.

Table E11-1
Projected Ethnic Populations (in 1,000s) by Age Group, United States, 2025

Age Group	Hispanic (1)	Non-Hispanic		
		White (2)	Black (3)	American Indian, Eskimo and Aleut (4)	Asian and Pacific Islander (5)
0–14	16,646	36,211	9,194	611	4,377
15–64	38,682	125,868	28,066	1,720	13,800
65+	6,105	47,260	6,268	338	2,670
Age-Dependency Ratio			55.1	55.2	51.1

Source: U.S. Bureau of the Census, *Projections, Series A - Middle, 2025*, Internet Release, January 2000.

a. Which ethnic group will probably have the highest dependency ratio in 2025? _____

b. Which ethnic group will probably have the lowest dependency ratio in 2025? _____

2. The calculation of dissimilarity indices are illustrated for two small university towns in Table E11-2 (neither town is highly segregated). Computations for the town of Amherst, Massachusetts are complete. Fill in the blanks to complete the computations of the dissimilarity index in Morgantown, West Virginia. (Use the fact that the first two columns of this table should total to 100% to derive the missing entries in those columns.) Then, answer the following questions about the results:

a. In which town are the tracts in which blacks reside more dissimilar from those in which whites reside? _____

b. Are blacks or Hispanics more segregated in Morgantown, West Virginia?
_____

c. From this example, which of the following statements best describes the meaning of a high dissimilarity index:

i. All neighborhoods in the city are segregated.

ii. All neighborhoods in the city are well integrated.

iii. At least some neighborhoods in the city are segregated.

iv. At least some neighborhoods in the city are well integrated.

Table E11-2
Segregation in Two Small University Towns, United States Census Data, 1990

| Census Tract Number | Black | | | Hispanic | | |
	Percent of Black Population Residing in Tract (1)	Percent of Non-Black Population Residing In Tract (2)	Absolute Value of Difference |(1)-(2)| (3)	Percent of Hispanic Population Residing in Tract (4)	Percent of Non-Hispanic Population Residing in Tract (5)	Absolute Value of Difference |(4)-(5)| (6)
Amherst, MA						
8203	17.96	19.23	1.27	27.95	18.70	9.25
8204	24.85	28.84	4.00	21.30	29.05	7.76
8205	15.74	18.53	2.79	11.79	18.76	6.96
8206	5.66	4.21	1.45	5.53	4.21	1.32
8207	13.41	11.04	2.37	13.19	11.04	2.15
820801	19.68	15.25	4.43	17.55	15.34	2.21
820802	2.71	2.90	0.19	2.68	2.90	0.21
		Total of Differences =	16.49		Total of Differences =	29.87
			÷ 2			÷ 2
		Dissimilarity Index =	8.2		Dissimilarity Index =	14.9
Morgantown, WV						
0101	12.30	10.61	1.69	12.85	10.63	2.22
0102	6.62	10.45	3.83	11.38	10.32	1.06
0103	11.65	7.48	4.17	6.67	7.62	0.95
0104	2.45	8.03	5.59	3.74	7.92	4.18
0105	0.79	5.03	4.24	5.69	4.89	0.80
0106	5.83	10.39	4.56	18.37	10.14	8.23
0107	15.18	5.94	9.24	4.72	6.24	1.52
0108	0.00	2.57	2.57	2.28	2.49	0.21
0109	18.85	10.27	8.58	5.53	10.60	5.07
0110		8.69		16.42	9.02	7.40
0118	3.31			12.36	20.13	7.77
		Total of Differences =			Total of Differences =	39.42
			÷ 2			÷ 2
		Dissimilarity Index =			Dissimilarity Index =	19.71

Source: U. S. Bureau of the Census, 1990 Tract Level Data Files.

PROPOSITIONS FOR DEBATE

1. The 2000 census demonstrates the difficulty of classifying the U.S. population on the basis of ethnic identity. Therefore, the Census Bureau should give up this undertaking as futile and meaningless.

2. Since most ethnic groups in the U.S. have similar demographic characteristics, it is safe to treat them as a homogeneous class.

3. Ethnic differences in mortality and health are solely due to socioeconomic differences between ethnic groups in the United States.

4. Ethnic differences in fertility rates are due to cultural and religious differences among ethnic groups and not socioeconomic differences.

5. Immigration and the increasing diversity of the U.S. population will decrease ethnic segregation in urban areas.

6. The United States is becoming a more divided nation because of the large concentration of immigration in a few states.

7. Segregation is no longer caused by overt discrimination and limited opportunities but simply because minority groups most often prefer to live with others of similar cultural background.

REFERENCES AND SELECTED READINGS

Anderton, Douglas L., Richard E. Barrett, and Donald J. Bogue. 1997. *The Population of the United States*. 3rd ed. New York: Free Press.

Austin, M. A. 1993. "The Kaiser-Permanente Women Twin Study Data Set." *Genetic Epidemiology* 10(6).

Banister, Judith. 1992. "Vietnam: Population Dynamics and Prospects." Bureau of the Census, *Center for International Research, Staff Paper no. 65*.

Bauman, Kurt J. 1999. "Shifting Family Definitions: The Effect of Cohabitation and Other Nonfamily Household Relationships on Measures of Poverty." *Demography* 36(3).

Bonvalet, C., J. Carpenter, and P. White. 1995. "The Residential Mobility of Ethnic Minorities: A Longitudinal Analysis." *Urban Studies* 32(1).

Bureau of Labor Statistics. 1996. "Testing Methods of Collecting Racial and Ethnic Information: Results of the Current Population Survey Supplement on Race and Ethnicity." *BLS Statistical Notes* 40.

Centers for Disease Control. 1998. *Health, United States, 1999*. DHHS Publication no. 99–1232. Washington, DC: Government Printing Office.

Edmonston, Barry, and Charles Shultze, eds. 1995. *Modernizing the U.S. Census*. Panel on Census Requirements in the Year 2000 and Beyond, Committee on National Statistics, Commission on Behavioral and Social Sciences and Education, National Research Council. Washington, DC.

Farley, Reynolds, and William H. Frey. 1994. "Changes in the Segregation of Whites from Blacks during the 1980s: Small Steps Toward a More Integrated Society." *American Sociological Review* 59(1).

Fishman, Robert. 1999. "The American Metropolis and Century's End: Past and Future Influences." *Housing Facts and Findings* 1(4).

Friedrichs, J. 1998. "Ethnic Segregation in Cologne, Germany 1984–94." *Urban Studies* 35(10).

Garner, C., T. Tatu, J. E. Reittie, T. Littlewood, J. Darley, S. Cervino, M. Farrall, P. Kelly, T. D. Spector, and S. L. Thein. 2000. "Genetic Influences on F Cells and other Hematologic Variables: A Twin Heritability Study." *Blood* 95(1).

Harris, C. D. 1993. "A Geographic Analysis of non-Russian Minorities in Russia and its Ethnic Homelands." *Post-Soviet Geography* 34(19).

Hayward, Mark D., and Melanie Heron. 1999. "Racial Inequality in Active Life Among Adult Americans." *Demography* 36(1).

Immigration and Naturalization Service (INS). 2000. *Legal Immigration, Fiscal Year 1998. Annual Report no. 1.* Washington, DC: Department of Justice.

Jargowsky, Paul A. 1997. *Poverty and Place: Ghettos, Barrios, and the American City.* New York: Russell Sage Press.

Kallan, Jeffrey E. 1998. "Drug Abuse-Related Mortality in the United States: Patterns and Correlates." *American Journal of Drug and Alcohol Abuse* 24(1).

Kass, Barbara L., Robin M. Weinick, and Alan C. Monheit. 1999. *Racial and Ethnic Differences in Health, 1996.* MEPS Chartbook no. 2. AHCPR Pub. no. 99-0001. Rockville, MD: Agency for Health Care Policy and Research.

Kesteloot, C., J. van Weesep, and P. White. 1997. "Minorities in West European Cities." *Journal of Economic and Social Geography* 88(2).

Lee, Sharon. 1998. "Asian Americans: Diverse and Growing." *Population Bulletin* 53(2).

Marger, Martin N. 2000. *Race and Ethnic Relations: American and Global Perspectives.* 5th ed. Belmont, CA: Wadsworth/Thomson Learning.

Massey, Douglas S. 1996. "The Age of Extremes: Concentrated Affluence and Poverty in the Twenty-First Century." *Demography* 33(4).

Massey, Douglas S., and Nancy A. Denton. 1993. *American Apartheid: Segregation and the Making of the Underclass.* Cambridge, MA: Harvard University Press.

Massey, Douglas S., Andrew B. Gross, and Kumiko Shibuya. 1994. "Migration, Segregation, and the Geographic Concentration of Poverty." *American Sociological Review* 59(3).

McEvedy, Colin, and Richard Jones. 1978. *Atlas of World Population History.* London: A. Lane.

National Center for Health Statistics. 1999a. "Deaths: Final Data for 1997." *National Vital Statistics Reports* 47(19). Washington, DC: Government Printing Office.

———. 1999b. "Highlights of Trends in Pregnancies and Pregnancy Rates by Outcome: Estimates for the United States, 1976–96." *National Vital Statistics Reports* 47(2).

———. 1999c. "Births: Final Data for 1997." *National Vital Statistics Reports* 47(18).

O'Hare, William P. 1992. "America's Minorities—The Demographics of Diversity." *Population Bulletin* 47(4).

O'Hare, William P., Kelvin M. Pollard, Taynia L. Mann, and Mary M. Kent. 1991. "African Americans in the 1990s." *Population Bulletin* 46(1).

Pannel, C. W., and J. S. Torguson. 1991. "Interpreting Spatial Patterns from the 1990 China Census." *Geographical Review* 81(3).

Pinal, Jorge del, and Audrey Singer. 1997. "Generations of Diversity: Latinos in the United States." *Population Bulletin* 52(3).

Pollard, Kelvin M., and William P. O'Hare. 1999. "America's Racial and Ethnic Minorities." *Population Bulletin* 54(3).

Ries, Peter. 1990. "Health of Black and White Americans, 1985–87." *NCHS Vital and Health Statistics Report* 10(171).

Rogers, Richard G. 1992. "Living and Dying in the U.S.A.: Sociodemographic Determinants of Death among Blacks and Whites." *Demography* 29(2).

Santelli, John S., Nancy D. Brener, Richard Lowry, Amita Bhatt, and Laurie S. Zabin. 1998. "Multiple Sexual Partners Among U.S. Adolescents and Young Adults." *Family Planning Perspectives* 30(6).

Soloway, Richard A. 1990. *Demography and Degeneration: Eugenics and the Declining Birthrate in Twentieth-Century Britain*. Chapel Hill: University of North Carolina Press.

South, Scott J., and Kyle D. Crowder. 1998. "Leaving the 'Hood: Residential Mobility Between Black, White, and Integrated Neighborhoods." *American Sociological Review* 59(1).

Spain, Daphne. 1999. "America's Diversity: On the Edge of Two Centuries." *Reports on America* 1(2). Population Reference Bureau.

Sugrue, Thomas J. 1996. *The Origins of the Urban Crisis: Race and Inequality in Postwar Detroit*. Princeton, NJ: Princeton University Press.

United States Bureau of the Census. 1993. *Population Projections of the United States, by Age, Sex, Race, and Hispanic Origin: 1993 to 2050*. Current Population Reports, Series P-25 no. 1104. Washington, DC: Government Printing Office.

———. 1998. *Statistical Abstract of the United States, 1998*. Washington, DC: Government Printing Office.

———. 1999. *Findings on Questions on Race and Hispanic Origin Tested in the 1996 National Content Survey*. Internet Release Revised March 23.

van Kempen, R. and J. van Weesep. 1998. "Ethnic Residential Patterns in Dutch Cities: Backgrounds, Shifts, and Consequences." *Urban Studies* 35(10).

Ventura, S. J., T. J. Mathews, and S. C. Curtin. 1998. "Declines in Teenage Birth Rates, 1991–97: National and State Patterns." *National Vital Statistics Reports* 47(12).

Waldinger, Roger. 1989. "Immigration and Urban Change." *Annual Review of Sociology* 15.

Wilson, William J. 1997. *When Work Disappears: The World of the New Urban Poor*. New York: Vintage Books.

Glossary

abortion   termination of a pregnancy after the implantation of the blastocyst (fertilized egg) in the endometrium (uterine wall) but before the fetus is viable. Includes both spontaneous and induced abortions. (chapter 7)

abortion rate   a rate whose numerator is the estimated number of *induced* abortions in a given year and whose denominator is some estimate of the at-risk population of *women*. Thus potentially there can be crude, general, and age-specific abortion rates analogous to birth and fertility rates. However, *abortion rate,* unmodified, usually means the number of induced abortions per 1,000 women aged 15–44, analogous to the general fertility rate. (chapter 7)

abortion ratio   a ratio whose numerator is the estimated number of induced abortions in a given year and whose denominator is some measure of the *pregnancies* at risk of being aborted. The at-risk population can be either the number of live births in the given year or the number of live births plus the legal abortions in that year. Abortion ratios can be either crude (for the total population) or specific (for an age or other category). (chapter 7)

age-dependency ratio   the number of people in the economically dependent ages (conventionally, younger than 15 and 65 or older) per one hundred people in the economically productive ages (conventionally, 15–64). Synonym: dependency ratio. (chapter four)

age heaping   the tendency of respondents to report age, or date of birth, as years ending in zero, five, or even numbers, sometimes especially avoiding numbers that are culturally taboo.

age-sex pyramid   see **population pyramid**. (chapter 4)

age-sex-specific rate   a rate referring to the performance of a subset of the population defined by age and sex. Examples: age-sex-specific death rates, age-specific fertility rates for females. (chapter 4)

age-sex structure   the composition of a population with respect to age and sex; the distribution of a population among categories defined by a combination of age and sex. (chapter 4)

age structure   the composition of a population with respect to age; the distribution of a population among age categories. (chapter 4)

aging of a population   increase in the median age of a population. (chapter 4)

ancestry   narrowly defined, the birthplace of one's parents; broadly defined, the *ethnic group* from which one claims biological descent. (chapter 11)

area of destination   in the context of migration, the area where the migration ended; the location of the host society. Synonym: place of destination. (chapter 9)

area of origin   in the context of migration, the area from which the migration started; the location of the donor society. Synonym: place of origin. (chapter 9)

at-risk population   that set of people who could have produced a specified kind of population event, for example, a death, a birth, or a migration. (chapter 1)

average   in statistical usage, the arithmetic mean, the total of all scores divided by number of cases. More casually, the one value that best represents all cases in a set. Another measure is a median, the score above which and below which one-half the cases fall.

baby-boom   in the United States, the increase in fertility that extended from the late 1940s through the early 1960s, peaking in 1957. (chapter 7)

birth control   measures taken to delay or avoid a birth, including contraception and induced abortion. (chapter 7)

cause of death   the principal cause of death as recorded by the responsible authority in the registration process. Ideally, the immediate cause (such as homicide, cancer, heart attack) as contrasted with secondary or contributing causes (murder motive, smoking, high cholesterol buildup). (chapter 5)

cause-specific death rate   a mortality rate indicating the number of deaths attributable to a specific cause per 100,000 population in a given year. (chapters 5, 11)

census   a complete count of every inhabitant of a given geographic entity at a given time. (chapter 2)

cohabitation   the living together of two persons of opposite sex in a conjugal, usually nonmarital, union. Sometimes includes same-sex couples presumed equivalent in social function to cohabiting heterosexual couples. (chapter 8)

cohort   generally, a set of people defined on the basis of experiencing some specified population event during the same short period of time. Thus a birth cohort is a set of people having similar birth dates and current ages, also known as a generation. When demographers use the term cohort unmodified, they usually mean birth cohort. (chapter 4)

cohort completed fertility   the average number of children born per woman in a birth cohort surviving the childbearing period. Can be measured by a *cohort completed fertility rate*. Synonym: completed family size. (chapter 7)

cohort completed fertility rate   the average number of children born per woman in a cohort by the end of their childbearing years. A measure of cohort completed family size. Analogous to a total fertility rate, but constructed for a real cohort, rather than a hypothetical one. (chapter 7)

cohort-component projection   a population projection in which each birth cohort is projected separately, resulting in a projection of age-sex structure as well as size. (chapter 4)

cohort perspective   the viewing of a population process longitudinally, as the cumulative life experience of a cohort. Used in cohort analysis or generational analysis. Contrast with **period perspective**. (chapter 8)

components of population growth   the only events by which a population's size can be influenced directly: births, deaths, and migrations. See **growth equation**. (chapter 1)

conception   the fertilization of an ovum by a sperm, marking the beginning of pregnancy or gestation. (chapter 7)

consensual union   a nonmarital sexual union that is relatively socially recognized and stable. (chapter 8)

consequences   effects.

contraception   measures taken to prevent coitus from resulting in conception. (chapter 7)

crude birth rate   the number of live births per 1,000 total population in a given year. Sometimes called simply the birth rate. (chapters 1, 7)

crude death rate   the number of deaths per 1,000 total population in a given year. Sometimes called simply the death rate. (chapters 1, 5)

crude rate   a period rate whose denominator is the total population. (chapter 1)

de facto population   the population physically present in an area at a given moment, such as a census moment. Contrast with **de jure population**. (chapter 2)

de jure population   the population that usually or habitually lives in an area. Synonym: resident population. Contrast with **de facto population**. (chapter 2)

demographic description   characterizing past or present populations in terms of their demographic variables, taken either singly or in combination. (chapter 1)

demographic transition   transition from a situation where fertility and mortality are high and uncontrolled to a situation where fertility and mortality are low and controlled. (chapter 3)

demographic variables   dimensions of variation among populations with respect to their size, growth and components of growth, and composition. (chapter 1)

demography   the scientific study of human population, its size and composition, dynamic life-course processes that change this composition (birth, death, marriage, migration, etc.), and relationships of population composition and change with social and physical environments.

density   see **population density**.

dependency ratio   see **age-dependency ratio**.

determinants   causes.

differential   in the context of studying the population processes, differences among the members of a set of compositional categories with respect to the incidence of the specified process. For instance, differential mortality, differential fertility, or differential migration.

disability adjusted life-years lost   the sum of years of life lost and years lived with disability, giving a total picture of morbidity and mortality impacts due to a specific cause. (chapter 6)

dissimilarity index   a measure of residential segregation based on comparing the distribution of members of a group among a set of residential areas in comparison with the distribution of nonmembers of that group. (chapter 11)

distribution   in a statistical context, the numbers of cases falling within a series of categories. In a frequency distribution, each category is represented by the absolute number of cases; in a percentage distribution, each category is represented by a proportion of the total cases. See also **population distribution**. (chapter 4)

diversity   see **population diversity**.

divorced   a marital status category, usually meaning currently not married by reason of civil dissolution of marriage from last spouse. (chapter 8)

doubling time   the time it would take for a population to double at a given annual growth rate. (chapter 3)

echo effect   the tendency toward repetition, one generation hence, of any span of abnormally high (or low) fertility, caused by the effect of the initial fertility level upon the age structure. (chapter 7)

emigration   migration out of a nation. See **out-migration**. (chapter 9)

empty-nest period   that part of the family cycle when adults remain in a household but all their children have left to establish their own residence elsewhere. (chapter 8)

epidemic   a mass outbreak of a disease that spreads and then disappears within a fairly short time. Where it appears in a large number of countries it is called a *pandemic*. Both terms contrast with endemic disease, which is a condition that more or less permanently affects substantial segments of a population. (chapter 5)

epidemiology   the study of the distribution of diseases or conditions in human populations. (chapter 5)

ethnic group   a group sharing a common subculture with unique cultural traits (e.g. language, religion) and, to some degree, a sense of community, ethnocentrism, ascribed membership, and distinct territoriality. (chapter 11)

European marriage pattern   the pattern that distinguished Western Europe during the eighteenth and nineteenth centuries, namely late marriage and large proportions never marrying. (chapter 8)

ever-married   a marital status combining (currently) married, divorced, and widowed. (chapter 8)

family cycle   the normal sequence of marital status and family formation changes occurring in a society, along with their timing. (chapter 8)

family planning   attempts by couples to regulate the number and spacing of their births. (chapter 7)

family-planning program   a government-sponsored effort to provide the information, supplies, and services for modern fertility control to those interested. (chapter 7)

family reconstitution   the linking of birth, marriage, and death dates of each married couple and their children, taken from administrative records (e.g. vital records or parish registers) into a chronology of vital events for family members. (chapter 7)

fecundability   the probability of conceiving per menstrual cycle among women who menstruate regularly and do not practice contraception. (chapter 7)

fecundity   the biological capacity of a man, a woman, or a couple to produce a live birth. (chapter 7)

fertility   the childbearing performance of individuals, couples, or groups as indicated by the frequency with which birth occurs in a population. (chapter 7)

fertility rate   see **general fertility rate**.

fertility transition   a part of the demographic transition in which fertility declines from a high, constant, and uncontrolled level to a low, variable, and controlled level. (chapters 3, 7)

fetal death   death of a fetus, usually after at least four weeks of pregnancy and including both spontaneous abortions or miscarriages—deaths before 28 weeks of pregnancy—and stillbirths—deaths after that period. (chapter 7)

forced or impelled migration   migration in which individuals are compelled by authorities or events to move. Includes flight or displacement and the creation of refugees. Historically also would include migration for slavery and involuntary indentured servitude. (chapter 9)

formal demography   the study of demographic variables separate from related nondemographic variables. To be distinguished from population studies. (chapter 1)

free migration   migration resulting from the initiative and free choice of the migrants, either individually or as a mass. Synonym: spontaneous, voluntary migration. (chapter 9)

frontier regions   in the context of world regions, those MDRs that have received large-scale immigration from Europe in recent centuries: North America, Australia, and New Zealand. (chapter 3)

general fertility rate   the number of live births per 1,000 women aged 15–44 (or 15–49) in a given year. Sometimes called simply the *fertility rate*. (chapter 7)

gestation period   duration of pregnancy. (chapter 7)

gross migration   the sum of migration into and out of a given area. In the context of migration streams, the sum of the migration streams in both directions between two areas. Synonym: volume of migration. Contrast with **net migration**. (chapter 9)

gross reproduction rate   the average number of daughters that would be born to a set of women during their lifetimes if they passed through their childbearing years conforming to the age-specific fertility rates of a given year. Like the total fertility rate but not counting sons. (chapter 7)

growth equation   the formula that specifies the components of growth during a specified time: $P_2 - P_1 = B - D + M$. Sometimes called (redundantly) the *balancing equation*. (chapter 1)

growth rate   the ratio of the total change in a population during a period to the average population (usually the midpoint population) during that period. (chapter 3)

historical demography   demography of pre-modern times that is based on a variety of early written records. (chapter 7)

household   a set of individuals who reside together, whether or not related. Commonly defined in censuses as those who make common provision for food and living essentials. (chapter 8)

hypothetical cohort   an imaginary set of people traced through a series of specified risks in order to detail the cumulative impact of those risks. This strategy is used in the construction of life tables and the computation of life expectancy, as well as the construction of total fertility rates. Synonym: **synthetic cohort**. (chapters 5, 7)

illegal migration   that migration which conflicts with the laws of a country governing entry or departure of migrants. (chapter 9)

immigration   migration into a nation. See **in-migration**. (chapter 9)

incidence rate   the number of persons contracting a disease as a proportion of the population at risk, per specified unit of time. (chapter 6)

induced abortion   an abortion that is assumed to result from action intended to cause it. (chapter 7)

inequality   an uneven distribution of population groups across categories such as income, opportunity, treatment, or status, generating or reflecting social or economic disparities. (chapter 11)

infant mortality   the mortality among live-born children who have not yet reached their first birthday. (chapter 5)

infant mortality rate   the number of deaths among infants under one year of age, per 1,000 live births in the same year. (chapter 5)

in-migration   migration into an area usually smaller than a nation. See **immigration**. (chapter 9)

intermediate variable   if a change in one variable results in a change in a second variable, which in turn results in a change in a third variable, then the second variable is called the intermediate variable. In the context of fertility explanation, intermediate variables are those proximate determinants of fertility that are intermediate between sociocultural and economic determinants on the one hand, and fertility itself on the other. (chapter 7)

internal migration   migration between parts of a nation or smaller geographic units. (chapter 9)

less-developed countries (LDCs)   those countries with technologically less developed or preindustrial economies. Synonyms: developing countries, Third-World countries. (chapter 3)

less-developed regions (LDRs)   world regions consisting largely of less-developed countries (LDCs). (chapter 3)

life course   the sequence of sociodemographic stages through which individuals pass from birth to death, usually with an emphasis on householding, marriage, schooling, and employment. Synonyms: life cycle, life history. (chapter 8)

life expectancy   the average (mean) number of years yet to be lived by people attaining a given age, according to a given life table. If the age is unspecified, it is assumed to be zero, in which case life expectancy means life expectancy at birth. (chapter 5)

life table   a table used for tracing the cumulative effect of a specified series of age-sex-specific death rates over a life cycle for a hypothetical cohort; the table used to compute life expectancy. (chapter 5)

longevity   the length of an individual life. Collectively, average length of life of a cohort. (chapter 5)

Malthusianism   based upon the writings of Thomas Malthus; specifically, believing that population tends to outstrip the means for its subsistence. (chapter 3)

marital dissolution   the combined processes of spouse mortality and divorce. (chapter 8)

marital fertility   the fertility of married persons. Synonym: legitimate fertility. (chapter 7)

marital status   one's status with respect to marriage. See **single, never-married, married, widowed, divorced**. (chapter 8)

marriage   legal recognition of a sexual union. The combined processes of first marriage and remarriage. (chapter 8)

marriage cohort   a set of people identified on the basis of being married at about the same time. (chapter 8)

marriage market   all the men and women who, at a given time and place, are potential marital partners for each other. (chapter 8)

marriage squeeze   a restriction in the marriage market caused by imbalance between the sizes of succeeding birth cohorts, combined with persistent norms regarding relative ages of brides and grooms. (chapter 8)

married   marital status currently married, usually even if separated. (chapter 8)

Marxist   based upon the writings of Karl Marx.

maternal death   female death associated with pregnancy, labor, or the puerperium (the period immediately following childbirth). (chapter 5)

maternal mortality rate   the number of maternal deaths per 100,000 live births in a specified year. Synonym: maternal death rate. (chapter 5)

megalopolis a term denoting an interconnected group of cities in connecting urbanized bands. (chapter 10)

menarche the beginning of the female reproductive, or childbearing, period, signaled by the first menstrual flow. (chapter 7)

menopause the end of the female reproductive or childbearing period, signaled by the cessation of menstruation. (chapter 7)

metropolis a very large and/or important city. (chapter 10)

metropolitan area a large concentration of population usually consisting of a central city and surrounding settlements. (chapter 10)

metropolitanization the relative growth of metropolitan-area population, compared with other population. (chapter 10)

migrant an individual who migrates. (chapter 9)

migration a change in residence (involving social reaffiliation) across some specified geopolitical boundary. (chapter 9)

migration pull attraction by a place of destination, for a migrant. (chapter 9)

migration push repulsion by a place of origin, for a migrant. (chapter 9)

migration stream the people who migrate from a given area of origin to a given area of destination in a given period of time. (chapter 9)

misreporting in a census, misallocation of an enumerated person among compositional categories. A form of content error. (chapter 2)

mobility in a geographic or spatial context, the quantity of movement among geographic units, including not only migration but also temporary moves such as commuting, transit across units, tourism, and seasonal movements. (chapter 9)

morbidity the state of illness and disability in a population. Specifically, the incidence and/or prevalence of a disease or disability in a population. (chapter 6).

more-developed countries (MDCs) countries with technologically developed, industrial economies. Synonym: developed countries. (chapter 3)

more-developed regions (MDRs) world regions consisting almost entirely of more-developed countries (MDCs). (chapter 3)

mortality the frequency with which death occurs in a population. (chapter 5)

mortality transition a part of the demographic transition in which mortality declines from a high, variable, and uncontrolled level to a low, constant, and controlled level. (chapters 3, 5)

natural increase births minus deaths. (chapter 1)

neo-Malthusianism believing (as Thomas Malthus did) in the tendency for population to outstrip the means for its subsistence and advocating (as Malthus did not) the promotion of birth control as a solution to this dilemma. (chapter 3)

net migration migration into an area minus migration out of that area. (chapters 1, 9)

never-married single in marital status and not having been married previously. (chapter 8)

nonmarital fertility fertility of persons not currently married. Synonym: illegitimate fertility. (chapter 7)

nuptiality the formation and dissolution of marriages and other stable sexual unions. (chapters 1, 8)

old-age dependency   the proportion of the population judged too old to be fully economically productive; usually measured as the percent aged 65 or over. (chapter 4)

out-migration   migration out of an area smaller than a nation. See **emigration**. (chapter 9)

parity   the number of children previously born alive to a woman. (chapter 7)

period perspective   the viewing of a population process cross-sectionally, as the combined experience of cohorts in a specified short period of time, normally one year. Employed in period analysis or cross-sectional analysis, usually involving period rates. See **cohort perspective**. (chapter 8)

period rate   a rate measuring the incidence of a population event during a specified short period of time, such as one year for an annual rate. (chapter 1)

population   a set of people residing in a given area at a given time.

population composition   the distribution of a population among a set of distinct status categories, such as sex (gender), age, and marital status. (chapter 1)

population density   the relationship between the size of a population and the size of the area in which it lives. (chapter 1)

population distribution   comparison of the sizes of populations resident in a set of geographic areas or other relevant categories. See **distribution**. (chapter 1)

population diversity   the variety of cultural groups represented, in significant proportions, within a population and the evenness of the population distribution across these groups. (chapter 11)

population events   individual events that alter the size or composition of a population. (chapter 1)

population explosion   a dramatic increase in population size; often, those increases associated with demographic transitions. (chapter 3)

population growth   change in population size, in either a positive or negative direction. Sometimes called *population change*. (chapters 1, 3)

population momentum   generally, the resistance to change in crude birth rates caused by an age structure resulting from the prior fertility regime. Currently, in LDRs, it is the lag between a decline of total fertility rates and decline in growth rates caused by large proportions of women still being in their childbearing years due to past high total fertility rates. (chapters 4, 7)

population policy   a series of measures taken by public authorities to influence the trend of population change, or principles offered as a basis for such measures. (chapter 1)

population problem   a believed consequence of a population trend or characteristic that is negatively valued. A social problem of which a population trend or characteristic is the perceived cause. (chapter 1)

population pyramid   a conventional form of bar graph representing the age-sex structure of a population, so named because of its normal pyramidal shape in LDRs. Synonym: age-sex pyramid. (chapter 4)

population reclassification   the process of changing population composition by moving members from one category to another, such as by aging or marriage. (chapter 1)

population register   the continuous recording of population events for individual members of a population in such a way that a current reading of all members' demographic characteristics is always available. (chapter 2)

population studies   the study of demographic variables, including their relationships with nondemographic variables. To be distinguished from formal demography. (chapter 1)

positive checks   in Malthusian theory, those checks on population growth operating through increase in the death rate. (chapter 3)

positive selectivity   migration in which those people with traits especially valued in the area of destination are overrepresented in the migrant stream. (chapter 9)

postpartum   immediately after the end of a pregnancy. (chapter 7)

prevalence rate   the number of persons having a particular disease at a given point in time per 1,000 population at risk. (chapter 6)

preventive checks   in Malthusian theory, those checks on population growth operating through decrease in the birth rate. (chapter 3)

primitive migration   the kind of migration caused by an ecological push, including wandering, ranging, and nomadic movements. (chapter 9)

projection   a population projection specifies the future size of a population by employing assumptions about future fertility, mortality, and migration. (chapters 3, 4)

pronatalist   advocating increased fertility. (chapter 7)

proximate cause or **proximate determinant**   the most immediate cause of some population process. See, for example, **cause of death** and **intermediate variable**. (chapters 5, 6)

race   an ambiguous term referring to a culturally defined social or ethnic group classified together on the basis of common history, nationality, or geographic distribution but with a supposedly shared unique genetic heritage. (chapter 11)

ratio   comparison of the sizes of two categories in a series by dividing one by the other. Examples: sex ratio, age-dependency ratio. (chapter 4)

refined rate   a rate whose numerator contains all of the specified population events in a given year but whose denominator contains not the total population but some subset more narrowly defining the at-risk population. Example: general fertility rate. (chapter 7)

refugee   one who has migrated in response to strong pressure because continuing to stay in the country of origin may have exposed him or her to danger of persecution. (chapter 9)

registration   the recording of population events on a continuous basis for all members of a population. This took the form of parish registers in Western history; it now takes the form of civil registration in current national data systems. (chapters 2, 7)

replacement-level fertility   the level of fertility at which a cohort of women, on the average, have just enough daughters to replace themselves in the population at current mortality levels. (chapter 7)

residence   the location with which an individual is affiliated, where he or she usually or habitually lives. (chapters 2, 9)

retrospective questions   questions asking about events that have happened in the past, perhaps the remote past. Sometimes employed in censuses or sample surveys, but not in registration of population events. (chapter 2)

rural   not urban. (chapter 10)

segregation   the policy, practice, or results of imposing a separation of social groups such as racial or ethnic groups, especially as a result of discrimination. (chapter 11)

selective migration   migration in which the composition of the migrant population differs from the composition of the specified resident population. (chapter 9)

sex ratio   the number of males per one hundred females in a population or a part thereof. Synonym: masculinity ratio. (chapter 4)

sex structure   the composition of a population with regard to sex (gender); the distribution of a population between the two sexes. (chapter 4)

single   not in a marital union, usually never-married in marital status. (chapter 8)

singulate mean age at first marriage   the mean age at first marriage which would produce a specified distribution of percentages single by age. A method of estimating mean age at first marriage from period marital-status data. (chapter 8)

size of population   the number of people residing in a geographical location. Synonym: absolute size of population. (chapter 1)

social demography   that part of population studies which specifies the relationships among demographic and sociological variables. (chapter 1)

specific rate   generally, any rate for some subset of the population rather than the total population (as in a crude rate). See **age-sex-specific rate**. (chapter 4)

standardization   a set of statistical procedures that control the effect of compositional factors that may contaminate the comparison of populations. (chapter 8)

suburbanization   increase in the proportion of the urban population living in rings immediately around central cities. (chapter 10)

survival   in the context of mortality, not dying. (chapter 5)

synthetic cohort   see **hypothetical cohort**.

theory   a clear statement of the hypothesized relationships among certain variables.

timing of marriage   conventionally measured by the average age at first marriage or the proportion ever-married by age. (chapter 8)

total fertility rate   the average number of children that would be born alive to a group of women during their lifetime if they were to pass through all their childbearing years conforming to the age-specific (female) fertility rates of a given year. (chapter 7)

underenumeration   undercounting population in a census. A form of coverage error. (chapter 2)

underpopulated   description of a geographic entity that would benefit from having a larger population size. (chapter 3)

universality of marriage   the proportion of a population which can marry that does. Distinguished from **timing of marriage**. (chapter 8)

unmarried   marital status combining single (never-married), divorced, and widowed. Synonym: nonmarried. (chapter 8)

urban growth   the growth of the urban population. (chapter 10)

urbanism   having a lifestyle characteristic of urban places. (chapter 10)

urbanization   as a condition, the proportion of the total population that lives in urban places. Synonym: degree of urbanization. As a process, the increase in this proportion. Synonym: pace of urbanization. (chapter 10)

urban place   a place having a relatively large resident population densely settled and surrounded by a less densely settled area. (chapter 10)

urban population   the part of the population residing in urban places. (chapter 10)

variable   a characteristic that varies from one unit to another.

vital statistics   processed results of registration of vital events. Strictly speaking, vital events are deaths and births only, but the term often is broadened to include other population events captured by a registration system, such as marriages and divorces. (chapter 2)

vital statistics method estimating net migration between censuses as the total growth between the censuses minus the natural increase between the censuses expected from vital statistics records. (chapter 9)

widowed a marital status of currently unmarried by reason of last spouse's death. (chapter 8)

years lived with disability years of life lived with, and lost to, health disabilities of known severity and duration. (chapter 6)

years of life lost how many more years persons might have lived if they had not died from a particular illness or cause. (chapter 6)

youth dependency the proportion of the population judged too young to be fully economically productive, usually measured as the percent under age 15. (chapter 4)

Index